Beyond ⌐roadway

Beyond Broadway

The Pleasure and Promise of Musical Theatre
Across America

STACY WOLF

OXFORD
UNIVERSITY PRESS

OXFORD
UNIVERSITY PRESS

Oxford University Press is a department of the University of Oxford. It furthers
the University's objective of excellence in research, scholarship, and education
by publishing worldwide. Oxford is a registered trade mark of Oxford University
Press in the UK and certain other countries.

Published in the United States of America by Oxford University Press
198 Madison Avenue, New York, NY 10016, United States of America.

© Oxford University Press 2020

Library of Congress Cataloging-in-Publication Data
Names: Wolf, Stacy Ellen, author.
Title: Beyond Broadway : the pleasure and promise of musical theatre
across America / by Stacy Wolf.
Description: New York, NY : Oxford University Press, [2019] |
Includes bibliographical references.
Identifiers: LCCN 2019017902 | ISBN 9780190639525 (hardback) |
ISBN 9780190639532 (pbk.) | ISBN 9780190639549 (updf) |
ISBN 9780190639556 (epub) | ISBN 9780190639563 (oso)
Subjects: LCSH: Musicals—Social aspects—United States. | Musicals—United States—
History and criticism. | Musicals—Production and direction—United States. |
Community theater—United States. | Amateur theater—United States. |
Dinner theater— Colorado.
Classification: LCC ML3918.M87 W65 2019 | DDC 782.1/40973—dc23
LC record available at https://lccn.loc.gov/2019017902

For anyone who has ever
participated in, worked on, or enjoyed
musical theatre
beyond Broadway

Table of Contents

Introduction

The first musical I ever saw was *The Music Man* at the Burn Brae Dinner Theatre in 1970 when I was nine years old. My parents, my seven-year-old sister, Allison, and I drove our dark blue Country Squire station wagon twenty minutes from our snug townhouse in Columbia, Maryland, to a plain brown building next to a big parking lot at the end of a curvy country road off US Route 29. We went to see the show because I was officially bitten by the musical theatre bug.

Like most Jewish middle-class children of the 1960s, I grew up listening to Broadway cast albums that played constantly in our house: *My Fair Lady, Man of La Mancha, West Side Story, Funny Girl, Oklahoma!, Camelot,* and more. My grandmother serenaded me with "Sunrise, Sunset" from *Fiddler on the Roof* whenever I slept over at her house. For my fourth birthday, my mother dressed me in a navy blue dress, black Mary Janes and white knee socks, and a navy cloth coat, and we went to Baltimore's Ambassador Theatre to see the movie of *Mary Poppins*. We followed the same routine when I turned six for *The Sound of Music*, this time with my identically dressed little sister in tow.

By third grade—one year before our dinner theatre sojourn (and the first year girls were allowed to wear pants to public school)—my mind was made up: I would be a Broadway star. Every day at lunch, while other girls were jumping rope or playing foursquare, my best friend, Marcie Pachino, and I made up dances to Broadway show tunes. (We also called ourselves Melissa [that was me] and Elizabeth [that was Marcie], longing for worldly, sophisticated names and not the diminutive ones we'd been given.)

I made my stage debut that same year as Peter Pan in our class musical. We didn't have auditions, but when our teacher, Mrs. Rigby, asked who wanted to play Peter, my hand shot up before anyone else had the chance. Marcie played Wendy, and I got to wear a green felt costume that one of the mothers sewed, and my Aunt Judy was the accompanist. After it was over, my grandfather said to me, "You did great and sang so loudly! And you were ad-libbing!" I didn't know if ad-libbing was good or bad. I just wanted to be on stage.

Beyond Broadway. Stacy Wolf, Oxford University Press (2020). © Oxford University Press.
DOI: 10.1093/oso/9780190639525.001.0001

The summer after my Peter Pan debut, my sister and I went to sleepaway camp for four weeks—Camp Ramblewood, a non-Orthodox, Jewish, all-around camp in northeastern Maryland near the Chesapeake Bay. Camp was fine, even for a nonathletic child and a passable swimmer, but the best part was getting to be in the musical: *The Music Man*. In fact, I don't recall playing any sports at camp—no memory of volleyball or softball and only a vague recollection of passing the deep water test in the pool and learning how to dive. No, my clearest memories of summer camp are being in a dark airless barn every day at "rest hour" after lunch, learning the music and choreography for "Seventy-Six Trombones."

I was one of the youngest campers who tried out, and I wanted to play Amaryllis in the worst way. I didn't get that part (now that I think of it, that was the first of countless shows in which I got cast but not in the part I wanted), but I did land the role of Gracie Shinn with a few speaking lines and the solo singing line, "In March I got a gray mackinaw," in the big production number, "Wells Fargo Wagon." I sang my line with gusto, having no idea whatsoever what a mackinaw was. I loved every minute of rehearsal, being around the big kids and learning music and choreography and going over it again and again until it was perfect. And then the night of the performance arrived, and the whole camp—kids, counselors, and staff—came to see the show. We performed in a cavernous multipurpose space called "the big top." The audience sat on the concrete floor, a few lights were strung up around the building, and we wore costumes assembled from whatever the theatre counselors could cobble together.

When my sister, Allie, and I were away at camp that summer, our parents moved our family from the city to the suburbs, from Baltimore, where our mother's family had lived for several generations and where we were surrounded by grandparents, cousins, aunts, and uncles, to Columbia, Maryland, 30 minutes and a world away. Columbia was (and is) a planned utopian city, built by the Rouse Company, a real estate developer and our father's employer, on what had been farmland in Howard County, halfway between Baltimore and Washington, DC. When Allie and I returned from camp to our new home in August, our parents had a surprise: we were going to see a production of *The Music Man* at the Burn Brae Dinner Theatre. Because I had performed in the show at camp, they thought it would be fun to take us to see a professional production. I could hardly wait.

Every moment of that night was magical for me, from getting dressed up, to entering the small vestibule of the theatre whose walls were covered with black-and-white photos of past shows, to choosing among a vast array of foods on the buffet table, plus cakes, pies, and pudding for dessert, all topped with whipped cream. The show thrilled me, and I could barely breathe for the whole two and a half hours. In part, I was affected because our table was right up against the stage, and I could almost touch the actors. And I was enthralled with the girl who played Amaryllis, Francine Applebaum, with her black corkscrew curls, shiny brown eyes, rosy cheeks, and turned-up nose. Most of all, because I had just performed in the show a few weeks prior, I could anticipate every line in the script, every note and every lyric in the songs, and I loved comparing each actor's interpretation, vocal inflections, and gestures with our production at camp. I noted that the boy who played Winthrop at Burn Brae used a much stronger, spit-filled lisp than David Gold, who was Winthrop at camp. The actor who played Marian at Burn Brae was an actual adult and older, of course, and her soprano voice was thick, rich, and full of vibrato. Jeanie Kramer, the teenager who was Marian in Camp Ramblewood's production, also had a great voice, but her Marian seemed less dreamy and trusting, more suspicious of Harold Hill until the very end.

Along with the cast and crew list and actors' bios, which I perused for days, the show's program advertised Saturday drama and dance classes for kids and teens held at the dinner theatre. Our parents enrolled Allie and me, and as I entered fourth grade, I began what would be my routine through elementary, middle, and into high school: Saturdays at the theatre. I met older kids and begged my parents to take me to see their high school productions of *Guys and Dolls* and community theatre productions of *Annie Get Your Gun*. The drama teacher, Toby Orenstein, also directed some shows at Burn Brae, casting kids from her classes, and so I played one of the Martas in the dinner theatre's production of *The Sound of Music* (like many long-running shows with children, *The Sound of Music* was double-cast) and one of the Siamese children in *The King and I*, in full racial drag of dark pancake makeup, thickly lined eyes, and a black wig. I returned to camp the following summer—a year after *The Music Man*—and played one of the secretaries in *How to Succeed in Business Without Really Trying*. By my eleventh birthday, I was a musical theatre fanatic, an obsessed Broadway star wannabe, and had performed in or seen shows at most of the musical theatre venues I visit in this book.

I'd never been to New York or seen a Broadway show.

* * *

As a national performance form, musical theatre—an utterly American, unapologetically commercial, earnestly popular, and middlebrow form of art and entertainment—is ubiquitous and has astonishing staying power

Figure 0.1. The audience begins to gather for the hundredth season of the annual Mountain Play in Marin County, California.

(Figure 0.1). Local productions of shows from *Oklahoma!* to *Thoroughly Modern Millie* cut across economic, racial, and geographic divides assuming the status of a national folk practice. Shows are handed down from one generation to the next, which is remarkable in a country of such diversity with so few common cultural experiences. Artists and audiences, both young and old, learn the Broadway canon and absorb the conventions of this distinctly American form of entertainment—and have a lot of fun doing so.

Musical theatre's liveness is anachronistic, almost primitive, a striking anomaly in the era of YouTube and new media platforms. Live performance's ephemerality—every single performance is different, never to be repeated exactly (and taped performances don't capture the intense immediacy of being there as a performer or a spectator)—means that musical theatre lives locally and intimately, building community in its place of performance.

"Broadway," as a globally recognizable brand, maintains its status as musical theatre's birthplace, but the form only persists in American culture thanks to local performances. Or put another way, when most people think about musicals, they imagine Broadway, New York City—bright lights and big city. But in fact the lifeblood of the musical is local, in productions at high schools and community theatres, afterschool programs and summer camps and dinner theatres. Local musical theatre is an underexamined, undervalued practice that touches millions of people's lives. *Beyond Broadway* illustrates the widespread presence and persistence of musical theatre in US culture, examining it not as an object or a cultural artifact (as much musical theatre scholarship does), but as a social practice, a doing, a live, visceral experience of creating, watching, listening.[1]

Moreover, local musical theatre sustains the Broadway musical. Were it not for local musical theatre, in fact, there would be no Broadway musical. Why? First, there would be no artists, as virtually every professional actor, director, choreographer, and designer began in a high school musical, a summer camp show, or a community theatre production in their hometown. Second, there would be no Broadway audiences, because a vast number of spectators go to see musicals on Broadway that they already know from seeing or performing in them at home. Third, there would be no Broadway repertoire, because licensing companies gain considerable profit through non-Equity and amateur licensing: a full 50 percent of their gross. Even a musical that financially fails on Broadway, which 80 percent do, can make back its investment through years of local productions at community theatres and high schools.

But local musical theatre is also an activity to be valued in and of itself for its contribution to individuals' lives and their communities. As Tim McDonald, President of iTheatrics, a company that develops short adaptations of Broadway musicals for kids, said, "I estimate that 99 percent of Americans will never see a show on Broadway. Their Broadway experience takes place in school theaters, community theaters and regional theaters . . . in inner-city schools, suburban schools and rural schools. These folks . . . have a great time putting on a musical for their community."[2]

The Broadway musical truly lives beyond Broadway.

Why does local musical theatre flourish in this country? Why do people continue to find this activity pleasurable? Why do they passionately engage in such an old-fashioned and slow artistic practice, one that requires intense, person-to-person collaboration? And why do audiences still flock to musicals in the towns where they live? What does local musical theatre *do*?

Beyond Broadway answers these questions by taking a journey that crisscrosses America, stopping at elementary schools, a middle school festival, afterschool programs, high schools, summer camps, state park outdoor theatres, community theatres, and dinner theatres. We go to California and Colorado, Maine and Michigan, Texas and Tennessee. What we find on this expedition is the ordinary abundance and extraordinary longevity of the musical as a thriving activity in US society that touches millions of people's lives. This book shows how a middle-class Jewish girl could imagine herself as a Broadway star without ever having been there.

The Tony Awards and Broadway

Near the beginning of the Seventy-Second Annual Tony Awards in June 2018, co-hosts Sara Bareilles and Josh Groban waxed poetic, delighted to be hosting the Tonys: "It's a dream come true for the both of us," said Bareilles, "because we're both theatre kids. In fact, here's the proof," as she gestured upstage toward the big screen behind them that displayed a photo of her as a teenager.[3] "Thaaaaat," she said, drawing out the word with a grin, "is me playing Fern in *Charlotte's Web* in Humboldt County when I was fourteen." Chortles from the Radio City Music Hall audience. The next photo appeared on the screen, of a little boy in some kind of pajama-looking animal costume with a hood and small ears sewn on, and Groban chimed in, "And here I am at age nine playing Mr. Mistoffelees in my backyard production of *Cats*." The audience roared with laughter, and Groban looked around the theatre and shouted good-naturedly, "Where is Andrew Lloyd Webber, where are you?" The camera panned to Lloyd Webber in the audience, looking bemused. "Eat your heart out, sir, eat your heart out," chuckled Groban. And the audience—thousands in the theatre and more than 6.3 million at home—continued to laugh with warm, knowing appreciation.[4]

But this trip down memory lane was only a pretext for the real event. "We know there are a lot of you out there who have photos of yourselves in school plays or community theatre," Bareilles said, and Groban went on: "We want you to go to Twitter and Instagram and post those photos using hashtag #tonydreaming. We want to celebrate YOU on the Tonys tonight." Bareilles concluded their spiel, "And throughout the show, we'll see photos of the presenters in some of their very first roles!"

The fans answered the call, and thousands posted photos of themselves on stage in *Grease*, *West Side Story*, and *Annie*, to name a few, and backstage, gathered in affectionate clumps of friends, their arms draped around each other. They posted sweet captions like, "Dreams are the result of hard work" and "Theatre will forever have my heart."[5]

On Tony night, Broadway's most glamorous, most New York-focused evening, the producers paid homage to local and amateur theatre and to professional artists' humble roots. The show provided the evidence that all actors start out in local productions and acknowledged that Broadway depends on local, mostly amateur theatre-makers. The gesture, surely an attempt to increase ratings (which may have worked: viewership was up one-tenth of a point over 2017), explicitly linked New York with the rest of the country, the professional with the amateur, Broadway with schools and community theatres.[6] The Tonys recognized Broadway musical theatre as US popular culture from coast to coast. This was Broadway looking to the local.

How does the local look back? How do local musical theatres converse with Broadway?

First, by way of the repertoire. Across the United States, community theatres, dinner theatres, afterschool programs, and the other venues discussed in this book perform the repertoire of musicals that originate on Broadway. Local theatre-makers eagerly await the release of licensing rights for new and popular shows and jump at the chance to do a show as soon as it's released. As we will see in Chapter 8, for example, the competition among Colorado dinner theatres to premiere a show in the region is fierce. Local theatres support and legitimate the Broadway repertoire, too.

As Broadway producers figured out that turning a profit on Broadway is against all odds, but making money through the licensing of local productions across the United States is a real possibility, shows are increasingly being written and developed for widespread productions. Disney's *Newsies*, for example, was never intended to enjoy a long Broadway run. The musical just needed to play in New York long enough to earn the "as seen on Broadway" imprimatur. For Disney, scores of local productions of *Newsies* were always the goal. In this way, local musical theatre, more and more, inspires the repertoire.

Second, the local looks to Broadway because original, canonical performances "haunt" all future productions across the United States. Well-known, popular, or iconic performances, which abound in musical theatre, leave a trace. It could be the original actor, like Patti LuPone as Evita, Chita Rivera as Anita in *West Side Story*, or Sarah Brightman as Christine in *The Phantom of the Opera*. As theatre scholar Marvin Carlson writes, audiences are "haunted by the memory of that interpretation, and all actors performing the role must contend with the cultural ghost of the great originator."[7] And not only actors. Original production concepts (Michael Bennett's single line across the stage in *A Chorus Line*); choreography (Jerome Robbins' bottle dance in *Fiddler on the Roof*); or set design (John Napier's huge, interlocking, rotating scaffold-as-barricade in *Les Misérables*) also create cultural memories. A production team—director, musical director, choreographer, designers, actors—almost always knows previous versions of the show they're doing through the cast album, the Broadway production, a movie version, or YouTube clips, so they must decide whether to try to emulate the original, to work against it, or to try to pretend it's not there.[8] The ghosts of Broadway can't be ignored.

Third, local theatre-makers respond to the symbolic weight of "Broadway" as an aesthetic benchmark. Whether or not local artists or audiences have been to New York City's Broadway, the idea of Broadway suffuses their expectations and judgments. "It's as good as Broadway" is the highest compliment paid to any performer or production anywhere.

Finally, Broadway is a real place, a street and a neighborhood, the mecca of musical theatre. This Broadway holds power for some, none at all for others, and its theatre offerings are exorbitantly expensive for everyone and inaccessible to many. In spite of astronomical and ever-rising ticket prices for a Broadway show on Broadway (plus the expense of traveling to New York), the presence of musical theatre is increasing and everywhere. Broadway may be out of reach, but Broadway musical theatre is not (Figure 0.2).

Figure 0.2. The Worthington High School cast of *Into the Woods* in Worthington, Minnesota.

Where We Are (1): Time + Musicals in the 2010s

It's the evening of January 20, 2006, and 7.7 million people across the United States are sitting in front of their televisions, watching the Disney movie *High School Musical*, already tapping their toes and humming along to "We're All in This Together." *High School Musical* would become a blockbuster, the most successful Disney Channel Original Movie ever produced. It would also launch a new era for Broadway-style musicals, exponentially expanding their visibility and popularity.

The 2010s, a decade of intense musical theatre enthusiasm and activity, provides the context for this book. While local musical theatre at community theatres, high schools, and summer camps existed and quietly flourished since the early twentieth century, renewed interest in the form skyrocketed in the early twenty-first century. Once an activity stereotyped as only for girls and gay/gay-seeming/proto-gay boys, participation in musical theatre became, in many settings, as acceptable as playing sports.

The terrain shifted with *High School Musical*, with its infectious score, relatable high school setting, and, most importantly, enormously appealing straight white male protagonist: the handsome star athlete (played by heart-throb Zac Efron) who's equally drawn to musical theatre performance as to basketball. His romance with the studious new girl in town (starlet Vanessa Hudgens) blossoms in the school's auditorium, as the two decide to audition for the high school musical. After its record-breaking premiere, the TV movie drew 6.1 million more viewers when Disney rebroadcast it the following night. The soundtrack was number one on the Billboard charts for two weeks and went quadruple platinum. Within six months, Disney created a stage version of *High School Musical*, which still enjoys thousands of productions each year. This story of the athlete who also loves to sing and dance wasn't unheard of in real life, but *High School Musical* blew open the secret and fully masculinized the desire to perform.

Just prior to *High School Musical*, though, the TV competition show *American Idol* (2002–16, 2017–18) transformed television, stardom, and musical performance, followed by *Dancing with the Stars* (debuted 2005) and *So You Think You Can Dance* (debuted 2005). These shows also paved the way for musical theatre's widespread popularity. According to John Koblin in the *New York Times, American Idol* "not only established itself as rating powerhouse but spawned a series of amateur singing competitions that strove to duplicate its success."[9] While not about musical theatre per se, the competitive reality shows valued musical theatre–style performance by people of all genders, races, and types, and made stardom seem accessible to anyone.

Other narrative TV series like Fox's *Glee*, which ran for six seasons (2009–15), and NBC's *Smash* (2012–13) and *Rise* (ten episodes in 2018) also featured characters across identities who found joy in performance, as show tunes transformed the school's losers into show choir winners. Episodes of *Buffy the Vampire Slayer* (1996–2003) and *Crazy Ex-Girlfriend* (2015–18) also relied on tropes and techniques of musicals. Truer to the musical theatre repertoire, live televised revivals of classic musicals, including *The Sound of Music Live!* (2013), *The Wiz Live!* (2015), and *Grease Live!* (2016), brought old shows onto people's screens and into their homes.

Movie musicals also proliferated in the 2010s, including film adaptations of the Broadway hits *Les Misérables* (2012) and *Into the Woods* (2014); the original musical *La La Land* (2016), which won six Academy Awards; the Disney-animated *Moana* (2016); and, of course, the "monster hit" *Frozen* (2013), which sold $1.3 billion in tickets worldwide.[10] (Rob Marshall's 2002 film adaptation of Kander and Ebb's *Chicago*, Tim Burton's 2007 film of Sondheim's *Sweeney Todd*, and Phyllida Lloyd's 2008 version of ABBA's *Mamma Mia!* foreshadowed this trend.) In 2017, on the heels of the success of *La La Land*, "roughly twenty musicals [were] in the works in studios," including original musicals (*The Greatest Showman* with Hugh Jackman, released in 2017) and adaptations of Broadway shows (*Wicked*).[11] "Music has a way of getting inside all of us and lifting us up," said theatre, television, and film producer Marc Platt.[12] *New York Times* writer Brooks Barnes explained that "there is an inherent entertainment proposition in musicals, a heightened emotional experience that people go to the movies to find."[13]

These mass media events returned musical theatre to the entertainment mainstream, inculcating millions of children, teens, and adults into the pleasures of a form that many critics said was dead by the mid-1960s. Though the live, staged Broadway musical was reinvigorated in the 1980s with the influx of UK-born megamusicals like *Cats* (1982) and *Phantom of the Opera* (1988), the televisual performances of the early twenty-first century could take advantage of the explosive growth of YouTube as an entertainment and communication platform. These shows wove musicals into the daily lives of millions on a scale unlike anything since the "golden age of the Broadway musical" in the 1940s and 1950s, when cast albums served a similarly pleasurable infectious function and held a similarly pleasurable inculcating power.

Even by 2010, the start of the decade, *New York Times* writer David Kamp identified "the Glee Generation." In the four years since the airing of *High School Musical*, he wrote, "The musical theater idiom has regained its currency, and is enjoying what may be its greatest popularity among young people since the pre-rock era. We're raising a generation of Broadway babies." He went on to speculate what influenced musical theatre's appeal: "Well, as cornball as they are, the *High School Musical* movies conditioned impressionable teenagers to enjoy entertainment in which appealing young characters erupt into song and dance." Kamp also asserted that youth are more tolerant, that a boy can like show tunes without being gay and "besides," he wrote, "What's wrong with being gay?" In the end, he quipped, " 'Theater geek' is a kind of oxymoron now, isn't it?"[14]

In 2015, the Broadway musical itself was revolutionized by *Hamilton*, Lin-Manuel Miranda's multiracial, hip-hop adaptation of Ron Chernow's biography of US founding father Alexander Hamilton. Not only did *Hamilton* win eleven Tony Awards, including Best Musical, and the Pulitzer Prize in Drama, and break all records for ticket sales on Broadway, in London and Chicago, and on national tour, but composer, lyricist, writer, and star Miranda's constant social media activity built connections between live musical theatre and fans' digital lives.

While these performances provide the background and setting of the historical moment, *Beyond Broadway* is not about the popularity of musicals on television, in films, on the internet, or on Broadway. This book is about live local theatre. Moreover, while the specific production examples in this book are contemporary (between 2012 and 2018), the types and venues of musical theatre—high school musicals, community theatre musicals, summer camp musicals, and so on—originated generations ago. *Beyond Broadway* connects that past and the present, demonstrating the persistence, the surprising resilience, and the power of local musical theatre to revivify itself year after year.

Where We Are (2): Community + Place

It's a Saturday night somewhere, anywhere in the United States. Two hundred people are in their seats, looking over their program for tonight's musical,

Bye Bye Birdie, the 1960 Tony Award-winning confection by Michael Stewart, Lee Adams, and Charles Strouse. This audience might be in a well-used fifty-year-old community theatre in West Windsor, New Jersey, or in a renovated high school auditorium with rows of new lighting instruments in Belleville, Michigan. They might be on a massive hillside in the sweltering heat of an Austin, Texas summer, or on the top of Mt. Tamalpais in Marin County, California, overlooking the foggy San Francisco Bay. They might be on rows of backless benches in a wooden barn in Clayton Lake, Maine, or on padded seats in a glittery dinner theatre in Johnstown, Colorado. We'll visit all of these places in this book.

Maybe the audience paid for their tickets (if so, not much more than the cost of a movie) or maybe the show is free. Wherever they are, it's likely that they've been here before, probable that they know someone involved with the show, and possible that they themselves have performed on this very stage. They're an audience of friends, family, neighbors, and people just out to see a play. The theatre is almost surely in their town or proximate to it, and their pleasure in seeing the show is enhanced by a sense of civic pride. They might be familiar with *Bye Bye Birdie*, its music ("Kids! What's the matter with kids today?") or story. If not, in a few hours they can add one more show to their knowledge base of the musical theatre repertoire.

Meanwhile, the kids or adults backstage nervously put the final touches on their makeup, adjust their headset mics, and run through the first few steps of choreography in a corner. They're not the same people they were three months ago. Some already knew the musical—maybe they performed in the show, or listened to the cast album, or watched a bootleg video—and some did not. But now, they all know *Bye Bye Birdie* backwards and forwards. When rehearsals started, some were acquaintances or friends because they worked on shows together here or elsewhere, and some were newcomers. But now, they're a cast, they're a community, they're a family.

The particular theatre where this production of *Bye Bye Birdie* is about to begin—wherever it is—is one organism in the local musical theatre ecosystem. Within one town—Brunswick, Maine, for example—you can find musical theatre performance at a variety of venues: a production of *Mamma Mia!* by the Brunswick High School players, *Mary Poppins* by the pay-to-play Midcoast Youth Theatre, auditions for *Once Upon a Mattress* at the community-run Brunswick Little Theatre, and advertisements for an upcoming production of *Hello, Dolly!* at the professional Maine State Music Theatre. Each venue is part of this ecosystem, saturated with that region's idiosyncrasies—how people dress (T-shirts and jeans? suits and ties and dresses?), how they speak (with what accents? in what languages?), what they ate for dinner (burgers? tacos? sushi?), how they got to the theatre (by car? bus? on foot? by bicycle?), how they engage with the show (talking back? sitting quietly? cheering loudly?). In other words, wherever this show takes place, it will take on the flavor and accent and racial, ethnic, and socioeconomic dynamics of the local setting's demographics.

People, too, are organisms in the local musical theatre ecosystem, typically moving across their community's venues. For example, kids perform in their middle school shows and also participate in afterschool programs. High school drama teachers during the school year work as camp theatre counselors in the summer. A director of one community theatre show is the producer for another and acts in another and designs another. And over years and generations, cycles continue: a child performer in community theatre plays a leading role in her high school musical and later opens her own studio. Her child learns to stage manage in her mother's studio, then oversees musicals at a summer camp, and so it goes. Each type of theatre feeds into the local musical theatre culture, and they all sustain each other. Many spectators attend shows at all of these places. Cycles repeat, too, as all of these venues produce musicals in predictable seasons—the spring high school musical, the Christmas season community theatre show, the outdoor summer musical—and often in connection with other local rituals, celebrations, and activities.

Musical theatre is at root a collaborative, communal enterprise. It brings people—theatre-makers and spectators—together in the same room at the same time, often across generations, to experience a story told through song and dance, once and only once, together. In this way, local musical theatre counters the anti-communitarian trends of contemporary culture noted by sociologist Robert D. Putnam, who writes in his book, *Bowling Alone: The Collapse and Revival of American Community*, that "the bonds of our communities have withered" over the twentieth century.[15] Putnam observes that our attachments to one another and to the places we live have declined precipitously. Involvement in PTAs, in civic organizations, in other group activities has decreased so much that people are, in essence, "bowling alone."

Putnam doesn't include musical theatre (or any of the arts, for that matter) in his influential, often-cited, often-critiqued study. If he had, he would have found a different picture, an America where kids and adults come together on a regular basis to sing and dance, well supported by their communities. Nonetheless, Putnam points toward the arts in his manifesto-like conclusion, noting "the favorable effect it [art] can have on rebuilding American communities" and that "art is especially useful in transcending conventional social barriers."[16] In addition, he adds, "social capital"—by which he means our reciprocal neighborly, civic, friend, and familial networks and connections—"is often a valuable by-product of cultural activities whose main purpose is purely artistic."[17] He urges "America's artists, the leaders and funders of our cultural institutions, as well as ordinary Americans" to "find ways" for many more people to "participate in (not merely consume or 'appreciate') cultural activities," including community theatre.[18] Some community-based arts practices, he argues, "produce great art, but all of them produce great bridging social capital, in some respects an even more impressive achievement."[19] *Beyond Broadway* documents many such practices and their "social capital" gains.

Where We Are (3): Technology

It's Tuesday at 4 p.m., somewhere, anywhere in the United States. A group of four high schoolers are gathered in a little clump hunched over someone's phone. One of them swipes the screen from right to left, and they watch a series of photos go by. Every few swipes, they pause or laugh. At one photo, they stop. Someone's hand touches the screen and moves to zoom in on the image. Longer pause. "I like this one the best," one girl finally says. "Yeah," agree the others, nodding all around. "Let's do it." They take one more look at the photo, then back away from the phone, which its owner puts down. The kids pick up paintbrushes and jars of watercolor paints in greens and browns and get to work on the backdrop of trees for the set of their school's production of *Into the Woods*. Except for the occasional glance at the design they decided to use as a model, no one touches their phone for the rest of the day. This is another of local musical theatre's paradoxes: It eschews technology while relying on and benefiting from it.

Our lives are mediated by technology, and some say that our screen lives are supplanting real life. As Sherry Turkle writes in *Alone Together: Why We Expect More from Technology and Less from Each Other*, "The ties we form through the Internet are not, in the end, the ties that bind. But they are the ties that preoccupy."[20] The effects are profound, according to Turkle: "When we misplace our mobile devices, we become anxious—impossible, really."[21] She describes 21st-century teenagers as "tethered" to their phones, constantly "on-call," communicating solely by texts, and reluctant to connect with another person in real time by speaking on the phone or meeting in person.[22]

Musical theatre defies this trend because participation requires face-to-face communication and spectatorship is live. People engage in a local, intimate, low-tech, hands-on activity in a globalized culture saturated by social media, screens, and big data. Theatre is "right here, right now," writes Lauren Gunderson, who was the most produced playwright in 2017–18.[23] She enumerates theatre's unique qualities: "Theater is not on demand. Rather, it asks you to show up on time and focus in order to experience the intimate intensity of its medium." Gunderson explains, "The fiction is happening to real people who are right in front of you. You can hear it, smell it, see their passion and pain only feet away from your seat." She concludes, "The emotionally and physically distinct power of being present for art is hard to document or measure, but it's apparent to everyone who has witnessed live performance's arias, embraces and thunderous ovations."[24]

Gunderson is spot on—and yet technology enables local musical theatre, too. First, YouTube and other online platforms allow anyone with a computer or smartphone to see any number of productions online, so Broadway has become universally accessible. Whether for pleasure or to find a set design model or to learn how different actors, both professional and amateur, played a particular role (as the high school students do in Chapter 3), technology is a source of information, cultural acquisition, and knowledge (Figure 0.3).

Figure 0.3. The director and techies at Memorial Theatre, Worthington, Minnesota.

Social media supports and connects fan communities through Instagram, Twitter, Facebook, and specific fan sites. Finally, licensors sell and rent an array of technologically based products—accompaniment tracks, choreography DVDs, digital scenic backdrops—as well as host online forums and discussion boards for prospective theatre-makers to ask questions and share resources.

Professionals and Amateurs

As the #tonydreaming invitation to home television audiences underlined, Broadway holds cultural power because it is the seat of professional theatre. Broadway represents the cream of the crop, the people who, by talent, skill, training, or luck, manage to make a living performing in or working backstage on musicals. As Pat Payne, managing director of the Candlelight Dinner Playhouse in Johnstown, Colorado, said, "Broadway is where you make it."

At the other end of the economic scale is the amateur, the one who does musical theatre not for money but solely for love. This is the original meaning of the word amateur, from the Latin "amator": love, from "amare": to love. The dedication and seriousness of one who does musical theatre for love and love alone deserve respect, which the Tony Awards' telecast invitation to post photos gestured toward, but the "amateur," especially in US culture, comes with a whole host of negative connotations and derogatory associations: the dabbler, the dilettante, the egocentric prima donna, the enthusiast who is embarrassingly delusional about their lack of ability. That image of the amateur is a stereotype that this book seeks to disprove.

The terms "professional" and "amateur" are opposites, but in the local musical theatre ecosystem, they exist along a continuum, as we'll see throughout this book.[25] To the outside eye and to most audiences, sometimes it's not obvious who is who. At theatres where kids perform—summer camp, theatre festivals, and elementary, middle, and high schools—the youngsters are all amateurs. While some kids do go on to professional careers, most don't. But their other-than-professional-musical-theatre future in no way diminishes the significance of this activity for social, emotional, and intellectual development and, simply, for pleasure.

The adults who work with these children and youth amateurs, though, are professionals. They're teachers in elementary, middle, and high schools, owners of dance studios, theatre directors and designers, and band and or-chestra directors. They earn their livelihood teaching, training, and working with kids, guiding them in the production of musical theatre.

Theatre workers in dinner theatres are also professionals. Though the ac-tors in the places we visit in this book are non-Equity—that is, the theatres are not bound by actors' union rules for salaries and working hours and conditions—dinner theatres nonetheless provide a living wage for actors, who also work as food servers for the meal that precedes the show.

Community theatres fall somewhere in the middle of this professional-amateur range, as certain leadership roles are financially compensated, some on the artistic team receive a small stipend, and, typically, the actors volun-teer their time, energy, and talent.

But as this book shows, whether or not one is "amateur" or "professional," being paid or making a living doing musical theatre, participants take it se-riously. Sociologist Robert Stebbins coined the term "serious leisure" to de-scribe how people can engage in an activity during their non-work hours with total dedication and commitment.[26] Stebbins and other scholars in the field of Leisure Studies have researched community orchestras and choirs, amateur artists and craftspeople to understand why and how their "hobbies" matter. Wayne Booth, a (professional) literary scholar who learned to play the cello in later adulthood, is an example of someone who pursued serious leisure. As he describes himself, "The amateur *works* at it, or at least has done so in the past, aspiring to some level of competence or mastery or know-how or expertise . . . they don't just dabble at something that they sort of enjoy doing occasionally. Instead, like any serious professional, they work at learning to do it better."[27]

In the twenty-first century, amateurs in many fields not only have fun partaking in their chosen activity, but they make a significant contribu-tion to society. Charles Leadbeater, a British thought leader, author, and former advisor to government, public, and private organizations, uses "pro-am" to label amateurs who are as skilled as professionals in their practices, be it gardening, computer repair, political activism, or theatre. In *The Pro-Am Revolution: How Enthusiasts Are Changing Our Economy and Society*, Leadbeater and Paul Miller argue that the old distinction between profes-sionalism ("a mark of seriousness and high standards") and amateurism ("second-rate," "a term of derision") is obsolete in the twenty-first century. As they write, "The Pro-Ams are knowledgeable, educated, committed, and networked, by new technology."[28]

Why have we not paid more attention to local and amateur theatre? The "pervasiveness of the commonplace," answers theatre scholar Claire Cochrane. She argues that amateur theatre is so common, obvious, and everyday that it seems to be unworthy of study. To my mind (and to Cochrane's, of course), nothing could be farther from the truth. The pervasive and the commonplace deserve our attention.

Licensing

Near the New Hartford, Connecticut, warehouse loading dock of Music Theatre International (MTI)—the largest licensing company for musicals in the world—sit fifty boxes of scripts and scores, ready to be shipped out. Inside these tightly packed brown lumps are the makings of a musical, maybe *Camelot, Caroline, or Change,* or *Chitty Chitty Bang Bang.* Soon, a UPS worker will load them onto a truck and they'll be taken to Brookings, South Dakota; Tupelo, Mississippi; and Roswell, New Mexico. A day or two later, the musical's director will open the box with excitement and anxiety: once the rights have been acquired, the licensing fee has been paid, and the scripts appear on the doorstep, there's nothing stopping them from doing the show. This book follows those scripts and scores to their destinations to see what happens and how they're brought to life on stage.

But first, let's go back. How did the stuff in these boxes get here? To answer that question, we need to return to New York, to the headquarters of MTI.

I didn't expect MTI to look like a normal office. They, along with Theatrical Rights Worldwide, the Rodgers & Hammerstein Organization, Samuel French, Tams-Witmark, and Broadway Licensing, hold the keys to the kingdom: permission to do a show and scripts and scores to rent. Throughout my life, teachers, directors, and colleagues told tragic stories about being refused permission by MTI or whispered about being afraid "they" would catch you casting across gender or race, or shut you down for cutting a line or setting a scene somewhere other than where the script specified.

Anyone who produces a musical, professional or amateur, deals with licensors. Even though most of the participants in local musical theatre are unpaid or minimally paid, the scripts, scores, and musical arrangements of every show must be licensed from the company that owns the property and that distributes profit shares to the composers, lyricists, and librettists. As noted earlier, amateur rights account for a full 50 percent of MTI's gross income.[29] This statistic is surprising because many people think that local productions at schools, community theatres, churches, and the like are just a sideline. On the contrary, these productions are key to the stability of the licensing industry. In this way, local musicals are central not only to the cultural life of the United States and the creative life of millions of people, but also to the financial solvency of Broadway musical licensors, and by extension, the composers, lyricists, librettists, and other artists who earn royalties.

How did this business come about? Ever since Broadway musical theatre entered the consciousness of mainstream American culture, children, youth, and adults have gathered to put on a show.[30] With the invention and distribution of LPs in the late 1940s, musical theatre found a place in American homes like never before. In the 1940s, 1950s, and early 1960s, the songs of Broadway musicals played on the radio and records sold millions of copies, lasting for weeks, months, or years on the Billboard charts. In 1949, for example, Perry Como's cover of *South Pacific*'s "Some Enchanted Evening" was a Billboard number-one pop hit, and in 1957, the cast album of *West Side Story* spent forty weeks at the top of the charts.[31] Broadway stars were regularly featured in *Life* Magazine and appeared on television shows. *The Ed Sullivan Show* (which aired 1948-1971) presented around 400 performances from musicals, including evening-long programs dedicated to popular Broadway composers.[32]

At the same time, the theatrical repertoire of Shakespeare, fairy tales, and Greek myths performed by community theatres, elementary, middle, and high schools, and summer camps since the early twentieth century began to shift to then-contemporary Broadway musicals such as *Annie Get Your Gun* (1946), *Finian's Rainbow* (1947), and *Kiss Me, Kate* (1948), as aspiring performers wanted to sing and dance to the hummable music they were coming to know. By the 1960s, musicals like *Oklahoma!* (1943), *Brigadoon* (1947), and *Bye Bye Birdie* (1960) were integral to the school and community theatre repertoire.[33] Whether well funded or scraped together from loose change, performed in a proper theatre or in a school cafeteria or in a found outdoor space, in front of an elaborate set with lights and costumes or on an empty stage, accompanied by a full orchestra, a single piano, or sung a cappella, Broadway musicals played on stages across America as quickly as they became known by way of LPs, national tours, or their movie adaptations.

Unlike Shakespeare or Sophocles, though, musicals' scripts and scores reside not in the public domain but are protected by copyright and controlled by licensors. As the Broadway musical theatre repertoire grew, so did the licensing companies' properties. Samuel French, which was founded in 1830, now owns the rights to big hits like *Grease* (1972) and *Chicago* (1975), and more recently, *Fun Home* (2014). The Tams-Witmark Music Library, which licensed the first high school musical, an operetta of *Robin Hood*, was established in 1925 and later bought the rights to *Cabaret* (1966) and *A Chorus Line* (1975). The Rodgers & Hammerstein Organization, formed in 1944, was the first licensing company owned by the musicals' own creators, eliminating a profit-scraping middleman.[34] Thousands of productions of the ever-popular *Oklahoma!* (1943), which until recently saw at least one performance somewhere in the United States each day, plus *Carousel* (1945), *South Pacific* (1949), *The King and I* (1950), and *The Sound of Music* (1959) channel profits into the Rodgers & Hammerstein Organization, as the pair's repertoire is a valuable cultural product that local artists, including schools and community theatres, want to perform. The Rodgers & Hammerstein Organization also owns *Annie Get Your Gun* (1946), *Footloose* (1998), *In the Heights* (2008), and many more titles. As Ted Chapin, the group's chief creative officer, said, "The so-called amateur [that is, any theatre that hires nonprofessional actors] is very important and increasingly important [to the licensing business]. In the old days, big shows wouldn't be done by schools or community theatres, and now there seems to be no end to what people can do."[35]

Until 1952, Tams-Witmark Music Library and the Rodgers & Hammerstein Organization controlled most of musical theatre licensing. That year, composer and lyricist Frank Loesser, coming off the success of *Guys and Dolls* (1950), opened a new licensing and publishing company, Frank Music Corporation, in order to control and profit from his titles, including *Where's Charley?* (1948) and, later, *The Most Happy Fella* (1956) and *How to Succeed in Business Without Really Trying* (1960).[36] In 1954, Loesser joined with orchestrator Don Walker (who worked on *Carousel* [1954], *Fiddler on the Roof* [1964], and many other shows) to found MTI to deal with Loesser's properties and to buy more shows to compete with Rodgers & Hammerstein and Tams.[37]

MTI chugged along for more than thirty years until 1988, when former entertainment lawyer and music producer Freddie Gershon bought the company. In 1990, Gershon teamed with Cameron Mackintosh, producer of *Les Misérables* (1987) as well as all of Andrew Lloyd's Webber's blockbuster megamusicals, including *Jesus Christ Superstar* (1971), *Evita* (1979), *Joseph and the Amazing Technicolor Dreamcoat* (1982), and *The Phantom of the Opera* (1988). This collaboration between one man with years of experience in the law and the music business and the other with intimate knowledge of producing musical theatre on a grand scale led MTI to become the largest musical theatre licensing company in the world. In 2017, Drew Cohen, president of MTI since 2007, was promoted to global chief executive officer, signaling the company's international aspirations.[38]

MTI hardly monopolized the ever-growing, increasingly lucrative licensing business, though. In 2006, former MTI president Steve Spiegel launched Theatrical Rights Worldwide, which bought the rights to many contemporary musicals, including *Big Fish* (2013), *Memphis* (2009), and the top-rated high school musical from 2014 to 2017, *The Addams Family* (2010). In 2017, another company joined the game: Broadway Licensing, whose president, Sean Cercone, formerly worked for Theatrical Rights Worldwide and helped to oversee that company's expansion.[39] Broadway Licensing owns *A Bronx Tale* (2016) and *High Fidelity* (2006) and is primarily engaged in developing new musicals for schools.[40]

As the catalog of musicals from which local theatre groups can select grows, schools especially have transformed the licensing industry. In the past, shows could not be licensed until after the Broadway production closed because, according to *New York Times* arts writer Jim Rendon, "Licensers were afraid that it would cannibalize business."[41] But the opposite has happened: School productions now make Broadway and touring productions all the more popular. As Sean Patrick Flahaven, the chief executive officer of the Musical Company, a partnership between Andrew Lloyd Webber's Really Useful Group and Concord Music, said, "The idea is to put it out there and to see if it drives business toward seeing the Broadway show or the tour."[42] *Aladdin* (the Junior version) and *School of Rock*, for example, were both released for school and amateur licensing while the shows still played on Broadway.

Disney, whose shows are licensed and distributed through MTI, is a major force in the national musical theatre ecosystem. Between 2004, when Disney began licensing its titles, and 2018, their shows, such as *Beauty and the Beast* (1994) and *The Lion King* (1997), were performed more than 250,000 times in more than ninety thousand productions. "These titles bring people to theatre," said Disney Theatrical Group president Thomas Schumacher. "They want to see a great show with a great title they know."[43]

As of 2018, MTI owned over four hundred titles (including eighty junior, school, and Theatre for Young Audiences editions), Rogers & Hammerstein owned a hundred, and Tams-Witmark owned over 150 (including five Young Performer's Editions). Theatrical Rights Worldwide owned 110 titles (including seventeen school and "Young@Part" editions), and Broadway Licensing owned twenty, along with three "JV" middle school editions.[44]

Though the big business of licensing might feel anathema to local, grass-roots productions, the opposite is true.

And so, MTI's offices, which occupy the second floor of a nondescript building on West 54th Street in Manhattan, bely the power they wield.[45] The walls of the small, brightly lit lobby are painted in bold colors and display posters of *Seussical, Les Misérables*, and other shows. Behind a counter sit two workers, typically recent college grads, who answer phones constantly and direct callers to the right extension. When I visited, one of the workers—a young woman in black pants, boots, and a short, stylish hot pink blazer—led me down a hallway that opened onto a large room with the walls lined with floor-to-ceiling shelves of neatly labeled binders and fifty cubicles arranged in foursquare shapes. The room buzzed with the activity of regular-looking people talking on the phone or tapping replies to queries on their computers.

A team of twenty people deals with the permission inquiries of *Avenue Q, Mamma Mia!, Once on This Island*, and more than 400 other shows whose licenses are distributed by MTI. MTI's clients are startlingly diverse in terms of geography, culture, race, and economic resources. Each staff member handles around a hundred calls a day (that's a total of two thousand calls a day!), answering questions ranging from "Where can I rent an Audrey II plant for *Little Shop*?" to "What is a great show for a cast of mostly girls (or mostly boys)?" to "How do I make the carpet fly in *Aladdin*?"[46] They work to move callers along quickly if possible to deal with the next person in the phone or e-chat queue. But for each person who calls—community theatre director, dinner theatre artistic director, high school drama teacher—the stakes are high: What show do we want to do this year, can we get the rights, and how much will it cost to license it?

I didn't expect the people I met there—senior vice president Carol Edelson, senior operations officer John Prignano, and the famous, visionary chief executive officer Freddie Gershon—to be so warm, helpful, and enthusiastic about musical theatre production.[47] Why did I imagine these people, who only want to encourage more musical theatre production from the tiniest theatre in Paducah, Kentucky, to a big performing arts center in Riverside, California, would be frowning gatekeepers? This tour was the first of six years of visits and conversations that upended my assumptions about musical theatre across the United States and surprised me at every turn.

After I recovered from my surprise that this place wasn't as magical or terrifying as Willy Wonka's Chocolate Factory, I could see that MTI is a business whose goals are to provide theatres with what they need to do a show from start to finish, to protect the musical as intellectual property and ensure that it's produced according to the creators' intentions, and to try to stay ahead of the amateur's DIY creativity curve to make money. As just one example: Once MTI realized that people could, would, and did videotape productions in spite of the warnings against it, they created a recording agreement that gives permission to tape the show for a nominal fee. And as various theatres' musical or technical limitations became known to the staff at MTI, they produced more materials to help people do shows, such as digitized music files to supplement or replace an orchestra and Broadway choreography instructional videos. "The Original Production," overseen by choreographer Jerry Mitchell (who worked on *Legally Blonde* and won a Tony for choreographing the revival of *La Cage aux Folles*), features videotapes of Broadway choreographers teaching their moves to future choreographers and dancers.[48] Purchasing the video for $399 buys you the rights to use the choreography, too, which MTI hopes will discourage choreographers from imitating (by copyright law, stealing) choreography they find on YouTube. MTI also hosts chat boards for people to share resources and ask questions about a show. All of the licensors offer similar products. In short, they've created and continue to build an industrial complex licensing support network, in which local musical theatre production and a national capitalist marketplace go hand-in-hand.

The Journey

On Interstate US 101 in California, State Highway 215 in South Carolina, and County Road 9 in Colorado, the scripts and scores are on their way. *Beyond Broadway* traces the journey of those scripts and scores across America, from the licensing house to the people who make theatre locally, from the most well-known and expected places to the most surprising and unlikely. What happens to the scripts and scores when they get there? Who are the people who do musical theatre and why? How is each musical brought to life on stage? How do productions become part of the fabric of community-building, identity-formation, leisure consumption, and love? In other words, how are musicals made and why do they matter?

After I visited MTI's corporate headquarters and imagined the boxes of scripts and scores spreading Broadway musical theatre across the country, I began my own journey. I started in Atlanta, Georgia, at the Junior Theatre Festival (JTF). Since 2003, more than four thousand middle school–aged children and their teachers and directors have gathered each January during Martin Luther King Jr. weekend to celebrate musical theatre at JTF. Produced by iTheatrics (the company that adapts Broadway musicals for kids), *Playbill*, and MTI, the convention features ninety school and community groups who present a fifteen-minute segment from a show that they rehearsed or performed at home for professional artist adjudicators' immediate feedback. The weekend also includes performance workshops for kids and producing workshops for adults, a showcase of musical numbers from new shows, and an elaborate distribution of awards, during which almost every group is publicly recognized. Fueled by progressive language and democratic affirmations, JTF is unabashedly profit-driven, since MTI licenses the very repertoire of musicals that the children perform. The kids who attend JTF find confirmation and community in an intense, emotion-filled weekend that celebrates musical theatre. JTF combines crass commercialism and heartfelt outreach in a masterfully organized, exuberant event.

The JTF experience, in all its big, loud, and hectic over-the-top glory, made me curious to look more closely at the afterschool programs whose kids attend JTF and the adults who run those programs and bring their young charges to the festival. I wanted to meet, talk to, and see in action the powerful mentors who occupy a crucial place in the national musical theatre ecosystem. In San Anselmo, California I found Marilyn Izdebski, who epitomizes a figure I call the "backstage diva." She is the female musical theatre director who runs afterschool and summer pay-to-play programs, teaching kids dance and theatre by directing them in three or more shows a year. Someone like her (and she's usually a woman) can be found in most US towns. This familiar person is a disciplined leader and charismatic educator who, though invisible in theatre history, teaches musical theatre–obsessed kids to sing and dance and act and shapes them into triple-threat performers. She also helps them to grow up.

The children and teens who perform in Marilyn's shows and who participate in afterschool programs are often the ones who go on to do musical theatre in high school. Virtually every high school in the country—more than 26,000—hosts a theatre program and produces at least one play and/or musical a year. The Educational Theatre Association's annual survey found that more than 37,000 high school productions took place in 2017–18, with more than 46 million people in the audience.[49] *Beauty and the Beast, The Addams Family*, and *The Little Mermaid* were the most frequently produced high school musicals that year, but another, very different kind of show ranked fourth: Stephen Sondheim and James Lapine's *Into the Woods*.[50] In part because its ensemble cast offers excellent performance opportunities for girls, this artistically challenging and emotionally complex show sees thousands of high school productions each year. I visited three public high schools in the Midwest—one small school in rural southwestern Minnesota, one tiny school in rural southern Ohio, and one medium-sized school close to Ann Arbor, Michigan—each with different racial and socioeconomic demographics and community issues. I saw their dress rehearsals and talked to the students about why they wanted to be in or work backstage on *Into the Woods*, what they experienced, and how their school and their community were changed because of the musical.

Many people who do high school musicals return to theatre as adults, maybe after college or settling into working life. What's the adult counterpart of the high school musical? Community theatre. Community theatres started in the United States in the early twentieth century to engage citizens in their towns, promote patriotism, and instill a sense of civic pride through performance. The label now applies to the thousands of amateur groups across the country that are typically run by a few paid staff but mostly operate on volunteer labor. One is the Kelsey Theatre, a consortium of twelve community theatre companies that rehearse and perform on the campus of Mercer County Community College in central New Jersey. I spent many evenings hanging out at this theatre, watching auditions, rehearsals, and performances and talking to people who elect to spend their time after school and after work making musical theatre, which some have been doing their whole lives. These well-established companies cast intergenerationally—it's not unusual to see six-year-old children and 70-year-old adults in the same show. These theatre companies, which proudly take on the label "community theatre," renew themselves through families and through webs of connections that spread to local high schools, community colleges, summer day camps, and the many other community theatres that are concentrated in the area.

In addition to the thousands of year-round community theatres across the country, many cities also support outdoor musicals, typically in unique natural settings. Zilker Summer Musical in Austin, Texas, established by the local Recreation Department in 1959, offers an annual free musical on a hillside that attracts thousands of spectators, many of whom would not otherwise see a play. The Mountain Play, in Marin County, California, has produced one show each spring since 1913 in a 3,750-seat amphitheater on the top of Mount Tamalpais (Figure 0.4). The Open Air Theatre in Washington Crossing State Park in New Jersey, which opened in 1964, presents thirteen shows each summer to more than eighteen thousand spectators. Each of these venues, all located in old and well-established state parks, also has a complex and fraught history in relation to state and local government. Coincidentally, these three organizations produced *The Sound of Music* in successive years—the perfect show for an outdoor theatre. When Maria sings, "The hills are alive with the sound of music," it was true: The hills *are* alive with the sound of music, though in California, Texas, and New Jersey, and not the Austrian mountains where the classic Rodgers and Hammerstein musical is set.

Also taking place in the summer, but at the other end of the scale from big civic outdoor community theatre, are musicals in the tiny, insular, homogenous culture of girls' non-Orthodox Jewish summer camps in Maine. Each

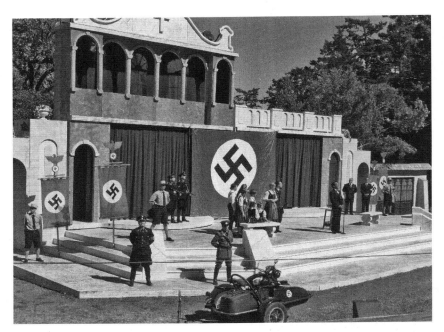

Figure 0.4. The Mountain Play's production of *The Sound of Music* on the top of Mt. Tamalpais in Marin County, California.

of these summer camps was founded by Jewish women—all early twentieth-century progressive educators—for socioeconomically privileged Jewish girls. Since the early 1900s, campers participate in theatre as a required activity alongside swimming, volleyball, and arts and crafts, so musical theatre shapes their experiences in profound ways. I visited four of these summer camps in the same state where Stephen Sondheim spent many summers at Androscoggin, an all-boys' Jewish summer camp. Over the course of their years at camp, most girls perform in seven musicals and make up the audience for forty more. In this consciously created community, the excitement, pressure, and camaraderie of musical theatre production creates an even more intense bubble in its midst.

Some of the most popular musicals at summer camp—and at all of the venues in this book—are Disney shows. In fact, by 2018, over 100 million Americans participated in or saw a Disney show.[51] Across the country, *Beauty and the Beast* alone has been performed more often than the four longest-running Broadway shows combined.[52] "Disney musicals are so pervasive, so woven into the fabric of Americana, that 38 percent of the U.S. population have engaged with a licensed Disney show either as part of the cast, crew, or audience," writes Ruthie Fierberg in *Playbill*.[53] Disney Theatrical Group's involvement in the local musical theatre scene includes the creation of kid-friendly versions of shows with supplementary materials, and since 2011, an ambitious philanthropic program to support musical theatre production in underserved public elementary schools.

I shuttled between Disney Theatrical Group's New York headquarters and Nashville, Tennessee, where they established their first Disney Musicals in Schools Program. I visited schools and met administrators, teachers, and teaching artists in Nashville, as well as the staff of the Tennessee Performing Arts Center, which oversees the program. I learned how schools across a range of racial and socioeconomic communities produce Disney musicals, and I saw kids perform Disney characters in, for example, *The Little Mermaid* and *Aladdin*. By loosening its famously tight grip on its product and allowing schools to produce their shows legally, Disney has at once increased revenue and become an instigator of social change and youth empowerment through musical theatre. President of Disney Theatrical Group Thomas Schumacher said that Disney's music "is the new American songbook . . . We are this new era of Broadway."[54] Disney's vision accommodates a populist agenda as they balance profit and corporate interests with philanthropy and grassroots artistic activism.

Each new place I visited delighted and engaged me. The more I traveled, the more I realized there were many more stories I could collect. But I decided to end my journey by going back to the beginning, in a way: to dinner theatre, the place of my own musical theatre origins. Instead of returning to Maryland, though, I explored the form in Colorado, where I was surprised to find four dinner theatres in close proximity to one another along Interstate 90. It also seemed fitting to end this project with the person who was my fellow traveler to summer camp and in Saturday afternoon drama and dance classes: my sister. Allie and I took a five-day dinner theatre road trip to Colorado's Front Range, where an unusually high concentration of this hybrid form of restaurant and musical theatre entertainment thrives. Though many people have heard of dinner theatres, only in certain parts of the country can one experience this unique activity, which combines profit motives with community investment by way of the Broadway musical theatre repertoire. Like the other places I traveled to for this book, dinner theatres in Colorado proved that the form flourishes beyond Broadway.

Many years after I sat as an enthralled 10-year-old watching *The Music Man* at the Burn Brae Dinner Theatre, and after spending a lifetime on both sides of the stage lights, I now attend musicals with a different set of critical tools but no less enthusiasm and joy. What's more, the analytical and interpretive skills that I use daily as a "professional" theatre studies scholar were formed in those early, foundational "amateur" experiences (as was, I suspect, my feminist perspective). How I see and hear, experience, understand, and am moved by musical theatre was shaped as much by the many local productions in which I was an actor, director, and dramaturg as by graduate school and professional training.

For this book, I saw hundreds of performances at schools, community theatres, and other venues (many of which, sadly, I didn't have space to discuss). I spent time in the library reading books and articles, in the archives perusing government documents, licensing agreements, and contracts, and on the internet chasing down facts and trying not to get distracted by every interesting theatre I couldn't visit or write about. Mostly, though, I spent time with people, observing production and board meetings, sitting in on auditions, watching rehearsals, going to performances, and witnessing award ceremonies. And I talked to people—more than 300 interviews in person or by phone, Skype, and email with producers, directors, choreographers, designers, stage managers, techies, actors, musicians, and spectators (both kids and adults in all of these positions and roles), as well as administrators, teachers, Disney executives, licensors, and summer camp theatre counselors and camp directors, among others. These interviews, I hope, establish a rich oral history and a present-tense account of a practice known and experienced for generations but as yet untold. Relying on the words of the people who do the work, I explain how local theatres operate economically, logistically, philosophically, emotionally, and artistically. The performances they produce form a vibrant, unacknowledged subculture of American theatre, culture, and society.

For the participant-observer method that was so central to my research, field notes—the handwritten, often hurriedly scrawled observations of who and what and when and where and how—were key. In those many notebooks, I recorded remarks made in passing, as well as a smell or the feeling of the air or the light, details that quickly fade from memory unless you write them down. Since I spent so many hours enclosed in rehearsal rooms, windowless studios, and dark theatres, I generated a lot of words about how musical theatre is made, trying to capture the wondrous way that productions are built from scratch, assembled minute by minute, hour by hour, day by day. No matter how many rehearsals I watched, I was always fascinated and curious, captivated by the process.

In these precious, often strange, and sometimes funny field notes, I later noticed that I jotted the phrase "notes are notes" at least fifty times. Why? Because when I observed rehearsals of songs, dances, and scenes—in a cold conference room in the Hilton Hotel in Atlanta when Maryland Children's Theatre rehearsed their excerpt of *Annie JR.* for the Junior Theatre Festival; in the Midtown Arts Center dinner theatre in Ft. Collins, Colorado, when the cast did their first stumble-through of Act 1 of *Ragtime*; in a steamy barn at a summer camp in Maine when twelve-year-old girls had their dress rehearsal of *Willy Wonka*—and many more, the same thing always happened. After the rehearsal, the director would say, "Okay, everybody, gather 'round for notes!" The group would assemble, pencils at the ready. Facing them, the director would try to decipher what was written while the actors were performing. Squinting at these typically illegible notes, which had been scribbled often in the dark, the director would offer general observations, positive feedback and encouragement, specific corrections, and criticism of the performances. No matter where I went, no matter the age of the performers, no matter the temperament

Figure 0.5. Eric, the director, gives notes to the Worthington High School cast following the dress rehearsal of *Into the Woods*.

of the director, I saw and heard this ritual of musical theatre production—the notes that a director gives to the cast—happen the same way every time (Figure 0.5).

I came to see how musical theatre production is a kind of folk knowledge passed down through embodied rituals, practice and repetition, and participation. We learn by doing. The stages of making musical theatre—selecting the show, holding auditions, learning music and choreography, blocking the scenes, working on characterization, fixing, polishing, running, building and loading in the set, tech, dress, performance, strike, and celebration—are remarkably similar no matter where you go. And yet, how these rituals are practiced is unique for every show, every time. It's always new and always feels fresh.

All of this adds up to what I call an "empathetic ethnographic" study.[55] What does that mean? I wasn't new to musical theatre production but had never visited the theatres I write about here until I decided to study them. I was (I am) an "indigenous ethnographer," insider and outsider both.[56] I tried to immerse myself in each theatre's culture, to be a compassionate participant-observer. As I met people, I was open about my project and its purpose. Throughout the research and writing process, I cultivated "critical generosity," standing beside the work and not above it, and emphasizing the positive aspects of what I witnessed.[57] Later, I shared many of these chapters with the people I quoted and described, opening a discussion about representation and responsibility. As I revised each chapter, I tried to account for their critiques and corrections, in line with a feminist ethnographic method of dialog and mutual enrichment.

This method—empathetic, indigenous, critically generous ethnography—foregrounds a relational way of knowing, so my connections to and collaborations with the people I met varied from place to place. The book itself, then, required an eclectic format and a range of foci, narrative structures, and voices.

Though all the chapters of this book are unified by musical theatre, each chapter begins in a different setting and takes the reader through a different sphere of activity of production and reception. These differences reflect my own distinct involvement with each theatre and what I experienced as an indigenous, empathetic ethnographer. In some settings, such as Marilyn the backstage diva's rehearsals and performances, I spent a number of days on two different trips six months apart. In some cases, I visited the theatre once as a spectator and interviewed people on the phone and exchanged emails. I spent many hours at Kelsey, the community theatre, over the course of six years. I tried to discern how these stories needed to be told. (As Stephen Sondheim famously said, content dictates form.)

In some accounts, I am in the middle of the action, recording the conversations and rehearsal activities I heard and witnessed. In others, I stand at a slight distance, trying to understand how things work, how people relate to each other, who has power and who does not. In different chapters, I use first person or third person narrative, sometimes told from someone else's perspective, sometimes from my own point of view. Some chapters are more journalistic, others are more traditionally analytical, and some are autoethnographic.

The musical theatre practices that I studied also varied in scale, from large omnipresent corporations like Disney to tiny summer camps that are closed to outsiders. To try to capture these variations, I've chosen different ways to focus each chapter. For the Broadway Junior chapter (Chapter 1), for example, I follow the adventures of two teens over a weekend festival. The backstage diva chapter (Chapter 2) is biographical, a life study centered on an individual and her influence on children's lives. The high school musical chapter (Chapter 3) is built around a specific musical, *Into the Woods*. Other chapters are defined by setting (outdoor summer musicals, Chapter 4) or by type of venue (dinner theatres, Chapter 8).

I also chose which stories to tell among the many hundreds that I heard or witnessed. For the most part, I picked the positive rather than the critical, negative, or resistant. To be sure, for everyone who finds community in local musical theatre, others feel excluded. For everyone who flourishes, others flounder or fail. People experience rejection, humiliation, frustration, competition, back-biting, nastiness, anxiety, cliques, and bankruptcy. They get hurt physically and emotionally. They lose their voices. They lose their confidence. Sometimes they lose their friends. Sometimes they lose their way.

But telling those stories hasn't been my goal for this book. I intended to document an aspect of musical theatre production history that seldom garners attention, much less sustained appreciation. My purpose was to shine a light on places and practices that have touched and shaped many of us (places and practices, in fact, fundamental to who we are) but to which scholars, critics, and ethnographers have not paid proper attention. I hope to encourage readers to notice the musical theatre in our backyards, to take a look at the sustaining, complicated, pleasurable, and powerful local practices that surround us.

This book, in its entirety, is a journey. It's organized as so many Americans actually experience musical theatre—namely, by getting in a car and driving to it. I invite the reader to start anew with each chapter, just as I started anew with each place I visited, discovering what was unique about this place, these people, these practices, these musicals.

I embarked on this book with an attitude of respect and curiosity and ended up feeling moved and inspired by those who make musical theatre locally, grateful for and appreciative of their contribution to society, to culture, to art, and to people's lives. I've surely been enriched and transformed by the people I've met and the performances I've experienced. I hope you, the reader, will feel that way, too.

Beyond Broadway is neither comprehensive nor quantitative, neither objective nor statistical. It's my journey, fueled by my questions, curiosities, and preoccupations. But I hope that the stories of the people I met who do musical theatre, sometimes for money but mostly for fun and for the love of it, will reveal something about the fabric of the United States, of people's desire to be creative, of their need to connect, to make something together, to entertain and be entertained. While the places I visited were specific, singular, and unique, I don't believe what happens there is unusual. Unusual, no. Remarkable, yes.

Figure 1.1. Student performers on stage in the all-conference session at the JTF, Atlanta, Georgia.

1

The Junior Theatre Festival and
Broadway Junior

1

Twelve-year-old Vanessa Jackson looked across the glass-walled, marble-floored lobby of Atlanta's Galleria Hotel at a sea of brightly colored "Junior Theatre Festival" T-shirts worn by kids who, like her, love to perform in musicals.[1] Multiple escalators moved up and down, carrying streams of kids, their red and black tote bags flung casually over their shoulders. She felt a little nervous, even though she knew that she was there with twenty classmates and friends from the Arbor Arts Magnet Middle School. They were, in fact, standing right next to her in a tight little huddle waiting for their director, Ms. Carter, to give them their T-shirts and folders with the schedule of activities and their room keys so that they could take their suitcases upstairs.

Vanessa closed her eyes for a moment and tried to breathe and focus, as her teacher had taught her to do when she got stage fright. She knew tomorrow would be here soon enough, so she tried not to worry about it now. She reminded herself that she knew every word, every note, and every step of "Seventy-Six Trombones," "Trouble in River City," and "Good Night, My Someone," which were the songs in their fifteen-minute excerpt from *The Music Man JR.* Tomorrow she, playing Marian the Librarian, and her friends would perform for a hundred other kid performers, their teachers and directors and parent chaperones, and two professional artist judges.

They already presented the whole show at home two months before in November and got a standing ovation both nights. Vanessa could sing the songs in her sleep and sometimes did. But at this moment, about to spend three nights away from her parents, who felt far away even though they were a short hour's drive away in a suburb on the other side of the city, she was nervous.

Vanessa was so involved with her own thoughts and fears of making a mistake that she didn't notice a tall, older white boy who tried to act casual as he came down the escalator, scanning the crowds of kids and munching on the

Beyond Broadway. Stacy Wolf, Oxford University Press (2020). © Oxford University Press.
DOI: 10.1093/oso/9780190639525.001.0001

apple that everyone got in their JTF tote bags. This was Daniel Davis's fifth time at JTF, but the fourteen-year-old felt more keyed-up every year, as the Jefferson Children's Theatre directors Sara and Bob cast him in progressively bigger parts, and he wanted more than ever to get noticed by the adjudicators when he played Corny Collins in their excerpt from *Hairspray JR*. Before they left home, Sara told him that she and Bob selected him and a few other kids to attend the first round of auditions at JTF for the choreography DVD that iTheatrics tapes in New York City. He was so excited to be getting his big chance but anxious, too, since this was his last year before he aged out of the Children's Theatre as a high schooler.

2

The JTF takes place in mid-January during Martin Luther King Jr. weekend, when more than four thousand children, aged eight to eighteen, from public and private schools, community theatres, private studios, pay-to-play programs, and children's theatres, and their teachers, directors, and chaperoning parents gather in a big hotel convention center in Atlanta to celebrate their participation in musical theatre (Figure 1.1). The huge event is produced by iTheatrics—a New York–based company that adapts Broadway musicals for kids, creating hour-long, age-appropriate versions of *Fiddler on the Roof, Godspell*, and *Legally Blonde*, among others—in collaboration with Musical Theatre International (MTI), Disney Theatrical Group, and *Playbill*.

JTF, which began in 2003, was the brainchild of Nicholas F. Manos, former president of Atlanta's now-defunct Theater of the Stars.[2] (TOTS was a non-profit Atlanta-based theatre from 1953 to 2013. It premiered the live stage version of Disney's *High School Musical* and produced *Annie* twenty-one times during its sixty years of operation.) As Manos tells it, after a large-cast, full-length production of *Annie* closed, he noticed how deflated the kids were. He wanted to energize them and believed that connecting them to a national network of kids who love musical theatre would do the trick.

In collaboration with Timothy A. McDonald, then MTI's education director and now the president and CEO of iTheatrics, they conceived of the festival, which started with twenty schools and 650 participants in the first year and grew quickly from there. By 2016, JTF featured festival headliner Darren Criss and sold out its six thousand slots in record time. In response to the Atlanta festival's growing popularity, JTF West opened in 2017 in

Sacramento, California, offering slightly different programing and boasting a more "intimate" setting for its fifteen hundred attendees.[3] By 2018, its fifteenth year, JTF welcomed 7,500 attendees representing forty states and six countries.[4]

JTF consists of numerous interlocking parts. Everyone trickles in on Friday evening, and each participant picks up a package of welcome materials: T-shirt, looseleaf notebook with a printed schedule of events, water bottle, and a tote bag filled with snacks. Each group is assigned a meeting room for an hour on Friday night to rehearse their fifteen-minute performance—a segment of a musical from MTI's Broadway Junior catalog that their teacher/director has chosen—which is the centerpiece of the festival.

Saturday morning is booked with ten or more concurrent sessions of eight or nine groups (each room designated as a color-coded "pod"), during which each group performs for all of the other groups in that pod and receives immediate feedback from two professional artist adjudicators. Strictly timed, these mini-productions take place in nondescript convention center rooms sans set, lights, and props, accompanied by fully orchestrated taped music played over loudspeakers. The costumes—such as they are—consist solely of jeans and the matching logo'd T-shirts provided by JTF.

Saturday afternoon is fully scheduled with workshops in singing, dancing, and acting for the children, and on producing, directing, and designing for their teachers and directors, as well as kids' auditions for various special performances. 2016's program included "Tech Olympics," in which students competed in a timed "obstacle course of technical theatre activities—ranging from performing a quick change and focusing a light to pre-setting props and taping the floor."[5] On Saturday night, they host an all-kids dance party.

Sunday morning gathers the crowd in an all-conference session with musical theatre writers or a few current young adult Broadway artists who have flown in to talk about their careers and answer questions from the adoring audience. The 2016 JTF featured designers and dramaturgs as celebrity guests. The festival culminates with a Sunday afternoon blowout event: a showcase of musical numbers from recently or soon-to-be released shows to pique interest, performed by selected children's theatre companies or school groups, now fully costumed and gloriously lit, and other, less polished numbers presented by various groups that were selected, assembled, and rehearsed during the festival. One group, called MVP ("Most Valuable Players"), includes kids whose teachers recommend them for their "enthusiasm." From my perspective in the audience, it was clear that some kids are chosen for "talent" or performance ability and others for being good teammates, a tension that threads through the entire weekend. The evening ends with an elaborate distribution of awards; almost every group there is publicly recognized in some way.

Over the years, as the numbers of participants have grown, so has the organizers' attention to detail. Led by director of programming Marty Johnson, they constantly strive to improve on the festival's structure and expand the offerings. For example, a few years in they instituted a welcome introductory session for first-time teachers and directors. They also added adult-facilitated "debriefing" sessions following each group's adjudication to allow the kids to talk about their feelings after the on-the-spot critique and blow off steam. Though JTF's team stresses celebration and community-building in their publicity materials and throughout the weekend, "feedback" is a key aspect of this subcultural event. It's not a competition, says Johnson, but as writer, blogger, and frequent JTF attendee Peter Filichia notes, "Well, yes, and no, for there are judges in each room who will speak plainly after a presentation" and "submit written evaluations that result in awards."[6] Still, the organizers want to emphasize the festival as affirmation that will carry the kids through until the next year.

One director, Relana Gerami, who owns and runs her own voice and per-forming arts studio, BATAVA (Bay Area Theater and Voice Academy) in League City, Texas, described readying her students for JTF: "We prepared our kids like little drill sergeants. They had their hair in buns and they were in little uniforms [jazz shoes, identical T-shirts]. I was like, 'I really over-prepared these kids.' And when they did their adjudication, Cindy Ripley (she's an iTheatrics consultant and primary resident music director), she just loved our kids and said that our kids were like the model group. And we were just like floored."

JTF combines crass commercialism and heartfelt outreach in a seam-less, exuberant event. The enormous project operates like a slick corporate machine, even with thousands of rambunctious singing and dancing kids spilling into hallways, taking over space typically occupied by business-people and their briefcases. Despite being fueled by progressive language and democratic affirmations, JTF is unabashedly profit-driven, since the reper-toire of musicals that the kids perform is chosen solely from MTI's Broadway Junior collection, which as of 2018 included forty-six one-hour musicals for middle-school kids and fifteen thirty-minute titles for elementary-age kids, adapted from full-length shows. In other words, schools and community theatres pay MTI around $500 to license the very shows from which they then perform excerpts at JTF, and MTI profits handsomely from Broadway Junior licensing. Many of the groups that attend JTF, whose registration cost $675 (in 2018) plus travel expenses, hotel, and food, receive no funding at home and rely on bake sales and JTF scholarships to enable their attendance and participation. JTF, as a microcosm of tween musical theatre across the United States, is a place of political, economic, artistic, and affectual contradictions.

3

In the Cobb meeting room at 7 p.m. on Friday night, Daniel tried to stay calm as Sara and Bob called everyone to attention. The little kids were tired—they had driven the nine hours from Norfolk, Virginia, straight through—but also wired from the excitement of being there, of staying in hotel rooms, and from the chocolate sundaes they had for dessert at Applebee's. Daniel was frustrated: This was their one chance to rehearse! And they only had one hour! Daniel knew that enunciating all of the words in "The Nicest Kids in Town" would be hard for him, and he desperately wanted to practice in the acoustically dead space of the conference hotel meeting room. The kids who were new to JTF were freaked out that there were no stage or lights or costumes, even though he had warned them that it felt weird at first to perform at JTF. "Just use your imagination," he'd said. He remembered the year they did Disney's *The Jungle Book* and they couldn't have any props or scenery so you couldn't tell where the trees were and where was clear space. "We just had to watch each other carefully and remember where the scenery was at home," he had told his best friend, Becca.

Daniel was an old-timer by JTF standards. He started coming to the festival when he was eight because his sister Julia was involved with Jefferson Children's Theatre. She had to watch him after school, so she took him with her on the bus to the theatre when he was in kindergarten. At first he didn't understand what they did there, though he saw how happy Julia was to be with her friends. It felt like a family and they were all nice to him, even though he was the tagalong brother. But when he saw her on stage for the first time, playing Adelaide in *Guys and Dolls JR.*, he was amazed. She didn't even seem like herself. He knew that he wanted to do it, too. He did his first show the next year when he was six and played a bird in *Once on This Island*

JR. Even though Daniel wanted a bigger part—even at six and the littlest kid, he wanted a bigger part—he remembered thinking, "I'm going to be the best bird I can be." He learned from the older kids that "you should always be energetic, even if you're in the back being a rock." He loved how everything came together for the performance and when their voices joined when they got all of the harmonies right.

Since then, Bob and Sara were like second parents to him, taking him to their house to start his homework when his mother worked a double shift and couldn't pick him up from rehearsal. He didn't mind going to their house for dinner or maybe to McDonald's if he was really lucky. But the best part was being on stage. He told Becca once, "When you're onstage, and you're doing this different part of you, playing a part, you forget the test you have next week . . . everything that's a burden, it just leaves. It's the best feeling ever."

But JTF was a whole different thing because even the little kids were good. He knew he had a huge advantage as a boy because there were few of them. He remembered his first year at JTF noticing that at the all-conference sessions, Marty or Tim said how happy they were to see boys at JTF, and whenever boys did anything—it didn't matter what—everyone cheered. He felt glad that people were applauding but really, he thought, we're actors and so are the girls. At the Children's Theatre, he sometimes felt bad because there were so many girls who were really good—and better than the boys—but there were more of them. Sometimes there was a part that a girl could do—and better than a boy—like Peter Pan, but the boy would get it.

Still, every year the festival got bigger, and there were more kids from performing arts academies and rich private schools added to the kids like him who went to public schools or who did afterschool community theatre. He overheard Bob and Sara talking on the drive that some groups had a lot of money and could spend more time rehearsing and less time fundraising than they had to do to get them all down to Atlanta.

Finally the kids got quiet, and the chaperoning parents chatting or looking at their phones or knitting settled down, and Sara said, "Everybody. We have fifty minutes left to rehearse. This is our chance to show them what we have. You worked so hard at home and this is what we've been waiting for." Jessica, a ten-year-old who was in the chorus, raised her hand. She was really good for her age and would play leading roles in no time, but she was always asking annoying questions. "Are we going to win a prize?" she asked. "Let's not think about that," said Sara. "Maybe we will and maybe we won't, but that's not the point. The point is to do your best." Jessica rolled her eyes, not trying to hide her disgust. Daniel exchanged looks with Becca, who played Tracy Turnblad, the star of the show. They were remembering the year before when their group won Best Ensemble for *Godspell JR*.

"Places!" Sara said, and everyone scampered to their opening sides "off-stage," waiting for Bob to hit "play" on the computer. The introduction to "You Can't Stop the Beat" rang out, and they ran to their places in three lines, six kids across, with Daniel and Becca downstage just in front of the group, as they had practiced again and again at home. But the stage area—just a section of the carpeted floor—was bigger than their stage in the community center, so their lines were messed up. Bob stopped the music. "It's okay, it's okay," said Sara. "This is a new space for us. Let's figure out where everyone should stand and try again." This is how it went for the next forty-five minutes until they got the positioning right, and the choreography worked with almost no mistakes, and the harmony sounded pretty good. There was no energy, though. They were going through the motions, but everyone was too tired. They needed an audience. When they performed the show in early December, they'd had a terrible, sloppy, slow dress rehearsal—even the little kids could feel how off they were—but then the performance was great, and everyone said it was as good as Broadway. But tonight, Daniel was bummed because he really wanted to get into his character, to feel Corny's charm and hamminess. But all they had time for was basic choreography. Oh well. He hoped he would get in the zone tomorrow.

4

When Stephen Sondheim and Arthur Laurents walked into Freddie Gershon's office in 1993, the Music Theatre International CEO couldn't have anticipated the gold mine that the Broadway Junior shows would become or how they would transform musical theatre for youth. This was the year before *Beauty and the Beast* premiered as the first Broadway show produced by Disney, which became Times Square's first family-friendly theatrical resident; the year before *Rent* transformed Broadway into a cool place for young people; and more than ten years before Disney's *High School Musical* would become a mass tween sensation for girls and boys alike, blowing the world of musical theatre performance wide open.

As Gershon tells it, Sondheim and Laurents came to talk to him about their worries about musical theatre's American legacy. They talked about how "no one knows the music of Broadway anymore" and that "Broadway's wonderful shows are going to be lost," Gershon told me. To be sure, Laurents, who wrote the librettos for *West Side Story* (1957) and *Gypsy* (1959, for which Sondheim wrote the lyrics), and Sondheim, whose musicals, including *Company* (1970), *Sweeney Todd* (1979), and *Assassins* (1990), were emotionally dark, musically difficult, and with presumably adults-only content, had financial interests as well as artistic ones in the perpetuation of musical theatre. Because only 20 percent of musicals run long enough on Broadway to turn a profit, artists rely on a percentage of fees from licensing of their shows. Gershon had an idea: "Let's adapt your shows for kids. Let's make them shorter and re-do the score to be in the range of young voices."[7] He wanted to start with *Into the Woods*, he said, "because, if I stick with Act I, it's a kid's show."[8] Sondheim agreed, and *Into the Woods JR.* was on its way.[9]

Gershon somehow knew that kid-friendly scripts and scores, ready for use by teachers and community theatre directors, would sell. He saw that there was a huge untapped market of elementary and middle schools and afterschool programs across the country, which, at the time, performed musicals that were expressly written for youth or, just as often, presented shortened, cleaned-up versions of Broadway shows that teachers cut themselves. Either way, Gershon's licensing business was losing out. If MTI could provide a "musical in a box," as he called it, schools would benefit by having ready-made, professionally edited scripts and transposed scores, and MTI and the artists whose work they licensed would profit for years to come. Gershon's prescience led to nothing less than a complete revolution in musical theatre production with kids. (In 2012, Gershon received a special Tony Award, which acknowledged his creation of the Broadway Junior shows.[10])

At the same time, MTI was busy digitizing its materials. The internet was relatively new in the early 1990s, and computer experts at MTI, including bookwriter/lyricist Robert Lee, now a professor in the Graduate Musical Theatre Writing Program at New York University's Tisch School of the Arts, and two of his colleagues used newly invented scanners, word processing and desktop programs, and Finale to convert extant scripts and scores, which were often incomplete or rife with contradictions. "It was an exciting time," said Lee, who worked in MTI's Music and Materials department from 1995 to 1998 and was at the forefront of this digitization project. They also developed ancillary products, such as "Rehearse Score," a proprietary application in which all of the music has been converted into MIDI (Musical Information Digital Interface) files, which teachers or directors can rent and use in rehearsal or share with kids to learn their parts.

Into the Woods was the first full-length musical that Lee and his colleagues digitized, a notable challenge with its intricate, complicated, and multi-vocal score. ("Our eyeballs were hanging out of their sockets," he told me.) Gershon surely suggested "juniorizing" *Into the Woods* as their first project because much of legwork had been done: Its digital transformation, which would make standardized, mass distribution possible as the first junior show, was already in process.

Gershon also knew that Sondheim's involvement would hold considerable weight with other composers and lyricists who might be skittish about shrinking their shows, and he wanted to move forward quickly—even before the full-length *Into the Woods* digitization process was completed. Next up then: *Annie*. With its charming story, its multiple roles for girls, including an expandable bevy of orphans, and a score with many songs already in a child's range, the 1977 hit was the perfect vehicle for junior adaptation. As Gershon anticipated, composer Charles Strouse hesitated when he approached him, but, as Gershon tells it, "I said, 'Steve Sondheim did it.' He said, 'Really?' and within seconds I got the three authors to agree to a junior version of *Annie*."[11]

The adaptation process that was later regularized began with *Annie*. A writer on MTI's staff (for *Annie JR.* it was playwright and lyricist Jim Luigs) drafted a sixty-minute script and revised the lyrics for shorter musical numbers. The digitized music files simplified transposition to melodies in kid-friendly keys and easier harmonies. All changes were approved by the original *Annie*'s creative team: composer Strouse, lyricist Martin Charnin, and librettist Thomas Meehan, with Luigs revising the new show as necessary. The ready-to-try version was sent to a school, community theatre, or musical theatre summer camp to get it on its feet to see if the script was easy to understand and follow and the music appropriate for kids' voices. They also included an "Accompaniment CD" that could replace a rehearsal pianist. (For *Annie JR.*, a full orchestra recorded the score, but for *Fiddler on the Roof JR.*, the second show, they opted for less expensive, synthesized music.)

MTI piloted *Annie JR.* in 1995 at a junior high school in the tiny town of Gowanda in upstate New York (pop. 2,800), directed by then-teacher Cindy Ripley (now iTheatric's lead educational consultant), who also wrote the first Director's Guide—a model for the how-to books that accompany every licensed Broadway Junior title.[12] Representatives from the home office went up to see the "prototype," and the event, according to Lee, was "a big to-do. The school went all out. They made T-shirts. They laid a red carpet in front of the school auditorium's entrance," and the tween cast and MTI dignitaries arrived in rented limos that they "rode for one block!" Lee said, "They sold it like it was a Broadway premiere. It's Broadway but for kids." The show was a success, and the MTI team felt, as Lee said, "We've got something here. This works." Gershon now had a real-life example to take to authors as evidence of the Juniors' viability.

MTI made an even stronger case with their next show, *Fiddler on the Roof JR.*, which was piloted at a school in Yonkers. "It was hilarious," said Lee, "to see a little kid wearing a big gray beard as Tevye. It was totally charming." But *Fiddler* also revealed the promise of an adult show's adaptation for kids: "*Annie* was fine, but it's still about kids. *Fiddler* felt more polished," Lee explained.

In the meantime, *Into the Woods JR.*, a more challenging adaptation than *Annie* or even *Fiddler*, was in development. Sondheim and James Lapine, the librettist and director of the original *Into the Woods*, along with a team of artists and educators from MTI, took the 1987 dark, deconstructive mashup of Cinderella, Jack and the Beanstalk, Little Red Riding Hood, and a gaggle of original storybook characters that Sondheim and Lapine created and constructed what they hoped would be the perfect junior script and score. Some necessary changes were apparent from the start. Gershon was certain the show should be Act I only, partly because that act ends with an age-appropriate "happily ever after," while the second act devolves into adults-only murder and mayhem, and because the junior shows had to be around an hour long. Among other changes, Sondheim dropped the lascivious, overtly sexual character of the Wolf and the violent and threatening "Witch's Rap," and cut the word "breast" from the lyric of "Giants in the Sky" to "minimize adolescent snickering."[13]

Through the winter of 1997–1998, about thirty schools across the country staged *Into the Woods JR.* and provided feedback to MTI, both positive (they liked its short, one-act length; the score worked for young voices) and negative (they missed the "Witch's Rap" and the character of the Wolf, both of which were subsequently put back). The struggle between what adults find appropriate for children and what children themselves want to perform arises because, according to children's literature scholar Perry Nodelman, adults carry their own assumptions about children and what they think children can handle. As Nodelman sees it, adults interact with children as if the adults' imagined, limited ideal is true—but it's not.[14] Thus, MTI's piloting process uses the experience of kids and the expertise of their teachers and directors to assess the level of difficulty and complexity of the show and to improve the material.

One of the pilot productions took place in the summer of 1998 at French Woods Performing Arts Camp, where they also recorded the songs on the demo tapes that would later be packaged with the Broadway Junior scripts. Michelle K. Moore, who was thirteen years old when she sang the role of the Baker's Wife, remembers that "they wanted the children to be able to learn the junior versions of the songs by listening to other children sing the songs! Some of the keys were changed & songs were cut short & adults don't sound like kids so hearing & learning from other kids would make it more relatable & that is where we came in!" French Woods' musical director David Weinstein oversaw the rehearsals, which took place at the camp, and they made the recording in a New York studio. Moore recalls that everyone took the process very seriously and worked hard to get the music and difficult harmonies perfect. She said, "I felt so cool, but most of all, I felt so respected. Not only were we getting this amazing experience, but we were also a part of something bigger. We were also helping other kids be able to put on shows of their own." She continued, "I learned what it was like to be in an environment where hard work & good work could get done while having fun & while feeling like I mattered. We were children who were able to rise to the occasion because of how well we were treated."

Sondheim and Lapine revised the show again, and the next junior version, which is the current officially licensed script and score, was piloted in 2002 as part of a special program for Washington, DC public elementary schools. One hundred forty-three children performed the show, with many more helping backstage at the Kennedy Center for the Performing Arts' Sondheim Celebration.[15]

The Broadway Junior imprint marks a musical as an adaptation of the longer and more challenging "real" Broadway show. As Nodelman writes of children's literature, its "use-value" lies in what's been excised, "those qualities that would make it 'adult' and therefore, presumably, unsuitable for child readers." The "very existence" of children's literature "as a genre implies an act of censorship," he argues.[16] But many think this shrinkage of "real" shows is preferable to creation of "children's musical theatre," which has no connection to adult musical theatre at all. Though the Broadway Junior properties are aggressively cut and censored, they do give kids the chance to play roles and sing music of the standard Broadway repertoire.

Over the next few years, MTI reached out to other composers and lyricists who agreed that trimming their shows for youth was well worth it to keep the properties selling, and the Broadway Junior catalog grew.[17] To bolster sales, in 2004–2005, McDonald developed and directed a national *Broadway Junior on Tour*, which included fifteen-minute segments of *Into the Woods JR.* and *The Music Man JR.*[18] Other new titles included *Seussical JR.*, Roald Dahl's *Willy Wonka JR.*, and Gilbert and Sullivan's *The Pirates of Penzance JR.*[19] In 2004, the Disney Theatrical Group began adapting their animated movie musicals into JR. and thirty-minute KIDS versions, which MTI distributed, expanding the catalog even more with musicals that kids already knew and loved, including *The Jungle Book JR.* and *KIDS*, *The Little Mermaid JR.*, *Aladdin JR.* and *KIDS* (both English and bilingual English/Spanish editions), and *The Lion King JR.* and *KIDS.*[20] From 1997 to 2005—the first stage of the operation—MTI licensed twenty thousand productions of JR. and KIDS shows.[21]

In 2006, McDonald left MTI (with Gershon's encouragement and blessing) to found iTheatrics, the company that creates all of the Broadway Junior scripts, scores, and supplementary materials (except for the Disney shows, which Disney Theatrical Group does in house), as well as organizing and producing the JTF. Musical theatre artists pay iTheatrics about $200,000 to adapt their show for kids. The process takes two years, and they typically have around eighteen titles somewhere in the pipeline at any given time.[22]

Other licensors followed the money and followed suit. In 2010, Tams-Witmark Library, Inc. contracted with iTheatrics to develop their Young Performers' Editions, including adaptations of *The Wizard of Oz* and *Bye Bye Birdie*, whose full-length version consistently ranks among the most popular titles for high schools. In 2012, the Rodgers & Hammerstein Organization launched the Getting to Know Collection, which includes *The Sound of Music, Oklahoma!, Once Upon a Mattress*, and *The King and I*. TRW (Theatrical Rights Worldwide) also licenses kid-friendly "Young@Part" and School Edition adaptations of their shows, including *Monty Python's Spamalot* and *Curtains.*[23] All of the companies produce and distribute supplementary materials similar to MTI's.[24]

From 2008 to 2018, the number of elementary and middle school musical theatre productions more than doubled, growing their share of licensing companies' income from around 10 percent to almost 25 percent.[25]

Moreover, according to Jim Rendon in the *New York Times*, "Educational licensing has reversed the fortunes of some shows."[26] *Seussical: The Musical*, for example, played on Broadway for only six months in 2000 and lost $10 million. Undaunted by the show's New York City failure, iTheatrics produced a junior version that became one of the most popular school shows in the catalogue, with more than 2,500 productions in 2016–2017.[27] As we'll see in the Disney chapter (Chapter 7), *The Little Mermaid* had a similar fate.

During the same decade, as discussed in the Introduction, Broadway musicals and Broadway-style musical theatre performances became increasingly visible (and cool) in popular culture, which drew more boys to the form. *Rent* (1996), *Spring Awakening* (2006), and *In the Heights* (2008), preceded by stage adaptations of Disney animated films like *Beauty and the Beast* (1994) and *The Lion King* (1997), attracted a younger and somewhat more diverse audience to Broadway who then wanted to perform those shows at school and at their local community theatres.[28] With the television debuts of *American Idol* in 2002, reality shows to cast Broadway productions like *Grease* (2007), and live televised productions, such as *The Wiz Live!* (2015), musical theatre's presence and influence expanded exponentially.[29]

Musical theatre's rising popularity was in part due to boys' increased interest in performing. While musicals always attracted a small handful of boys, the numbers increased dramatically in the first decade of the twenty-first century with Disney's *High School Musical*—both the movie in January 2006 and the live musical in September 2006 only nine months later and the fastest development of a stage musical in theatre history. *Glee* premiered in 2009, and combined with *High School Musical*, made singing show tunes cool.[30] Mickey Rapkin writes in *Theatre Geek*, his book about Stagedoor Manor, the famous musical theatre summer camp, that in the 1980s, they "had to offer substantial scholarships just to get boys through the front door."[31] As noted in the Introduction, in 2008, Stagedoor Manor built a new boys' dorm and added twenty beds because the interest among boys increased fourfold that year.[32] *Hamilton* set a new record for young people's interest in—that is, obsession with—musical theatre, and the blockbuster's fans cross gender, race, sexuality, socioeconomics, and location.

Figure 1.2. Student performers present their 15-minute Broadway Junior excerpt for professional artist adjudicators at the JTF.

5

On Saturday morning, Vanessa sat between Lisa and Stephen on an uncomfortable chair in the Marquee Room, where their group plus seven others in the purple "pod" were performing. The room was packed with antsy kids sitting in rows of chairs with their groups. The ones had who performed already were restless and veering toward rowdy. The ones who were yet to go were fidgety and anxious, which Vanessa knew included her, though she was trying, really trying to sit still. The adults sort of tried to calm the kids, but there were so many more kids than adults, and the adults were nervous, too, so the room felt to her like it was literally buzzing (Figure 1.2).

Vanessa was surprised by how different the groups were. Some were really good, with a lot of kids doing complicated choreography perfectly. Some groups seemed a little sad, with maybe only ten kids who looked nervous and unsure of themselves. Vanessa now could see how talented their group was, though Ms. Carter said that "there is no such thing as talent, only hard work."

Though Vanessa had never been to JTF because her parents wouldn't let her travel alone until she was twelve—even though her grades were always good enough and she always made her bed and helped with the dishes with no complaints—she knew everything about JTF because the kids at her school talked about it nonstop year round. When Ms. Carter picked *The Music Man JR.* for the fall show, the kids started guessing what she would include in the 15-minute JTF version. Some of the older kids helped to put together the script and with rehearsal, too. Lisa and Kate, twin eighth-graders who had taken ballet and jazz and tap lessons since they were four, made up the dances. Some groups just performed fifteen minutes from the middle of their show, but Ms. Carter wrote a new mini-musical that told the whole story. Vanessa was glad that she would get to sing a verse of one of her solos, the beautiful "Goodnight My Someone," and she loved the big group songs like "Seventy-Six Trombones"—led by Juan, the eighth-grade boy playing Harold Hill whom she had to pretend to be in love with—and "Wells Fargo Wagon." When Stephen played Winthrop and sang with a lisp, it cracked up everybody every time.

At the beginning of middle school in sixth grade, Vanessa wasn't a "theatre geek"—that was what the other kids in the show called themselves—but doing two shows this year "brought her out of her shell," her mother said. She played soccer in elementary school, and she still played in an afterschool league, though she was starting to like doing theatre more. She knew they gave awards at JTF, but she didn't think about theatre as a competition. She told her parents at dinner one night, "It's more about art . . . theatre isn't for competing and being the best. It's for telling a story." Also, she tried to explain that when you play soccer, "it's the same every time. Theatre, you do different plays, and it's different every time."

Even before the play, though, Vanessa knew about theatre because her parents took her to see a lot of musicals at the performing arts center, like *The Lion King, Jersey Boys*, and *Wicked* (her favorite). Like those Broadway shows, she expected Mr. Miller, the band teacher, to play the piano and lead the student musicians for their shows at school, but it turned out that all of the music for the show was taped. Her friend Emma, who played the violin in the school orchestra, was sad not to do the musical. It was cool in the end because it sounded professional, and it saved time because they didn't have to practice with the band, but she wished Emma could do the shows, too.

When the group before them entered the "stage" area, which wasn't a stage at all, but just the front of the room with a few cubes to sit or stand on, Ms. Carter motioned to them and they all stood up, moved out of their rows, slipped out of the room, and lined up in the hallway. "Quiet!" Ms. Carter hissed. It was hard to stay calm, lined up and with hands to the side like they had practiced. The door was partly open, and Vanessa could see a bunch of little kids doing a song from *Honk!* They were cute, she guessed, but she was too nervous to watch their performance carefully. Ms. Carter had told them that one of the most important things about JTF was being able to watch other groups and learn from what they noticed, good and bad. She also told them to congratulate other kids when you saw them in the halls. Vanessa would watch carefully after her group performed, she decided. The adjudicators talked to the little kids, but she couldn't hear what they were saying. It seemed like it took forever. Then, finally, she heard over the loudspeaker, "Introducing Arbor Arts Magnet Middle School and *The Music Man JR.!*" and everyone in the room turned to look at them and started clapping, and they walked to the front of the room in the straightest line ever.

The fifteen minutes went by so fast, Vanessa didn't even know what happened. She was sweaty and glanced at Lisa "Ethel Toffelmier" on one side and Juan "Harold Hill" on the other, both breathless and grinning from ear. Everyone was clapping and cheering, and Ms. Carter was practically jumping up and down. They did well.

The adjudicators—a woman named Cindy in a bright flowy shirt and short hair and a man wearing big black-framed glasses and skinny jeans whom she heard was a director from New York—came around from behind their table covered with score sheets to talk to their group. Vanessa was even more nervous for the adjudication than she had been for the performance. Now professionals would tell them how they did (Figure 1.3). She knew from talking to kids in other groups that sometimes the adjudicators were really nice—too nice, some said, "sugarcoating it," Kate had told her. "They would be much harsher and more honest with adults," she said. Vanessa also heard that sometimes the adjudicators didn't like the part of the show that was performed, though it wasn't the kids' fault, and that sometimes groups brought in scenery or wore costumes, which was against the rules, but they didn't get in trouble for it. But now, all the kids and Ms. Carter and the other teachers and parents leaned in as the judges spoke.

"Great job!" Cindy began. "You have so much energy and spirit and seemed to be having fun. I really liked that."

"Yeah," said the man, whose name turned out to be Alan. "I loved the choreography, especially that awesome wheel formation in the middle of

Figure 1.3. Following their performance, the student performers listen to the adjudicators' comments at the JTF.

'Seventy-Six Trombones.' Who did that?" Kate and Lisa grinned broadly. "We did," they said in harmony. "Good work! Keep doing that!" Alan enthused.

"Let's try something," said Cindy. "You, Marian, what's your name?" She looked at Vanessa, who was remembering the section of the choreography that she liked best: when they made a bridge with their arms and everyone went underneath it. Vanessa looked up at Cindy.

"Vanessa?" she answered.

"Vanessa, yes, hi! Let's go to the beginning of your song when Amaryllis is playing the piano. Oh, and Amaryllis," she looked at Alexis, "Nice job miming the piano! So, Vanessa, come and stand here. You, too, Amaryllis." Uh oh, I'm in trouble, thought Vanessa. She was trying to remember what Ms. Carter had said: learn every minute. Cindy said, "The song is beautiful—you have a lovely voice—but who are you singing to then?"

"Um."

"Is it to Amaryllis?"

"No." She knew she was supposed to be pretending to sing to someone she was going to fall in love with. Which she said.

"Yes!" said Cindy, nodding energetically. "Then why are you looking down at Amaryllis playing the piano?"

"Um."

"She's teaching Amaryllis to play the piano," shouted Kate, coming to her rescue. Vanessa wasn't normally shy, but she didn't know what she was supposed to say.

"Yes, true," said Cindy, "but that's not who she's singing the song to. Instead of looking down, look up and out, and imagine someone you know and love is sitting all the way in the back of the room. Let's try it."

Vanessa took a breath and was waiting for the music to start. "No, just sing a cappella," Cindy said. "Try it now."

"Okay." Vanessa looked down like she always did and then caught herself, looked up, imagined her mom in the back of the room, and sang, "Good night, my someone, good night, my love." She heard her voice carry over the heads of the two hundred people in the audience, and for a moment she became someone else, became Marian. Everyone was looking at her. She felt different, and she knew it was good. When she finished, everyone was smiling at her. Cindy was beaming. "Amazing!" she said. "Did you feel it? Wow! That's acting! That's how to do it." Cindy turned to the whole cast of *The Music Man JR.* sitting on the floor. "I hope you all can see what a difference it makes if you project your energy up and out. It's a great thing for everyone to keep in mind, no matter what show you're doing."

After it was over, they walked to a different room to "debrief" and talk about how they felt about the performance and the adjudication. Vanessa wasn't sure whether she should be happy or sad. She definitely thought that Cindy's coaching was good. Did that mean that Ms. Carter didn't direct her well enough? Or that she hadn't been expressive enough? Then Sydney came up to her, frowning. "What's wrong?" Vanessa asked. Sydney scowled, "The adjudicators didn't say anything to me. They didn't notice me. It didn't even matter that I was there."

6

iTheatrics created and licensed many Broadway Junior shows without a hitch, but a few proved challenging. *Hairspray*, Marc Shaiman, Scott Wittman, Thomas Meehan, and Mark O'Donnell's effervescent adaptation of John Waters's campy gay cult film, has catchy and singable music, a "nostalgic" 1960s setting, a large cast with broadly drawn characters, and an expandable ensemble that gets to do a lot of singing and dancing. It also features an unconventional protagonist: a "bigger in size than the other girls" teenage girl.[33]

Hairspray is about racial integration in Baltimore in the early 1960s. In the musical, teenager Tracy Turnblad wins a place on a television dance show and insists on bringing her African American friends to perform on the show, too. There is shock and outrage from the racist white characters, but Tracy and her friends rule the day. It's a lively, tuneful, feel good show with a progressive, liberal message.

The cast, according to the creators' intentions and the cast list on MTI's website, includes white characters Tracy, her mother Edna (who in Waters's film and in the full-length version of the musical is played by a man in drag, but is female in the Broadway Junior edition), Tracy's best friend Penny, evil girl Amber Von Tussle, and her eviler mother, Velma. The African American characters include Seaweed, who is Penny's boyfriend, his sister Little Inez, and Motormouth Maybelle, the classic black female show-stopping belter. The musical also requires a mixed-race chorus.[34]

Hairspray JR. was popular from the start (as is the full-length show, which is frequently produced all over the United States). It was so appealing, in fact, that schools and kids' theatres everywhere wanted to do it, even those without any African American students. In Plano, Texas, in 2012, a pay-to-play program (much like Marilyn Izdebski's studio in Chapter 2) performed the show with an all-white cast because, as the president of the theatre's board of directors said, no black actors auditioned, and "he wasn't one to bow to 'political correctness' or deny the actors a chance to do a fun show."[35] The theatre wrote to MTI for permission to do the show with an all-white case and received a letter of dispensation from Shaiman and Wittman, a shorter version of which can now be used as a program note in any production that lacks African American actors:

> Dear Audience Members,
>
> When we, the creators of HAIRSPRAY, first started licensing the show to high-schools and community theatres, we were asked by some about using make-up in order for non-African Americans to portray the black characters in the show.
>
> Although we comprehend that not every community around the globe has the perfectly balanced make-up (pardon the pun) of ethnicity to cast HAIRSPRAY as written, we had to, of course, forbid any use of the coloring of anyone's face (even if done respectfully and subtly) for it is still, at the end of the day, a form of blackface, which is a chapter in the story of race in America that our show is obviously against.

Yet, we also realized, to deny an actor the chance to play a role due to the color of his or her skin would be its own form of racism, albeit a "politically correct" one.

And so, if the production of HAIRSPRAY you are about to see tonight features folks whose skin color doesn't match the characters (not unlike how Edna has been traditionally played by a man), we ask that you use the timeless theatrical concept of "suspension of disbelief" and allow yourself to witness the story and not the racial background (or gender) of the actors. Our show is, after all, about not judging books by their covers! If the direction and the actors are good (and they had better be!) you will still get the message loud and clear. And hopefully have a great time receiving it!

Thank You,

Marc, Scott, Mark, Tom & John

The authors and MTI also wrote a letter to all licensees forbidding the use of blackface: "By signing below, you agree to inform the director of your production that such use of make-up is strictly prohibited." And they drew a line in the sand.

Shortly thereafter, Tim McDonald wrote a foreword to the *Hairspray JR.* Director's Guide, which all those who license the show receive. He describes the development of the original *Hairspray* for Broadway, and how eager he was to adapt the show to a Broadway Junior version. Then, in what reads like an effort to calm nerves, he extolls the virtues of the show: "the authors and producer did a brilliant job [with the Broadway Junior version] . . . The show fearlessly embraced the civil rights movement in a way that was wonderfully accessible. And the show was fun, fun, FUN!"

But there's more. For teachers and directors who haven't purchased the licensing yet and who are debating whether or not they can do the show without black children, iTheatrics' education advisor Cindy Ripley answers queries on the MTI website personally, gently discouraging an all-white cast: "Greetings," she writes (off the public chat site) to anyone who inquires, "As you know, the *Hairspray* story is about integration and the civil rights issues of the 1960's [sic] and one of the very best ways to learn about historical events is to experience them live onstage with singing and dancing. That being said, to cast authentically, you need to have some African American kids, namely 2 strong female leads and one male at least. Some may do it differently and certainly have." She includes Shaiman and Wittman's letter as well as McDonald's and signs off, "Such a great show, but not for everyone! Cindy."

Though the groups that want to do an all-white *Hairspray JR.* are happy—the show is indeed fun, fun, FUN!—online debates rage about Shaiman and Wittman's decision. Some rebuke them for prioritizing profits over the integrity and political message of the show.[36] Back in Plano, local high school teacher Karen Wilbanks objected to the production: "My shock is, why do you choose the play if it doesn't fit the cast of people?"[37]

But *Hairspray* has another challenge written into its libretto: Tracy's body. The Plano production also cast a thin girl as Tracy and padded her. Chat boards light up with these conversations. Must a director cast an "overweight" girl (whatever that means)? Is this role not a rare chance for a not-skinny girl to play the lead? In middle schools, as everywhere, typecasting still sadly reigns. What are the ethics around padding Tracy? Is that merely costuming or is it another version of blackface?[38]

As long as the show is licensed, which is happening to the tune of thousands of productions a year, the debate will continue. Kids will have a lot of fun doing the show. And the creators and MTI will keep making money.

7

"Finally!" Daniel said to himself as he took the stairs two at a time to get to the Saturday afternoon choreography auditions on the Terrace Level of the hotel. "My chance to get to New York City!" He held a precious Golden Ticket in his hand, named after Willy Wonka's Golden Ticket (a little silly, he thought), but really a ticket to be able to audition to dance on the DVD that gets sent to all of the teachers and directors who do new shows. He didn't know any kids who were ever chosen, though he'd seen a lot of the DVDs, which Sara often consulted as she created the choreography for their shows. When he got to the room—a huge ballroom with rows of chandeliers on the ceiling and a big wooden dance floor in the middle—Daniel's heart sank: There were a million kids standing around. (He later found out that 850 kids were called for the first round of auditions, chosen by their teachers/directors.[39]) Some of the kids had fancy jazz shoes, but he just wore his sneakers. He hoped no one would notice that they weren't even real Converse but imitations. "Hey," a boy, who looked about his age, greeted him.

"Hey," echoed Daniel.

"Is this your first time with a Golden Ticket?" the boy asked.

"Yeah," said Daniel

"Cool," said the boy, smiling. "Don't be nervous. It's fun. I'm Marcus."

"I'm Daniel."

"Cool," Marcus nodded.

After a minute, Steven Kennedy, the man in charge of choreography, got up. He gestured to a bunch of adults nearby, whom Daniel guessed were the judges, to get ready. "Hi, everybody. Welcome! We're going to teach you a combination for *Fame the Musical JR.*, which we're launching next year." Everyone cheered. "Yeah, it's great. Everyone form lines across the room so we can see all of you. I'm not gonna lie: this combination is pretty difficult, and it goes fast. But do your best. Even if you can't get all of the steps, look like you're having fun. That's just as important to us as getting the steps right."

Steven nodded and suddenly the room was filled with the song "The Junior Festival," better known as "Fame!": "Fame! I'm gonna make it to heaven/ Light up the sky like a flame." Loud. "Jenny is going to do it first so you can see the whole combination," Steven shouted over the music. A skinny blond lady wearing worn-out jazz shoes got up and launched into a Broadway dance combination. Daniel felt his heart racing as he noticed a double turn, high kicks, and some other movements so fast he could barely follow. This is so hard, he thought.

Steven and Jenny broke down the combination, which was only four measures of eight counts, but there was a lot of movement crammed into that short time. Daniel followed carefully, repeating every step as best as he could. He only started dancing this year, so he didn't know the names of all the steps. Everyone was quiet and focused, except one little girl who kept trying to ask questions. Steven looked at her. "We don't want to see you raise your hand," he said, nice but firm. That's kind of mean, thought Daniel, but he understood. They want listeners. They want kids who are professionals. Or else they won't want to work with you.

After around twenty minutes of going over the steps, Steven and Jenny and the other adults were ready to watch. "Remember," Steven said again. "Have fun." Right, thought Daniel. He knew that most everyone there was way better than him. Marcus whispered, "You know they do this like a profes-sional audition because in New York, Steven teaches 18 dances in four days and then they film everything in two days!" That explains it, thought Daniel.

The Jefferson kids were never expected to learn choreography so quickly, much less anything this hard. He did what he could and tried to smile and look enthusiastic, but it was rough. I'm so bad, he thought. Usually he felt that he had a better chance at getting cast because there were so few boys, but this time he knew it didn't matter. And later, when the callback list was posted on the JTF app, his name wasn't on it.

Daniel tried to squelch his disappointment and left to find the rest of the Jefferson kids, who were doing workshops, and Sara and Bob, who'd gone to a workshop with a Broadway lighting designer to learn how to light a show in an old theatre space with only a few ancient lighting instruments.

As he walked across the forum of the convention center, he saw groups of kids all over the place, some talking but most singing and dancing in big circles, happily oblivious to the other groups also singing their loudest. He tried not to feel too bad. He knew he was lucky to audition with a professional choreographer and, really, to be here at all. He looked at the younger kids singing in circles and remembered when he was younger and happy just to be around other kids who love musicals.

8

The Broadway Junior scripts and scores differ from full-length versions in a number of ways attuned to the needs of young people's performance.[40] First, teachers and directors who work with kids need a show that is shorter in duration. The sixty-minute format (or thirty minutes for the KIDS shows) is designed to fit into a school day's schedule. And given the complexity of producing a musical, a shorter show is much more manageable for a school or community theatre or children's theatre. Dialog is reduced, as many classic musicals feel too talky and the book scenes are too long for a contemporary audience of adults, much less kids. Songs are transposed to keys that are comfortable for kids' voices, the harmonies are simplified, and the songs are shorter. Because most children's voices can't sustain a song for three minutes, the lyrics are edited to capture the essence and meaning of the song in a minute or so.[41] For *The Music Man JR.*, for example, which Vanessa's school performed, six songs were cut, including Harold Hill's song of seduction, "Marian the Librarian," and several love songs.[42]

Do the Broadway Junior adaptations oversimplify musicals in a condescending gesture to the young people who perform them? Yes and no. On the one hand, these adaptations are just that: drastic revisions of Broadway shows that shortchange kids' learning the full score, grappling with fully formed characters, interpreting extended book scenes, and navigating complex emotional or political issues. On the other hand, Broadway musicals, as a commercial and mainstream art form, were never meant to be a frozen repertoire; they are rather, as theatre scholar Bruce Kirle argues, "works-in-process."[43] Many classic musicals were written for specific performers, and songs were added, cut, moved, or rearranged throughout the out-of-town (now extended preview) run. Directors of revivals often reconceive the show, as director John Doyle did with Sondheim's *Sweeney Todd, Company, Passion,* and *Pacific Overtures,* as well as with *The Color Purple* and *Carmen Jones,* and the Fiasco Theatre Company did for *Into the Woods* and *Merrily We Roll Along.* Other directors, with permission of the licensors, trim the dialog of scenes that feel too long for contemporary (adult) audiences. In other words, Broadway musicals are closer in spirit and intention to Shakespeare than to Beckett (whose estate is notoriously strict and litigious), though in practice, they're not in the public domain, so changes are forbidden without permission.

Shows for young people need larger casts to accommodate as many kids as possible, whether in a school, community theatre, or afterschool program. Characters with names and lines are at a premium, so minor parts might be divided into multiple roles in a junior script. Ensembles are given as much as possible to do, including musical numbers and being on stage in general. Finally, the Broadway Junior scripts have their own look: the font is larger, and the spoken text and musical score appear in order of the show, not as musical librettos usually are printed, with all of the spoken text followed by all of the songs. Some licensing companies only send "sides"—a modified script that contains only a specific character's cues and lines—but the Broadway Junior scripts are entire scripts, clear and easy to navigate.

Every Broadway Junior license also comes with an elaborate ShowKit, which includes, first, a Directors' Guide—essentially a teacher's manual (not unlike what textbook publishers write and include with an order) for producing musicals. Virtually any adult—with theatre experience or not—can pick up this guide and follow step-by-step instructions on how to hold auditions, cast a show, run rehearsals, and produce the show, including ideas for building inexpensive sets and costumes. The ShowKit also contains multiple copies of "Family Matters," a brochure with ideas for fundraising tips and ways to get families involved in the production; CDs—one fully orchestrated accompaniment for performance and one demo rehearsal CD with children's voices so that actors learning the songs can sing along; a choreography DVD with ideas for staging musical numbers; piano vocal score; and 20 student scripts.[44]

MTI's ever-expanding Broadway Junior and Broadway KIDS licensing business is exceedingly lucrative. For artists, the $200,000 that they pay iTheatrics to adapt their musical for kids is a drop in the bucket of what they might see in returns. Licenses for a popular show for kids can earn $1 million or more a year. *Annie*, for example, in its various incarnations, saw thirteen thousand productions globally from 2013 to 2018.[45]

iTheatrics (and their colleagues at the other licensing companies) have also developed a plethora of ancillary products designed to help musical theatre directors at any level. Schools can license spoken "partner" tracks to help young actors learn their lines. They can request a free "Broadway Junior CertifiKIT": MTI's press agents will send show listings to local papers announcing the production and will provide a personalized "Certificate of Excellence" signed by the musical's authors that can be framed and displayed in the school or theatre's lobby. Most significantly, MTI's music accompaniment materials are flexible and can accommodate any school or community theatre's resources and needs. At JTF, all of the music, from the adjudicated sessions to the all-conference musical numbers, is recorded and played through a sound system. Many schools use these fully orchestrated CDs (or MP3 files) for their productions, which come with the ShowKit, eliminating the need for any accompanist, even a pianist. In addition, MTI licenses partial tracks with specific instruments missing. The idea is that if a school has some musicians—say, violinists and cellists—the students can play their parts and the recording fills in the other instruments. (As we'll see in Chapter 3 on high school musicals, schools with big marching bands might have more horn than string players. At East Clinton High School in Ohio, they rented the string tracks to support the large student band of brass, woodwind, and percussion players.)

The absence of musicians means that a crucial aspect of the musical theatre production experience is missing. Not only do kids lose the opportunity to confront the challenges and experience the satisfaction of this stage of the collaborative production process, but they're inevitably led to believe that musicians don't matter and that you can do a musical without players, karaoke-style. Still, countless schools would not be able to do shows at all were it not for the accompaniment recordings. This material both enables and downgrades musical theatre production at the same time.

MTI maintains a multifaceted, increasingly robust website for all of their shows (not just the juniors) with, for example, maps of locations of future productions, forums for discussions, and sites to rent or lend sets, props, and costumes.[46] The site also offers MTI Show Support: online help and advice from master teacher Cindy Ripley, who sometimes responds in real time.[47] Directors can also find an "Audition Central" link for each show with all of the characters listed, each with a "breakdown" (character description, gender, vocal range), excerpts from the script and score to use for auditions, and casting suggestions.[48] On *The Music Man JR.* site, for example, MTI advises, "The role of Marian is a different twist on the traditional leading lady. [. . .] Your Marian must have an amazing voice, be an excellent actor, and be able to move well. She must also have an air of confidence that draws Harold and your audience to her. [. . .] Female. Range: G3–G5."[49]

Schools and afterschool programs and community theatres that produce musical theatre with children interact with MTI and its subsidiaries across a continuum of intensity. Most groups buy the license and get the scripts and do the show on their own without further engagement with the company. Other groups take advantage of the supplementary materials of MTI, especially when the group is young and new. Schools or community theatres that started doing musicals after 2006 find MTI's extra materials alongside the script licensing and are more likely to buy additional materials. In fact, on the website, when you click on an MTI title (either the full-length show or the Broadway Junior version), a song from the show begins to play immediately, inundating you with an infectious show tune melody. All in all, MTI is striving to make musical theatre production possible for any situation, even as they make money hand over fist in the process.

9

Vanessa might have dozed off had it not been for the flashing lights, loud and pulsing music, and four thousand screaming kids at the Sunday afternoon Student Awards presentations. She had been up late with her friends and some other kids they met at the dance party. The other kids were from a community theatre and went to different schools in the same town and complained how no one at their school got it or understood why they did shows. And they sang at the party, too (how could they not?). Kate told Vanessa that the awards would be kind of fun and kind of boring, depending on which award their group got. She said that all of the groups got an award for something, but some were more for effort than excellence.

Vanessa was also thinking about yesterday afternoon's all-conference session with some of the *Newsies* cast members and how nice they seemed. The girl—the only one in the show—was funny and smart. Someone asked Andrew Keenan-Bolger, the star, how he got started, and he just said to work hard (which she did), do a lot of theatre (which she did), and come to JTF (which she did). Alan Menken (who wrote the music for *Aladdin* and *Beauty and the Beast* and a lot of other shows) played the piano and talked about the songs he wrote, which was fun, also. Every once in a while she thought about her parents or her math homework, but it was hard to think about anything but musicals, musicals, musicals during JTF.

All of a sudden, she heard "Arbor Arts Magnet Middle School!" being announced, and their school name and *The Music Man JR.* was showing on the two big screens on either side of the stage. "We won, we won!" Ms. Carter said, as she raced up the stage to collect the award. They won for Excellence in Acting! Vanessa and her friends were jumping up and down and screaming and giving each other high fives. She couldn't believe it! They won! Ms. Carter held the trophy over her head and then pointed to the kids from her school. Everyone was snapping photos with their phones. After everyone calmed down, the awards continued for a while. By the time it was over, Vanessa thought Kate was right and that every group had won something or other.

Sitting on the other side of the huge hall, Daniel was awake and alert in spite of the late night with his new friends from the choreography audition. It had been really fun hanging out. He really liked Marcus, and they already texted each other a bunch of times and sent photos of what they were doing. Daniel knew the awards were long. Based on their adjudication, he didn't think they were going to win anything. In fact, he felt his Golden Ticket audition, even though it was humiliating, was the best thing that came out of the festival this year. Daniel heard the ping of his phone and looked down to see if it was from Becca or Marcus or his mom, but then all the Jefferson kids were screaming, "Bob and Sara! Bob and Sara!" Bob and Sara won the Freddie G. Teacher Award! "Eow!" shouted Daniel, joining the cheering. Bob and Sara ran up the long aisle to stand on stage with 10 other teachers who were chosen to go to New York next summer to see shows and watch rehearsals and learn about directing musicals. It was amazing. If he couldn't get to New York, he was psyched that Bob and Sara got to go.

10

As a microcosm of musical theatre for youth, JTF reveals the extraordinary power of community and common cause as well as the troublesome aspects of this vibrant social practice. Feelings of affirmation and celebration dominate the festival, as this weekend is the high point of the year for many groups, their attendance enabled by nonstop fundraising, and their performances created and rehearsed for this single showing. At JTF, young performers' love for musical theatre is honored and supported. Many experience a rare kind of solidarity that they never knew existed beyond their own group.

Still, there are cracks in the veneer, problems embedded in the very culture JTF purports to build and sustain. First, the unrelenting dominance of "Broadway" offers an unfulfillable promise of professional success. Young stars currently appearing on Broadway do interviews during the all-conference sessions. Posters, T-shirts, buttons, and mugs from Broadway shows cover tables and shelves of the pop-up souvenir shop. And of course, the Broadway repertoire provides the material for each performance and so organizes JTF's musical and theatrical world. Unsurprisingly, many of the participants say they have Broadway aspirations. While a desire for stardom is the entry point for virtually every performer and the common thread of every Broadway story (since the beginning of time), what does it mean that this event fuels such unrealistic hopes and dreams? Perhaps the desire for stardom is a natural part of pre and adolescent development. JTF tries to democratize these desires, to give as many kids as possible a chance to shine. It rewards effort and spirit as well as vocal strength and stage presence, but few if any of these kids will actually become Broadway performers.

Second, despite its display of community and emphasis on the simple joy of performance, JTF is haunted by economic inequity. Colorful, identical JTF T-shirts and homogenous fashion choices of twelve-year-olds can't hide the different funding circumstances of the participating groups, which range from wealthy private schools to underserved public schools and backyard community theatres. Some groups fundraise all year not only to be able to attend the festival but to do their shows at home, and their directors are volunteers at the community theatre or are teachers who spend extra unpaid time after school producing the play.

JTF navigates other troublesome features that go beyond the quality of the individual child's participation and that touch on larger issues of musical theatre production. For example, as noted earlier, there are no musicians at JTF. All of the music is played from recorded tracks—the same tracks that MTI includes with its Broadway Junior licenses. On the one hand, providing fully orchestrated tracks makes performing a Broadway musical accessible to any group; on the other hand, it devalues the crucial component of music and conveys the sense that the music is a luxurious add-on and not integral to musical theatre performance.[50]

Moreover, JTF's key sponsor, MTI, sees big profits from this event, which is tied to the licensing machine that enables these productions in the first place. The festival is both the beginning and end of a cycle of production that depends on and profits the licensors. To participate in JTF, groups must license and perform a title from MTI's Broadway Junior catalog, which includes Disney musicals. That is, they've already paid the company to do the show. Though extensive, the Broadway Junior catalog excludes the hundreds of musicals that are owned by other licensors, including the Rodgers & Hammerstein Organization (*Cinderella, The Sound of Music, Annie Get Your Gun, In the Heights*), Tams-Witmark (*The Wizard of Oz, Bye Bye Birdie*), TRW (*The Addams Family, All Shook Up*), and Samuel French (*Chicago*). JTF never hints that other musicals exist outside of MTI's catalog. In this way, a select repertoire stands in for all musical theatre, and JTF blocks the possibility of kids' exposure to more shows.

And then there is gender. JTF, like all youth theatrical projects, is dominated by girls, but rather than allow the festival to be a place of girl power, the adults fetishize boys and go overboard to welcome them. When I attended the festival, girls outnumbered boys ten to one, and this gender disparity and the presence of boys in musical theatre were addressed on numerous occasions. In the all-conference sessions, boys were met with huge rounds of applause with each appearance, and several speakers, including composer Alan Menken, Disney Theatrical Group president Thomas Schumacher, and the cast of Disney's *Newsies*, who flew in for the day (the show was running on Broadway then), talked about bullying and offered advice to musical theatre–inclined boys. The organizers of JTF have yet to find a way to support boys, whether gay, proto-gay, or straight—though they're all queer by virtue of their participation in this feminized activity—without fixating on them to the detriment of the many girls who are equally dedicated to performance.

The Broadway musical theatre repertoire exacerbates the problem, with too many male parts and heterosexual romance narratives. The repertoire itself, like it or not, relies on and reinforces many negative gender stereotypes—especially female stereotypes—and is unrelentingly heterosexual. On *The Music Man JR.* website, for example, in addition to providing a basic sense of the character and the necessary vocal range, MTI describes Marian: "The character progresses greatly during the show, starting as an uptight librarian and transforming into a beautiful and trusting young woman. [. . .] She will also need to be comfortable kissing two boys—Harold and Charlie Cowell, which requires a certain amount of emotional maturity. Finally, take some time during auditions to try different pairs of Harolds and Marians until you reach the perfect match."[51] MTI is not to blame, for indeed, this is how the character of Marian is defined. But who wants a 12-year-old girl to learn that the books and intelligence associated with a librarian make her "uptight" and prevent her from being "beautiful and trusting"? And why should a fine young actor have to "be comfortable" kissing two boys?

These stereotypes appear in high relief when 4,000 kids of every shape and size and race and ethnicity perform excerpts in a short period of time. I found it positively painful to watch the repetitive performances of mincing femininity and awkward heterosexuality during the adjudicated sessions at JTF. In 2013, the year of *The Little Mermaid JR.*'s debut, 23 groups performed excerpts from the show, and I was horrified to witness girl after girl sing—usually with great charisma and forcefulness—about wanting to sacrifice herself for a boy. Even edgy musicals like *Hair* (Tams-Witmark), *Rent* (MTI plus a PG-13 rated School Edition), and *Spring Awakening* (MTI)—all less frequently produced in afterschool programs and never by middle-schoolers—present conventional and conservative gender roles that often demean or diminish women.

As for racial and socioeconomic diversity at JTF, white girls were the most visible demographic, but every group included students who looked to be of different races, and a number of groups were predominantly kids of color. The groups that participated included elementary and middle schools, which ranged from the wealthy Gwendolyn Brooks Middle School in affluent Oak Park, Illinois, to several Title I schools in Georgia. The community theatres also ran the gamut, from well-established pay-to-play companies to free programs offered to every child in the community who wants to participate.

And whether schools or community theatres were rich or poor, every teacher and director to whom I spoke expressed passionate dedication to kids and to musical theatre, believing with equal force in the pleasure of the art form and its value in young people's emotional development. The festival, which is growing every year in both locations, proves that the Broadway musical—at least this version of it—is alive and well across race, geography, and socioeconomics.

Of the thousands of schools, community theatres, private studios, and afterschool programs that produce musicals across the country, close to 100 of them participate in JTF. On the one hand, it's a tiny fraction of all of the children who sing or dance on stage each year. But it includes almost 7,500 children from forty states and six countries across gender, race, ethnicity, and class. That's not nothing.

11

At 9 a.m. on Monday morning—too early for a non-school day—Vanessa stood in the hotel lobby, which now felt familiar, since she had walked through it ten times a day all weekend. She looked around at all of the kids slouched against pillars or sitting on the floor or on their suitcases or duffle bags, waiting to go home, whether by plane or bus or car. Everyone looked tired, even the circle of girls who were leaning into each other and singing "For Good" from *Wicked*, which was everyone's favorite sad song when leaving your friends. It felt like a million years ago when she sang "Goodnight My Someone" during the adjudication. She touched her tote bag with her notebook inside. She wondered what show Ms. Carter would pick for the next year and if she could possibly get the lead again.

She glanced up the escalator and saw a tall, older white boy coming down. She remembered seeing him perform in *Hairspray JR.* in their pod. He played Corny Collins and totally hammed it up. He was so good—not a fantastic voice or a great dancer, but funny and bouncing off the walls with energy. Just as he got off the escalator, she stepped up to him. "Hey, you're Corny Collins," she said. "You were great." He looked very pleased and not the least bit embarrassed. "How did you—?"

"You were in my pod," she said.

"Oh yeah! Now I remember," he replied. "You played Marian the Librarian! You were amazing! And you took direction so well! When Cindy coached you, you were awesome!"

"Thanks!" Vanessa answered happily. "You were awesome yourself."

Someone called Daniel's name from across the lobby. He turned his head— "Coming!" he shouted, and then looked back at Vanessa, "I gotta go. But I'll see you next year, right?"

"Yeah," Vanessa nodded and smiled. "See you next year!"

Figure 2.1. A scene from *42nd Street*, Marilyn Izdebski Productions, San Anselmo, California.

2

Backstage Divas

The Backstage Diva: A Story

Once upon a time there was a little girl who loved to dance. Each morning she jumped out of bed and slipped on the worn, faded ballet shoes that were the last thing she took off before she got under the covers at night. She chasséed across her bedroom, she twirled into the kitchen for breakfast, she did piqué turns to grab her coat and book bag. In school all day, she read aloud when the teacher called on her, she calculated math equations, and she stared out the window and tapped her feet beneath the desk, going over the steps she'd learned the day before.

Then one day, everything changed.

Her father died, but he didn't believe in life insurance. She and her mother had to move from a three-bedroom house to a one-bedroom apartment. Her mother starting smoking and drinking and going out with other men. Then her mother told her they couldn't afford dance lessons anymore. The little girl could barely speak. She was devastated. She was in a total panic.

The next day after school, she went to the dance studio as usual, but she waited after class to tell her teacher that they had no money, her mother couldn't pay for dance classes, and she had to stop coming to class. She held back a sob as the tears streamed down her face. Her teacher looked up, dropped her clipboard, and gave her a hug. "That's okay, Marilyn. You come here after school every day, you help run the desk, and you can keep taking dance classes."

Years passed, and as little Marilyn grew up, her passion for dancing only grew. She felt most alive on stage and most at home at the studio. At school, no one knew what was going on with her family. No one knew that she was scared and lonely sometimes. No one knew that she worried about her mother.

But it was different at the studio. Though she felt she could tell her dance teacher anything, she didn't have to. Her dance teacher knew how she felt just by looking at her. She knew when Marilyn needed a hug or to talk or to be left alone. Marilyn felt safe, and more than that, she loved to dance and be with other girls and boys who loved to dance.

But then, something terrible happened.

Beyond Broadway. Stacy Wolf, Oxford University Press (2020). © Oxford University Press.
DOI: 10.1093/oso/9780190639525.001.0001

When Marilyn was sixteen, her mother died. She was sent to live with a neighbor and then was taken in by a family that loved her and became her family for the rest of her life. Her uncle, who was her legal guardian, did not want her to dance. But she knew she would never stop dancing or doing theatre no matter what he said or thought.

Marilyn said to herself, "Do you want it [this tragedy] to make you do bad things or do you want to do good things?" She kept dancing, went to college, studied theatre, and became a performer and a teacher. She never forgot the importance of her dance teacher and how much the studio mattered to her as a girl. She knew she had to do the same thing for other children.

But what did that mean? She wanted to teach children to dance. She wanted to direct them in shows. She wanted to make a place for children to feel good about themselves, a place where no one would mock them or make fun of them for any reason. A place where no one is too short, too tall, too big, or too small. She decided to open her own studio.

Marilyn never meant to be a businesswoman. But as the years went by, more parents heard of her studio and sent their children to Marilyn to do shows. Some kids loved the stage and some were shy and scared. Some wanted to be stars and some just needed something to do after school. She took them all and tried to draw out the light she saw in each child.

She learned how to do everything, from balancing the books to directing and choreographing new shows to dealing with overly involved parents. You might say that she built her brand. Over the years, Marilyn honed her craft and developed her methods. She wrote a memo with audition instructions for the kids: "Choose an uptempo, happy, personality-filled song ('Tomorrow' is not a good choice.)"; "Have your hair off your face!"; "Do the choreography for your song—don't just stand there and sing!"; "SMILE!!! HAVE FUN!!!" She wrote a letter to parents about casting: "I am directing musicals. The production numbers are the show-stoppers of all musicals. Therefore, the music and dance are most important to me. Those cast in the chorus represent the largest and most important part of my shows." About the few speaking or principal roles, she explained, "I cast them on the basis of the level of excitement, interest, humor, and just plain stage presence that I see at an audition. These roles are never pre-cast." She learned she needed to add, "Nor are they 'earned' by being in previous shows, taking dance lessons, or by being my dearest friends." She repeatedly said, "Theatre and doing musicals is an ensemble effort." She required parents to supply parts of costumes—leotards and tights for the girls; pants and shirt for the boys; and ballet shoes, jazz shoes, and tap shoes. Finally, she asked parents to volunteer a few hours of their time to help out in some way. For herself and her team of helpers, she created a 50-item list and schedule of tasks that needed to be accomplished for each show.

Marilyn's reputation grew. Many kids stuck around for years performing in Marilyn's shows. Some of her loyal following returned from college to help out in the summer, just to be around her. She knew which shows worked for her kids, which she repeated with a new crop of kids after those who had done those shows aged out.

Her energy never seemed to flag. For every show, for auditions, rehearsals, and performances, she brought the same intensity, drive, and passion. And the children answered her with undying dedication. The diva's "toughness comes out of performance, which is often a triumph over personal limitations or disaster," writes theatre scholar John Clum.[1] That was true for Marilyn. She became a backstage diva and lived happily ever after.

Meet Marilyn

When I arrive at the theatre—a barnlike building on the leafy campus of the San Francisco Theological Seminary in San Anselmo, California, nineteen miles north of San Francisco—to watch the dress rehearsal for *42nd Street* (Figure 2.1), a petite, bright-eyed woman with perfect posture in her mid-60s quickly strides across the floor to greet me. She wears black yoga pants, a black zip-up sweater, a black scarf around her neck, white athletic socks, and black clogs—her uniform and the only way I ever saw her dressed. Her dark hair is in a bun with a pencil stuck through it and a pair of reading glasses hangs around her neck. Even though we'd only spoken on the phone a few times, she approaches me with a wide smile, one arm outstretched to hug me and the other carrying a small, fluffy white Maltipoo (Figure 2.2). "This is Bobbi," she says, as I lean in to pet the dog and see that one of her eyes is sewn shut and her little pink tongue droops sideways out of her mouth. "She got in a fight with another dog that bit her in the face," Marilyn informs me matter-of-factly. She lost one eye but is "doing really well half-blind and only bumps into walls occasionally." (Full disclosure: When I met Marilyn, I misidentified the dog by gender and by breed: I thought he was Bobby, a male Shih Tzu! Fortunately, Marilyn corrected my error in an earlier draft of this chapter.)

If you ask any kid who performs in musicals in Marin County, California, how they got started in musical theatre, the answer would be "Marilyn."

Figure 2.2. Marilyn (with Bobbi) talks to the performers during tech/dress rehearsal for *42 Street*.

I meet her after having followed the trail of crumbs—or rather, musical theatre–obsessed kids—from Redwood High School's well-respected drama program (which produced *Into the Woods*, the subject of Chapter 3) to the Mountain Play's annual event (we'll visit there in Chapter 5), which brings together all of Mill Valley to see a musical six miles up on Mt. Tamalpais. In the bios of the kids in the Mountain Play's production of *The Sound of Music*, they all thanked Marilyn. I finally land here, in the two-hundred-seat Playhouse she rents for shows five times a year. Everyone knows Marilyn. And they only refer to her by her first name. In Mill Valley, she is a living legend.

Marilyn produces six shows a year, two each in the fall, spring, and summer for different age groups. She typically casts sixty to a hundred kids aged seven to fifteen in a show, always in elaborate costumes—even the chorus members have several costume changes—and sometimes tap shoes. During the school year, the children rehearse in her studio once a week for three hours for ten weeks and then move to the Playhouse for tech and dress rehearsals and the performance. Children often do their first "Marilyn show" when they are seven or eight and continue through middle school, performing in twenty or more shows. Most of "Marilyn's kids," as they call themselves, go on to do high school musicals and community shows, and a few become professional actors, usually in the Bay Area. Some return from college or as adults to help out in the theatre. Marilyn has directed 153 shows, including *Evita* four times, *Annie* six times, and *Guys and Dolls* seven times.[2] Over her forty-year career, Marilyn estimates that she's worked with ten thousand kids.

Though Marilyn Izdebski herself is quirky and unique, her role in her community is not. The female musical theatre director who works with kids after school and on the weekends, who teaches them dance or drama, and who directs them in shows can be found in most American towns. She is typically a disciplined leader and dependable mentor who shapes musical theatre–obsessed kids into triple-threat performers. As one of her young performers said, "We all give credit to Marilyn."[3]

The backstage diva is singular and generalizable, idiosyncratic and typical. Marilyn is the star of this chapter, but there's also Jordan Nelson in Casper, Wyoming; Relana Gerami in League City, Texas; Judith Ranaletta in Rochester, New York; and Toby Orenstein in Columbia, Maryland, who was the backstage diva of my childhood and adolescence—just to name a very few. You could drop a pin anywhere on the map of the United States, in any city or town, and find such a woman. We can recognize her. We know this type. And we know that she is a powerful force in the indoctrination and training of young people. Though most of those kids won't become professional performers, that doesn't diminish her importance. On the contrary, all of her kids are profoundly shaped by her.

The very descriptor "backstage" might seem anathema to the "diva" who typically is the star, who takes up space, and whose performance is the center of attention. But "diva" is the perfect moniker for these women, who, though they labor backstage, occupy a starring role in the lives of musical theatre kids and are a force in the afterschool artistic life of their community.

In addition, they perform every day during rehearsals with a diva's intensity and charisma, whether they're giving line readings, demonstrating a piece of schtick, instructing the actors where to go and when and how, yelling about a missed cue, or waxing poetic during an opening night pep talk. Their work—that is, their performance—takes place under the watchful eyes of the children and the backstage crew, which is made up of local friends of the theatre, star-struck parents, and dedicated former performers who return as young adults to work backstage. These women might be considered what literature scholar Wayne Koestenbaum calls "local, private divas," who, as he writes, "glamorize the local (the slow, the tenacious, the microscopic, the incremental)"; that is, the painstaking, patience-demanding work of directing musical theatre with kids.[4] Just as the diva makes the aria look effortless even as she works hard to sing it, the backstage diva seems naturally to connect with and motivate her kids.

The character of the backstage diva has appeared in popular culture as, for example, the Miss Patty in *Gilmore Girls* (2000–07), Idina Menzel's and Kristen Chenoweth's characters in *Glee* (2009–15), or the drama teacher in *High School Musical* (2006). In *Bunheads* (2012–13), she was the studio owner, played by Kelly Bishop, who originated the (diva) role of Sheila in *A Chorus Line* (1975), to contrast with the show's protagonist, played by Sutton Foster, who was meant to be a kind of anti-backstage diva. Though certain larger-than-life aspects of the fictionalized character resonate with actual backstage divas, the many women I've met aren't frustrated performers like their fictitious counterparts. Rather, the backstage diva's ambitions are grander somehow, to create and sustain a place, a home in the local and national musical theatre ecosystem. She sees her role as nothing less than shaping children into people.

A Brief History of the Backstage Diva

Marilyn follows a history of female dancing instructors and drama coaches who built cottage industries of theatrical production over the years. We can trace her roots back to a handful of women who taught social dances to youth in private homes and community spaces in the American colonies in the eighteenth century.[5] By the end of the nineteenth century, women frequently operated schools of dance that bore their name.[6] Dancing in America originated as a social activity and entertainment form, but in the early twentieth century, thanks to women like Margaret H'Doubler, who argued for dance's educational value, and Isadora Duncan, who "stirred new consideration of dance as a serious form of artistic expression," dance achieved an elevated status and was deemed worthy of collegiate study.[7] These ideals trickled down, leading to dance's inclusion in K-12 public school girls' physical education programs and the opening of private children's dance studios. Additionally, in the late 1920s, Americans started going to the movies, and with the 1927 release of *The Jazz Singer*, the first musical film, a broader segment of society was exposed to musical comedy and theatrical dancing and soon wanted to learn how to dance like their on-screen idols.[8] By the 1940s, most towns boasted at least one community dance school—typically run by a woman—offering some combination of modern, tap, ballet, ballroom, acrobatics, and baton classes.[9]

Backstage divas also emerged during the children's theatre movement that took off in the 1920s. In that decade, the Junior League Association, run primarily by women, added children's theatre to its national agenda. By the 1940s, the League had opened over a hundred children's theatres in cities across America, from Portland to Chicago to Nashville. Some programs primarily presented extant shows to children audiences. However, by the 1930s, thanks to theatre educator Winifred Ward, many had started offering Creative Dramatics classes where children could "develop plays out of their own thoughts and imaginations and emotions" under the supervision of a (typically female) teacher.[10] Creative Dramatics was popular into the 1950s and 1960s and has remained at the core of many twenty-first-century early childhood theatre programs.

Locally, women began opening children's theatre studios, sometimes on their own and sometimes through organizations like Parks & Recreation or the YMCA. Irene Belcher, for example, opened her first children's theatre studio in Muncie, Indiana, in the 1930s, and was Muncie's "first lady of the theater."[11] Mary MacMurtrie directed the Juvenile Players in Burlingame, California, in the 1920s with the support of a Parent-Teacher Association.[12] When she moved to Arizona in 1931, she independently founded the Tucson Children's Theater.[13] MacMurtrie was the community's "Marvelous Task Master," as a tribute to her read. She "was a professional, and in this world of amateurs and self-styled prophets, that is no small thing."[14] This remains the very definition of a backstage diva: She is a professional in a world of amateurs.

A 1948 *Dramatics* magazine article acknowledged this trend, stating that privately owned children's theatre studios were "the answer for those who want to be their own bosses and engage in free enterprise." The article went on, "A person of integrity and inspiration can develop a sound business based on the creative needs of children, since this appeals to thoughtful parents, and in the long run builds on the respect of the community."[15]

These pioneers in dance and theatre education paved the way for backstage divas like Marilyn who went on to combine theatre and dance, introducing private children's musical theatre education in the second half of the twentieth century. By the late 1960s and early 1970s, youth musical theatre classes were offered by dance studios and music conservatories. Some programs added one musical theater workshop or dance class, while others expanded their offerings more broadly and became comprehensive performing arts schools. Some studio owners made these changes because they wanted to offer a more "well-rounded" arts education.[16] Others knew about the new triple-threat demands of Broadway and felt comprehensive training would better prepare their top students for the profession.[17] Still others lived in towns where public school arts programs were lacking, so they sought to fulfill a need in their communities.

By the mid-1970s, more women opened performing arts studios that offered musical theatre classes from the start, like Marilyn, who launched her school in 1978 with a mounting of *Oliver!* Marilyn is one of several early backstage divas who taught musical theatre to youth by directing them in canonical Broadway titles and producing full-scale productions.[18] The children learned the skills of music, dance, and acting by rehearsing for a show. This approach began around 1960 as hit Golden Age Broadway musical titles became available for amateur licensing. Unlike Creative Dramatics classes, which led children to devise original plays, musical theatre classes like Marilyn's asked students to bring extant shows to life in the most "professional" way possible. As a result, in the rehearsal room, the backstage diva started functioning less like a teacher and more like a director.

Female-operated full-service arts academies multiplied in the 1980s, 1990s, and into the early 2000s.[19] Studios emerged with "Broadway Bound," "Triple Threat," or "Show Biz" in their names. The "About Us" page of their eventual websites typically feature the founder's biography, which, while always unique, highlights how much backstage divas have in common with one another. Rhonda Cato, for example, is the director of Magic Curtain Productions in East Orlando, Florida. In this city the median age is 32.1 years, 14 percent of the population lives below the poverty line, and 37 percent of the people are Latino.[20] Rhonda taught theatre part time and one day said to her daughter, "Why don't we get a group of your friends and we'll work on the song, 'Hard Knock Life' [from *Annie*]?" Seven little girls showed up at her house, and they practiced once a week for two months and sang for the school talent show. The girls loved it, wanted to do more, and told their friends, and soon there were ten to twelve little girls at her house twice a week. Rhonda started looked for a rehearsal and performance space and found one at a bowling alley for free. Youth bowlers—teenagers with earrings and tattoos, as she described them, "came in and they sat down and were mesmerized by my twelve little performers, and that's when I said, 'There's a place for arts in East Orlando.'" She directed shows and soon her little program grew to thirty-five kids, with numbers increasing each year. In 2013, Magic Curtain opened their own space with a hundred-seat theatre, voice room, dance room, and drama room.[21] Most women started their programs for the same reason: They saw a need for and interest in youth arts in their communities, and they wanted the Broadway musical repertoire to be at the center.

Directing musicals is only one of the backstage diva's many responsibilities. She oversees the business from top to bottom, working year-round as an independent contractor of sorts. The backstage diva is often a real estate genius, finding some unused space and figuring out how to repurpose it as a theatre. She advertises her business, balances the books, negotiates with licensing companies, and always stays several years ahead, planning for the theatre's future. The backstage diva guides techies, makes sure the dressing rooms are orderly, and mollifies parents when they get too helicopter-y. She balances artistic aspirations and financial pressures, and channels her creativity into shaping kids into triple-threat performers. An artist with equal measures of good sense, patience, clarity, and business acumen, the backstage diva's labor is logistical, physical, and emotional.

Marilyn, like other backstage divas, relies on the income from students' tuition for her livelihood. Though many of Marilyn's students are wealthy, others are not, and she never turns away a child who can't afford to pay: "Because dance almost was taken away from me at a young age, I make it a policy that if someone wants to dance, they will dance." Many backstage divas run low-cost or free programs, such as Jordan Nelson, who directs Casper Children's Theatre in Casper, Wyoming;, Becky Lovins, who is executive director of the Portsmouth Area Arts Council & Children's Theatre in Portsmouth, Ohio; and Amy Browning of First Stage Theatre Company in Huntington, West Virginia.

Evita Auditions

The day of *Evita* auditions, which are held in the theatre at nearby Redwood High School, starts with twenty-one twelve- to fifteen-year-olds—almost all white kids—singing. The Andrew Lloyd Webber and Tim Rice 1979 sung-through musical that made Patti LuPone a star follows the story of Eva Peron, who went from poor country girl to the rich and powerful wife of Argentina's president. It's a serious and adult-themed show with a lot of dance and a fantastic role for a girl. Marilyn directed the show four times in her career, and this time, like the others, she would divide the part into three "Evas" at different stages of her life, and then double-cast each of the roles. That way, six girls would be cast as Eva.

Two volunteer parents man a small table in the theatre's windowed and sunlit foyer, helping the kids fill out audition forms with their name, parent or guardian's contact information, age, height, school and grade, musical theatre and dance class experience. On the bottom of the form, a "contract" reads, "DO YOU UNDERSTAND THAT YOU ARE MAKING A COMMITMENT TO THE ENTIRE SHOW AND ARE WILLING TO ACCEPT WHATEVER ROLE YOU ARE ASSIGNED? AND TO DO YOUR VERY BEST TO GIVE IT LIFE?" Each child then receives a number and goes into the theatre. Every child will be cast in the pay-to-play production, and though Marilyn already knows most of the kids, she wants to convey professionalism from the start with a performance of anonymity.

In the theatre, Marilyn sits behind a work table set halfway up the audience, and Bobbi, the Maltipoo, sleeps on it, amid her papers. Marilyn's former student and current assistant, Siena, props an iPhone on a tripod to tape the auditions (though I don't think Marilyn ever looked at them), and Judy, Marilyn's friend and musical director of thirty years, sits ready at the piano on the auditorium floor downstage right. I settle myself in the row behind Marilyn, not wanting to get in her way but hoping to peek over her shoulder to see what she will write on each child's audition sheet.

With no "good morning," welcome, preamble, or introduction whatsoever, Marilyn calls "number one!" and a small girl with long straight blond hair in a pale pink Juicy T-shirt, jean shorts, and white Converse sneakers stands and walks slowly up the stairs onto the stage. "My name is Abby," she says, barely above a whisper, "I'm fourteen years old and in the eighth grade and I go to Marin Catholic"—introducing herself as Marilyn expects them to do—"I'm singing 'Tomorrow' from *Annie*." I think I detect Marilyn take a breath (recall that she recommends singing an uptempo song and not "Tomorrow") and sit a little taller in her seat, as if willing Abby to be brave. Or maybe that's how I feel. Abby looks over at Judy, who plays her starting note. Abby, trembling visibly, squeaks out two lines of music on pitch—"the sun'll come out tomorrow. Bet your bottom dollar that tomorrow, there'll be sun" and stops. Everybody waits for her to go on, but she doesn't. That's what she has. "Thank you," the girl says, already relieved that it's over. "Thank you, Abby," Marilyn replies, curtly, as Abby leaves the stage. Marilyn writes something on her notepad. The twenty other kids sit in the audience quietly. No one applauds because, as Marilyn has told them, "It's not a performance."

One by one, Marilyn calls their numbers, and the kids go up on stage and sing their song. Some get through a line or two like Abby, and others present entire numbers with several verses, but Marilyn never cuts them off. A girl named Jessica in a sundress and a ribbon holding a thick dark ponytail stops after one line of "Maybe" from *Annie*, frowning. "It's in the wrong key," she says to Judy. "Can you play it lower?" Judy immediately transposes the song down a few notes, and Jessica continues with confidence and energy, belting out the wistful, downbeat song. Another girl, Zoe, wears a long flowy black skirt, red blouse, character shoes, and a flower in her hair, which was pulled back severely in a bun, looking remarkably like Eva Peron. "You're not dressed as Eva, are you, Zoe?" Marilyn asks the girl when she walks onto the stage. "No, Marilyn," a tall and mature-looking Zoe answers. "I just wanted to wear a skirt and dance shoes." "Okay," says Marilyn, looking dubious. "You all know enough not to audition in costume, right?" The kids all solemnly nod. Zoe sings "Hard Knock Life" from *Annie*. For every child, Marilyn keeps the same impassive face and when they finish, she thanks them politely but coldly.

At the same time, though, there is a feeling of cozy and casual insiderness among the kids, with jokes flying back and forth whenever Marilyn stops to take a phone call or answer a question. Perhaps there is elevated hilarity because of the nervousness of auditions? Even with six girls to be cast as Eva, the competition is stiff and they know it.

After an hour, they take a five-minute break. David, one of the kids who auditioned, approaches Marilyn, who's sipping (now melted) iced coffee and talking to Siena. He has curly blond hair and wears madras plaid shorts and an Izod collared shirt. "Excuse me, Marilyn?" he says. He tells her that his little brother, who is in the concurrent younger kids' production of *Once Upon a Mattress*, "really wants to play the kitten in the show." Marilyn looks at him sharply, "David, it's not appropriate for you to tell me this. I'm going to pretend that this didn't happen." And the boy slinks off. Just as Marilyn teaches the kids to audition in a way that she considers professional, she also expects them to practice certain rules of theatre etiquette. And as she promised, the next time she speaks to him, it's as if nothing happened.

Marilyn scores the kids with two numbers, one for singing and one for personality, from 1 through 10, though no one gets a 10. A lot of kids get a 7, which seems to translate into 70, C, satisfactory. She invites me to sit next to her so I can see her in action. Sometimes I guess her scoring correctly, but often not. Even in these tiny, two-minute performances, there are vast differences among the kids. Some of them are calm, relaxed, and confident. Others seem terrified, even stricken. Some have strong voices and others cannot sing on key at all. Some project their energy into the house and others shrink into themselves.

When they move on to the acting segment of the audition, teaming kids to read a page (or less) of a scene, more differences emerge. Some of the best singers also speak clearly and loudly but display no expressiveness in their acting. Some of the off-key singers are strong actors and convey a sense of a character. Even at twelve years old, there are significant differences in their ability to read aloud. Some have already memorized the scene, which Marilyn made available to then in advance, and are able to look up. Others read haltingly and can't pronounce some of the words. Some of the kids have good physical control. Others wander around the stage and display nervous physical tics. Somehow, Marilyn sees through this strange condensation of preteen embodiment to each child's potential to play Che or Eva or another role in eight weeks' time.

After all of the kids sing and read, Marilyn drops her brusque façade. "Thanks everyone! You did a great job! Siena will call you this evening if you're called back. See some of you tomorrow and everyone on Wednesday for our first rehearsal! Bye!" And the kids gather their backpacks and move from the auditorium's dim light to the bright California day.

The next afternoon, they hold callbacks. The theatre is filled with giddy energy of the three boys and ten girls who know they have a shot at the leading roles of Eva or Che. After downing her last sip of coffee and dumping Bobbi onto my lap, Marilyn calls all of the kids onto the stage together, and each sings a scale so that Judy can test their range. They return to their seats, then one by one, each girl goes up on stage and performs the first few lines of Eva's famous song, "Don't Cry for Me, Argentina." Marilyn repeats every time, "I want to see the passion!" Each kid starts strong. Some can keep the intensity as they sing the challenging intervals of the music, and others' energy flags or they can't reach the low notes at the end of the phrase, "I kept my promise / Don't keep your distance." After each one, Marilyn says, "Good!" She's different today during the high-stakes callbacks, encouraging and warm.

After all then girls sing and return to their seats and Marilyn is about to move on, she notices one girl who is crying. "What's wrong, Callie?" Marilyn asks. "She thinks she did badly," replies Zoe, consoling her friend. Marilyn drops her clipboard, and moves down the aisle to put her arm around the weeping Callie. "I was looking for acting, not singing, Callie," Marilyn says softly to the girl but loud enough for all to hear. Then she turns to everyone: "By the way, girls, this is a really difficult song. It goes up and down and the intervals are hard." Judy adds, "We're all friends here. We've been cracking all day." When the boys sing for the role of Che next, Marilyn reminds them, "I'm looking for intensity, for acting," and Judy adds, "This is not a singing audition. This is an acting audition and you're a pop star."

All morning, I see the kids absorbing Marilyn's lessons as they watch her and take their cues from her, struggling to see themselves through her eyes, to decipher what she wants. The backstage diva is the gatekeeper of young, tender, and fragile egos. She greatly controls kids' lives and their sense of themselves.

After ninety minutes of moving the kids in and out of roles, having them sing Che, Eva, the girlfriend, and Peron, and putting them in different combinations to sing together, Judy leans over to Marilyn and whispers, "We're not going to figure out anything by having them do more," and she consults her list to make sure that each child had the same number of chances to sing. Marilyn stands up. "Thank you, everyone! See you at rehearsal tomorrow when we'll give you your parts!" And the kids leave.

"I'm looking for energy and a little kernel of characterization," Marilyn tells me, stacking the audition sheets. "Some of them understand the character and have an aspect of the character in them. The words are then just something that the character says. That one," she said, tilting her head towards a girl with a pixie cut and unusual poise and confidence on her way out the door. "She could read the phone book in the character of Eva. She *gets* the character. A great acting exercise is to use Ann Landers' letters and have them perform them in different kinds of characters—Valley Girl, Queen, etc. [I'm trying to see if] they have enough that I can work with." Do their past roles matter? I ask. "Not really, because kids change so much that each time is different," she replies. "Occasionally if a kid hasn't had a lead and I see the potential, I'll see if I can give them a chance."

When the theatre is empty, Marilyn, Judy, and Siena put their heads together to cast the show, since rehearsals start the next morning. They go through the kids one by one. "David was so quiet," Siena says. "I could barely hear him."

"I think he has potential," Marilyn counters.

"I don't know," Judy muses. "I don't know if we can get it out of him."

"I like Tara for one of the Middle Evas. She surprised me," says Judy.

"Hmmm," Marilyn says. "I think she gave a great audition but I don't know if she'll do any more than what we saw. Let's cast her as the girlfriend. I want to give Jessica a chance as a Middle Eva." Judy raises her eyebrows, presses her lips together, and continues, "And what about Tara's mother? She won't be happy."

"I know," answers Marilyn. "She lives through her kid. It's okay, I'll handle her."

"What did you think about Zoe?" Siena asks, but before she finishes saying her name, the three of them shout in unison, "Older Eva!" "She's going to Broadway, that girl!" Siena said. Marilyn and Judy nod, grinning widely, imagining Zoe on Broadway.

"That boy, Zach?" Judy goes on. "His brother is a star baseball player [but] this kid is not athletic at all. Let's make sure he has something to do."

"Yes!" replies Marilyn. "Now I know why he looks familiar! He looks just like his brother. But skinnier. I thought he did well. I was thinking about him for Magaldi."

"Great!" Judy responds. They go through the rest of the kids and assign each a role and they're done.

The next day when the kids arrive for the first rehearsal, Marilyn will give them a piece of paper with the cast list on it, facedown. She'll give them a speech about "appropriate responses to casting and making lemonade" and give them the signal to turn the paper over.

"Casting is an art," Marilyn tells me. Still, her attitude about auditions has changed over the years. "In my early career, I would make auditions very strict and serious and the kids would be so anxious and in tears. Over the years, I've mellowed and now I try to keep it light and relaxed, and then they get serious and focused when they get up there." She adds, "They have plenty of time in their lives to feel bad about auditions. I want them to have a good experience." She tucks Bobbi under her arm and strides out the door.

Rehearsals

Rehearsal #1: *Once Upon a Mattress* and Acting

A few days later, on a chilly, foggy, northern California June morning, a line of cars drop off twenty still sleepy seven- to twelve-year-olds at the high school to rehearse for *Once Upon a Mattress*. This 1959 comedic, lightly feminist revamp of "The Princess and the Pea," by Mary Rodgers and Marshall Barer, starred Carol Burnett on Broadway and in two popular television versions in 1964 and 1972. There's some adult humor that Marilyn downplays, emphasizing instead the show's broad slapstick style.

Marilyn starts the day by going over the scene they'd blocked the day before, with the second cast watching from the house. (As noted, she double-casts every show to provide more kids with opportunities to play bigger parts and to ensure that no one child has ownership over any part.) Marilyn warns the actors, "If you don't remember your entrance, you'll owe me a $100 gift certificate to Starbucks." Everyone giggles nervously and glances toward the coffee cup perched on the edge of the stage next to her set of keys, the stacked script pages, which Siena hands to her one by one, and a tall stool that is ignored the entire day.

Next Marilyn calls both casts on stage to teach them how to do a stage slap, demonstrating how the slapper makes a big, wind-up gesture and creates the sharp skin-on-skin sound by clapping their hands together just beyond the face of the slappee, who screams and recoils in pain. Everyone laughs as they try it out, some falling on the floor after they get "hit." "Good! Great!" Marilyn shouts above the din. She looks down at one kid who lies on the floor curled up laughing, about to tell him to get up, but then shrugs and turns to work with another.

Then the second cast goes to sit in the audience, and Marilyn continues Act 1, Scene 3, when Winifred, the bold, disheveled true princess enters the castle courtyard after having swum across the moat. All of the lords and ladies recoil in horror at the "dripping wet" girl, "a few slimy weeds clinging to her purple gown," as the stage directions read.[22] Marilyn shows each child where to stand and where to move and when and how to how to react to Winifred. The Queen, played by Missy in this cast, repeats the line, "You swam the moat?" three times, with ever-increasing shock. Marilyn demonstrates the intonation she wants to hear from Missy, who imitates Marilyn dutifully in her own voice. Marilyn loves it. She also shows Hannah, who plays Winifred, how to respond with a wide, pleasant smile and a shrug.[23]

The children are eager, some tentative and some bold. They want to please her. In contrast to a rehearsal process with adults—or even with high schoolers—Marilyn doesn't try to draw out the kids' own ideas about the characters. She's directed this show many times in the past. She knows how each role should be played, how the jokes need to land, and the meaning, inflection, and emphasis of each line for maximum effect. She corrects and coaches the young actors to make their gestures bigger. Above all, she calls for "passion." The kids follow her instructions as best as they can and imitate her schtick, willingly being disciplined into a certain way of playing a role— or trying to. In the end, each child's rendition of the character remains entirely their own. Throughout the day, there is a lot of laughter and praise from Marilyn and quick transitions between silliness and seriousness.

Rehearsal #2: *Once Upon a Mattress* and Choreography

After a short break, the children eat cupcakes that one mother brought for her daughter's birthday, and Bobbi jumps to attention to scarf up all of the sugary crumbs on the floor. The kids sing "Happy Birthday" with great enthusiasm and multi-part harmony, and Marilyn glances at the DVD of a 2008 production of the show to jog her memory of the choreography for the next part of rehearsal. She gathers all of the children into a circle on the floor. "What's a triple threat?" she asks. The kids chew on their lips and avert their eyes. She answers, "It's a performer who can sing and dance and act— what you need to do in musical theatre!" She tells them they are going to learn "The Spanish Panic," one of the big ensemble numbers in the show. "If you're learning dance for the first time, it's so much fun," she exclaims. "If you haven't had much dance, this is your chance to see why I love it so much." Marilyn's enthusiastic set-up ensures the kids' engagement, and it works like a charm. They can't wait to get started.

Marilyn commands all of the kids to stay on stage, even the ones who aren't in the song: "I want all of you to learn this so you can have practice dancing." She stands in front of them and slowly demonstrates eight counts of the song's first line. "Watch me first," she says, as the kids are antsy to try it. The movement includes low kicks, pivot turns, and shuffle-ball-changes, and starts and ends with the performers' hands on their hips. "Let's go through it together," she says. She counts slowly and repeats the choreography, and the children follow her. Some execute it perfectly the first time, having watched and absorbed the movement. Others' feet get tangled. She repeats it over and over, endlessly patient, and most of the kids start to get it, clearly pleased with themselves. Lauren, a fourteen-year-old who is helping with this show (and who performed in Marilyn's 2008 production of *Once Upon a Mattress*) moves among the kids to correct their movements. Marilyn says, "Let me see it," and turns around to watch them. Lauren steps to the front so that the kids can watch her. They run through the tiny dance phrase altogether. "Great!" says Marilyn. "Great start! Now, I don't want to see any dead arms. Your arms should be relaxed but alive. And smile! This is a funny dance! Do it again." After twenty minutes, they've learned the first verse of the number. Some are performance ready, most have a ways to go, and a few might not ever get it right.

At 12:30 p.m., Siena gestures with her watch, signaling thirty minutes left in their time. "We made a great stab at this," Marilyn says, stopping midway through the song so they can run everything they worked on that day. "That was fantastic," she says. Through the morning, the children and Marilyn create the play line by line, gesture by gesture, note by note. At the same time, the kids learn the ways of Marilyn. As for Bobbi, she spends the day walking up and down the aisle of the theatre, sleeping on the edge of the stage on Marilyn's script pages, or sitting in my lap.

Marilyn, like all backstage divas, aims to strike a balance between strict training and gentle nurturing, between making the best possible show and helping the kids to feel good about themselves. She readily acknowledges that kids possess different aspirations, different skills, and different levels of maturity. Other backstage divas express similar sentiments. Amy Browning of First Stage Theatre Company in Huntington, West Virginia, said, "We worked a lot on jazz squares [one of the easiest dance steps] . . . some kids are really good at it, some kids couldn't find their feet." Anne Kessler of Curtain Call Performing Arts Center, in Mount Laurel, New Jersey, remarked, "I never say to a kid, 'You can't do that. That's too hard.' You say, 'You can do this. Let's give it a try. Let's try it a different way. If it's not working, how can we make that work?'" Relana Gerami of the Bay Area Theatre and Voice Academy in League City, Texas, said, "We always explain . . . to the kids that criticism is not bad." She added, "I'm very honest with everyone, and sometimes they can't take it . . . I've learned how to find the ones who can and can't." She summed it up: Most kids "want discipline. They want to know that they messed up. But they also want to know that they did well."

Like Marilyn, other backstage divas have well-honed methods of working and expectations for their kids. Jennifer Boesing, director of Youth Musical Theatre Company in Berkeley, California, just across the bay from Marilyn, directed *Sweeney Todd* that same summer. She never gives line readings but asks each actor to think about what they are saying, a slower process that requires the child's independent interpretation. Jennifer wants kids to "connect with each other on stage." Neva Garrett, who directs Holly Performance Academy in Dahlonega, Georgia, said, "We're always on them, 'Don't look bored, don't look bored.'" Anne Kessler of Curtain Call Performing Arts Center recounted how she talks to the kids during rehearsals: "I'm like, 'So today we have to nail down this little song passage [that] we're having trouble [with]. We're gonna repeat it like five or six times until our muscles, our vocal muscles, remember how to do it.'" She went on, "It's no different than . . . batting practice where you're practicing your swing . . . There is athleticism in performance, and I try to make those connections."

Rehearsal #3: *42nd Street* and Dress Rehearsal

The dress rehearsal of *42nd Street* at the Playhouse two nights before the show opens in early November is controlled chaos. The show, with music by Harry Warren, lyrics by Al Dubin and Johnny Mercer, and book by Mark Bramble and Michael Stewart, is a 1980 confection, which opened on Broadway the same year as *Barnum* and revivals of *The Music Man, Camelot*, and *West Side Story*. Set in 1933, *42nd Street* is the backstage story of a girl from Allentown, Pennsylvania, who becomes a Broadway star. It's a perfect Marilyn vehicle, with a large cast of colorful characters and many chorus numbers (Figure 2.3).

I arrive at the theatre before the kids but after Marilyn and her crew of adult helpers. The place is buzzing with many volunteers: two people deal with a new sound system and will eventually get the kids fitted with body mics and then do a sound check to make sure all of the channels are working. Five women organize an astonishing array of costumes, tap shoes, and feather boas into small, curtained-off, makeshift dressing rooms backstage. Another pair of women prepare signup sheets to order T-shirts and DVDs of the show. Two men in their early 20s adjust the floor-to-ceiling canvas backdrop—a sun yellow background over which "Pretty Lady" in large silver 3-D lettering is painted below an image of a 1930s iconic blond pin-up girl. One stands on a ladder to make sure that the backdrop hangs evenly and is steady. Later Marilyn would yell at the kids, "You can't stand right behind the curtain! You're punching it!" Judy helps the other musicians—a younger guy on a drum set and another middle-aged guy on a synthesizer—to unpack and set up in a little cordoned-off section downstage left. Finally, there are three women in their twenties—all former students, Marilyn's assistants and stage

Figure 2.3. A glittery musical number from *42nd Street*, Marilyn Izdebski Productions.

managers—who stick to her like glue, then scamper off to take care of whatever she says need to be done.

Everyone is here because of the kids, because of musical theatre, and because of Marilyn, the backstage diva. She herself wears many hats, adopts many roles, and plays many characters as an artist/educator/entrepreneur. She can do everything and is the leader and the one calling the shots, administratively, artistically, and emotionally, but she relies on a big loyal crew of parents and friend volunteers to help out.

Marilyn has completed many other tasks to prepare for this rehearsal, including designing the lights and setting the cues (skills she learned on the job—who else was going to design and focus lights for her in those early days?), and before that, organizing the rehearsal schedule and, of course, directing and choreographing the show. She might find this production a bit easier because she's done *42nd Street* five times before. She keeps a list of fifty preproduction tasks of varying degrees of logistical complexity, which she seldom refers to since she's done so many shows over the years. As one teenager who performed in thirty-one Marilyn shows said, "There really aren't that many people who could do all the things that she does. She choreographs them . . . she designs the lights, she basically stage manages them, and for one person to do all that is outstanding."[24]

When the kids start arriving, the air shifts with their noisy, nervous, frenetic energy. Some of the adults turn their attention to child wrangling, directing the sixty performers aged seven to fifteen to their dressing areas and urging them to change, put their makeup on (or ask for help to put it on), and get into costume. From the floor, which is the theatre's stage, banks of seats rise on three sides, and Marilyn goes up to the booth to finalize the light cues and ready the sound system. Bobbi stands center stage, looking a little forlorn until the drummer scoops her up and delivers her to Marilyn in the booth.

Tech/dress is the rehearsal when, on the one hand, everything—all the different components of musical theatre, including costumes, lights, and sets—comes together, and on the other hand, the artistic work of the past months—learning music and lyrics and choreography and developing character and polishing scenes—seems to be forgotten in the disorienting adjustment to a new space and the addition of a lot of "stuff." During tech/dress rehearsal, the show starts to feel more real, but somehow more unreal, too. You're faced with a seemingly uncrossable distance from past rehearsals to near-future performance, so you need someone to help you make the leap past this scary, unnerving place. You need someone charismatic and strict and encouraging and confident and organized. You need the backstage diva.

Now down from the booth and pacing the stage, Marilyn wears both a headset to communicate with the stage manager backstage and follow spot operators, which she never takes off the whole night, and a mic to talk to the kids, so her voice is audible through the theatre's sound system. It is a little unsettling because you hear her voice but don't know if she is in the booth or backstage or in the audience. But wherever she is, the kids know she sees and hears everything.

The kids sprint out from the dressing rooms, whose floors are now littered with everyday costumes of T-shirts and jeans, Velcro'd sneakers, and slip-on Uggs. The kids in the ensemble are thrilled with their costumes for the opening number: The boys wear black tuxedo pants, a white shirt, and a black vest, and the girls wear a hot pink satin twirly skirt that hits just above the knee and a pale pink short-sleeved satin overshirt, tied at the midriff, both over a black tank leotard and nude tights, which provide the base for all their costumes. On their feet, character shoes with taps (the boys, too), and in their bunhead hair, a big pink flower blossom. The kids dance onto the stage floor, the boys practice and tap their steps quietly, and the girls spin around in their skirts or look for an adult to help fasten the flower in their hair.

The older kids know to corral the younger ones to sit in the center section of seats to show Marilyn they're ready. They are almost all girls, mostly white, including a few who might be Jewish, plus a few South Asians and Latinas. There is one boy with Down syndrome. Incredibly fresh-faced and phone-less, they sit together in mixed-age groups, talking, singing, or playing clapping games but not loudly. The older girls keep an eye out for Marilyn to see when she will be want to begin.

Marilyn commands the kids in the chorus, who are seven, eight, or nine years old, to come onto the stage before they start the run. "Fernando," she calls to her tech assistant, "I need some more light down here so they can see where to go." She shows them how to stay in the light. "Thank you, Marilyn!" they all chant. Then she gestures toward all of the kids to gather and they do a big group warmup, a singsong, handclapping game called "Bumble Bee," which everyone seems to love and which calms and focuses them. "Okay, kids," she says, looking around the big circle. "Tonight is the first time on this stage with costumes and makeup and lights. That's a lot! But you've worked hard and you're ready. Even if you mess up, try to keep going no matter what. Do your best!"

"Thank you, Marilyn!" the kids chime in answer. There is a noisy scramble, made noisier by their tap shoes, as they go to their places for the start of the show. Marilyn climbs up to the booth, and I follow, carrying Bobbi, who'd wandered onto the stage again. Marilyn calls "Places!" over the loudspeaker, and the theatre goes dark. The music starts, and the lights bump up to 100 percent on "one," and before my eyes can adjust to the light, I see what looks like a million kids in tap shoes dancing onto the stage. Were there this many kids before, or did they multiply backstage? Then, just as quickly, the lights and sound cut out, and Marilyn yells, "Hold! Exit the stage, please, quietly, quietly." And they do, except for the din of 100 taps echoing loudly in the barnlike structure. Then they start over and this time the lights and sound hold, and rows and rows of kids enter, tapping and singing. Some are terrific dancers and some uncoordinated, some are focused and some in outer space, and most are somewhere in the middle. They are very small and there are many of them. The choreography is baby Busby Berkeley style—simple, crisp, designed to look good with a lot of people doing it in unison. After the first few glitches, Marilyn allows the performers to keep going.

In the first book scene, the girl playing the ingénue lead, Dorothy, the fourteen-year-old Lauren who helped out with the little kids' *Once Upon a Mattress*, is a good twelve inches taller than the boy playing her boyfriend. It is very strange in that adolescents-on-stage way, but they act the scene with confidence, focus, and expressiveness, looking each other in the eye.

Then another chorus number and the throngs of kids dance on again in new, equally vibrant costumes. Over the course of the show, the chorus is featured in at least eight numbers, each with a different costume of feathers, sequins, or scarves, and silk gloves and flowing skirts for the girls, and satin vests with glitter and rhinestones for the boys. Perfect for this show, these costumes in their dance recital glory also signify the backstage diva aesthetics. I can imagine how a seven-year-old who likes to sing and dance would love every minute of this—wearing eight different fancy costumes in one night. They would feel like a star, even if they were one of fifty kids. The colors through the night are crazy, and getting this many children on and offstage so many times in one show is a superhuman feat, only possible because of the several traffic-directing and voice-shushing adults backstage. Still, each blackout for a scene change—and there are many of them—is long, not because there is a lot of scenery to move, but to give the mass of kids time to exit.

Choreographically, the show is impressive. Marilyn is an expert at staging movement that flatters a lot of little bodies, unifies the ensemble, and is varied enough for visual interest, too. Their default position is hands on hips, which works well because the performers are planted on two feet, their hands still and not fidgeting or waving their arms. It is effective and gives a feeling of power and stability. Some of the boys—who stand out because there are fewer of them—are fine dancers. The many tap numbers are charming to witness in a 21st-century performance, and the kids seem to love it.

In the middle of Act 1, the little boy playing Abner misses an entrance. The kids on stage in the scene wait. And wait. This pause brings Marilyn down from the booth. "If he doesn't come in, someone can say, 'I hear Abner coming,'" she teaches them how to cover. The boy finally wanders out sheepishly. She says, "Jason, what happened?" Jason is silent and looks around for an escape route. Marilyn: "Did you go upstairs?" "Yea." "That's why you need to look at the cue sheets." "Thank you, Marilyn," Jason murmurs. Then she marches away, and they continue. No one can get away with anything here, I note. She knows everything. But it is two nights before they open, so it seems like the kid should know his entrances.

Marilyn turns her headset to a different channel so she can talk only to Siena, who also wears a headset and remains down on the stage floor. Through the show, Marilyn talks nonstop from the booth, barking instructions to Siena: "What is she doing? Tell her to go backstage now!" Sometimes Marilyn switches the channel so she can be heard through the theatre: "Kristy, don't play with your hair on stage!" "Everyone, use your arms! They're not dead animals! No dead arms! No dead arms!" "Cassandra, you have to exit stage left!" "Leora, your hands are not on your hips!" Siena frequently walks onto the stage, with the action continuing, to reposition or respace the kids and help them make corrections as they happen.

Then Act 1 is over, and Marilyn bounds onto the stage from her perch in the booth, leaping down the five sets of stairs onto the stage floor. "Sit," she says, her voice still booming through the headset mic. Her lithe arms gesture to the kids, who are sweaty and fussing with the scarves and picking at the beads on their costumes. The children sit down immediately, all hands in laps and sitting upright. This is clearly a practiced posture for them.

"It's very good," Marilyn says, making eye contact with each and every child. "You've got the steps. Your arms are relaxed but don't look like dead animals. You're dancers!" The kids look pleased and relieved. "You're all looking up— well, almost—Julia, can you make sure to look up and not at your feet?" Julia nods solemnly and, somehow, none of the kids look at her. "But this is what I need now in Act 2: passion! I need to see that this is the best night of your life! This is all you ever wanted to do: dance! And here you are doing it!" She pauses for a moment, letting it sink in. "Also, remember, you are entertaining the people in the theatre, on this side and this side and this side," as she points to the three banks of seats." Another pause. "Let's go!" she yells, and heads back up to the booth. All of the kids yell back, "Thank you, Marilyn!" then leap to their feet and put their hands on their hips, ready to start Act 2.

Through the run, I sit in the booth with Marilyn and with Bobbi, who sleeps on the table next to the light board. Marilyn simultaneously manages to watch the kids perform; take notes on specific choreography or blocking mistakes, including a kid sitting a mere few inches too far stage right; run the lights; change and write new cues if she doesn't like them; communicate by headset with Fernando about some lighting instruments that aren't focused right; answer texts on her phone from another assistant; and occasionally shout instructions to the actors. The backstage diva is a fully embodied, totally focused machine, moving among and doing what would normally be the jobs of five different people, at least.

After the run is over, including a lengthy curtain call, the kids sit on the stage floor. Already down from the booth and standing in one of the aisles, clipboard in hand, Marilyn steps forward and says, "Act 1 was fifty minutes and Act 2 was forty-two minutes." Cheers and applause erupt. They know that they should want the show to be as short as possible and that their goal is to pick up the pace and keep it moving. Scraping a few minutes off the previous night's run is good, the first measure of the rehearsal's success. "We got through tonight very well. I have a few notes that I'll give to you as you're getting changed, but kids, great job! Please hang up your costumes! I'll see you tomorrow!" The kids didn't expect more detailed notes or praise. Marilyn knew from years of experience that they were too tired and nothing would sink in. Better to walk them through their mistakes just before the next night's final dress rehearsal. More applause, one more "thank you, Marilyn!" as the kids start to disperse. "Wait a minute!" shouts one of the mothers, and she explains to the kids, who now suddenly seem distracted and fidgety, how to place their orders for T-shirts and DVD copies of the show, the memorabilia that is tied in to the experience from the start.

For a moment I forget where I am and what year it is. Something about this person, this place, and this evening seems out of time, innocent, or from another time. What is it? Except for Marilyn's phone, which she mostly uses to communicate with her assistants, there are no phones at all. The kids seem innocent and fresh-faced, no snarkiness or whispering behind hands that I could see. There are many small children around, and the adolescent girls act motherly and responsible. In addition, the show's aesthetics are classic and even old-fashioned. The painted backdrop, the dance recital costumes, the classic choreography feel simultaneously familiar and fresh. To be sure, it's familiar and old to Marilyn and fresh and new to the kids. The backstage diva draws the kids to her time, her frame of reference, her way of doing things and making musical theatre.

Marilyn's intense long-term investment in her enterprise since 1978 and the dedication of the students over several generations have made Marilyn her own brand. But more than that, in the community, Marilyn has become synonymous with musical theatre itself. The kids don't refer to the shows they do by title or creators: They aren't doing Sondheim shows or Rodgers and Hammerstein shows, they do "Marilyn shows." They count the number they've done, collecting them like Girl Scout badges—"ten," "twenty," "thirty"—and the number of years they've worked with her—"I started dancing with Marilyn when I was eight and now I'm twenty-five." When I ask some of Marilyn's students if they do shows at their schools, one of them says that she does but that "the school plays aren't nearly as good as the Marilyn plays." One girl said, "She cares about us so much. We're like her kids. It's such a family." Like a community theatre, her studio is a meeting ground for kids from different schools around the region.

On opening night, the kids' families and friends, dressed in their theatre-going best and weighed down with congratulatory bouquets of flowers for the young stars, mill around the stage, sensing the children's nervous excitement. Volunteers scurry around backstage, braiding hair and tying ribbons, sewing loose seams or taping up hems. When it is time for the show to start, the packed-house audience settles in their seats. The house lights go to dark, the music begins, and the kids dance onto the stage. The lights come up, shining on the children who worked so hard for weeks and weeks to make a show.

Where is Marilyn then? In the back of the house, watching quietly? Getting dressed for a post-show greeting? Among her own friends and family in the audience? No. She is in the booth, Bobbi by her side, headset on, running the light board, working. And tomorrow she will start rehearsing for the next show. She is, after all, the backstage diva.

Performance

Over her forty-year career, Marilyn directed *Gypsy* six times. In Arthur Laurents's script, the opening scene of *Gypsy* features a vaudeville director and performer, Uncle Jocko, auditioning two (intentionally) awful child performers—one who plays the flute and one who dances wearing a dress made of balloons. Brief vignettes introduce the musical's vaudeville setting as a sad place for performers who, even as children, are without talent and washed up. Then Mama Rose barges in with Baby June and Louise, who perform "Let Me Entertain You," much to Uncle Jocko's fury.

In the script, the first two performances are short, thirty-second sketches meant to show the audience that Uncle Jocko is a sellout whose girlfriend's little sister is already guaranteed to win the night's talent contest, and that Rose is deluded enough to believe that this theatre is legitimate. Most of all, the first scene shows Rose as a woman who takes charge wherever she goes. The two-minute opening tells the audience what this show is about: a mother who is so hungry for her children's success that she refuses to see the truth right before her eyes.

In Marilyn's 1993 production, the opening scene clocks in at eight minutes, as she alters the musical for her own needs. First, rather than post the scene's setting ("Uncle Jocko's Kiddie Show Seattle") in a Brechtian-style placard set on an easel as most productions do, Marilyn has two perky little girls in red smock jumpers and white short-sleeved blouses carry the sign on stage. They sing-shout the 1927 classic song, "I'm Looking Over a Four-Leaf Clover," with a simple dance that ends with a curtsy (and wild applause and cheering from the audience). Marilyn makes a new musical number out of what's typically a scene-setting sign placed on an easel.

Then, she uses the musical's overture, which she moved from the start of the show to within the first scene, for several elaborately choreographed numbers. Ostensibly these are different groups auditioning for Uncle Jocko, who stands all the way downstage, his back to the audience. The first, performed to the instrumental "Everything's Coming Up Roses," features twenty tapping teenagers (eighteen girls and two boys) in white satin vests with white bowties over a red leotard for the girls and black pants and white shirt and bowtie for the boys. The second number finds twenty-four of the littler girls, including the "Four-Leaf Clover" duo, in the red smock jumpers with white lace trim and white knee socks and ballet shoes, executing a simple dance to the instrumental "You'll Never Get Away from Me." The little ones curtsy and move upstage (again, after roaring applause). Two short solo songs follow, so that by the time Uncle Jocko speaks his first line in the show, "Everybody— SHUT UP! . . . All mothers *out*," there are fifty bodies on the stage, singing and dancing their hearts out. Marilyn has mastered the art of finding ways to use more of her students and to feature them early in the show.

Another example: Near the end of Act 1, Tulsa, a young man in Rose's troupe who is about to elope with the younger daughter June, demonstrates the song for his new act that he's been working on for Louise, who is secretly in love with him. In "All I Need Is the Girl" as written, Tulsa sings and dances with a broom, which he imagines to be the dancing partner he needs and whom Louise desires to be. It's a solo song and dance, with Louise as the audience. In Marilyn's production, during the first solo verse, all forty-four members of the ensemble, in red leotards, white sailor collar with a red ribbon trim, mid-thigh white shorts, white knee socks, and black tap shoes, slink onto the stage and sit upstage and around Tulsa on different levels of the set. At the end of the first chorus, Tulsa sings, "All I need now is the girl," and announces, "Then my back-up comes in," and twelve of the seated girls (and one boy) stand and start tapping in call and response with Tulsa, taps ringing through the theatre. At the end of the next verse, Tulsa commands, "Follow me, Louise," and the rest of the girls pack the stage, thirty-two of them tapping away and twelve more standing on the upstage platform. Finally, they all sing and dance the final verse together.

What functions as Tulsa's fantasy solo in most productions, made painful through Louise's unrequited desire for him, becomes a rousing ensemble tap song, a big production number. But it doesn't matter. The diva's "public images and careers often involved negotiations between convention and transgression," writes cultural studies scholar Alexander Doty.[25] More important than conveying the pathos of the scene is the need to give a score of enthusiastic tapping girls a lot to do. And Marilyn succeeds brilliantly.

Legacy

When kids reflect on Marilyn's influence on their lives, which typically lasts for years, they tend to use the same words that she uses to encourage them: passion, love, dedication. Many say they appreciate her "tough love" because the shows are so good. One teenage girl exclaims, "I had so many people coming up to me after that show and saying, 'You guys are so amazing, this was amazing. I saw this on Broadway, it was, it was like, I could compare them, they were unbelievable.' And I just, all of I could think of was, yea, we did some of it, but Marilyn was the one who pushed us to that level."[26] Another puts it, "She wants the show to get done but she's so kind to people and so loving underneath this like rough, like go-getting exterior. She's such a sweetheart underneath it all."[27] Marilyn is at once the harshest critic and the most supportive mentor. She coaxes from the child performers their most intimate feelings and expressiveness; she touches nerves; she touches bodies; she demands discipline and tends to badger, even nag. Another teenage girl says, "She's dedicated her entire life to this."[28] Siena adds that from Marilyn, "I've learned so much about how to be in the world."[29]

When she was working, Marilyn was the center of the action, and everything started and stopped with her. Every decision, large or small, was hers. The business bore her name, and her professional reputation depended on her close contact with children and her decisive vision as a teacher, director, choreographer, and guide. For years—right up until she retired—she said she wouldn't: "I don't want to ever retire. If I didn't have this, if I didn't have all these amazing kids around me, I don't know what I would do."[30] Her students saw her in the same way; as one girl said, "She'll be directing from her hospitable bed when she's 110," and, "She just kind of seems timeless to me."[31] Another added, "We always joke about, she's going to be ninety-two with a walker, doing a pull back." The girl concluded, "She'll do it until it's not enjoyable anymore."[32]

Marilyn directed *Gypsy* one last time before she retired. After the show, she gave a teary speech about her life and how much the studio meant to her.

But it wasn't quite over.

In a rough, unedited homemade video, a petite woman in her mid-sixties wearing black yoga pants, black clogs, white ankle socks, and a black hoodie emblazoned with "The Music Man" on the back faces a wall of mirrors in a nondescript dance studio. Along the edges of the room and reflected in the mirror, the camera captures shelves filled with file boxes, a bulletin board with photos and announcements, several music stands, an electric piano, and a ballet barre. She faces away from the camera and toward the mirror, her movements reflected there. Marilyn's dark curly hair is gathered in a small clump on top of her head, a few stray tendrils at the nape of her neck falling over the chain that holds a pair of reading glasses perched on her nose. She holds pages of instructions from which she reads and points to various locations on the shiny wood floor. "Kiss today goodbye, the sweetness and the sorrow," she hums the first lyric of the eleven o'clock number from *A Chorus Line*. "And Leslie crosses over here on 'what I did for love,'" Marilyn says, as she takes a few steps downstage right. Then she moves back to where she started, "Evvie, you cross forward on 'Look my eyes are dry, the gift was ours to borrow,'" and she makes the move she's choreographed for the girl. Marilyn works through the song this way, singing the lyrics lightly, speaking directions, moving, telling the camera on which foot to step. When the song is over, she looks up, concluding, "It's not hard." Which, for Marilyn's choreography, it's not. Not for the backstage diva.

Figure 3.1. The cast and human "trees" in *Into the Woods* in Wilmington, Ohio.

3

High School Musicals and *Into the Woods*

Enter Milky White

A tenth-grade girl in white pants and a long-sleeved white shirt and big cow-bell around her neck.

A papier mâché figure on wheels.

A twelfth-grade boy in a white jumpsuit and a half-mask on his head, holding two sticks with cardboard hoofs at the end.

Six boxes covered with paper and painted white—one big rectangular box as the body, four long, thin boxes as the legs, a smaller, flatter box for the head with paper ears attached.

Two kids bent over and covered with a white sheet, with the front one holding a rubber cow head.

Every high school production team of *Into the Woods* must meet the challenge and pleasure of creating Milky White, one of the stars of the show.[1] In 2018, there were hundreds of Milky Whites and hundreds of high school productions of the musical (Figure 3.1).

Stephen Sondheim and James Lapine's *Into the Woods* is a classic story of journey and transformation. The characters include fairy tale figures—Cinderella, Little Red Riding Hood, Rapunzel, Jack (and the Beanstalk), and a witch, of course—plus some invented types: the Baker and his Wife, who represent a typical contemporary urban American couple, and Milky White, Jack's cow, who meets an untimely death near the end of Act 1, having served as the vessel for the Witch's potion.

The musical opens with "Once Upon a Time," and the characters sing their wishes: Cinderella to go to the ball; Jack's mother for money to live; the Baker and his Wife for a child.[2] The characters leave the village to go into the woods to fulfill their desires. By the end of Act 1, all of their wishes have been granted, and they sing happily "Ever After," except for Milky White, now dead.[3] Act 2 unravels all that's been done because the characters, though they sing, "I never thought I'd be so happy," are hardly satisfied but want more.

Beyond Broadway. Stacy Wolf, Oxford University Press (2020). © Oxford University Press.
DOI: 10.1093/oso/9780190639525.001.0001

Also, they must deal with the repercussions of their Act 1 deeds.[4] The community disintegrates, many die, and the remaining characters form a new nuclear family at the end.

When the show opened on Broadway in 1987, it was almost universally panned. *New York Times* critic Frank Rich, despite being one of Sondheim's most vocal champions in the early days when only the most sophisticated playgoers were fans, wrote, "Unfortunately, the book is as wildly overgrown as the forest."[5] Rich admitted that "the conception is brilliant, and sometimes the execution lives up to it," and praised the clever lyrics and some of the performances.[6] Still, he declared, "The confusion breeds stasis; the show stands still during the huffing and puffing of voluminous plot information. Worse," he went on, "the convoluted story has a strangulating effect on the musical's two essential sources of emotional power, its people and its score." He said he didn't care about the characters and the "numerous songs" often felt "truncated."[7] *Into the Woods* won three Tony Awards but ran for only 765 performances.

No matter. Sondheim believed the show would be a moneymaker in the long run. In *Look, I Made a Hat*, he reflects that "at one point in the collaborative joy of our early discussions I brashly predicted that if the piece worked, it would spawn innumerable productions for many years to come, since it dealt with world myths and fables and would therefore never feel dated."[8] Sondheim felt that the show "would appeal to schools and amateur theatres as well as professional ones, especially in conservative parts of the country which are hesitant to support shows that deal with contemporary themes in contemporary ways and use four-letter words (there are none in the show). I predicted that ITW could be a modest annuity for us, and I'm surprised to say I was right."[9] He *was* right—to the tune of hundreds of productions a year.

And so we journey into the woods . . . sort of . . . to the Midwest to see the dress rehearsals and performances of three high school productions.

Like this musical, high school is a classic story of journey and transformation. Young people start in ninth grade, typically at age fourteen, and through various trials and tribulations, begin to form into the adults they'll become. Ninth graders look up to older kids. Many students who have never participated in theatre before high school see the annual musical and want to get involved. Theatrical production often occupies a vibrant subculture in high school.

As with the other venues in this book, the Broadway musical repertoire is rendered local in each and every high school production of *Into the Woods*, as it participates in area political discussions and reflects community values. For example, at Garrison Forest School, a small private girls' school in Baltimore, Maryland, *Into the Woods* helped to ease racial tensions roiling the city and the school soon after the death of Freddie Gray, a man who died from injuries incurred after an arrest and ride in a police van. At the racially diverse school, tensions ran high, and the musical helped to mitigate them.[10] At the San Francisco Jewish Community School, *Into the Woods* served as a way to reinforce Jewish values. Theatre teacher Dylan Russell wrote in the program, "Many aspects of our modern world push us towards individualism and focus on 'me' but we remain bound to our community." At Redwood High School in Larkspur, California, the musical gave the graduating seniors a chance to expand their theatrical repertoire beyond the program's more typical edgy, serious, non-musical theatre fare.

In this chapter, we travel to three public schools in the Midwest—in Minnesota, Ohio, and Michigan; two small and rural, one midsized in a small town; all in politically conservative communities; all supportive of the arts (in principle more than funding)—to see their final dress rehearsal and performance. At other high schools across the country that I visited for my research, I observed earlier stages of the process—auditions and rehearsals—or was solely a spectator and paying patron, but here I wanted to see high school productions when it all came together, to witness the last push to get the show to performance.

The Jimmy Awards

In addition to the fictional representations in the TV movie *High School Musical*, the TV shows *Glee* and *Rise* and occasional episodes of other shows (*Ugly Betty*, for example), and documentaries such as *Most Valuable Players*, *Purple Dreams*, and *I Can't . . . I Have Rehearsal*, high school musical theatre earns national visibility at the annual Jimmy Awards.[11] Since 2009, eighty high school students have gathered in New York City for nine days of master classes, private coaching sessions, and rehearsals with professional Broadway artists to prepare for the National High School Musical Theatre Awards, or the Jimmys. Named after Broadway theatre owner and producer

James M. Nederlander, affectionately nicknamed "the Tonys for teenagers," the Jimmy Awards culminate in an evening of musical numbers performed on a Broadway stage, with a handful of college scholarships awarded to a select few.[12]

The intense, serious, and dedicated young performers who are lucky enough to land an all-expenses-paid trip to New York are selected each year by forty regional competitions, smaller versions of the Jimmys, like the Applause Awards in Florida and the Jerry Awards in Wisconsin.[13] Aside from the allure of the Jimmys, these regional awards recognize the achievements of high school musicals, and the stakes are high in areas with large public high schools and sufficient resources for specialty teachers. An estimated hundred thousand students at fifteen hundred high schools compete for prizes and recognition at these events.[14]

The eighty high-schoolers who make it to New York hail from all over the country, with more students coming from large, usually wealthy public high schools. Though mostly white, the finalists include a few African American and Latinx performers, and less frequently, an Asian American student. (Though physical markers of race and ethnicity like skin color, for example, are not accurate identifiers of one's heritage or culture or identity, such visible markers matter nonetheless because of the politics of casting in the professional, amateur, and school theatre worlds.)

The Jimmys earn well-deserved attention: a few articles in the *New York Times* leading up to and following the event; feature stories in local papers about the New York–bound finalists; an annual piece on NPR; the previously noted documentary *Most Valuable Players*. But they represent a tiny fraction of the high-schoolers who participate in musical theatre across the United States, in programs wealthy or barely funded, in schools rural, suburban, or urban. Thousands of schools that take their annual high school musical quite seriously never show up on the award program's roster.

Moreover, the Jimmy Awards, documentaries, and TV shows show musical theatre as competitive and akin to sports. These contests work well in a film or TV narrative, as they create conflict and suspense and feature ecstatic winners and heartbroken losers. Ordinary high school musical life has some of these elements, especially the competition of auditions and the stress of getting the show ready to open. But more typically, young people rehearse and perform the show in their own community solely for their friends, families, and neighbors. The high school musical speaks from and to local concerns, and students' performances are inflected by their personalities and roles within the school's culture. And this happens almost forty thousand times a year.[15]

Why High School Musicals Matter: The Students

At the 2017 Florida Association for Theatre Education's annual conference, arts commentator Howard Sherman, who writes frequently about musical theatre in schools, especially on censorship, casting, and copyright, suggested that "theatre is a place where students who may not fit some arbitrarily perceived model of 'typical' can find others who are like them at their cores." These students are "drawn together by a need to express themselves or support the expressions of others, rather than by throwing or hitting a ball into or over a net, or a wall, or a hoop." He summarizes, "School theatre is teamwork without fractures and brain trauma."[16] The collaborative communities created by school drama programs offer not only a sense of belonging, but also opportunities for self-expression not found in other extracurricular activities.

Sherman also points to the larger developmental benefits of theatre. He writes that participation in theatre teaches students "that they should not be afraid to stand in the spotlight and say what must be said, or to shine a harsh light on transgressions, on injustices that must be stopped." [17] In short, he says, theatre "makes them better people, and better citizens."[18]

In addition to theatre's social and psychological benefits, participation in the arts has been linked to patterns of academic growth that remain consistent regardless of the student's socioeconomic background. A 1999 study found that students involved in theatre throughout their high school careers had higher reading proficiency levels than their noninvolved peers, with nearly 20 percent of theatre-involved students reading at high proficiency by grade twelve. The researchers attributed this pattern to the fact that "theater is a language-rich environment [that] actively engages students with issues of language."[19] Student musicians who play in the orchestra of high school musicals are likely to reap academic benefits, too, since those consistently involved in instrumental music throughout their high school careers show higher levels of math proficiency by grade twelve, including lower socioeconomic status students.[20]

Education experts agree on theatre and music's positive influence on students, but specialists in Theatre-in-Education (TIE)—a subfield of Theatre

Studies that sees theatre as a tool for social change, community building, and individual empowerment—privileges student-generated plays over extant musicals. These scholar/educator/activists believe that when students make theatre from their own experiences and begin with their own stories, they experience a deeper and more meaningful connection with the work. TIE scholars tend to dismiss the Broadway canon out of hand, assuming that musicals, which require rote learning of music and choreography and often feature simple, flat characters, shortchange students' creativity and personal attachment to the material. But divisions between the social/political and the aesthetic/artistic disappear in the musical theatre classroom or rehearsal hall, and students do feel empowered rehearsing for *Shrek* or *Anything Goes*.

In an extended ethnographic study, TIE researcher Kathleen Gallagher compared two drama classrooms. In one, students devised the play based on their own stories, experiences, and imaginations. The goal: to "instrumentalize" drama for "some social function."[21] In the other classroom, the students rehearsed and performed Andrew Lloyd Webber and Tim Rice's musical, *Joseph and the Amazing Technicolor Dreamcoat*. The goal: to "activate" theatre as a "craft" in order to produce "an effective performance."[22] Gallagher describes how the students in the *Joseph* class "were not exploring their own ideas nor how they connected, or did not connect, to the plot of the musical. They were coached in singing and dancing, aiming for flawlessness and professionalism."[23]

Nonetheless, Gallagher's team of researchers was surprised to see that "personal exploration was happening" at the *Joseph* rehearsals.[24] "It didn't take us long to realize," she writes, "that this easy aesthetic/social split was a seductive but inaccurate description of a more complex reality."[25] The "social" classroom edged towards the aesthetic and the "aesthetic" (musical theatre) classroom offered kids ways to engage that mattered to them.

Another case study found that for a student who was also an athlete, being in the musical allowed him to "express many facets of his personality," which he felt he couldn't do in other school situations.[26] The student said, "With sports, you have to be this one, angry, mean person [. . .] but with theater, it's just being yourself and letting everything out of you."[27] Another observational study found that the student cast of a high school production of *Les Misérables* had "its own internal culture, with distinctive ways of thinking, feeling, and acting." The musical established a culture that rewarded hard work and that welcomed "strong emotions as part of the process,"[28] with the support of engaged and caring adult mentors.

Being a spectator also benefits students. A 2017 study found that fourth- to twelfth-grade students who went on a field trip to see live theatre reaped significantly more educational benefits than those who saw a movie of the same story. The researchers argued that theatre's liveness—the "in-person experience"—bolstered students' empathy and established stronger emotional connections.[29] Another study that examined musical theatre's ability to affect emotion noted that "a significant change was observed in attitudes targeted by the show," concluding that "musical theater may be a promising method for promoting attitudinal change."[30]

All of this happens through the process of doing a show, any show. But if the material is thought-provoking and artistically challenging, the benefits multiply.

The Theatre Teacher's Annual Challenge

Each and every year, high school theatre directors confront the daunting task of choosing a show for the annual musical, which, even from a catalog of hundreds, can be tough. They need a show that is appropriate for the local culture and achievable given the number of students available to cast and their abilities. Directors know their population and take care to pick a show to amplify students' strengths, often choosing a musical with specific students in mind to cast. This dynamic is unique to high school musical theatre.

Directors also need to choose a show that kids will get excited about because it's a long-term commitment. The schools I visited had been working on the show for four months, rehearsing after school and occasionally on weekends. They were constrained by Christmas vacation, sidelined by bad weather, delayed by shooting threats. Kids have jobs, family obligations, and other school activities. The high school musical has to fit into teenagers' lives.

Interestingly, budget constraints seldom hamper musical theatre production because of enormously creative and enterprising teachers who volunteer countless hours to get the show up. According to the Educational Theatre Association, in 2012, high schools spent about $300 million on theatrical productions, but that figure doesn't include volunteer labor and materials purchased by teachers (who are not reimbursed).[31] Each of the schools I visited operated on a shoestring budget and all pulled off excellent productions, though the teachers were exhausted by the end. (Just imagine what a little money in support of the arts could do.)

Dramatics magazine, which since 1938 has published a yearly survey of most frequently produced plays and musicals, found that high schools started doing musicals after 1960. Every year from the 1960s to the 2000s, *Bye Bye Birdie* was among the top five shows.[32] In the 2010s, *Beauty and the Beast, Into the Woods*, and *Grease* ranked at the top.[33] *The Addams Family* was released in 2014 and for the next three years was the most produced high school musical. Steve Spiegel, president of Theatrical Rights Worldwide, which licenses the high school hit show, explained its popularity: "the cleverness of the script, the number of major roles for women and the familiarity of the characters. And, in dealing with acceptance and tolerance, it brings forward a wonderful message that is universal and appreciated by all ages. And it shows an honest portrayal of families . . . flaws and all . . . surrounded by love."[34]

Although *The Addams Family* was panned by critics when it opened on Broadway in 2010, it proved to be critic-proof: It ran for 759 performances and launched a national, then international, tour.[35] Then, with amateur productions, the show recouped its initial investment. As *New York Times* critic Charles Isherwood wrote, "The assumption that the American musical theater canon is unofficially protected for posterity by critics in New York thus crumbled into dust."[36] *The Addams Family* is not an anomaly: Many shows that teens favor were rejected by New York critics. Isherwood observes, "Show-tune-crazed students across the country, it is clear, have their own opinions. For them the American musical theater is not a carefully edited collection of golden oldies but a living organism, and the newest shows are a primary source of their excited devotion to performing."[37]

Among the biggest challenges for a high school theatre director: a dearth of boys and the overabundance of enthusiastic, skilled, and talented girls. As writer Lucy Huber put it in a gone-viral tweet: "High school girls in musicals: Ive [sic] being going to theater camp since 1st grade and taking professional voice lessons since I was 10, so excited to be townsperson #3 this spring! HS boys in musicals: The drama teacher cornered me after Alegbra [sic] 2 and said I had to be Shrek."[38]

In 2018, *Beauty and the Beast* moved up to number one, *The Addams Family* was number two, *The Little Mermaid* came in third.[39] Most of the musicals that high schools produce, such as these, rely on conventional gender stereotypes—often, the woman sacrifices herself for a man—and are built around a heterosexual romance and, typically, a happily-ever-after marriage.[40] Perhaps that's why *Into the Woods* was number four.

Over the years of doing this research, I've had countless conversations with frustrated high school theatre directors who want nothing more than a show with a lot of girls' parts, empowering roles for them, and a non-heterosexist narrative. "When do you think the rights to *Wicked* will be released?" I've been asked again and again. I suspect that this is one reason *Into the Woods* is so frequently produced at high schools (and, in fact, *Into the Woods* was the most represented show among the nominees for the 2018 Jimmys). Even though the music is exceptionally difficult for young people to sing, it contains understated heterosexual romance and a lot of good parts for girls.

But choosing a show that works for the students is just one consideration.

Censorship and Controversy on High School Stages

In "Who Cares About Censorship on School Stages?" Howard Sherman suggests that "many schools view their productions as community relations, frequently citing that they want to appeal to audiences 'from 8 to 80.'"[41] In selecting high school musicals, educators must consider both the educational needs of their students and the entertainment desires of audience members from a variety of age groups and belief systems. As community-wide gatherings, musicals catalyze conversations and controversies about what material can and should be presented on the high school stage.

Sondheim's *Sweeney Todd*, for example, has caused controversy because of its portrayal of a murderous, throat-cutting barber. In Woodbridge, Connecticut, a month before the opening of Amity Regional High School's March 2013 production, members of the community arranged a protest. They were concerned about the show's depictions of violence in the wake of the devastating school shooting in Newtown, Connecticut, in December 2012. Sherman, a graduate of Amity, spoke on behalf of the show: "The themes of *Sweeney Todd* are not murder and cannibalism and rape [. . .] the theme of *Sweeney Todd* is about the uselessness of revenge."[42] The next week, Amity High School's principal confirmed that the show would go on.

Les Misérables is another show that often comes under scrutiny because of the presence of guns on stage. In the week following the 2018 school shooting in Parkland, Florida, the Philadelphia-based student cast and crew of William Penn Charter School's *Les Misérables: School Edition* sat down to consider the unwanted but impossible-to-ignore new context for their production, which was set to open that weekend. The violence in Florida elevated the stakes of the show, especially because some Penn Charter students had met victims of the Parkland attack at a summer camp the previous year. One actor noted that she wanted to "wield her performance like a hammer, as a means of acting against gun violence." She said, "I think 'Les Miz' is one of the most important things I can do for myself, for my family and friends, that can best help the whole gun situation."[43]

Representations of homosexuality trouble other communities. In November 2013, the Trumbull (Connecticut) High School Thespian Society found out that their production of *Rent: School Edition* had been cancelled because of the "challenging issues" in the musical.[44] Trumbull High's Thespian Society president Larissa Mark organized a protest against the decision, noting, "I think the main reason why *Rent* is so important is that homosexuality, drug use and disease are not 'issues' in the twenty-first century . . . they're part of our lives. It's not fiction to us."[45] Finally, after a week of student protest and pressure from local government officials, Trumbull High's principal allowed the production to take place.[46]

The approved school edition of the Tony Award– and Pulitzer Prize–winning musical *Rent* has been edited for profanity and sexually explicit material.[47] Nonetheless, the Trumbull High School production was not the only time *Rent: School Edition* faced pushback: In the year following the release of the school edition, at least three more controversies arose across the United States.[48]

Theatre educators often choose *Rent* precisely for its frank discussion of contemporary themes. In 2009, at Corona del Mar High School in California, theatre teacher Ron Martin picked the musical (the School Edition) in response to a Facebook video that showed Corona del Mar students using homophobic slurs.[49] The production was later cancelled, allegedly because the principal objected to the show's homosexuality.[50] In a slightly different case, the 2013 production of *Rent: School Edition* was allowed to go ahead at Southold High School in Long Island, New York, but only after the school administration made changes to the licensed script to make it "sensitive to the community as a whole."[51] Among these modifications was the casting of a female student in the role of Angel, a male drag queen. Sherman objected to this decision, noting that he feared "depth [would] be intentionally lost, in service of obscuring the homosexuality that is essential to the character."[52]

Objections to "homosexual themes" were also at the root of the cancellation of South Williamsport High School's 2015 production of *Spamalot*. Although the administration initially denied that they cancelled show because of its gay content, an email later released under Pennsylvania's Right-to-Know law revealed that the principal was "not comfortable with *Spamalot* and its homosexual themes [. . .] drama productions are supposed to be community events."[53]

Race and ethnicity also prove to be divisive in high school musicals. The use of the N-word in Stephen Flaherty and Lynn Ahrens's *Ragtime* has led to several controversies in high school theatre programs. In 2008 a school in Chicago cancelled its production, while in 2015 a high school in Minnesota substituted the word "Negro" to calm community members' objections.[54] When Cherry Hill High School East of New Jersey faced pushback during the school's 2017 production of *Ragtime*, student cast members spoke in defense of the unaltered script, as did Brian Stokes Mitchell, who starred as Coalhouse Walker Jr. in the 1998 Broadway production. Mitchell said that the show "is about terribly ugly things that happen to people and how they surmount that [. . .] [T]o take the ugly language out of *Ragtime* is to sanitize it and that does it a great disservice."[55] Ultimately, Cherry Hill High School allowed the use of the N-word in the production and addressed the controversy in the classroom. Before seeing the show, "the 2,200 students in grades nine through 12 [talked] about the themes from *Ragtime* in two English class periods and one history class."[56] The superintendent said, "This is not a discussion that will end when the curtain closes for the final time on *Ragtime*."[57]

A different crisis arose in Ithaca (New York) High School's 2018 production of *The Hunchback of Notre Dame* when a white actor was cast as Esmeralda. Frustrated students argued that the role should have gone to a student of color: "Esmeralda is a Roma, [. . .] it is her oppression, and that of her people, which allows her to better understand the perspective of the Hunchback."[58] One senior, who is African American and auditioned for the show, expressed her disappointment: "It shows you that theater wasn't made for you [. . .] if you can't get the parts that are written for you, what parts are you going to get?"[59] When the school cancelled the show in response to the student protests, national news platforms publicized the controversy, including Breitbart, which ridiculed the students' objections. The extremity of the response only strengthened students' resolve: "If we want to make a change we have to start somewhere."[60]

When the cast list for Pioneer High School's 2018 production of *In the Heights* was released, students were conflicted. One cast member at the Ann Arbor, Michigan, school, a non-Latinx senior cast in the leading role of Nina, said, "I was really disappointed that there weren't more Latinx students cast in leads. On the flip side, I think [Pioneer Theatre Guild] is taking a good step towards diversity. The cast has roughly a 70 percent majority of people of color in the show, whereas last year we only had a handful of people of color acting in the show at all."[61] The production came on the heels of multiple controversies regarding casting of *In the Heights* in 2016, both at the college level (a production at UCLA was disputed)[62] and at the professional level (Chicago's Porchlight Music Theatre's production was protested when a white actor was cast in the lead role, Usnavi).[63] *In the Heights* lyricist and composer Lin-Manuel Miranda weighed in, saying that non-Latinx casting is permissible at the high school level—but not at universities or community theatres:

> When I see a school production with not a lot of Latino students doing it, I know they're learning things about Latino culture that go beyond what they're fed in the media every day. They HAVE to learn those things to play their parts correctly. And when I see a school with a huge Latino population do *Heights*, I feel a surge of pride that the students get to perform something that may have a sliver of resonance in their daily lives. [. . .] High school's the ONE CHANCE YOU GET, as an actor, to play any role you want, before the world tells you what "type" you are. Honor that sacred time as educators, and use it to change their lives.[64]

These struggles underline the importance of high school musical theatre in a community. The high school musical is a ritual, an annual performance of the community's investment in itself and in its kids, in the Broadway repertoire and the pleasure of song and dance. As Sam Minge, musical director of East Clinton High School's production of *Into the Woods*, said, "Seeing the community turn out like they do makes me smile. They pack the house and it's a great mix in the audience. There are parents, teachers and community members who get dressed up like it's a night on Broadway, and then we literally have farmers who come from the shop in their Carhartts to watch some high school kids do Sondheim in the small town theater serving popcorn and soda at intermission. It's a little slice of Americana in the best sense."

Why *Into the Woods*?

Into the Woods is a hard show to do—much harder than any others on the top ten list—which many high school directors don't realize until rehearsals are well under way. The music is enormously complex—the score is densely interwoven, with little dialog and few separate and unique musical numbers. The second act is violent and disturbing and contains adult themes. Technical challenges abound, from how to stage and represent Milky White's body, to how to build Rapunzel's tower, out of which long hair must flow, to how to make the Witch vanish in a flash and a puff of smoke. And yet, these very challenges make the show appealing. Students hone their musical skills; actors have a lot to chew on; the backstage tech kids are faced with interesting problems (and can make good use of other schools' Instagram and YouTube posts). As Ava, the stage manager at Belleville High School, said, we're "taking other people's ideas and building off of them."

The charm of the musical is easy to identify. First, because it's based on fairy tales, the story is accessible. Second, *Into the Woods* is an ensemble show with a group of lively characters and not just two or four leading roles. Third, though it lacks a traditional singing and dancing chorus, *Into the Woods* offers opportunities to expand the cast by adding other fairy tale characters (as they did at all three schools I visited) or trees or flowers (which they did at East Clinton High School). Fourth, any character can be played by an actor of any race. Fifth, romance is secondary or comically portrayed in the musical, more a display than central to the narrative. As Emma Watkins observes, "Courtship rituals are undermined in Cinderella's Prince; the Witch is a central female character not in pursuit of heterosexual romance; the significant marriages in the first act come apart in one way or another."[65] *Into the Woods* also asks for dramatic makeup, character masks, and elaborate costumes—it's a big and fun show.

Moreover, there are a number of excellent roles for girls: the Witch, Cinderella, the Baker's Wife, Jack's mother, and Little Red, and the smaller roles of the Stepmother and Stepsisters, Rapunzel, and the ghost of Cinderella's mother. Jack can be cast as a girl, as she was at East Clinton High School (and I know of one production in which a boy played the Witch). Further, these roles don't adhere to hypernormative forms of femininity. Even the princesses are not "normal."

And yet, the show is hardly a model of feminist musical theatre. Peter C. Wood, who reads the show through Susan Faludi's *Backlash*, argues persuasively that "this play, like much of popular culture in the mid-1980s, is manifestly antagonistic toward female desire and attempts to create a fantasy of domestic existence."[66]

From a musical theatre history perspective, *Into the Woods* is the lynchpin between old-school Rodgers and Hammerstein and newer, edgier musicals like *Rent* or *Spring Awakening* that many schools won't do; none of the three conservative-leaning schools in the Midwest that I visited would do those shows. *Into the Woods* is a compelling example of a show whose content is neither nostalgic nor risky.

The teachers at each of the schools I visited chose the show because their program is growing and they believed the kids were ready for the challenge. For the teachers, *Into the Woods* raised the bar either musically or because of the seriousness and complexity of its message. The students were excited about the choice since many knew the movie version, though none previously knew Sondheim's work, except for Rebekah in Michigan, who's likely to major in musical theatre in college. Students' key referent is the show their school did the year before and the year before that. That's how they're pulled in, by what they see happening at the school. The local history within a three-year period forms the students' frame of reference, more or less.

We'll follow *Into the Woods'* plot chronologically with performance examples from each school's production. For each of the three towns, I've highlighted the contribution of three students to show the range of reasons that kids do musical theatre, what they gain from participation, and how it shapes them and their school community.

Worthington High School, Worthington, Minnesota

Worthington (pop. 13,000) sits in Minnesota's southwest corner, an hour from Sioux Falls, South Dakota, and a little more than three hours from Minneapolis. The small town is just off I-90, which in this part of the state is a sparsely trafficked, perfectly flat and straight highway. On both sides of the road in every direction, silos and barns punctuate the flatness and mark the presence of farms, and in mid-March, a dusting of snow covers the ground from a storm the previous week. (Somehow on my 10-day research trip, I managed to miss bad weather—snow in Minnesota, floods in Ohio, ice in Michigan—that either preceded or followed me.) Worthington has the most racial and ethnic diversity in the state outside of the Twin Cities metropolitan area. According to 2018 Chamber of Commerce records, Worthington's largest employer is JBS Pork, a leading meat processor in the United States and Canada. The school district employs the second largest number of people, 545 employees. Of the top ten employers in the area, 59 percent of jobs are in production and manufacturing, 12 percent of employees work for the school, 11 percent work for commercial stores like Walmart, 9 percent work in the health industry, and 11 percent work in city administration and community service.[67] The economy is struggling.

Worthington High School is small, with 823 students in the school and 3,209 in the district during the 2017–18 school year.[68] The school is located in a residential neighborhood of small tidy houses, adjacent to a bigger road with grocery stores, gas stations, and Walmart. Memorial Auditorium, where the students perform the annual high school musical, is one block from the school. The charming and beautiful 680-seat art deco theatre was built in 1931 and has a brand-new, large, and airy lobby.

Eric, the play's director, is not a teacher at the school but was hired to oversee the production. His day job is teaching theatre and music at the local community college. When I arrived, he gave me a backstage tour, including Milky White's plaster head and the Prince's horse-drawn coach. A platform painted to look like an open book occupied half of the stage floor raked at eleven degrees, which meant that the upstage section was tall enough for the Witch to melt into. "The students freaked out when they stepped onto the platform," Eric said, gesturing toward what looked like a dangerously steep slope, "but that's the height I needed below the platform to disappear the Witch, and they wouldn't let me cut a trap door into the floor." He shrugged, grinning. "It's fine. The actors are getting used to it now."

Two floor-to-ceiling, huge, gorgeous, realistically twisty trees framed the proscenium. The "tree" stage left could rotate to reveal Rapunzel's tower. Next to the trees, two "rag curtains" made of strands of all shades of green fabric tied together formed long strands that looked like a dense, leafy forest. Eric designed the set, and his father (a former high school theatre teacher whose last production before he retired was *Into the Woods* [Eric played the Baker]), Charlotte, the student stage manager, plus a few more volunteer dads (including Charlotte's) helped him build it the previous weekend.[69] All week after school, the ten dedicated tech students were coming and going to help put on the finishing touches. The hung backdrop, which was the only part of the set rented rather than built, revealed a dark and scary woods scene. The school paid MTI a $365 licensing fee per performance, plus $600 to rent the scripts and scores for two months, and Eric requested another $100 to rent the materials for an additional month because he wanted the kids to have their scripts in hand before their Christmas break. The set was built on virtually no budget.

In addition to the funding that the school provides, which, according to Eric, is generous for a public high school, a small *Little Mermaid* costume rental operation supplements their coffers. Three years ago, the students built costumes for their production of the Disney show, which turned out so well that they now rent them out to other schools and community theatres all over the tristate Minnesota/South Dakota/North Dakota area. Just as often, they trade the costumes for ones that Eric needs for the next show that another school owns. "It's a blessing in disguise," he said. "Mostly to get the costumes here and there is a management problem, which takes a lot of time to manage, but now one school just sends it to the next. It got us seed money for the program." This was just one example of Eric's enterprising spirit and knowhow.

Eric, who sports a beard, big glasses, and an intense, sunny energy, grew up two hours from Worthington, but he feels himself to be "from another ZIP code." An out gay man with progressive politics and connections both theatrical and personal to the Twin Cities, he found a place for himself directing musical theatre at Worthington High School as an insider-outsider, someone who understands the community and also sees his mission as supporting the students who might chafe against their parents' conservative values and politics. He described the town as "all of the things that are American in one place . . . 60 percent voted for Trump *and* they like the arts." Moreover, unlike most of the teachers I met during my travels, Eric also does freelance directing and acting at local theatres. He plans to go to graduate school and direct professionally. As much as he enjoys teaching and directing teenagers and exposing them to theatre, he also sees this work as his own training ground.

Eric decided to do *Into the Woods* because he felt the students were up to the challenge, and he knew he had enough strong performers to cast it. Like every high school theatre director, Eric knew in advance who would audition, whom he wanted to be able to cast, and what they could carry. The numbers were larger than he anticipated, as they were for every school I visited—there was much enthusiasm for this show. Though not everyone who auditioned was cast, Eric added horses and birds and townspeople to expand the scripted cast of twenty to thirty-two roles in the show. He knew they could pull it off.

About half an hour before the 4 p.m. start of the dress rehearsal, many people were busy. The thirty-two student actors were downstairs in the not-quite-large-enough dressing room, getting into costumes and makeup with the help of five volunteer mothers and four students who combed out the wigs and organized the other costumes on labeled racks. In the theatre, Erin, the lighting designer—a professional freelancer from Minneapolis and a friend of Eric's who came to Worthington for a few days to help out, volunteering her time and sleeping on his couch—rehearsed cues with stage manager, Charlotte. Three students knelt behind Rapunzel's tower stage left, trying to make it turn smoothly. Two others painted the final touches on the fireplace of Cinderella's house. The musicians—a bass, percussion, and two-keyboard combo of a middle school band teacher, a math teacher, an English teacher who is also a mother, and two students—tuned their instruments. The conductor—the young and earnest, brand-new middle school orchestra teacher—glanced over the score, nervous because this was his first musical.

Moments later, the director of the Nobles County Public Library stopped by to pick up the $6 tickets for giveaway tie-ins for a new program about fairy tales, then Eric moved up to the balcony to watch the run. He settled himself, flanked by two women on either side, including the costume designer, who also taught at the community college, a mother whose child had graduated but still wanted to help out with costumes and makeup, and two more mother volunteers who took notes as Eric dictated them during the show. For a high school musical, human capital of time and expertise matters more than dollars.

Eric had only one more day to rehearse the kids before opening. The next day was a Wednesday and all school activities had to end by 6 p.m. so that students could participate in religious activities. How could he squeeze in one last dress rehearsal? He also wanted elementary school students to see the show, so he arranged for them to be bussed in to see Act 1 in the morning, then got his cast and crew excused from classes in the afternoon so they could run Act 2 and be done by the evening. Other teachers supported the show and allowed the students' absences. "We're not getting anything done in the robotics club these days because half the club is in the musical," the teacher who advises that group said.

"Once Upon a Time" and the Role of the Stage Manager

The first line of *Into the Woods*, "once upon a time," launches the audience into the world of fairy tales, both the Brothers Grimm familiar ones and the new ones invented by Sondheim and Lapine.[70] The musical's fifteen-minute opening "Prologue" introduces the musical's three main plotlines and their characters, establishes Act 1's style as a "fast-paced farce," and provides the backstory for Cinderella, Jack and his mother, and the Baker and his Wife.[71] For most productions, including the many I've seen at high schools, the opening reveals three separate tableaux, one for each story, set in a parallel line downstage. The actors in each family stand or sit in front of a flat that is painted or partially rendered in 3D furnishings to look like a house's interior as within a large book. The Narrator stands downstage right, gets the stories going, and provides the narrative threads between them.

The opening of this musical is complex and challenging for any cast, students or adults, amateur or professional. There are a lot of words that introduce three separate stories whose details are crucial if the audience is to have any idea what's going on, fairy tales or not. Cinderella sings, "I wish to go to the Festival," and the Baker and his Wife sing, "I wish we had a child," and Jack sings, "I wish my cow would give us some milk."[72] The music at times is discordant, with surprising melodic jumps and few repetitions to aid either performer or audience. Further, the actors must coordinate their fast-moving and wordy lines with the other actors across a broad proscenium, and the timing is tricky. Most of the lyrics are sung by individual characters, so actors can't depend on others to support them during the scary first few minutes of the show.

Eric coached the students to spit out their words, which they often remembered to do. Yet as I observed the enthusiastic, well-rehearsed, if sometimes (understandably) nervous actors at all three schools, I was struck by the difficulty of this opening and wished for these students a rousing ensemble number or an easy comic scene to help them get past the first few anxious minutes of solo singing. When Sondheim predicted this musical's popularity with schools, he surely neglected to consider how young actors would struggle with its first moments.

The opening is complicated technically, too. Lights come up on each "house" when that character's story is being told—Cinderella, then Jack and his mother, then the Baker and his Wife, who are visited by Little Red. She asks for bread and sweets to take to Granny, and heads off, initiating the "Into the Woods" theme. The Witch then comes to the Baker's house, and explains, in a hilarious rap number, the Baker's family's curse and the recipe for lifting it. By the end of this fifteen-minute opening number, everyone has gone "into the woods."[73]

At Worthington High School, all of this coming and going was controlled by the stage manager/production assistant/assistant director: the calm and competent Charlotte. A young woman with big, stylish glasses and a long curly mane of hair, she is, like most stage managers I've known (especially those who are women), both soft-spoken and self-assured, seldom without her headset and clipboard (the stage manager's costume). Charlotte is a triplet; one sister played Cinderella and the other was on the tech crew. She lives on a farm, which her family has owned for generations, thirty minutes from the school.

Charlotte got involved in theatre in her freshman year with a production of *Anything Goes*, working on the tech crew. She loved building the set, making something from nothing, and then seeing what she made on stage as part of the play: "You don't have your name stamped on it, [but] you know people are going to remember. It's a really good feeling, looking at a set and going 'wow, I helped with that.'"

After the first year, she "wanted to do more, because I absolutely love musical theatre and I wanted to feel like I had a bigger hand in it." Eric also saw her potential and asked if she wanted to be the stage manager and assistant director, and she agreed. From the first day of auditions, she was responsible for making sure that all of the forms were filled out and that everyone was ready to go. Eric also asked her "without spying exactly" to keep an eye on how students behaved as they were waiting to audition. He wanted to cast students who would be diligent, disciplined, and kind to each other.

Charlotte also kept track of all thirty-two actors' blocking: "I've got my binder and it's got pretty much every single thing about the show in it, every single bit of blocking written three or four times every time something changes." Eric comes to rehearsal with the blocking sketched out for each scene, built around tableaux and stage pictures that he wants to see. Then he tells the students "to connect the dots" by finding motivation, a through line, and reasons to go from here to there. For *Into the Woods*, the choir teacher who usually does the musical direction for the singers was on maternity leave, so he taught them the music, too, with Charlotte by his side, or she took students aside to practice scenes separately. And he designed and built the set with Charlotte's help.

Through the rehearsal period, Charlotte went to the scene shop whenever she could to help build Milky White from papier mâché layered on a wooden frame. Once they got access to the theatre a few weeks before opening night, she spent a frigid, snowy Saturday with Eric and his father soaking brown paper in water and then twisting and wrapping it around the chicken-wire frame of the two trees that dominated the set. When the "trees" dried, their texture looked like real tree bark. The next week, when the whole production moved into the theatre, she called the show, as Erin, the professional lighting designer, taught her. On headset, she told the student who ran the light board when to go to the next cue and the students moving the set when to go. At the end of each rehearsal, Charlotte instructed the cast where to be and when, and she reminded them to turn off and store their mics, to put away their costumes, and, before each show, to check their props.

Charlotte's involvement in the play allowed her to see the school's limited resources and to wish (like the characters in the show) for more space and a bigger school. In 2016, and again in 2018, the district voted down a referendum to build a new school. According to one 2011 article, "As most rural Minnesota districts have shrunk, Worthington added some 500 students in the past five years, for a total enrollment of more than 2,550."[74] The facility was overcrowded and they were in desperate need of more space. In fact, even with a relatively new wing of the building with band and chorus rooms, the school lacked an auditorium or appropriate space for performance, which is why they performed at Memorial.

Charlotte voted for the new school referendum without telling her parents, even though she knew that they—or most certainly her father—voted against it. She added that her parents were supportive of the triplets' pursuit of theatre and that her father "does his best to support everything we do," chauffeuring them to and from rehearsals, and volunteering to help build the set. "I'm not a really big believer in just going with whatever your parents believe," she told me, then had to run off to call places.

Increasing diversity in the town has led to tensions among white farmers, Karen—an ethnic group from Burma (Myanmar)—refugees, and Latinos, most evident in the school referendum's split vote. From 2001 to 2011, the number of Hispanic children in the school district increased from 20 to 45 percent.[75] The district has adjusted to address the economic and social pressures faced by these students by offering English language-learner classes, and by employing a Hispanic graduate of Worthington schools to serve as "a confidante, an academic advisor and a tutor willing to help out before or after school."[76] Nonetheless, "graduation rates and test scores for Hispanics still lag far behind those for white students."[77] The Karens and Latinos own small houses or live in rental housing, so their property taxes are much lower (or none at all) than the white families who have owned large tracts of land for generations and pay much more. Many of these families, including Charlotte and her sisters', didn't support a new school building, for which they felt they would be paying more than their fair share.[78]

Into the Woods seemed the perfect show to do here and now, Charlotte said. She noted the resonances between their lives and the play, including the struggles between parents and children that *Into the Woods* represents so wistfully. She also saw the defeat of the Giant as a powerful symbol for her community's debate surrounding the failed referendum. In *Into the Woods*, "people didn't think about the needs of others . . . it wasn't until [the characters] worked together and . . . thought back to their own personal experiences and how they could use those challenges . . . to try to overcome the [Giant]." The musical gave her a place to think through local struggles and, just as importantly, to assume a leadership position in the school (Figure 3.2).

"Hello, Little Girl" and the Role of the Wolf

The characters go into the woods, each on their own quest, including Little Red, who sets out from the Baker and his Wife's house with a basket full of bread and sweets for her granny. She soon encounters the Wolf, played at Worthington by Noah. He sings "Hello, Little Girl" and follows Little Red around the stage as she meanders toward her grandmother's house. The song is in two modes: the first a bright, major mode, vaudeville-like melody that he directs towards Little Red, "Hello, little girl, / What's your rush? / You're missing all the flowers," which she answers with quick determination, "Mother said, / 'Straight ahead' / Not to delay / Or be misled."[79] For the Wolf's second tune, in alternating verses, he sings to himself in a minor, blues mode, scheming how he will eat the grandmother first and then the girl, "tender and fresh, / Not one lump."[80] The humor of the number emerges through the double entendre of the Wolf's hunger for Little Red, which Sondheim wrote

Figure 3.2. Milky White, Jack, the Baker, and the Baker's Wife in *Into the Woods* in Worthington, Minnesota. Note the "rag curtains," "bark" on the "tree," and sharply raked platform.

to be heard as both literal and sexual. He sings, "There's no possible way to describe what you feel / When you're talking to your meal!"[81]

Eric, like many high school directors of *Into the Woods* in conservative communities like Worthington, intentionally downplayed the sexuality of the song. Noah wore a rubber wolf mask on the top half of his face and biker gear, which gave him a cartoonish appearance. He and Ellie, who played Little Red with girlish innocence, were on opposite sides of the stage for most of the song. Their only physical contact was a sweet waltz, which suggested nothing more than courteous friendship. Noah's Wolf was more charming than menacing; even his howl at the end, which Eric coached him to extend and make more animalistic, made him funny rather than threatening.

The show was Noah's fourth musical. He's an experienced musician with perfect pitch, owns several guitars, and also plays alto saxophone, cello, keyboard, harmonica, dulcimer, recorder, and ukulele. Noah's mother, who works as the administrative assistant to the school's principal and also helped out with the show, was delighted that her son, who's on the autism spectrum, could participate in the musical. She didn't know what a big role he had because he learned his lines and music at home entirely on his own.

Eric respected Noah's musical ability and gladly cast him as the Wolf. He also cast other students with learning or emotional challenges, believing that musical theatre gives opportunities to kids like Noah who might not otherwise be able to share their talents. Eric focused on "put[ting] [Noah] in a situation where he can succeed" by casting him in a role where Noah's own movement was "part of who the character is . . . [so that it] doesn't look out of place, it just looks character driven." Eric explained his philosophy of casting as asking, "What does this performer have that's innately already part of the character [so that] when they get nervous and default to their own self, it's related to who they're playing?"

"Giants in the Sky" and the Role of Jack

As the musical goes on, the adventurous and friend-seeking Jack climbs up, then down, the beanstalk and sings "Giants in the Sky." The patter song takes place midway through Act 1 and details Jack's adventures in the land of Giants. After Jack returns to the familiarity of home, he wishes—like most of the characters in the musical—for a life in between fantasy and reality.[82]

The number gives the actor playing Jack a chance to express the character's enthusiasm as he recounts his trespassing travels skyward.[83] Kaw Doh, who played Jack, captured the character's ingenuousness and eagerness perfectly. Eric staged the number with Kaw Doh taking full advantage of the stage, revealing Jack's excitability. He roved all over the upper platform, ran from side to side and sang out to the audience to tell his story. During the Wednesday morning performance of Act 1 for a packed house of fourth- and fifth-graders bussed in from the nearby elementary schools, the children, who were almost all kids of color, cheered especially loud for Kaw Doh. Maybe they appreciated the character's mischievousness and maybe they recognized themselves in a person of color on the stage. During his preshow welcome, Eric primed the audience of young spectators and possible future performers: "This could be you in a few years!"

Kaw Doh, who is a Karen refugee and a newly minted US citizen, made his stage debut as Jack. He's a musician, plays in a band, and plans to go to college and major in music, but he had never done theatre before. When he auditioned and was cast as Jack, he noticed similarities between himself and the character. Over the months of rehearsals, he said, "Maybe I've become more like Jack. My friends say I'm the same as him!" It didn't even feel like acting to him.

Eric required the students to map out their character's motivations in the show and objectives for each scene. He distributed a worksheet with questions based on Uta Hagen's famous Method acting techniques focused on given circumstances, relationships, and objectives, and he discouraged the students from watching clips of the show online. Eric very much wanted them to create the characters for themselves. In fact, he taught the actors the music before Christmas break so "they don't listen to the cast album and pick up bad habits."

Kaw Doh didn't tell his parents that he was in the show until a few days before the performance, when he handed them their tickets. "They liked it!" but he wasn't sure how much his mother, who speaks little English, followed the story. "She was proud of me, though," he said.

Kaw Doh was one of three students of color in the play. Maria, who is Latina, played the Stepsister Lucinda, and Jenna, an Asian American, was in the ensemble. Although the school's population is 60 percent minority, and the ninth and tenth grades are predominantly students of color, most of the students involved in the theatre program are white. Eric originally cast two more Latinas in the show, but much to his dismay, both dropped out before rehearsals started because their parents feared deportation. The parents of one, though they felt somewhat secure in Worthington, didn't want their daughter to draw attention to their family by performing publicly in a big community event. The other worried that her family might have to relocate at a moment's notice and didn't want to have to quit the play later, leaving the production in the lurch. Eric understood but was tremendously disappointed.

Worthington's racial diversity made the national news in an article in 2011 that outlined the school district's struggle to support non-English speakers, especially Latinos. When I asked what's the key issue in the town, everyone answered without missing a beat, "diversity." "Our traditionally white, male-dominated culture is adjusting to an influx of people of color," one mother said, "which is all for the good." Kelly, a tall, brown-haired, articulate junior who gave up basketball to play the Witch (and was at first a little reluctant to "act ugly" in the role, according to one of the mothers who helped with makeup), found the musical a perfect metaphor for their school and town. "The Giant represents a force bigger than us," she said. "That means our differences. So we have to come together to overcome it."

Whatever people's politics, the show brought them together. As Tammy, the managing director of the space, told me, "This is my favorite event that we program—the high school musical."

East Clinton High School, Sabina, Ohio

Sabina, Ohio (pop. 2,540), the home of East Clinton High School, is an equidistant hour's drive from Cincinnati and Columbus and a little closer to Dayton. The school is surrounded by the vast corn and soybean fields of southern Ohio. According to a 2018 study, 17.5 percent of the population has a bachelor's degree or higher and the median household income is $48,675.[84] From 2003 to 2008, a DHL hub was located in nearby Wilmington, where the historic Murphy Theatre—site of the high school musical's performance—is located. DHL's closure resulted in the loss of nearly ten thousand jobs, decimating the local non-farming economy.[85] Everyone is white, and there is little concern with the immigration issues that were so important in Worthington. People in East Clinton are more concerned with poverty—around 60 percent of the 380 students are on free/reduced lunch—and the opioid crisis.

The teachers know everyone and everything in this small community. Kristi Grover, a math teacher who's overseen the musical's production for thirty years, said, "I would hope to think that everybody here [in this rehearsal] is well fed, but I'm sure I would be kidding myself." She regrets that there is a small costume fee to participate in the musical, but adds that ticket sales subsidize the fee for students in need.

The fifty students in the cast of *Into the Woods*, who ranged from eleven to eighteen years old, arrived damp and chilled on the rainy afternoon of their final Thursday night dress rehearsal. The teachers and some volunteer parents had loaded some of the cast and crew into their cars at the school to shuttle them fifteen minutes to downtown and the theatre, stopping at McDonald's to grab some food for dinner. Some of the older kids had cars and drove themselves and their friends.

The hundred-year-old Murphy Theatre fronts Main Street and sits next to Jen's Deli, a funky and popular café, and across the street from the General Denver Hotel. The theatre sported an old-fashioned lettered marquee that read, "East Clinton HS *Into the Woods*, Fri and Sat 7 pm." The red-carpeted lobby has an embossed tin ceiling, which workmen on ladders had polished earlier in the day. Back in the day, the venue played "host to vaudeville, lectures, minstrel shows, movies, high school graduations, band concerts, plays and even church services," according to its brochure.[86] Touring musical groups and movies dominate the current season.[87]

The high school musical is a huge annual event in the town, and no one doubted that both nights of the show would be entirely sold out. The theatre's manager needed to make sure they had more than the usual amount of popcorn and soda as well as a few extra kids to work behind the concessions counter. The 769-seat house has two wide aisles and a balcony with two follow spots in the back. To light the show, Kristi gave a marked-up copy of the script to the theatre staff's tech guy, and he figured out where to put some cues and also operated the light board. Fathers of two ninth-grade girls in the show manned the follow spots, looking at their copies of the script by flashlight to anticipate who had the next solo and needed to be brightly lit. Both men performed in this very theatre twenty years earlier when they went to East Clinton High School. One also helped to assemble the straightforward two-level set, which was designed, built, and painted by students in art classes. According to Sam Minge, the school's thirteen-year band director and the musical director of *Into the Woods*, many students "never leave the county." The next night, the house was packed with several generations of families who owned farms and spent their entire lives here.

The musical was created by a team of teachers. Kristi chose the show in consultation with the other teachers. They all agreed that the musical theatre program was getting stronger each year, and, as Sam said, "the kids are up to it." "The show is a big emotional investment," Sam explained. "You need to know your community and you need to know the kids." Kristi oversaw all aspects of the production, including dealing with Music Theatre International (MTI) and figuring out the budget, and she did some of the directing. In addition to her work as the director, she also acted as the producer and resident "control freak," as she calls herself, with responsibilities ranging from creating the program to "pick[ing] up the [prop] ear of corn from a grocery store that ordered it in for us." Veteran high school English teacher Steve Wages—whom Harper, who played the Narrator, complimented, "We do real work in his class"—blocked most of the scenes and coached the actors. During the performance, Steve, a big soft-spoken guy with a mustache, worked as the nominal stage manager, decked out in a headset and overseeing the maelstrom of so many students, including little ones, backstage. First-year choir teacher Laura Nichols, who looks more like a student than a teacher, with stick-straight brown hair, bright eyes, sneakers, and blue jeans, took on the role of assistant director, and she did a lot of actor coaching ("character advice," Sam called it) and the choreography.

During the dress rehearsal, Sam, the music director—tall and thin with dark hair, a warm smile, and a gentle voice—was in charge. He oversaw an orchestra of students on woodwinds and brass, while Laura controlled Sinfonia, the computerized string tracks that they rented from MTI for $1,450 because they don't have a string section to play the show live. But, Sam said, they wanted as much live music as possible. Marching band is big in East Clinton, due in large part to Sam's energy and enthusiasm—he's grown the program by leaps and bounds—with one-third of the student body involved, including virtually all of the kids in the musical. They have two concert bands, a competitive marching program, and an electronic music class. In Worthington, Minnesota, the orchestra was seated backstage and watched the action on a large screen that the theatre's tech director rigged with a video camera out front. But in East Clinton, the orchestra sat on the floor in front of the stage, and Sam's conducting was visible to all of the student performers, who tried to stay in character as they watched him for cues and cut-offs. After their dress rehearsal, he gave most of the notes.

Kristi, who has vibrant blue eyes and curly strawberry blond hair, conveys equal degrees of shrugging exhaustion and ever-renewable passion for theatre and dedication to the children. She's committed to doing a musical each year, both to expose kids to culture that is lacking in Sabina and to encourage them to step outside of their shells. She is willing to cast complete theatrical newcomers in major roles, which means she sometimes must answer questions like, "How do I learn all of these lines?" She is aware of who is coming from a rough home life. Kristi grew up close by, and notes, "I guess I was a poor child. I was a farm kid. I didn't know how poor I was; I don't think these kids know either." Before opening night, she leads a prayer: "I'm very thankful," she says to the kids. "Now don't make me cry, 'cause I do that a lot."

Kristi wants everyone to be included, so any student who auditions in middle or high school is cast, but she notes that with a show as big and challenging as *Into the Woods*, "we have a lot of responsibility resting on very young shoulders—very inexperienced shoulders." Many eighth-graders were in the cast, including the girl who played Jack. A number of students were athletes, such as the Baker's Wife, who is a softball player. The boy who played the Baker was in his first show ever. Sam explained, "Kids run the gamut in ability and when they get involved. Sometimes they audition as seniors and it's like, where have you been for the past four years? And some started as Oompa Loompas in *Willy Wonka* and now are leads." Because *Into the Woods* lacks a traditional chorus, many of the younger students played trees or flowers. The spare but more-than-adequate set was wonderfully filled out with human trees scattered across the stage (see Figure 3.1).

Kristi is also sharp with the kids. At the end of their Thursday night dress rehearsal, she noted the old adage about a bad dress rehearsal, but couldn't contain her frustration. "We'll stage the curtain call, even though after tonight's rehearsal, you don't deserve a curtain call," she reprimanded the kids, who looked at their laps, unable to meet her eyes.

"Agony" and the Role of Cinderella's Prince

Further along in Act 1, two new characters appear who are, of course, central to fairy tales and thus to *Into the Woods*: the Princes. In Sondheim and Lapine's riff, Cinderella's Prince and Rapunzel's Prince—and that's how they're identified, by the woman each desires—are brothers, bound by the pain of the unrequited love they both endure. The Princes meet in the woods, as one is trying to woo Cinderella, who ran away from him after the ball, and the other wants Rapunzel, who is locked "high in a tower."[88] They share their stories in a hilarious, campy duet, "Agony," in which each tries to outdo the other's whining.

Sondheim used 6/8 meter for the song to imitate the style of a barcarolle, or a song sung by Venetian gondoliers. According to John Franceschina, Sondheim "composed with a monotonous accompaniment . . . and easily flowing melody [which] provides [*sic*] an ironic background to the princes' misfortunes."[89] One sings, "Agony—! Far more painful than yours," and the other joins him, "Agony! Oh, the torture they teach!"[90]

The song, which critic Frank Rich described as its "own self-contained joke,"[91] was even funnier than usual in East Clinton's production because the Princes were played by real brothers—Liam, a senior, and Danny, a sophomore—a fact known by everyone in the packed-house audience. Their voices have a similar timbre and they physically resemble each other. Most importantly, they felt comfortable hamming it up together, as the song requires. They practiced at home and tried to think of funny gestures and ways of mirroring each other to enhance the comedy of the song, Liam told me. Each time he and Danny rehearsed and performed the number, the blocking was a little different, depending on how they felt and how their energy bounced off one another, Liam said.

Liam began performing in "musical," as East Clintonites call it (with no article), in ninth grade. "Of course I was going to finish out all four years doing musical," he said. But his primary commitment was to orchestra and marching band, like almost all of the students involved in the show. East Clinton, with less than four hundred students in the high school—so few that they include middle school students in the show (Liam's younger twin sisters also performed, one as Jack and one in the ensemble as a flower)—is too small to have stereotypical high school cliques, several of the students told me. But the population does divide roughly into two groups: the one-third who do band and the rest who don't. The band students attend band camp before school begins in the fall, spending long hot days outdoors working on the many musical numbers and formations, the August "corn rain" floating onto their heads, clothes, and instruments. Marching band's season of football games, pep rallies, local parades, and competitions runs from September to November, but the students take band as a class year-round.

Liam's involvement in music began as a child: "I've kind of been involved with everything musical since I was a little kid at my grandparents' church and all through school.[92] I picked up the recorder in third grade to learn to read music, and that was the first instrument I played and I loved it." For this family, and for many others in this community, singing in church developed their love for music and theatre, and it taught them, from a young age, how to sit still and pay attention. Far from detracting from appreciation for music and theatre, church enhances it. For a family Christmas present last year, Liam's parents got tickets to take their five kids to Chicago to see *Hamilton*.

Near the end of *Into the Woods*, after a tryst with the Baker's Wife, Cinderella's Prince stumbles upon Cinderella wandering alone in the woods. She confronts him: "I'm not your only love, am I? [. . .] My father's house was a nightmare. Your house was a dream. Now I want something in between." They agree to part amicably. He leaves with, "I shall always love the maiden who ran away," and she answers, "And I the far-away Prince," and he darts offstage, with the same silly arrogant stride.[93] Liam could connect the Prince's bittersweet ending to his own imminent high school graduation and departure from the comfort of school and band and a big and loving family. Soon he would be off to college to study nursing. He hopes to live by his class's senior motto: "Never forget where you came from, but never let that hold you back from where you want to go."

"It Takes Two" and the Role of the Baker

Shortly after the Princes' "Agony" in Act 1, the Baker reluctantly accepts the help of his wife in procuring the items to remove the curse. Earlier, though, at the start of *Into the Woods*, he insists on going it alone, singing, "The spell is in on my house." She answers, "No, the spell is on our house," but he embarks on the quest alone anyway.[94] The Baker now needs his wife to remind him which objects they need and to scheme how to get them. Before the second midnight, they have the cape and the cow and the hair, and the Baker's Wife, though she failed to nab Cinderella's slipper, believes that she can acquire it the next day. Optimistic, they find new affection and commitment in their jaunty love duet, "It Takes Two."

The song is ABABC in form, with the Baker's Wife singing her melody (A) first, then the Baker (B), and then they repeat. For the (C) section, he joins first to her tune, underlining that she's the correct and stronger one, but then they sing a new melody (in harmony) together, which represents their necessary synergy. The triplet-laden song conveys a constantly moving and syncopated feeling and suggests a lilting dance.[95] She sings, "You've changed. You're daring. You're different in the woods." He answers, "I thought one was enough, / It's not true: / It takes two of us." By the end of the number, they agree that "we'll get past the woods" and return, "safe at home with our beautiful prize."[96] Consistent with the farcical style of Act 1, the song sounds more like one between buddies than a romantic duet.

James played the Baker, in his first acting role—his friend Harper persuaded him to audition—and Jenny, the softball player, played the Baker's Wife. The pair presented a sweet connection, and according to James, they worked hard to achieve it, not unlike their characters' challenge to get on the same page and to trust each other. Jenny comes from a strongly religious background and she didn't want a boy to touch her. James respected her wishes, but they both knew the song needed to show the couple's love for each other, so they found likely places to sing to each other or join hands in a friendly way. Like "Agony," the number didn't have specific blocking and varied with each rehearsal and performance, but there were certain lines when the actors, coached and choreographed by teacher Laura, always made physical contact or looked at one another.

James is the only out gay student in the school. He said that his sexuality, his college ambitions, and his serious musicianship (he plays percussion in marching band and concert band and wants to go into music as a living after college) caused him to see the community from an outsider's perspective.

James comfortably performed the Baker's heterosexuality in the production. And though I didn't meet other out gay male students on my travels, I did observe a wide range of performances of masculinity. Sociologist C. J. Pascoe, in her book on masculinity in high schools, notes that high school theatre, especially musical theatre, tends to be "a space of liberation and relaxation" for boys both gay and straight. Pascoe writes, "Drama is notoriously a fag space in high schools. The ironic result of this connection is that the insult disappears. Not only does the insult disappear, but drama becomes a space where male students can enact a variety of gender practices."[97]

In addition to downplaying the romance between the Baker and his wife, the East Clinton production eliminated other sexually suggestive moments. For example, one of the running gags in the show is when the Witch reminds the Baker of her curse on his fertility and points her staff at the actor's groin, and he recoils in mock pain. (After this schtick, some fourth-graders in Worthington gasped and wanted to know, "How did they do that?"—that is, how did the Witch hurt the Baker with her staff? Ah, the magic of theatre!) But in the East Clinton production, Abigail, who played the Witch, pointed her staff at James's chest. He shrunk, as if she punched him, but there was no connection between her thrust and the sexual meaning of the curse.

Another example: When we meet Rapunzel wandering in the woods after her mother, the Witch, has released and expelled her from her tower in retaliation for Rapunzel's affair with the Prince, the actor typically carries twin babies, the result of their tryst. But in East Clinton's production, she was childless, which eliminated the implication of sex when the Prince manages to climb the tower to be with her. Like the Worthington production, the East Clinton version tamped down on any sexual suggestiveness between Cinderella's Prince and the Baker's Wife's ("Moments in the Woods") and the Wolf and Little Red ("Hello, Little Girl").

As the Murphy Theatre manager predicted, the place was packed that night and the line for popcorn at intermission so long that they almost had to delay the start of Act 2. Everyone in the town, it seemed, came out to see the show, and many people greeted each other warmly. "It's as good as Broadway!" I overheard more than a few people say.

Act 2: "Once Upon a Time" and the Role of the Narrator

The opening of Act 2 of *Into the Woods* resembles Act 1, with the Narrator intoning, "Once upon a time" even before the lights come up. At first it seems that we are starting again with new stories to follow the "happily-ever-after" finale in Act 1, which was "to be continued," as the Narrator had announced.[98] In Act 2, the characters open with, "I never thought I could be so happy," but quickly reveal that they have new, unfulfilled wishes. Moreover, they have to face the consequences of their actions from Act 1: an angry, widowed Giant is seeking revenge in their midst. As Rich wrote in his *Times* review, "In Act II, everyone is jolted into the woods again—this time not to cope with pubescent traumas symbolized by beanstalks and carnivorous wolves but with such adult catastrophes as unrequited passion, moral cowardice, smashed marriages and the deaths of loved ones."[99] In a high school production of this musical, the young actors must attempt to rise to adult challenges, which Rich described as "dilemmas of conscience, connectedness and loss."[100]

As in Act 1, the Narrator's Act 2 opening line sets the tone and prepares the audience for what's to come. We've returned to the world of fairy tales and books, with a Narrator (Rich: a "post-modern anti-narrator"[101]) as our guide, who continues to provide the connections among the different stories as the characters return to the woods, until (spoiler alert!) the Narrator is fed to the Giant midway through the second act. The casting choice for the Narrator varies in different productions, though the role is often played by a tall blond boy in a cardigan sweater and loafers. Surprisingly, in spite of the overabundance of girls involved in most high school's musical theatre programs, few productions cast a girl in the role, so I was glad to see that they did so at East Clinton High School.

Harper played the Narrator with an impressive, fierce possession of the stage. Perhaps because she had a speech impediment as a child, perhaps because she is a student leader and activist at East Clinton, or perhaps because she is the marching band's drum major, which requires attention-getting skills, she took absolute charge of the stage and the story. She wore a long lavender gown that suggested the fairy tale setting. This production placed her in the world of the characters to recount their tales, rather than clothing her in contemporary garb that would have her looking back to stories of the past. Or maybe this was what the school had available or what she wanted to wear. Harper took an often-overlooked character and made her a central figure in their production.

Harper and her best friend, Abigail, who played the Witch, as well as James and Liam, feel themselves to be leaders at the school. In their tiny, rural community, they take their studies and their music—orchestra, that is—seriously. During rehearsals for the musical, they also felt responsible for the younger kids, helping them learn their lines and music, giving them direction and coaching and encouragement. As role models, they always needed to demonstrate cooperation and a good attitude. Outside of the production, Harper helped to organize and run an anti-bullying weekend in the fall. She has progressive politics, which are unusual for this town, and sees herself as a political activist. She plans to go to college but can't leave the county now because of money, so she'll start at a community college and "work my scholarship butt off" to find money to pay for her education.

Harper explained how her participation in musical theatre enabled her to work on her articulation and overcome her inability to pronounce her r's. She went from a shy and withdrawn child to a confident, outspoken young woman. As the drum major for all four years of high school, Harper held one of the highest honors in the school. To a degree, Harper played a similar leadership role in *Into the Woods* that she does in the school community. While the Narrator is rejected from the community, though, she is graduating and possibly, in time, leaving to strike out on her own.

Like the students in Worthington, the young actors at East Clinton felt a connection between the show and their community. Kristi noted that the students think the first act is "just the fairytale story," but in a discussion with one of their teachers, they were encouraged to see the second act as, she said, "Life . . . the woods is life; you have to go out there, stand up for yourself."

After the curtain call, which was met with an immediate standing ovation and roaring shouts of appreciation, the actors exited the stage and ran around the outside of the theatre in their costumes to reappear in the theatre's elegant lobby, where they formed two long receiving lines. In this way, each person in the audience could congratulate them on their outstanding performance on their way out of the theatre and into the chilly night.

Belleville High School, Belleville, Michigan

For the production of *Into the Woods* at Belleville High School, in Belleville, Michigan (pop. 3,872), teacher and director Larry Koch—a twenty-seven-year-veteran teacher with bright blue eyes, a balding head, and an easy, slightly shy smile—held an all-day, in-school dress rehearsal on Thursday, which allowed teachers to bring their English classes to see one period's worth of the show. The student performers ran the show twice that day, once in the morning and once in the afternoon. Then, after Larry's notes and his teary-with-pride pep talk, they went home at the end of the school day to rest for Friday night's opening. As is the school's custom, the cast wore dressy clothes to school—the boys in suits and ties, and the girls in nice dresses or pants. About ninety minutes before curtain, four volunteer parents arrived to help set up the box office, stack the programs to be distributed by student volunteer ushers, and arrange a long table to sell cookies, candy, soda, water, and coffee.

Belleville, which some consider a small town and others a bedroom community of Ann Arbor, is thirty minutes from there—the home of the flagship campus of the University of Michigan—and forty minutes from downtown Detroit. A lovely lake, which was a river until Henry Ford had it dammed in 1924, occupies the middle of the downtown area, and wealthy Detroiters once built their summer homes there.[102] According to the *2012–2016 American Community Survey*, the median household income was $45,737, 16.4 percent of the population was below the poverty line, and 85.9 percent had at least a high school education.

According to Larry, "Belleville has changed over the last twenty-seven years since I began teaching [in 1991]. Formerly, the community was mostly white and blue collar. For the past fifteen years or so [since the early 2000s] there has been a flight from Detroit and Detroit Public Schools to the suburbs." He described Belleville as "a cute town" and said that more restaurants and businesses are opening every year. Also, the community has shifted politically. Larry noted that twenty-seven years ago, "It was like the Bible Belt." But now the school has a Gay-Straight Alliance, and two girls in the show were a couple and thanked each other in the production's program. School principal Stacey Buhro said that the area has a wide socioeconomic range—of the school's eighteen hundred students, 40 percent are "economically disadvantaged." Its racial makeup is 52 percent African American and the rest white. Stacey, like a number of teachers and staff, grew up in the town, went away to college, then returned there to teach. Former students include Nick Taylor, who directs the three-hundred-member marching band and directed a formidable student orchestra for the show. (Much of the *Into the Woods* cast also plays in the marching band, like the students at East Clinton High School.)

Belleville hosts a theatre program with extraordinary racial diversity, and more than half the kids in the show, both in leading roles and in the chorus, were of color (Figure 3.3). More often, even in a racially diverse school, white students dominate a musical theatre program. The mother of Jordan (who played the Wolf and Cinderella's Prince and is on the autism spectrum), who is white, said she used to notice race on stage, when, for example, parents in a play were a different race than their children. "Now," she said, "I don't even think about it. Any kid can play any role and that's that." Belleville's vibrant and diverse theatre program dispels assumptions about musical theatre's dominant whiteness.

In addition, because Belleville is much larger than the other schools I visited, the theatre students tended to self-identify as their own group. In her book *Jocks and Burnouts: Social Categories and Identity in the High School*, Penelope Eckert found that performing arts groups, specifically concert choir, self-segregated. As one student in her study said, "Concert Choir is like an individual part of school . . . It's like they all do their stuff . . . that group of

Figure 3.3. The Baker's Wife, the Baker, Milky White, and Jack in *Into the Woods* in Belleville, Michigan. Note the "moss" covered steps and realistic "tree."

kids, and they get things done."[103] At Belleville, being in the musical, even if it was a student's first play at school, won them entry into this group.

Unlike Worthington and East Clinton, whose schools rent a city-owned theatre because they lack an auditorium, Belleville High School has an eight-hundred-seat auditorium, built in 1968. A wide, sunny, and airy lobby looks onto a large, walled courtyard, and the theatre is a standard high school fare, with many rows of seats and a wide proscenium.

Larry readily admitted that he chose *Into the Woods* solely because the students wanted to do it: Rebekah, a charismatic, articulate African American senior who played the Witch, said she "bugged him to do it for four years!" As Larry wrote in the program's Director's Notes with wry, self-deprecating, self-correcting humor, "Our persistent BHS students ~~wore me down~~ [*sic*] . . . convinced me . . . to take a deeper, more concentrated look." He realized that the show is a mirror, noting, "We can see a part of ourselves in almost every one of these characters, good and bad. THAT was exciting to me. So, yeah, to use an expression, it gets deep. Plus the music is so darn catchy." Like many other high school directors of this musical, Larry didn't fully appreciate the complexity of the show, the amount of music to be learned and its difficulty, and the number of bodies to move around on stage. The reasons that *Into the Woods* is such a good vehicle for high school students are precisely those that make it so challenging: a lot of roles and a lot of music. Although they started rehearsals seven months earlier, there were many interruptions, including bad weather, shooting threats that caused the administration to close the school as a precaution, and a big district-wide robotics contest the week before the musical's tech rehearsal that took over the entire arts wing of the building, including the theatre and the scene shop, which had to be emptied of all in-process set pieces.

Nonetheless, they managed to build a beautiful set, which Yvette, a trained set designer and self-labeled stay-at-home mom, worked with a crew of twenty eager and dedicated students to construct. She told them, "You can make anything from trash and cardboard." They'd fashioned two towers, one that revolved to reveal Rapunzel's window and the other with a shimmery opening for Cinderella's mother's spirit. Around two-thirds the way upstage, three steps rose from the stage floor to a platform (not unlike the two levels in the East Clinton production), which covered the remaining one-third of stage space. The steps looked like real stones embedded in moss. Larry and his team of teacher assistants staged the show to make good use of the levels and the wide proscenium stage.

Like the other schools I visited, Belleville had little funding but at least one adult with expertise and the time and energy to work with an ample crew of young people. High school musical theatre's backstage, design, and tech work attracts at least a cast's worth of students who love theatre but don't want to perform. Yvette grows the program each year: "I tell them, when they're about to graduate, they need to bring two more students to replace them."

Act 2: "We're Not That Miserable!" and the Roles of the Lighting Designer and the Stage Manager

Midway through Act 2, the characters' lives are in danger, threatened by the angry lady Giant whose husband fell to his death when Jack chopped down the beanstalk. She wants to kill Jack in retaliation, but the characters wonder if they can sacrifice someone else. In this scene, they're all fighting, and they disagree about how they should respond. The dialog is quick and crisp, with lines volleyed back and forth across the stage. In the Belleville production, the Giant's voice, played by a student, came through the sound system, and she was imagined to be offstage right, so the actors spoke (well, shouted) their lines in that direction.

In an attempt to strike a bargain, the Witch asks the Giant, "Excuse me. Would you like a blind girl instead?" "What?" scream the Stepsisters, who were blinded in Act 1 by Cinderella's bird friends. The Stepmother yells, "How dare you!" at the Witch. "Put them out of their misery," the Witch quips, and the two Stepsisters shoot back ("bitter," as the stage directions instruct), "We're not that miserable!"[104] Their punchline provides a brief moment of hilarity in an otherwise emotionally difficult scene. The Giant responds with a growl, and the ground seems to shudder, indicated by pulsing lights and the actors pretending to lose their balance and fall down. The intricate moment combined acting, precisely coordinated among the 10 students on stage, with lighting and sound cues, the purview of Yvette's tech kids.

The enthusiastic tech team included Carlos, a serious, dark-haired, ROTC-bound senior from Colombia, who was the show's assistant lighting designer. Yvette's husband is a professional lighting designer for industrial shows. He designed the lights during a few visits to the school and mentored Carlos, who ultimately took control. (The school's proximity to Ann Arbor and Detroit provides a steady pool of professional artists.) Because of competing demands on the space, they had to hang and focus the lights before the set was finished, guessing where the actors would be. For the production, a student follow-spot operator picked up the actors if they failed to walk into the light. Various cues lit the cyclorama ("cyc") curtain in different hues to set the mood for each scene.

Carlos came to the United States in seventh grade when his mother married an American. The move was difficult for him, he said. But when his older sister got involved in theatre tech and he saw the Belleville production of *Little Shop of Horrors* his freshman year, he was "inspired . . . to take a bigger role." In his first show, he "only had one cue, which was to move a couch," but he has since taken on more backstage and design and tech responsibilities over his four years of high school, helping to build and light both *Willy Wonka* and *Man of La Mancha*. He practically glowed when he talked about what participating in theatre has meant to him. "When you, in the audience, or me, in the lighting spot, get to see what the performers do, how much love they put into the character, all the emotions that go into it, it's truly magical." He believed that *Into the Woods* carried an important message for their community: "Everyone has been in a situation where they want to give up, or where they don't know what to do, and there is a Giant, so to speak . . . that's why it's an important story."

Carlos's cues were called by the stage manager, Ava, who, like Charlotte in Worthington, oversaw a cast of twenty-seven actors and a twenty-five-member backstage crew. Ava, a white girl with straight brown hair, an easy smile, and that no-nonsense stage manager air, was convinced to join the tech crew by Carlos during her sophomore year. During *Willy Wonka*, she realized "it was really something I wanted to invest my time in, so I did." She suddenly became the stage manager for *Willy Wonka*, though she had no experience. "She just got thrown in," said Yvette, grinning. Ava added, "It was rough at first, I didn't really know what I was doing, [but] the community that we had, they all helped build me [to] where I am now." Now Ava is among the student leaders in the theatre community: "I thrive in the theatre. I come alive here."

For both Carlos and Ava, as well as a number of other students, the musical provides them with a sense of belonging and purpose. Feeling included also mattered to Victoria, the biracial (Puerto Rican and African American) girl who played Lucinda and spit the perfectly timed line, "We're not that miserable!" Victoria is a freshman, who noted, "Being African American in the arts, especially in theatre, is kind of hard 'cause I know that as I get older, it's gonna be harder for me to get the parts that I want," she said. "It'll always be harder for me as a person of color." Nonetheless, she aspires to a life in the theatre, and although a freshman, had extensive theatre experience: This was her fourteenth show. She started performing in community theatre with her mother, who was "a big influence" on her, when she was ten. Like her peers, Victoria found *Into the Woods* meaningful. "In the Act 2 Finale, we tell the audience, 'careful what you say to children,'" she said. "And I think that's more important now than ever, because children nowadays, we have to pre-pare them for the future . . . we're so stuck in our technology . . . we don't com-municate with each other and we don't read enough to know what's going on in our world."

Many Voices at Belleville High School

To get to know more of the kids, I hosted an all-day, marathon discussion with students in the cast and crew of *Into the Woods* on the Friday of their opening, which confirmed for me the power of the ensemble and the strong bond among these students. We continually added chairs to our circle in the sunlit lobby, as they came and went during their free study and lunch periods, confessing that they were "curious about what [their peers] had to say about the show." Multiple performers emphasized the "big family" back-stage, where students looked to peers and teachers alike for advice on de-veloping their characters and memorizing the complicated Sondheim lines, where "every little detail is super important." The friendships fostered by *Into the Woods* spanned all four grades: Carly, a white junior playing Little Red Riding Hood's Granny, was quick to say that although the freshmen "are young" and "they're not going to know everything," she has "gotten some great advice from some freshmen this year that has helped me so much with this role."

We talked about what being in the musical means to them, how it complements their fall involvement in the marching band (which is a big thing at Belleville, as at East Clinton High School), what their families think about their passion for musical theatre (some are supportive and some not so much). Michael, a white boy who shared the part of the Narrator with a white girl, said that *Into the Woods* allowed him to "take a written part and really express myself through that, and that's something I didn't really have throughout growing up." While his family initially thought he was "crazy be-cause of the ridiculous hours I spend practicing," he noted that they would all be in the audience that night, including relatives who made the four-hour drive from Pittsburgh, Pennsylvania. A member of the tech crew said that it was immensely gratifying to see "what we've done, with what little we had to do it with . . . the friends that came and saw the show thought we spent thousands of dollars and hundreds of hours on this set, but really we've spent—yes, the hundreds of hours—but we haven't really spent that much [money]." The spotlight operator said that she enjoyed the process because they were part of "something bigger, together."

Except for Rebekah (the Witch) and Anthony (the Baker), every one of the actors said they're shy. Michael (the co-Narrator) suggested that introverted teenagers are drawn to the stage because "they don't get as much attention, and they don't get to show a certain side of themselves as much as they'd maybe like to. So when they go onstage, they can express themselves." The actor playing Cinderella, who has anxiety, added, "When I'm onstage, I feel like I can step outside of who I am normally, and I can be open . . . even if I mess up, even if I do something wrong, [the audience] won't know." She equated her experience onstage to Cinderella escaping her stepfamily to go to the ball: "When I'm shy in school, that's kind of how Cinderella should act when she's being with her family . . . but when she's away from her family, she can be more open and more excited and happy." One actor summarized their experience this way: "High school is a lot of self-discovery—like, who am I? . . . People don't really know who they are in high school. But for people onstage, they are given a character, and they can do anything they want with the character, and nobody's going to judge them . . . they know exactly who they are."

"Last Midnight" and the Role of the Witch

In Act 2, the transformed Witch is beautiful but powerless, a mere mortal like the other characters. Still, the actor who plays the Witch gets a lot of stage time in Act 2 and sings "Lament" ("Children Won't Listen") and, later, "Last Midnight." In between those two powerful solos, the community begins to disintegrate. The Baker's Wife and Cinderella's Prince have a tryst, a "Moment in the Woods," after which the Giant kills the Baker's Wife. (Yes, like a typical slasher film, the woman is killed for her sexual desire and activity.) The Giant also kills the Narrator and Rapunzel, and the Steward kills Jack's mother after she yells at the Giant. Imani, who played Jack's mother, was hilarious in this scene, playing her as the stereotype of the black matriarch who gives attitude and suffers no fools, familiar from Tyler Perry movies. Imani rolled her head and pointed her finger imperiously, delighting in her portrayal of the character and the appreciative laughs she got from the audience. But then she was killed off, the Giant still unappeased.

The remaining characters—the Baker, Cinderella, Little Red, Jack, and the Witch—blame each other for their unfortunate situation in the angry, aggressive "Your Fault." There's murder and mayhem in the land.

The Witch decides that she can't abide the community's hesitations. Her final song in the musical, "Last Midnight," is a haunting, minor-key waltz, a tour de force opportunity for the actor, after which she disappears in a cloud of smoke (or steps into a trap door, or jumps off the upstage edge of a platform, or exits by walking off the stage, depending on the set and the production's technical capabilities and budget). The song expresses the Witch's refusal to join the small, fragile community in their quest to kill the Giant. She sings, threateningly, "You're so nice. You're not good, / You're not bad, / You're just nice. I'm just right. I'm the Witch. You're the world."[105] The song is harsh and dissonant, its insistent rhythm a beating heart. [106]

Rebekah, who played the Witch, began the song on the upstage platform in a spotlight, dressed in a dark purple gown that set off her dark skin and flowing black wig, whose long locks she occasionally flipped over her shoulder in a flirty comic gesture. In this song, she spit accusations at the other characters, who cowered in fear and confusion downstage of her. Over the course of the song, she moved downstage, and in the last verse, waltzed in diagonal lines, covering the central downstage area. Toward the end of the number, she sang directly to the audience, then moved quickly upstage for her last few lines, "Give me claws and a hunch, / Just away from this bunch / And the gloom / And the doom / And the boom / Cruuuunch."[107] Then Ava called the smoke cue, a big white puff shot out of the floor, and Rebekah disappeared.

Rebekah inhabited the character—a role she longed to play since she started high school—with joyful bravado, and she brought the house down with this number. She is singular in her community, not unlike the Witch. A star in the theatre program, who played Dolly Levi in the nonmusical production of *The Matchmaker* in the fall, Rebekah is respected and admired, and is headed off to the University of Michigan for college. But unlike the Witch, who refuses to play well with others, Rebekah is also seen as a dependable leader, as someone who helps the younger actors and the teachers, too. Larry gave her the title of "student director." As the cast warmed up for their opening night, for example, Rebekah urged them, "Enunciate and look out!" Throughout the rehearsal process, Rebekah offered suggestions to other actors, and after the show closed, the soon-to-graduate Rebekah kept the crew together by organizing regular outings to the local ice cream shop. The musical provided a place for this young woman—like others in this chapter on and off stage—to assume a leadership position and to be regarded with respect.

"No More" and the Role of the Baker

After the Witch exits, the four remaining characters—Little Red, Jack, Cinderella, and the Baker (and the Baker's infant child)—come up with a plan to entrap and kill the Giant (with the help of Cinderella's bird friends. As Little Red asks Cinderella in amazement, "You can talk to birds?"). The Baker must find a way to live without his wife, who, he's come to understand, was his support and the real force in their household. "No More" is his last big number in the show.

Anthony played the role of the Baker. Like Rebekah, he is African American and well known in the school as an actor who's taken on several big parts over his high school years. He's also going to college and plans to include theatre and music in his studies. His first role was Sancho, Don Quixote's sidekick in *Man of La Mancha*. He also played Barnaby Tucker in Belleville's production of *The Matchmaker*. Anthony said that he used the example of these two previous characters and their friendships with men as a foundation for building chemistry with the Baker's Wife. He told me that he and the actor playing his wife "know each other, we're in band together . . . there's nothing wrong with bringing some of that inner friendship we have onto the stage."

In addition, the Baker was his first serious role, a character who grows and changes over the course of the show. "I had to find my serious side and play the character fully," he said. Because Anthony is most comfortable as a comic actor, he also had to "tone it down at times . . . I was trying to come in touch with some emotions that could bring both comedy and sadness, happiness, tears, laughter, all that stuff into one."

"No More" is the Baker's emotional climax in the show, his reckoning with his fatherless past and push toward his future as a father himself. It's his last big number, a duet with the Mysterious Man, the Baker's father, played by

Daniel, a studious senior and a swimmer, whose coach told him, "I wish all of my swimmers showed the same dedication to the sport that the theatre students have about the play."

Daniel was among the handful of students at each school who also play on one or more sports teams. At Worthington, Kelly decided to quit the basket- ball team in her senior year to play the Witch, her first show at the school. At East Clinton, Jenny, who played the Baker's Wife, juggled softball practice with musical rehearsal. "It's keeping me in shape!" she said, when I passed her in the hall, dressed in her costume for that night's opening. The adults at all three schools were keen to help kids do both theatre and sports, if they wanted to. Still, it seemed that more students were juggling music, part-time jobs, or home responsibilities with the show than athletics.

Like many of the students in Belleville's production, Anthony plays in the marching band. Carol, the now-retired choir teacher who returned to the school to vocal direct the production, said that playing an instrument ensures that the students can read music, but that skill doesn't necessarily translate to singing. In band, "they can hide behind their instruments," she explained. As singers, they're unprotected and vulnerable. The students who make that transition well are almost always the ones who sing in church. "Like Anthony," she said, nodding toward the actor who was putting on his makeup and joking with the other kids. "He's accustomed to moving between his instrument and the voice. And he's fearless."

The actor playing the Baker must convey several significant emotional turns during the song, which is as word-filled and musically complex as any in the show. Anthony sang the number in a thick timbre to express his depth of feeling. For the first part of the song, he and Daniel sang toward each other but also directed their energy outwards, as Larry had coached them to do. Once alone on stage, Anthony stepped all the way downstage and sang the last verse closer to the audience than any other scene in the show, revealing the character's pain and determination.

Anthony developed his character using the various tools that typify techniques of musical theatre acting for teenagers in the early twenty-first century. He started with himself, asking, how am I like and not like this char- acter? In what ways does he remind me of myself? And not? Some of the students, like Victoria, who played Lucinda, considered whether or not they would want to be friends with the character. "Is she someone I would like?" Victoria asked herself. Then, as Anthony and the other students explained, they used acting exercises like writing character biographies and thinking about the character's goals and objectives for the whole show and for each scene. The pair of Narrators, for example, concocted an elaborate backstory that they were a homicidal couple temporarily sidetracked from murder to narrate this story.

Anthony's key tool for character development, though, was YouTube. He watched different productions, and explained, "I watched the Broadway show to see how he did it, I watched the 2002 revival to see how their actor did it, I watched some school versions, to see how their Bakers were doing it, and definitely took some ideas and planted them with my own experience." Anthony studied each actor's physicality and gestures, he listened to their vocal inflections in each song, and he noted their timing for jokes. He paid attention to actors' choices within each scene and their character development through the whole story.

Anthony's description of his use of video and his engagement with other actors' portrayals of his role was repeated by almost every student I met. They all watched a lot of different versions of productions and pulled bits and pieces from performances that they liked. As they explained the process, each felt the work—an imitative bricolage—to be entirely creative and individual, and each felt ownership over the role. It's a different way of thinking about musical theatre acting than my raised-on-Stanislavsky generation.

As Sam, East Clinton's music teacher, said, when students

get on the internet or otherwise view other performances (especially professional or collegiate ones) they are being exposed to a higher level of performing and can learn from and emulate it. I think it's part of being creative with what you have in a small school. Our kids love to be involved in the creative process. . . . By doing the research and thinking about their character, they are not only doing that and applying knowledge, but they are becoming stakeholders in their own production. With us not having a drama teacher, it makes up for a resource we do not have by utilizing what we do have.

But it's not only that kids use different tools to learn how to act in the early twenty-first century. It's that musical theatre, Broadway musical theatre, plus countless other productions, are always available to them. They may not set foot outside their county, but they know what a Broadway production looks like and thanks to their high school programs and their teachers' pedagogical practices, they know how to own it themselves. In this way, the national repertoire is transmitted to a local context.

"Into the Woods"

Into the Woods ends with the ensemble's reprise of the title song. In Belleville's production, the twenty-seven actors entered for the finale by the side and back doors of the auditorium. They strode through the house, occupying the aisles and singing directly to the audience, their faces beaming with their opening night triumph. The faces of parents, family, friends, and fellow students beamed as well. The theatre was filled half with African Americans and half with white people and a smattering of Latinos, all there for the same reason: to celebrate the kids. Just as the onstage community gathers at the end of this musical, the offstage community assembles to see the show.

The feeling of a show performed in a school differs from a civic auditorium. This building is the students' home day after day. They've practiced on this stage and watched rehearsals for hours in these seats. When families and friends come to see the show, they're coming to a school building after hours, merely visiting. Parents may have tracked rehearsals every day or may just show up to see the performance. They may come to the show every night or just this once on opening night. They're likely surprised by what their kids can do; the teachers are surprised, too, and maybe the kids surprise themselves.

In addition to the students' familiarity with the space, Belleville's proximity to Ann Arbor means the production doesn't hold the weight of a large community occasion. To be sure, it's a big school event and everyone is excited, but its sphere of influence is narrower than in the more isolated towns of Worthington and Wilmington, where the high school musical is performed in a public venue and carries broader civic significance.

Still, whether the performance takes place at school or in town, more than 26,000 US high schools do a show each year for almost 50 million spectators—that's more than three times the fourteen million people who see a Broadway show on tour.[108]

By the time the students arrived at the second chorus of "Into the Woods," the entire cast was on stage, spread across the wide proscenium. The final moments of this musical, like the opening, resemble each other in virtually every student production of the show: the costumes are colorful and the lights are bright. The kids are perspiring and elated. The teachers are slumping with exhaustion and elated. Most schools bring the backstage crew on stage for recognition and applause during the curtain call, and they're tired and elated.

I wonder if this was what Sondheim wished for?

Figure 4.1. Rehearsal for *Next to Normal*, with director Kat left, in silhouette, and the set being built, Kelsey Theatre, West Windsor, New Jersey.

4

Community Theatre

Scene 1: The Kelsey Awards

Time: Mid-August, a Sunday night
Place: The Kelsey Theatre, Mercer County Community College, West Windsor, New Jersey
Dramatis personae: Kyrus (emcee), Frank (director), Kat (director), and everyone who does Kelsey shows

When I drove into the parking lot of the Kelsey Theatre—a community theatre in central New Jersey—for the first time, I knew that it was a special night and not an evening of rehearsals or even a performance. It was a humid mid-August evening, and anyone who could be at the Jersey Shore was there, an hour's drive away, strolling the boardwalk and eating caramel apples and soft serve ice cream. But here, on the green and sprawling campus of Mercer County Community College, in a parking lot tucked in between a row of tennis courts, the gymnasium, and a courtyard of classrooms, groups of enthusiastic dressed-up thespians in their twenties put the finishing touches on their makeup or popped mints or checked their phones one last time before they went inside. They leaned on cars, looking excited and nervous in their suits and ties or short dresses and high-heeled shoes, as if they were going to a prom. They gathered into a _West Side Story_–esque clump and strode across the parking lot, and I followed them.

Past the small patio, and through the tiled-floor, show-postered, institutional-feeling lobby, we walked up a small flight of stairs and into the theatre. The sound level was deafening, as if every one of the 383 people there was talking at once. Ten minutes before show time, some people sat in their seats, but most were milling around, greeting each other with high-pitched shrieks and damp hugs. From a distance, it might have looked like the Tony Awards before the cameras roll. It was the annual Kelsey Awards.

The Kelsey Theatre was named for New Jersey's Secretary of State from 1870 to 1897, who purchased land in Trenton to open the School of Industrial Arts in 1901, which was the precursor to Mercer County Community

Beyond Broadway. Stacy Wolf, Oxford University Press (2020). © Oxford University Press.
DOI: 10.1093/oso/9780190639525.001.0001

College. A consortium of twelve community theatres that rehearse at the college and perform at Kelsey was formally established in 1995, though some of the groups date back to the 1950s.[1] Each company produces two shows a season, and with the addition of the three shows that the college produces, and various kids' shows scattered through the year, the theatre is lit and local audiences are entertained fifty weekends a year (Figure 4.1).[2] Though the directors, musical directors, musicians, choreographers, and designers receive a small stipend for their work—little more than what gas costs to drive to and from rehearsals and performances—the actors (what one producer calls "the talent") participate voluntarily, for the love of it: the original meaning of the word "amateur."

The theatre is close to where I live, so I spent many hours there over the years of research for this book, observing auditions, watching rehearsals from read-throughs to tech and dress, seeing shows, and talking to people. And after my research officially concluded, I continue to see shows, now with a deeper appreciation of the theatre makers' dedication, passion, and expertise. But my initiation to the place began not with a performance, not with a rehearsal, not with an interview, but with the most insider activity of any subculture: an awards ceremony.

A little past 7 p.m.—the show started early because they had a lot of awards to get through—the house lights went down and everyone, including those who'd lingered in the parking lot, found their seat. The night alternated among the distribution of awards, a musical number performance from each of the season's shows, and patter from the host, jack-of-all-trades Kyrus.[3] A tall, slender, and elegant African American man and a social media specialist at a digital marketing agency by day, Kyrus not only wrote and directed the Kelsey Awards show, but he oversaw the Kelsey Theatre Facebook page, served on the board of the Pennington Players (one of Kelsey's resident theatre companies), and was always rehearsing for or performing in a show as a director or actor. Early in the evening, someone joked, "Welcome to the Fifth Annual Kyrus-Has-Free-Time-on-His-Hands Awards," which was funny because Kyrus does indeed seem to be everywhere at once and surely has not one minute free.

Awards were decided by popular vote, open to anyone willing to log on to the site and cast a ballot. The categories ranged from the expected "Outstanding Villainous Performance" and "Outstanding Lighting Design" to the more unusual "Outstanding Debut Performance," designed to encourage further involvement at Kelsey; "Outstanding Young Performer," because there are a lot of kids involved; and "Outstanding Ensemble Performer," honoring someone who gave a great performance in the chorus of a show. A handful of people, especially stage managers and designers who work with several of the companies, earned multiple nominations in the same category for different shows.

Since that first time, I've attended more Kelsey Awards, gradually recognizing many of the people and understanding some of the jokes. In that first year, though, I felt like I'd landed on a distant planet, and as much as I tried to decode what was happening, I was mostly baffled by this locally specific subculture. I noted the numerous jokes about race, many of which Kyrus lobbed; for example, "The cast of *Kiss Me Kate* is here, or, how many white people can you fit on a stage?" The loud laughter in response revealed, I guessed, the mostly white theatre community's anxiety about race. (Since 2012—my first Kelsey Awards—they've produced more shows that feature actors of color, including *In the Heights, Memphis, West Side Story*, and *Miss Saigon,* which won Outstanding Production of a Musical at the New Jersey Community Theatre Association Awards in 2017.) Other jokes were about "straight white men," another under-represented demographic in the community theatre scene. "Pennsylvania," a mere fifteen minutes away, was also a frequent target. Kyrus warned early on, "If your phone goes off, you'll land in community theatre hell, aka Pennsylvania." People laughed because so many of Kelsey's artists live or work or do community theatre in Pennsylvania. Other Kelsey artists are involved with many of the New Jersey community theatres within an hour's drive of the place.

This once-a-year event enables the Kelsey theatre community to perform itself for itself, to demonstrate its vibrancy, both artistic and emotional. The evening featured, as Kyrus announced, "Special appearances of people who will never make it to Broadway." The night was thick with the feeling of friendly competition among the groups—as one presenter quipped, "All of us Kelsey folk getting together in one room pretending to like each other," but most award recipients expressed sincere gratitude. Director Kat, wearing a vintage black dress and boots and a jaunty velvet cap over her long dark hair and bangs, accepted an award for *The Secret Garden.* She went up to the podium holding six-month-old baby Olive, who was born during rehearsals for the show. "I want to thank my amazing cast and also my husband who made it possible for me to do this show. And," she said, looking down at the baby, "I want to thank Olive for being such a good baby!" Director and actor Frank, in khaki pants and a button-down shirt, wiped his brow and offered a sweet and heartfelt tribute to Dottie, recently deceased, who'd provided props for all of the companies for thirty years and whose daughter remained an active Kelsey choreographer. He warned with mock fear that "only Dottie knew" what lived in her basement, and "she could find you anything you needed for a show."

The evening's performed musical numbers ranged from *Anything Goes* to *The Hunchback of Notre Dame*, and those honored were of all ages and races. The Outstanding Romantic Leads award went to a gay male couple in *The Boy from Oz*, one black actor and one Italian (a well-represented ethnicity in central New Jersey). When they accepted the award, Andre, the African American actor, said, "It's cool that we got to play gay men in a real relationship, not an over-dramaticized relationship. I know that's not a word, but it's an Andre word." He laughed, almost drowned out by the crowd's cheering and applause. Every person who accepted an award thanked their fellow artists for their dedication and the Kelsey community for being so welcoming and "my second family."

In many ways, Kelsey is typical of a community theatre operation. Over forty thousand people see shows at Kelsey each season, and over a thousand community members participate in them onstage and backstage.[4] What makes the theatre unique are aspects that make any given community theatre (and every theatre that we've visited in this book) unique: what happens to the national musical theatre repertoire in this venue, including the specific operational practices, the local dynamics of production and reception, and, of course, the personalities involved. Like all community theatre, Kelsey's participants include what frequent Kelsey actor John Zimmerman called, "Butterflies and bees. The butterflies do one show and fly away. The bees return year after year. Community theatre needs both."

In this chapter, we dip into a year's worth of activities and follow the work of three busy and well-respected directors, Frank, Kyrus, and Kat.

Rewinding a year, we find the board of one of Kelsey's twelve companies choosing their two shows for the season. This is where it begins.

Scene 2: A Board Meeting of the Pennington Players

Time: *A year earlier, a Monday night in late August*
Place: *A conference room in the Hopewell Community Bank in a strip center, Ewing, New Jersey*

Dramatis personae: Kyrus *(president), Jenn (vice president), Wayne (treasurer), Alan (past president), Frank (board member), Beverly (board member)*

Kyrus, Frank, four more Pennington Players board members, and I—a guest and observer—settled into chairs around a conference table in a bland meeting room at the Hopewell Community Bank.

Wayne, the organized and cheery treasurer of the Players, which was established in 1951 and the oldest among the companies, got right down to business. "Let's talk about the season. Did we get any strong proposals?"

"Well," said Alan, the Players' past president, occasional Kelsey actor, Wayne's longtime partner, and the more serious of the two, "We got a few from people who've never done shows at Kelsey, including someone who included the first scene of a new play he's writing." Everyone looked around dubiously. They welcomed proposals from anyone but needed an extant musical and preferably a well-known one to be able to break even financially. As Leah Hager Cohen writes in her book on a community theatre in Boston, "The organization's utmost goal is not to produce great theater or make outsiders feel welcome (although these are certainly among the goals) but something more Darwinian: to survive."[5]

"Anyone know what Playful Productions is thinking about?" asked Jenn, referring to the newest company, run by Suzanne, Ruth, and Nancy.

"*Little Shop of Horrors*," chimed in Frank, whose day job is an associate director for an oncological pharmaceutical company. "And actually, I might direct it. Suzanne doesn't know the show so she wants to listen to the cast recording again, and they need to make sure they can afford to build or rent the plant," he added, referring to the musical's carnivorous flower. "But I think they'll decide to do it."

"That would be a good show for you," said the ever-optimistic and generous Jenn. "A new challenge. What about Lou and Kate?" meaning the married couple who lead PinnWorth Productions, their company a combination of their last names.

Wayne answered, "I heard they're planning *Sunday in the Park with George* because it's a show that Kate wants to design, and Lou loved the recent revival and wants to direct it. We got a proposal for *Miss Saigon*. Thoughts?"

"Could we get the actors? We've never done a show that needs so many Asian actors," asked Alan.

"Well," said Beverly, who'd just been the hardworking producer for the Players' sold-out run of *The Diary of Anne Frank* and was the only Asian

American on the board. "They did *The King and I* last year at the Walnut Street Theatre, and they got a great turnout for auditions."

"Yeah," said Wayne, "but they're in Philly and they're professional: they pay."

"Yes," Beverly said, "I still think that there are a lot of little Asian girls singing the music from *Miss Saigon* in their bedrooms, waiting to be able to audition for this show."

"Do you think we could get the rights? And what about flying in a helicopter?" asked Alan. They all looked at Jenn, who held the position of vice president that year. "I think we can do it," she said, "because I know we'll get huge audiences. And of course we wouldn't really fly in a helicopter." She paused. "Would we?" And everyone laughed.

Wayne continued, looking through his small stack of proposals. "Someone wants to do *The Sound of Music.*" Everyone groaned. "It's kids!" Everyone groaned again. "Alright, okay," he said. "I know we're still recovering from the last time we did *The Sound of Music*. Why does someone always want to do *The Sound of Music*?" More laughter. "Even though," he went on, "Kitty would love another big, classic musical with kids," referring to Kitty Getlik, Kelsey's artistic director and manager, who started working there as a stage manager in 1978 and became artistic director in 1995. They all knew that children on stage meant families and friends in the audience and sold-out houses.

They went through the rest of the proposals, some from frequent Kelsey directors, others from actors who had been in one show, but none besides the new and unfinished play from someone no one knew. They made sure that all of the budgets were within the $20,000 limit and looked reasonable. They tossed around a few ideas for extra publicity for *Pippin*, which Kyrus was directing this season. Beverly talked about how reading a scene from *Anne Frank* at Barnes & Noble bolstered ticket sales. They decided to sleep on the show selection and talk about it by the weekend.

After the meeting, I asked Wayne how he thought they would make the final decision. "Eeny-meeny-miny-mo and what show do we like," he told me. A few days later, they decided to do *Into the Woods*, which Kyrus had proposed to direct and to which we'll return later.

A Brief History of Community Theatres

While there were "amateur theatricals" during the Colonial and Revolutionary War times in the United States, an identifiable community theater "movement" was not under way until the late 1800s. The Footlight Club, in the Jamaica Plain neighborhood in Boston, is the oldest continuously operating community theatre in the United States, founded in 1877, even before the label came into usage. Playwright, director, and activist Louise Burleigh coined the term "community theatre" in 1917 to describe local, amateur theatrical activities that involved citizens in their towns, promoted patriotism, and aimed to instill civic pride through performance. Burleigh and other advocates saw community theatre as a unique opportunity for the masses to be civically engaged through active participation in art.[6] Fellow proselytizer Percy MacKaye described community theatre in 1917 as a "civic festival," a "ritual of democratic religion," compelled by people's "aspiring, playful, creative, child-like, religious instinct."[7]

Community theatre developed alongside the professional "little theatre" movement in the early 1910s and 1920s.[8] Little theatres often used amateur performers and therefore "planted the seed from which other amateur theater forms grew," including schools and community theatres. Theatre scholar Jennifer Chapman writes that the little theatre movement "introduced the idea that amateur theater [could] have a powerful impact on its participants and broader grassroots community."[9]

Later, in 1959, Wisconsin-based arts advocate and educator Robert Gard asserted that community theatre has a universal "life-meaning": it draws "the attention of the people" and inspires them to "active participation in theater-making in their communities."[10] "Community theatre is the very front skirmish line in the battle of the theatre arts to overcome public apathy and to gain, or regain, their proper share of the attention of the people," Gard wrote.[11]

From the start, musical theatrical entertainments were a staple of the community theatre repertoire, from vaudeville to variety shows, operettas to early musicals. By the 1950s, soon after a musical opened on Broadway, producers formed a touring company, and then released amateur rights for community groups. The production of Broadway musicals, directed, choreographed, and performed by your neighbors, increased the national visibility of and interest in musical theatre. Previously, people could listen to cast albums and see Broadway stars on television variety shows, such as *The Ed Sullivan Show*. They could play the piano and sing songs from Broadway at home using piano-vocal scores. But community theatre productions transformed the Broadway musical into a homegrown phenomenon.

Today, every state is host to numerous community theatres that together produce thousands of musicals a year, from *South Pacific* to *Rent*. As of 2014, the American Association of Community Theatres (AACT) represented more than seven thousand community theatres across America, with a combined 1.5 million volunteers. These theatres produce over 46,000 productions every year, entertain an audience of 86 million people, and rely on a combined annual budget of over $980 million.[12] And AACT is not even an all-encompassing organization; there are many community theatres unaffiliated with AACT (including Kelsey) that currently operate across the country. Community theatre is pervasive throughout America.

As a locally flavored national phenomenon, every community theatre incorporates the quirks and qualities of its local theatre scene, and because most community theatres depend on ticket sales for income, they choose shows that will appeal to their audience demographic. StillPointe Theatre in Baltimore, Maryland, for example, programs an edgy repertoire of "groundbreaking, thought-provoking, wild art" that has included *Murder Ballad, Batboy the Musical*, and *Sweeney Todd* "in true Baltimore style" for an urban audience.[13] In contrast, the family-owned and -operated Hale Center chain of four theatres in southern Utah attracts thousands of spectators a year—they claim to have more subscribers than any theatre in the country—to see shows like *The Little Mermaid* and *Legally Blonde*. Their shows are double or triple cast, which allows them to do eight to ten performances a week for several months, to mostly sold-out crowds.[14]

The Kelsey Theatre is another example. Located in Mercer County, New Jersey, Kelsey is at once close to and far away from Broadway, tucked between New York City (sixty miles away), Philadelphia (forty miles), and the Jersey Shore (forty miles), and located in the most densely populated state in the country. But 24 percent of the county's total area is farmland and it feels quite rural in many parts: This is New Jersey, the Garden State.[15] Our location matters, because as close as we are to New York City, no one at Kelsey really cares about Broadway in a day-to-day sense. Theatre—including community theatre—is intimate and local.

Another important aspect of Kelsey is the fact that it's a consortium of twelve companies, so plays and musicals happen constantly and on a breakneck schedule, which Kitty Getlik, Kelsey's artistic director and manager, schedules, manages, and oversees, with help from her assistant, Amy

Bessellieu. Each show runs for eight performances over two weekends on Friday night, Saturday matinee and night, and Sunday matinee. After the curtain falls on the second Sunday afternoon, the cast and crew have three hours to strike the set. Sometimes the two companies will coordinate if any set pieces work for both shows, but typically, the whole set gets removed to backstage or to the dumpster. Then, by the early evening, the next show loads in. The crew and cast have five nights (including load-in) to build the set, hang and focus lights, deal with sound and other technical issues, make sure that costumes fit and that props are in place, and rehearse on stage before opening night. Often, six or seven productions are in rehearsal somewhere on MCCC's campus at once.[16]

Scene 3: Auditions for Playful Theatre Productions' *Little Shop of Horrors*

"If a director casts a show well, their job is 99 percent done."

—common theatre knowledge

Time: One month later; mid-September, a Monday evening
Place: Blackbox theatre classroom at MCCC
Dramatis personae: Frank (director), Shannon (musical director, married to Frank), Elizabeth (their eight-year-old daughter), Mike (music director), Nicole (choreographer), Nancy (stage manager/producer), Ruth (stage manager/producer), Suzanne (producer), and many nervous actors

Frank, the frequently pacing director, and Shannon, the frequently smiling music director (and his wife), and Nicole, the frequently moving choreographer, settled into hard folding chairs behind a table, a neat stack of *Little Shop of Horrors* scripts in front of them. As Frank had said at the Pennington Players' board meeting, Playful Theatre Productions decided to mount Alan Menken and Howard Ashman's campy send-up of a B-horror movie, *Little Shop of Horrors.*

Shannon, who by day is a middle school band teacher and a professional French horn player, placed eight-year-old daughter Elizabeth in a nearby desk-chair combo, with crayons and a coloring book. Elizabeth had been dragged to Kelsey since she was an infant and was entirely capable of amusing herself during long evening and afternoon rehearsals. Five weeks from today, she would climb inside the puppet to play the person-eating plant Audrey II. Mike, the other music director and a fulltime musician, sat at the piano. In the hallway around the corner from the small studio/classroom/blackbox theatre, Suzanne, one of Playful Theatre Productions' producers, handed out audition forms that asked for each person's contact information, performance experience (or they could attach a résumé and a head shot), and, just as important, time conflicts for the next seven weeks.

Ruth, the stage manager, peeked her head in the room. "People are here," she said. "Great," said Frank, relieved that people were showing up to audition. Even though he knew from years of experience that people always auditioned, it was always a little nerve-wracking, especially for a show like *Little Shop*, which he loved, but which wasn't as well known as shows like *Les Miz*. "Bring the first one in," he said, and Ruth disappeared for a moment, then returned and sat by the door, ready to escort each person out and fetch the next one.

"Hi everybody!" said Maria, with a big smile and a wave. She was wearing a yellow sundress and her dark hair was pulled back in a matching headband, not inappropriate for the character but not in costume, which Frank hated. They all breathed a sigh of relief to see her there first thing in the evening. "Maria!" Frank greeted her warmly. She bounced up to the piano and put her music on the stand. Mike chuckled. It was "Adelaide's Lament," a song from *Guys and Dolls*, which they had done together at a different community theatre six months earlier. "Yeah," Maria grinned, now standing in the middle of room. "I thought I'd do a song that I already know." Then Mike played the introduction, and they were off.

As she performed the song, which was beautifully and expressively sung and charming and confident from start to finish, Frank, Shannon, Nicole, and Mike nodded and smiled, which was easy at the beginning of the night and with someone who gave a great audition and whom they knew. As the evening proceeded, they had to work harder to smile and nod and maintain a kind face. Frank sometimes felt his face would freeze from smiling, but he knew it was important to make every person auditioning feel comfortable and welcome. Maybe someone who wasn't cast in this show might be cast in another or even want to help out backstage on this show. But more than that, Frank wanted the experience of auditioning—which he saw as a tiny performance—to be positive for its own sake, and for everyone who auditioned to feel appreciated.

Maria finished, belting out the last phrase, "Bad bad cold!" with her arms extended. Mike finished with a run on the piano. "Thank you, Maria!" said

Frank, very pleased indeed. "Can you hang out for a few minutes and once we have a group, we'll do dance auditions?"

"Sure," she chirped.

"Oh, wait a second," said Frank, looking at her audition sheet and frowning. "You're going away in October?"

"Yeah, I have a weekend that I need to go to Pittsburgh for work," she replied, with an apologetic shrug. "It was planned a long time ago. But it's only that one weekend I'll be away."

"It's fine," answered Frank. "Just good for us to know now," and he glanced toward Ruth, who made a note of it.

After Maria left, they all shared a look. She was terrific and would surely be cast as Audrey. "She's perfect," Shannon leaned over to whisper to Frank, as the next actor entered.

They heard four more actors sing, and then Frank turned to Nicole. "Should they dance?" he asked. "Yes!" she said, ready to do her part. Ruth went out into the hall and returned with the five who just sang. For *Little Shop*, they only needed seven adult actors, which made their task much easier than casting a big show or one with children. They were looking for strong singers and comic character actors for Audrey, Seymour, and Orin, Audrey's sadistic dentist boyfriend, and an older man to play Mushnick, the plant shop owner. They also needed three "triple threat" women who could sing and dance and act—preferably African American—to play the Urchins, the Greek chorus who narrates the show and comments on the action.

Nicole made the dancing section of the audition intentionally tough. Though only the Urchins needed to dance well, Nicole believed (and Frank agreed) that actors reveal a lot about how they manage pressure and anxiety when they have to dance in an audition. Yes, they wanted to see who could pick up the choreography fast and perform it well, but more importantly, who could fake it and appear to be having fun. They needed an easygoing and playful cast for this over-the-top show, people who weren't afraid to look silly. Frank and Shannon sat back to watch, Mike was ready at the piano, and Nicole stood up.

"Everyone good?" she asked, as she gestured to them to spread out in the mirrorless room behind her. Their expressions ranged from smiling anticipation to grimacing terror. "No one needs to worry. Just have fun." The scared ones didn't look persuaded. "Let me show you first," and she turned to face them, then nodded to Mike, who started to play the jangly introduction to the title number. "Five, six, seven, eight," said Nicole, and executed two eight-count phrases that included side-steps, twirls, swaying hips, and sharp head-turning looks in different directions. None of the steps were technically difficult but they happened fast and with little repetition. "Uh oh," said Arnold, Maria's gray-bearded sixty-five-year-old father, who was auditioning for the role of Mr. Mushnick, when Nicole finished demonstrating.

Nicole smiled warmly. "Let's try it," she said, and turned around with her back to the actors. She went through each step slowly, then repeated again, then added another and another. The actors watched her intently. Maria was having fun. Arnold looked tortured. Finally, they got through the sixteen counts. "Let's see it!" said Nicole, turning to face them and backing up into a chair. "Ready? Here we go. Five, six, seven, eight!"

They went through the combination a few times; some of the actors improved each time through, and others were simply unable to grasp what Nicole did. "Good, good!" she encouraged. "That's great, everybody, thank you!" Frank added, "We'll be in touch tonight or first thing tomorrow about callbacks."

Before they called in the next person to sing, Frank, having gotten a little impatient with all the time it took to teach and go over the dance, said, "Nicole, do you think we need to see all of that? Can we do something shorter with the dance and then have the callbacks for the Urchins do more tomorrow night?"

"For sure," she said. "We're only really looking for three dancers."

"Yeah," said Shannon, "and we already found one in that first group: Tia." They agreed that Tia was fantastic and that Nicole would only teach one phrase of eight counts.

By the end of the evening, forty actors auditioned. Their singing ranged from barely on tune but with a lot of spirit, to perfectly sung but with little expressiveness, to excellent but not right for this show. The actors who were Kelsey regulars knew the ropes of auditions. They came in, handed their music to Mike, stood in the center of the room, and started singing. Typically, the song wasn't from the show but was in the style of the show. But new people auditioned using whatever knowledge they possessed from previous experiences in school or other community theatres or maybe even from the many TV or film representations of auditions in the classic, intentionally dreadful and wonderful audition montages: *Waiting for Guffman, High School Musical, Lady Bird, Glee,* or *Rise,* to name a few. They might not have a song prepared or it might be one from the show. They might come in costume or too dressed up to dance. They might offer a long explanation about their choice of song or apologize for having a cold. After each one left the room, Shannon asked Mike for the highest note of their song, so that she could note their range.

The team was so certain and pleased about Maria as Audrey that they offered the part to her that very night and asked her not to tell anyone or post it on Facebook. For the next night's callbacks, then, they could concentrate on casting Seymour, which they knew would be tough because they had a number of good men who were all very different from one another. Whoever played Seymour would, in some ways, define the show. They hoped that Arnold would want to do Mushnick. They knew already that he would be hilarious—an Italian playing a Jewish man (Arnold told me, "I grew up in a community with a lot of Jewish people, so I had that sound in my ear, you know")—and that Nicole could get him through the one dance in "Mushnick and Son." And they knew he would love being in another show with his daughter, Maria, with whom he'd performed in many shows over the years since she was a kid. They called back eight women—all very strong—for the Urchins, including a few white women, a few African Americans, and one Latina. They needed to see and hear different combinations to get the right trio.

The next night all of the actors were ready to go when they began callbacks promptly at 7. The creative team could barely suppress their excitement because they knew they were going to get a strong cast. Frank could already see the show taking shape in his mind. At callbacks, they tried out various combinations of "Seymours" with Maria to see if there was good chemistry between the actors. She was such a warm and generous actor that she connected with several of the men, but Frank and Shannon liked the quirkiness of the combination of her and Jarad.

After callbacks, Frank, Shannon, Mike, Nicole, Ruth, Nancy, and Suzanne settled in with fresh cans of Coke and bags of chips to make some decisions. Audrey and Mr. Mushnick: check. They loved Tia, Cat, and Nikema for the Urchins (Figure 4.2). Then came Seymour.

"I thought Mark sang well," opened Mike.

"Yeah, but I think he's too handsome to play a nerd," offered Nicole.

"What about Nick?" asked Ruth. Suzanne and Frank exchanged glances. A pause.

"What?" Ruth prodded. Suzanne sighed and said, "We heard he missed a lot of rehearsals for Pierrot Productions' *Oklahoma!* and Pete got frustrated and swore he'd never cast him again."[17]

Figure 4.2. The Urchins and Seymour rehearse for *Little Shop of Horrors.*

Ruth's mouth formed an astonished "o." "They had 150 people try out for that show! People came from everywhere, all the way from North Jersey! I remember that they cast actors who are typically the stars in the ensemble and newcomers as the leads—people we'd never seen before! He was so lucky to get cast!"

"Right, well, apparently he was also cast in PinnWorth's *Sweet Charity* and the rehearsal schedules conflicted," explained Suzanne. The group exchanged a tight-mouthed look again, knowing that over-eager actors sometimes auditioned for two closely scheduled shows and then bailed on one of them, leaving the whole production in the lurch. They shook off the fear that one of their actors might audition for PinnWorth's *Memphis* the next week and quit before they'd even finished blocking Act 1.

Shannon brought them back to the task at hand. "Hey, what about that guy . . .," as she turned back the pages of her notebook to see what she'd written about him. "Ray? I've never seen him before. Is he new around here?"

"I think he did some shows down in South Jersey, Cherry Hill," said Suzanne. "Was he good?" she asked, since she'd been out in the hall the whole night.

"Yeah, he was really good," said Frank. "What's he done?" He found Ray's form, and the résumé and head shot attached. "Oh, yeah, he did this show in college! That makes sense." Everyone took a minute to imagine new Ray in the cast.

Shannon broke the silence. "Do we feel we have to cast Vince?" referring to one of the Kelsey regulars who was a key member of the theatre community.

"Well, he's just not right for this part, and I'm sure he knows it," answered Frank.

Shannon said, "We haven't said it, but I think we all agree that it should be Jarad." Everyone nodded and Ruth added one more name to the cast list.

Shannon went on, "I'm concerned that we don't have anyone with a strong enough voice to play the plant." She looked toward Frank, "Did you reach out to Tim?" referring to a well-known teacher at one of the local high schools with a dynamic tenor voice.

"Well, I know he's directing a production of *Ain't Misbehavin'* at his school," Frank replied. "I can call him and see if he can do it. The voice of Audrey II isn't much rehearsal time."

"That would be good," Shannon said, knowing that Frank preferred not to solicit actors or cast those who haven't auditioned. But she also knew that African American men with voices in that range were rare in the community. "For this role, we just have to recruit," she added, and everyone nodded in agreement.

Why Community Theatre?

Why do people decide to participate in community musical theatre? By the time they reach adulthood, many people who have participated in or seen musicals as youth are passionate about them and elect to dedicate countless hours outside of their workday to participate in amateur productions. What community theatre advocate Virgil Baker wrote in 1952—"The motivating force that keeps a community theatre alive and functioning is the desire of the individuals who compose it for a fuller, richer, life experience"[18]—is borne out by Kelsey artists. As Kyrus said, "It's a release. We work nine to five, and then we have a choice: go home and watch TV or take the opportunity to be someone else and do something. And a live audience, nothing beats it." What's more, he added, "There's nowhere else I would be able to direct *Into the Woods!*" Pat, who worked in Princeton University's admissions office and performed in several Kelsey shows, said, "I love performing. It's a stress relief. Something I do for fun." Many talk about the "creativity" and "opportunity for expression" that musical theatre allows.

For some, it's the specific show that draws them. *Les Misérables* got a huge turnout, for example. Both *Miss Saigon* and *In the Heights* attracted many local performers of color who sought an infrequent chance to be in a show with Asian and Asian American and Latinx characters. As *Miss Saigon*'s producer and director Lou said, "The Asian American community was thrilled for this rare opportunity, and they came from everywhere to audition." A few performers see community theatre as a stepping stone to a professional career or a welcome return to nonprofessional theatre after leaving a performance career behind.

Some people—especially women—have to juggle children and jobs and school and to be able to participate. Cat, who played one of the Urchins in *Little Shop*, is a single mom. Nikema, another of the Urchins, said, "My kids are great," she said. "They know I need to do this. It's a lot of time but I need to do this." Her fourteen-year-old daughter sat in the theatre and did her homework during their long Wednesday night tech rehearsal. Some women tell stories of husbands who were unsympathetic to their desire to do theatre. One Kelsey regular said, "My husband wasn't having any of it. I wanted to do theatre and he didn't want me to, so I divorced him, and started doing community theatre again."

On the other hand, Kat explained how her husband, though "not a true lover of theatre," adjusted his work schedule to accommodate her passion for directing. "I was pregnant right after I agreed to direct *The Secret Garden* for Pierrot," she recounted. "He supported me and encouraged me to continue with the show stating that 'we would make it work.' I gave birth midway through the rehearsal process to our daughter Olive and returned to rehearsals with Olive in tow just a week after she was born with Tim there for support." For her next directing gig, the baby was older and "more mobile," and they would often "exchange baby duty at the theatre," or Olive would stay with Kat and her husband "would bring his work to the theatre to help." "It was a juggling act," she said. "It takes "sacrifice and dedication . . . to balance both a show and a family."

Just as often, one member of a family gets involved, and before they know it, the whole family is "roped in" and more or less living at the theatre. Jody, who won a Kelsey Award for Best Debut Performance, talked in a teary acceptance speech about how she drove her daughter to rehearsal night after night, and after watching for hours and days, decided to try out for a show herself. Children "catch the musical theatre bug" after being dragged to rehearsal by one or both parents (Elizabeth is a case in point) and decide they want to work on a show, too. Whether onstage or backstage locating props or building sets, generations of families stay involved across productions and across the years. As Donna said, "If my husband didn't come to the theatre to help on the weekends when I'm here, he would never see me." Kelsey is an uncommon setting in contemporary society that fosters family engagement and multigenerational connections.

Many of Kelsey's artists are regulars, the returning "bees" that actor John referred to. Maria, for example, auditions for any show that fits her schedule. "As soon as one show is over, I'm auditioning for the next" at Kelsey or another community theatre or, in the summer, the Open Air Theatre (see Chapter 5). She explained, "I keep meaning to take voice or dance lessons, but I just like rehearsing and performing and there is always another show that I want to do." A corps of Kelsey theatre-makers are lifelong participants. Producer Pete joked, "I've been doing community theatre since the earth cooled," and went on, "I've been here since the early 80s . . . I've been doing it for a long time and I've done every aspect of it. I keep telling myself that I'll retire but then I say one more year, one more year."

For many Kelsey artists, the limited time frame of doing a show adds to their enjoyment. As Kyrus said, counting on his fingers as he talked: "One: You're choosing it. Two: It's fulfilling in a different way than your day job. Three: The constraints make it satisfying: This is all the time we have; it can't go on forever; it can't be like your normal job. Four: There is pleasure in having to balance." One study of community theatre artists found this to be true: Participants calibrated their energy across the rehearsal period and its temporary nature increased their commitment.[19]

Everyone is aware of how their actual paid job impinges on this voluntary labor. Kat said, "It's a time commitment, and your job has to allow it." The actors, she added, "can't get here until 7 at night and they all have jobs and they have to get up in the morning and so can't be here all night." While the time limit of hours, days, and weeks until the show opens puts pressure on everyone, these boundaries also provide a kind of emotional safety net, since the end is always in sight. Community theatre artists put other parts of their lives on hold temporarily, knowing that they rehearse, perform, and then the show is over . . . until the next show.[20]

Scene 4: An Early Rehearsal for *Little Shop of Horrors*

Making the shape of the show in music, dance, and acting

Time: 1 week later, late September, a Thursday night
Place: same as Scene 3, a blackbox theatre classroom at MCCC
Dramatis personae: Frank (director), Shannon (musical director), Mike (musical director), Ruth (stage manager), Maria (Audrey), Jarad (Seymour), Arnold (Mushnick), Tia, Cat, and Nikema (the Urchins), Ruby (costumer)

Fifteen minutes before the second rehearsal for *Little Shop* began, the actors started drifting in. (Frank, Shannon, Mike, and Ruth were already there, setting up the room, moving the piano, getting their scripts and music ready.) Maria looked like she'd come straight from her job in an accountant's office, still dressed in a skirt, blouse, and heels, and a bit distracted. Jarad had time after his job (he was a middle school teacher) to go home and change and eat dinner. Tia, a student at the college, had been studying in the library and walked across campus to this building. Arnold, retired from his career as an elementary school assistant principal, had spent the morning playing golf and the afternoon running errands. They knew that Frank started on time (and, thankfully, finished on time), so they changed their clothes and shoes, threw away their gum, put their phones on silent, took out their scripts and pencils.

At 7 p.m. sharp, Frank, who'd been looking over his notes and blocking diagrams, ignoring the six actors as they arrived, said, "Okay, everybody, let's get started. Here's the plan," and he pointed to the board where the list of scenes and songs they planned to work on were listed (and which he erased one by one through the night). "Shannon will teach the opening number. Then we'll block the first scene. That might take the whole night, but if it doesn't, everyone except the Urchins can go and we'll work on 'Somewhere That's Green.' Okay? Great!" he answered himself before anyone else responded. Cat, who'd never done a show with Frank, whispered to Tia, "Does he not do any warmups?" "No," Tia whispered back. "He says there's too much to do and we need to warm up on our own. I sing to warm up on my way and get here early enough to do some stretches. And he doesn't do any of those bonding theatre games either."

Mike sat behind the piano, Shannon stood next to him behind a music stand, and she gestured for the actors to stand in a semicircle facing her and the piano. They held their music, pages stapled together or in a looseleaf notebook, pencils in the other hand or tucked behind their ear or stuck in a pants pocket. "Let's just sing it through once and see what anyone can get of your parts. When the parts divide, Cat and Jarad, you go up, Tia, you go down. Everyone else stay on the melody and we'll hear the balance. Don't worry if you can't sight read. Just follow along as best as you can. The harmony is mostly in thirds and it's easy to get. Ready?" and she looked at Mike. He started playing the introduction to the boppy, faux-1950s song, Shannon raised her hands, and they started singing. They got through the first two lines, and she stopped them. "Good start. Let's go over those harmonies in the second line to get them right now. Mike, will you play the top line?" Frank, who was pacing back and forth, head down but listening intently, suddenly chimed in, "The music from the revival is better than the original cast album." Shannon added, "And if anyone needs a CD to learn the music, Mike and I can make one for you." "Can you play our part again?" Jarad asked, and Mike plunked out each voice part and the actors sang along.

They spent an hour working on the song, learning each note and phrase and line, going back over it again and again, with comments from Shannon ("Sopranos, you sound a little sharp here"), Mike ("This part should be a little louder and faster"), and Frank ("Be sure to enunciate. The lyrics are funny and we need to be able to hear them"). For the actors, it was a lot to learn, but everyone was focused and each time they did it, the song sounded a little better and, after an hour, pretty close to perfect. Shannon hoped they'd practice at home to absorb the material because she wouldn't have time to work with them in such a concentrated way on this song again.

"We're done!" Shannon announced. Frank was ready: "Take a quick break, and then we'll block this number. Five minutes! Ruth, can you set up the flower shop?" Everyone grabbed their phones and water bottles. Some went to the bathroom or outside to get some air. Some, including little Elizabeth, who'd been quietly coloring the whole time at a table along the wall, not a peep out of her, grabbed some Doritos from the big bag Ruth brought. Within four minutes, everyone was back. Jarad arrived breathless, having jogged from the theatre in the next building. "I wanted to see how tech was going for *The Secret Garden*. The set is cool," he said. "Get your tickets!" said Ruth. "We can all go see the whole show this weekend."

Break over, Frank turned to the group. "The opening," Frank explained, "is super important. It tells the audience that this is a spoof of a fifties horror movie. It's campy but it's also scary. It's impossible to be too big or too silly. Your acting should appear to be improvisational, but it can't be improvisational. In rehearsal, have fun! But once we lock it, it has to stay locked." Everyone nodded. Those who'd worked with Frank before knew he was true to his word. He'd give you the blocking, encourage you to play and try stuff, then decide what he wanted—and that had to stick.

"This is the flower shop," Frank said, as he circled the room and pointed to different areas on the floor. "We'll have a counter, here," as Ruth adjusted the table that she'd preset from the sketch he gave her. "Then rows of flower pots there," pointing along the walls. "Up here," as he walked upstage and spread his arms, "We'll have some windows and the Urchins will pop up at different points. And the door will be down here," as he crossed to downstage left. "So, Mushnick, you start behind the counter," he looked to Arnold. "Seymour," he said, and Jarad looked up. "You're sweeping here. Audrey," and Maria stood at attention, "You're about to enter, so you're outside the door all the way stage left," and she moved where he pointed. "Urchins, you're behind the window, ready to pop up. Go to your places." Everyone scribbled Frank's instructions in their scripts and moved to where he'd told them to go.

He talked through the scene, noting who moved where on which line. "Maria, on your first line, you enter the shop and cross behind the counter to hang up your coat and purse. Jarad, when she comes in, drop the broom and then fumble as you try to pick it up. Arnold, you can probably look to each of them and shrug or shake your head—know what I mean?" The actors wrote down everything he said that pertained to them. Once they blocked the scene and went over it a few times—probably by the end of tonight's rehearsal—no one would look at their pencil notes again, though they wouldn't return to this scene for a few weeks until they did a stumble-through of Act 1. Ruth logged down every instruction, even though, she said, "Frank keeps detailed notes on the blocking and I probably could just use his script." Still, the stage manager's script becomes their bible. They would refer to it if anyone forgot where they were supposed to go, or if Ruth had to cover for an absent actor. As rehearsals moved along, they'd add notes on lighting and set changes and props to this script.

"Let's try it," Frank said. Everyone went to their places at the opening, and they went through the first three minutes of the scene. "How does that feel?" Frank asked, and everyone nodded. "Any questions?" and everyone shook their heads. "We're going to keep going," he said. "Too much repetition is death to this kind of thing. If between now and Saturday, you can get off book, it will be great so that the repetition will be useful." They worked through the rest of the scene like that, and it was slow-going and intense. Like the music, it was a lot for the actors to take in. Common theatre lore says that one minute of a scene in performance requires around an hour of rehearsal. Frank liked the look of it—a dark-haired Italian American Audrey and blond and round-faced Seymour, the three African American Urchins, who each possessed her own style, and short, gray-bearded, sixty-five-year-old Mr. Mushnick. "Pacing has to be super-fast. Not speed of the actual lines but the delivery. No air between the lines. Keep it clipping along. Including some overlap. Let it flow together like a real conversation," he coached them.

Before they ended for the night, Ruby showed up with a rack of 1950s-style dresses and a tape measure and pulled the women into the hall one by one to talk about costumes. Frank was happy when she came to an early rehearsal because it meant the actors could get a sense of their costumes, which always helped with characterization. Ruby worked with many of Kelsey's companies and grew a huge collection of costumes. She used to keep them in her basement and then moved them to her garage, until her husband "wanted to put the car in the garage—imagine that!" she laughed. Her daughter rented her a nearby storage space where the costumes are kept. "I love theatre and I love costumes and I can't imagine not doing this. I'm seventy years old and dragging all of these costumes around all the time, but when I go to the show and see my ideas and my costumes on stage and I see how important it is that each character looks just right, I love it."

At 10 p.m., as they were putting their scripts away and gathering their stuff, Cat approached Tia. "I don't know what I'm doing in this scene," she said quietly, glancing toward Frank. "I just nodded that it felt fine because everyone else did."

"You're good," Tia said. "Just learn your lines and see if you can figure out what you're doing. If it doesn't work and looks stupid the next time we do it, Frank will change it."

"Okay," Cat said, somewhat calmed.

Just before the actors left the room, Frank spoke privately to each one, giving them the attention that all actors crave, starting with Jarad: "Who's the bad guy in this show?" Jarad: "The plant." Frank: "No, it's you. The plant doesn't do anything. It's just reactive. You're the one who does everything. We need to see little bit of the kind of guy who would feed people to plants. If you're just a sad sack, then it's boring. Go through the script and think about where he shows that he's an evil person, [especially] towards the end."

Then Frank turned to Maria, who was waiting for him: "A lot of what I've said is the silly part of Audrey. But I want us to approach Audrey as the smartest person in the room all the time but she just doesn't show it. You know those people who seem dumb but then they say something and you realize that they've been paying attention all the time and know more than anyone? Think about how smart Audrey might be."

Finally, Frank caught Cat, Tia, and Nikema just before they walked out the door. "You can do whatever you want through the whole show. The more you do what's unexpected, the funnier it will be. Goof around and have fun. That's basically the whole story." He added, "You can do a lot of ad-libbing. I love your characters. So play with it and we'll tell you if it doesn't work." They nodded and exchanged grins.

Serious Leisure

Much happens in this deceptively simple interaction among people in a room for three hours on a Thursday night. What they have in common—the only thing, in fact—is the desire to make musical theatre, to take the words in the script and notes in the score and bring them to life on stage.

Well, it's not quite true that they only have that one thing in common: They also all have jobs in the daytime. They've come to this rehearsal after a full day in the office, in the classroom, waiting tables, running errands, or caring for children. These theatre-makers leave their jobs, studies, and children behind when they get to rehearsal. They talk about "creative expression," about the "release," about the pleasure of singing and dancing. At the same time, they work hard when they're rehearsing. Community musical theatre defies the traditional opposition between work and leisure.

In some ways, participating in community musical theatre is clearly a leisure activity. First and foremost, it's voluntary. In *Hobbies: Leisure and the Culture of Work in America*, Steven M. Gelber writes that "from the participants' point of view the single most important element in defining leisure activity is . . . how freely they have chosen to do it."[21] He goes on, "It is not what, but why and when something is done that makes it leisure. Therefore, one person's livelihood"—in this case, participating in the creation of a musical—"can be another person's pastime." He terms this kind of pastime "productive leisure."[22]

In other ways, community musical theatre requires considerable labor. One study of nonprofessional musicians parsed out their feelings of work and play. Even when music "is not connected to their occupation," the musicians perceived their activity as "work." "They 'work' at their 'play,'" the study concluded.[23] Kelsey's theatre-makers express a similar sentiment. Their work at rehearsals is voluntary and creative, intense and temporary. Perhaps the best way to describe their pursuit—the nonprofessional's dedication to their practice—is what sociologist Robert A. Stebbins calls "serious leisure."[24]

While the term "serious leisure" acknowledges the commitment of the theatre-makers at Kelsey, it somehow fails to capture the joy, the laughter, and the playing around that happens there, too. The activity of rehearsing for and performing a musical, which need not be silly and lighthearted in topic or subject matter, but which, importantly, gathers people to sing together and dance together, is, quite simply, fun.

Scene 5: A Later Rehearsal for *Into the Woods*

Fixing problems

Time: *3 months later, December, a Thursday night*
Place: *Band rehearsal room, MCCC*
Dramatis personae: *Kyrus (director), Mike (musical director), Vianna (stage manager), John (The Baker), and the cast of* Into the Woods

Stephen Sondheim's and James Lapine's 1987 fairy tale mashup *Into the Woods* (which we visited at high schools in Chapter 3) presented different challenges and pleasures for Kyrus, the director and choreographer, and for Mike, the musical director for both the performers and the orchestra for this musically dense and difficult show. (Mike also worked with Frank and Shannon on *Little Shop of Horrors*.) The cast was big, and their ages ranged from high school to mid-sixties. They scheduled as many rehearsals as they could for just a few people to work on small sections, but there were many big group scenes, too—one of the reasons that *Into the Woods* is such a great musical. The most difficult part of the show was the regularly reprised title song with many of Sondheim's words per minute and complicated choreography, which Kyrus created.

Over the past four weeks of rehearsal, *Into the Woods* had taken shape. It seemed almost magical, perhaps more so when you only rehearse three days a week, rather than all day every day, as professional theatres do, or every afternoon or evening, as many high school and college theatres do. At the start of every rehearsal, after warm-ups and a group affirmation, Kyrus and Mike first had to go back over what they did in the previous rehearsal for whoever was absent. With a big show, even when actors note all of their conflicts on their audition sheets, it's inevitable that someone will be missing from almost every rehearsal, and Kyrus and Mike tried not to feel frustrated. They reviewed and then moved on. The details got filled in, and it started to look and sound like a show.

From the start, because everyone in the cast already knew the musical—Sondheim fanatics that they were—Kyrus was aware that some of the actors already had ideas for their characters, and he was committed to letting them find their way "organically." For the first rehearsal for the early scene in which Little Red visits the Baker and the Baker's Wife's house to fill a basket with bread and sweets to take to her granny's house, for example, Kyrus didn't plan in advance, but had the actors say their lines and then move when and where they wanted. He watched. They stumbled through the whole scene in a few minutes. Kyrus said, "Let's start again." Everyone moved back to where they started. He cocked his head and said, "John, why don't you start over there? And Julie, there? And then on your line, Kerry, you can cross down to them and make it more emphatic, like you're demanding the sweets?" They tried it out a few different ways and then agreed which one felt the best. Sometimes Kyrus asked Vianna, the stage manager, to write down the blocking, sometimes the actors made a note, and sometimes he just assumed that everyone would remember.

At later rehearsals, he'd likely make changes or ask them to try it differently, but early on, he was more concerned that they get off book. Also, they spent more rehearsal time than usual on the music for *Into the Woods*, which Mike wanted them to perfect early and not develop any bad habits. Some of the cast couldn't read music at all and only a few could sight read, so Mike gave them audio files of their parts. Kyrus and Mike thought the actors were practicing their music at home—at least the ones who had time—but the whole cast needed to be in the same room to make the complex phrases of Sondheim's melodies and harmonies fit together (Figure 4.3).

In the meantime, as the actors rehearsed, the design and tech team worked with Kyrus to figure out what kind of set, lights, and costumes the show

Figure 4.3. Portrait of the men of *Into the Woods*. Photo credit: Kyrus Keenan Westcott.

needed, and how it would look. Because Kyrus wanted a "classic [production] with some contemporary touches" and "didn't want to set it somewhere else"—he'd scoffed about a production that was set in the attic of a house where a child discovers hidden toys—Brian, the set designer, knew what they had to build: trees in the background, a tower for Rapunzel, another tower for Cinderella's dead mother's ghost, a puppet of Milky White. By week four, Kyrus felt pressure to keep the actors on task. In a few weeks, he would spend hours and hours—all night, as it turned out—with Vicki, the lighting designer, writing cues, so for now he left it to Brian and his team to work out problems. About creating smoke to make the Witch disappear without violating the theatre's fire codes, Kyrus emailed the whole design and tech team: "Do what you want, just make it look cool."

Last week they ran all of Act 1, including the title-song, big-ensemble finale, which they were returning to tonight. Kyrus had choreographed it last week—unlike acting, dance required precise preplanning and then teaching the steps—but a few people had been missing. Worse, the whole cast was starting to get antsy because Christmas was coming and there would be a ten-day break in rehearsals. Kyrus and Mike had insisted on a longer-than-usual rehearsal period for the show because too many people would be away over the holidays. They wouldn't rehearse again until after the New Year. Kyrus wanted tonight's rehearsal to be a good one.

Kyrus started rehearsal as he always did. "Circle up, everybody!" he called, and the actors gathered in a circle, arms around each other. "Alright, gang, this is our last rehearsal before the holidays. Let's stay focused. All good? Everybody give me a thumbs up and say we're good." Kyrus's pre-rehearsal "thumbs up" ritual is a symbolic moment of transition. Though he doesn't call it that, it's a pause when he is asking the actors to mentally shift from their day job to rehearsal and to feel connected to the other actors, the creative team, and the show. The group stepped back to release their arms and, altogether, raised their thumbs to mirror his. Kyrus found these affirmations important as a director and when he was acting in a show, too, which he did as frequently as he directed. Being an actor helped him as a director because he was aware of the challenges from their point of view. He always tried to imagine how he would feel as an actor getting his own corrections or notes.

Their first attempt at the long and complicated ensemble number was a disaster. Everyone bumped into each other by the third "into the woods," no one remembered to sing, and the actors all looked at each other accusingly. Kyrus adjusted the spacing and told them, "There won't be collisions if everyone moves with confidence. If you hesitate, you'll crash." "And please sing," Mike added, and everyone grinned sheepishly. They tried it again. And again. Then Kyrus tried a different tactic and asked them to start on the other foot. "You just made it so much harder!" whined the actor playing the Stepmother. "Not if you were in marching band!" answered the actor playing the Narrator. Others chimed in, "Yes! You got it!" laughing as they remembered their high school marching band routines. (As we saw in Chapter 3 on high school musicals, marching bands contribute to the national musical theatre ecosystem. As a side note, director John Doyle, who created the technique of actor-musicianship, said that when he moved to the United States, after having directed numerous actor-musician productions in the United Kingdom, he was surprised by the number of American actors who not only played instruments but also could move and play at the same time. He eventually figured it out: marching band!)

After another fifteen minutes of working on the number with little improvement, Kyrus said cheerfully, "Okay everybody, take five," and as the actors dashed out to the bathroom or to check their phones, he opened his diagram-laden notebook to turn over a fresh page. Without missing a beat or revealing any anxiety whatsoever, he re-choreographed the number. When everyone came back from the break, he replaced the movement of the entire song with simpler steps (though he never said that the new choreography was easier), and everyone learned it quickly, and it worked.

At the end of the night, Kyrus gathered them together again. "Such great work, guys!" he said. Nodding toward Mike, "We're really pleased. Get some rest and Merry Christmas. We're going to Uno's if anyone wants to meet us there for pizza and beers." He wasn't lying: Both he and Mike were happy with how things went that night, and they felt fine about the holiday break. From this point on, every rehearsal would be about identifying and solving problems, fixing, and polishing until they moved into the theatre for tech—and like always, everything would fall apart.

Community

The "community" of community theatre refers to the local community—the region—and to the group's unity, onstage and offstage, unplanned and intentional, which happens when people make musical theatre.[25] The very process of making theatre is, as producer, actor, and Pennington Players board member Wayne said, "forced camaraderie." Indeed, creating a musical is intense and intensely bonding. Jarad, who played Seymour in *Little Shop*, said, "It is like a family. We spend so much time together and we're all working for something, for the same goal of making a great show, together. We have to depend on each other and we're very vulnerable. By the end, it's just devastating for it to be over." Nikema added, "Yeah, postpartum." Pat, who performed in *Dogfight*, which Kat directed, said, "Our cast got close. We're all on different tracks in life, which is cool. We're building friendships." He liked that they "became a community through the work."

But that bonding doesn't always happen. Playful Theatre Productions producer Ruth told me, "Sometimes a cast is close and sometimes there are struggles and people don't get along, and then there are other casts where everyone gets along perfectly fine but it's all business. They come to rehearsal and put in their time but aren't interested in more than that." I asked, "Is the show better if the cast is close?" "Yes," she answered without hesitation, presuming that offstage emotional connections will bleed into the rehearsal room and onto the stage.

Frank, though, sees it differently. He told me, "I've seen casts that love one another like family and give so-so performances, and casts with massive amounts of repressed loathing transform that into dynamic performances onstage . . . After all, a community with conflict is still a community, and sometimes the conflict hurts but sometimes, in a strange way, it helps."

For some Kelsey artists, "community" is the most important aspect of "community theatre." Of course, one can be active in church (and many are) or volunteer or play in a basketball league. Community theatre is another nondomestic space where one can socialize and make and sustain friends. "Readymade friends," as Pennington Players board member and actor Alan said.

Community theatre can also be an entrée into life in a town. When Jay Stevens moved to this area of New Jersey (Pennington Borough, next to the church on Main Street) in 1961, for example, neighbors immediately started coming over to ask her to participate in what was then the Pennington Theatre Club. She "went to paint a set one day" and then "was hooked." She explained, "I was new and people were nice to me. I had little kids and so did they." Jay's involvement was motivated by her desire to belong and to build a social life. "Just like a bowling league," she said. The love of theatre soon followed. She dedicated herself to doing backstage work for the Players for more than fifty more years.

Jay's story is a familiar one. Christina, who played Cinderella in *Into the Woods*, moved to the area after graduate school to take a job teaching at a local girls' private school. Though she hadn't done theatre since college, she auditioned for the show, landed an excellent role, and has been performing in shows at Kelsey nonstop since then. "I was excited to be in *Into the Woods*, and I loved it. But I didn't expect that I would want to keep doing theatre and would make so many friends," she told me.

Some Kelsey artists are primarily motivated by the desire to perform (or direct, choreograph, stage manage, or design) but find community anyway. The Pennington Players' production of *In the Heights*, for example, which Kyrus directed, Rachel (a high school teacher by day) choreographed, and Mike musical directed, gathered Latinx actors from miles away who were thrilled to do the show. More than half the cast was new to Kelsey; some were new to community theatre altogether. To extend the production's reach,

Kyrus led talkbacks after all of the performances, which also gave the actors a chance to talk about how much doing the show mattered to them. One woman in the ensemble said, "I used to dance. But then I stopped dancing to be a cheerleader. Worst mistake of my life. Rachel made us become a family." Another chimed in, "I live the farthest from here. I don't like leaving. I want to stay with my cast." And the young man who played Usnavi: "We're not acting on stage. It's how we are."

Scene 6: Tech/Dress Rehearsal for Pierrot Productions' *Next to Normal*

Time: 3 months later, March, a Tuesday night
Place: The Kelsey Theatre, MCCC
Dramatis personae: Kat (director), Pete (musical director), Judi (lighting designer), Akira (stage manager), Jen (actor who plays Diana), Ronnie (actor who plays Dan, the husband), Morgan (actor who plays Natalie, the daughter), and the rest of the cast and run crew of Next to Normal

Kat arrived at tech/dress for *Next to Normal* exhausted from the night before when the baby didn't sleep for more than twenty minutes at a stretch. She had been in the theatre all day yesterday, Monday. She managed to get a day off work to set cues with Judi, the lighting designer, and to make sure that the levels on Brian's set were all correct and as she wanted. She'd somehow managed to scour her closet for her favorite plaid jumper and grab matching tights and boots and her lucky houndstooth newsboy cap.

Next to Normal (music by Tom Kitt, lyrics and book by Brian Yorkey) won the 2010 Pulitzer Prize and three 2009 Tony Awards, including Best Musical Score. It follows Diana, a woman with bipolar disorder who imagines that she sees her son, who died as a toddler, alive as a teenager. The dark, disturbing, and deeply affecting musical follows Diana's emotional struggles and the toll it takes on her husband and her teenage daughter, who is actually alive and starved for attention. It's an edgy show for a community theatre.

Kat wished she didn't want so many light cues in this show, but the set was simple and spare and she wanted to use as few props as possible. "This is an abstract show," she said. "I'm anti-props, literally, and we're only using what's necessary. If they can live without it, we cut it." She needed lights, then, to differentiate among the spaces—Natalie's room from the psychiatrist's office from the kitchen. She hadn't seen the show on Broadway, but Pete, the producer, had seen it a few times and sent her some photos. That set was built on scaffolding with platforms at different heights and included neon lights, and though she knew Brian's design was simpler than on Broadway, she liked the hard, industrial feeling of the New York set and lighting design and wanted to capture that aesthetic in her production, too.

Though Kat was tired, she was ready and prepared. She, Judi, and Brian did everything they could yesterday with no bodies on stage, focusing the lights on paper plates taped to music stands to approximate where the actors would be. Now they needed the actors on stage and to see if they could make the crosses in time and if it looked as good as she imagined. She also knew that this might be a plodding and tedious rehearsal when she might doubt her concept, and the actors might feel frustrated and anxious if it went too slowly and they felt they weren't really rehearsing. It was so important to be upbeat and organized and keep everyone in a good mood. She brought cookies for their break midway through the night when everyone's energy would be flagging.

Jen, Ronnie, and Morgan were already in the dressing room getting into their costumes and makeup. They'd had the day off on Monday but were a little stiff and sore from Sunday afternoon, when they helped to strike the set of *Legally Blonde* and to load in their set under Brian's watchful eye and with the help of four teenage boys whom Brian wrangled to come over to the theatre. More accurately, the actors had helped the boys, who expertly connected poles and platforms and built several sets of stairs for the set at lightning speed. Kat had asked them to leave the lowest-level platform from the previous show, which they could use, too, and also a set of chairs and a kitchen table that would also be perfect for *Next to Normal*.

The minute after *Legally Blonde's* curtain call ended on Sunday afternoon, everyone got to work striking the set and then loading in *Next to Normal*. Because both shows had small casts, they needed all hands on deck. "Everyone has to come and pitch in," said Ruth, one of Playful Theatre Productions' producers. "That's community theatre." The *Next to Normal* cast knew that the faster they could strike the old set and load in the new one, the sooner Kat and Judi could focus lights, and then add actors, who needed every moment to adjust to the stage, the steps, the platforms. They did rehearse on stage one night last week in the middle of the previous show's run, but that was it.

At 7:30, Kat peeked backstage into the dressing rooms. "Are you guys ready? Can we do a mic check? Is everyone okay?" They glanced around to make sure they weren't forgetting anything, grabbed their water bottles, and went out onto the stage. Akira, the stage manager, was waiting with their headsets, which the men and Morgan tucked into the back of their pants, and Jen ran the cord under her dress and put the little console in the back elastic of her pantyhose.

Up until then, everything in the show had been meticulously rehearsed. Kat had a reputation for detail and precision, and it was well deserved. And she had strong feelings about originality, too. Before they started rehearsing *Next to Normal*, Kat told the actors, "There are other productions floating around: Don't go watch it. You can get your own ideas. We invent together." Other Kelsey directors understand the creative process differently. Lou, for example, who directed *Sunday in the Park with George*, which Kate designed, wanted the show to emulate the 1984 original Broadway production as much as possible: "The closer we get to what they did on Broadway, the happier I'll be," he said.

Trained first as a choreographer, Kat begins with stage pictures that she designed, which encapsulate the emotional dynamics of each scene. She blocks the musical by asking the actors to move from one stage picture to the next. Pat, who performed in a production of Pasek and Paul's (the creators of *Dear Evan Hansen*) *Dogfight* that Kat directed, said, "She comes in with a very clear idea of what she wants . . . She says, 'Okay. This is your spatial relationship with this other actor, and this is how that energy should feel, and how that space should feel, [then] organically, the specifics come together.'"

Kat supplements these spatial relationships with biographical and psychological exercises that help the actors develop backstories for their characters. Pat, who played an unnamed Marine, said, "She asked us a slew of questions— you know, 'What's your full name?' 'Are both of your parents in the picture?' 'How many siblings do you have?' [. . .] and then we went around, we were exchanging answers, and it was really surprising to see how much overlap [there was between character backstories], and how they kind of fit together."

Starting with their first blocking rehearsal, Kat has the actors repeat each moment until they get it right. They stick with each beat until it's precise and polished, then they move on. She videotapes the scene's final version each night for the actors to be able to refer to it and review every gesture, vocal nuance, and facial expression because they know they won't revisit that scene for several weeks. Pat told me that the process is "really focused . . . If it doesn't feel right, she wants to do [it] again, even if it's a short little piece of a scene . . . she's made it very clear that once we have done a scene, because we do it so thoroughly, the expectation is that, now, any time that we run that scene, it will be at that level."

Kat, like Frank, downplays the community building that some other directors, like Kyrus, prioritize. She told the *Dogfight* cast that the show was not "just to have matching T-shirts and bake cookies together." For auditions for *Dogfight*, which drew over a hundred people that they whittled down to twenty-four for callbacks, the actors "were given numbers to wear and referred to by number instead of by name, and our callbacks were all filmed. Halfway through the night, half of the actors called back were dismissed," said Pat. He added, "I think this no-nonsense sort of approach made the expectations clear from the start."

Kat's working method gives her cast—in *Next to Normal, The Secret Garden, Dogfight,* and the many other shows she's directed at Kelsey— confidence. They know that she has high expectations and if she likes what they're doing, then the show is good. They trust her, Pat said. The same holds true for Frank and Kyrus on every show: absolute trust from the cast.

The cast of *Next to Normal* was nervous and excited tonight—the first time they wore costumes and started to really feel like their characters. "It's a great night and a scary night," said Morgan, a little jittery. "I look in the mirror and I look like Natalie now." Akira called "places" and the actors went to their first spot, which was each character's "home base": Diana down center stage; Natalie in her "room" on the second level; Dan at the "kitchen" table, just left of center. Pete, the musical director, looked down from the orchestra "pit," which was a small balcony-like area above the stage, far stage right and just behind the proscenium, and raised his arm, and the band started to play. Kat sat next to Judi in the booth at the back of the theatre, watching intently and sometimes whispering cues to her. Though there was a small run crew for the show, mostly people who'd auditioned for the show and weren't cast but wanted to be involved anyway, Judi ran the light board herself because there wasn't time to record the cues in enough detail for someone else to follow. And Akira was too busy with other tasks to be able to call the cues anyway.

They managed to get through the first ten minutes, remarkably, and Kat and Judi widened their eyes and smiled at each other. The lights looked good and helped to tell the story. Yesterday's long workday was paying off. Then, during the next scene, Kat whispered to me, "You know what I'm talking about because you know theatre, but when I say dry tech or wet tech no one knows what I'm talking about." As if on cue, she suddenly she put her hand on Judi's arm and yelled toward the stage, "Hold, please!" The actors stopped singing and shielded their eyes to see where Kat's voice was coming from. "Hang on, everybody," she said, bounding down the auditorium's steps. She walked onto the stage, her boot heels clicking on the floor. "Does everyone know how to find your light? It's okay, has anyone not had that experience of having to walk into your light? We have a lot of specials in this show and no follow spot, thank goodness. But that means that you have to feel your light yourself—it won't go to you. Otherwise, we won't see you!" She pointed to the sharply outlined square on the floor, and moved into it. The light reflected off her big glasses. "You can see your nose. You can feel the light on you. If you're not in it, if that happens, try to glide into the light." Then she had all of the actors try it. "Good," she said, and jogged back up to her place. "Let's keep going. Pick it up at the start of 'Perfect for You.' "

They got through Act 1 with only a few stops for adjustments of lights or set changes or coordination with the band. After the last note of "A Light in the Dark," the lights faded to black, the house lights came up, and Akira yelled, "Take ten!" Everyone took one of the cookies Kat brought, drank some water (or tea for Jen), sat down somewhere in the audience, and checked their phone. Kat ate a cookie, too, called home to make sure the baby was alright, and talked to Pete about some notes she'd taken about the tempo of a few songs. She looked towards Akira—Kat would swear she had an internal clock set for ten minutes—who nodded and said, "Places for Act 2!"

Act 2 went equally well—flawless, almost. Ronnie went up on his lines a few times. The lights cut out in the middle of Jen's biggest song. The sound was uneven throughout because the kid running the sound board didn't know the show and who sang when. The band played too slowly for the reprise of "It's Gonna Be Good." Morgan stumbled down the stairs and almost fell. Still, they would not be here all night, and every person in the theatre was relieved. Kat quickly blocked the curtain call, and then thanked the actors and told them to change and come out and sit in the house for notes.

"Guys, you're doing great. I know it's a brand-new set," she opened. Then, she praised them for being so professional. Aside from the one-line pep talk, her corrections were specific: Lift your arm on this line, turn your head on that note, cross one moment earlier, and so on. When they were done, she said, "Go home and get some rest! We have one more dress rehearsal tomorrow, then invited dress on Thursday. You're ready!"

Jen lingered. "Can I talk to you?" she asked.

"Of course," Kat replied, trying not to glance at her watch.

"I just feel like I'm not there yet," Jen said. "I know the music and my lines but I feel like I haven't found the character's pain yet. I feel like something's missing." Her eyes filled with tears. "And I don't want to disappoint you."

"Oh, honey," Kat said, putting her arm around Jen. "You're doing an awesome job! What are you saying? I can see Diana's pain! Try not to worry. You've got it, you're just anxious because this show is so hard. But you really do have it and you're ready. Go home and drink some tea. We need an audience now . . . crying *their* eyes out."

Kat was glad that Jen felt comfortable talking to her. She felt her role as a director to be expansive: "I'm a therapist and a counselor as much as an artist," she told me. "I need for everyone to feel safe; they need to trust me to not let them make fools of themselves and they need to trust each other." With a risky show like *Next to Normal*, this was especially true.

Kat drove home feeling the combination of exhaustion and anxiety she'd come to recognize as that mid-dress-rehearsal-but-before-opening-night feeling. Her work was nearly done now, as an artist, as a counselor, as a teacher and guide. It was up to the actors and the crew to do what they'd been preparing for all these months. She knew they would.

And she hoped they'd have a decent audience for opening night.

Professionalism

Community theatre is the purview of the amateur. Because Mercer County Community College is the physical home of Kelsey and provides in-kind support for the production companies, Kitty Getlik, Kelsey's artistic director and general manager, works full-time for the college, as does Amy Bessellieu, the administrative specialist, and Kate Pinner, the technical theatre coordinator, who also teaches theatre at the college and is the co-producer of PinnWorth Productions, one of Kelsey's resident companies.[26] But no one else at Kelsey makes a living doing shows. In our culture, the professional typically disdains the amateur, in spite of the countless ways in which the amateur theatre feeds the professional theatre.[27] Arts commentator Howard Sherman condemns this derision: "[T]hose whose lives and careers take them away from the arts, but whose love of performing doesn't abate, become part of a maligned yet integral part of the theatrical ecosystem which, when spoken of by most professionals and media voices, is summarily disparaged."[28] He urges "everyone," meaning the professional theatre artists who read his posts, "to stop using 'community theater' as a punch line or a punching bag."[29] Sherman praises the inclusivity of community theatres, which often produce large-cast shows that many professional companies cannot afford to do. At community theatres, big casts drive the all-important ticket sales.

How do we measure the achievements of the amateur? How do we disconnect success from monetary compensation, from a salary? Is it through strong ticket sales? Good reviews? The artists' own sense of accomplishment? Kelsey Awards? It depends.

For some directors at Kelsey, the goal is "professionalism," which Kat, for example, uses to motivate her cast and crew. Professionalism is aspirational and tied to behavior and comportment, commitment and effort.[30]

Kat relies on the term "professionalism" frequently and consistently. "I want this production to look fully professional," she'll offer at the first read-through, or, "Thanks, everybody, for being professional and quiet backstage" during tech. With every set of notes she gave to cast of *Next to Normal*, she praised them for "being professional," as if by saying it, she knows they will rise to the occasion. Pat, an actor, described Kat's approach: "I think that the professionalism she emphasizes also comes with expectations; that after we've learned something once, we're to go over it on our own and have it show-ready."

Frank, in contrast, doesn't use the term, though he still maintains the highest standards for dedication and excellence. He said, "What we do is fundamentally *different* from what the professionals are doing, and trying to duplicate what they do—with larger budgets, different levels of commitment and expertise, different audience expectations, and even different levels of control over the material—is not a good idea." He went on,

> Our goals are different . . . no community theatre production has ever been 'better than Broadway,' no matter what our grandparents tell us after the show. ☺ But we can give audiences experiences that the professionals cannot and never will be able to give them, and for me at least, it's wise to focus on the ways we can take advantage of our nonprofessional status rather than fight it. And ultimately, responsibility, efficiency, dedication, and focus are not the sole domain of the professional.

Kelsey directors display their professionalism—whether or not they use the term—in "credibility, relevance, and competence."[31] Leisure

Studies scholar Chris Rojek suggests that these qualities matter because they tell "others about who we are, what we hold to be valuable and how we can make a difference."[32] For example, Kelsey's directors all convey a self-reflexive sense of their working practices. Kyrus said, "I tell [the actors], 'Practice at home; rehearse at rehearsal.'"[33] Frank told me, "We just don't have time to mess around. I want the actors to arrive ready to start . . . I'm interested in them as performers and that's their job when they come here."

At Kelsey, however serious the directors are, everything has to be tempered with gentleness and with fun. Rehearsals must be enjoyable, and the performers' time must be respected. Choreographer Nicole said, "In our world when so few experiences are live, it's scary to be up there doing a show. Anything can happen." Frank said that he wants people to have a good time—even as they are working hard—because if they don't, they may never return to Kelsey or, worse, quit in the middle of the show. The directors know that in the end, no one is under any obligation to participate. "The intrinsic rewards [are] from the activity itself, " one study of amateur musicians found.[34] Like them, amateur theatre makers typically enjoy rehearsal as much as performance but won't tolerate boredom. In addition, each company's producers hope that first-timers will audition for another show or get involved backstage and truly become a part of the community. As Wayne said, "We want to make people feel welcome so they stay and don't just do one show and leave."

From Kitty's point of view, commitment is crucial. She told me, "There is no place else in my life and probably no place else in your life where you can be part of a group of people and every single one of those people is . . . trying their best to make the absolute best show they can possibly make and to do the absolute best at what they do for that show. Anywhere else you go there are going to be people who are phoning it in. There are going to be people who are giving about 80 percent. In community theatre they are giving 110 percent, and they are all invested in this performance. And you're not going to find that anywhere else."

John, a regular Kelsey actor who played the Baker in *Into the Woods* and Tevye in *Fiddler on the Roof*, saw it differently: "It all comes together on opening night because it's the first time when the stakes are the same for everyone. Up until then, everyone is differently committed. Some don't give 100 percent until performance. Some give 100 percent from the first rehearsal. On opening night, you have to be there and do it."

Scene 7: Enter the Audience

<u>Time</u>: *any weekend of the year, Fridays and Saturdays at 8 p.m., Saturdays and Sundays at 2 p.m.*
<u>Place</u>: *The Kelsey Theatre*
<u>Dramatis personae</u>: *Kitty (artistic director and general manager), the audience, the cast and musicians and stage crew, the volunteer ushers*

Whenever I enter the Kelsey Theatre's lobby, I usually see Kitty in the box office, dispensing tickets and chatting with the people she knows when they come to the window. Small groups gather there and outside in the little courtyard, chatting and waiting for their friends or family to arrive or munching on the Philly soft pretzels or M&M's that are sold from a concessions table. Some spectators hold bouquets of flowers for performers.

A portion of Kelsey's audiences remain consistent from show to show: a majority of sixty-five-plus-year-old white subscribers, who come in couples and groups, whether they're friends who subscribe together or come by bus from one of the retirement communities in the area. "It's a great way to see a lot of theatre," one patron told me enthusiastically. "We can see seventeen shows for shows for $185. That's a great deal!" Many are sophisticated spectators, who, before retirement, lived closer to New York City and were frequent Broadway theatregoers. Some of Kelsey's artists worry that the subscribers' tastes are conventional and "entertainment"-oriented, but subscribers are the bread and butter of each weekend's audience. For their part, return patrons often recognize actors from previous shows, but few are aware of the significant differences among the administration and organization of Kelsey's twelve companies or the directors' working styles. They just come to see a show.

I've been surrounded by many such spectators over my years of seeing shows at Kelsey. They're typically engaged and curious and positive—"New Yorkers, essentially," as Kitty described them—though I heard a little whining about *Sunday in the Park with George* ("I don't like Sondheim. His songs don't stick with me") and even about *Into the Woods*, when, predictably, a section of the audience assumed the show was over at the end of Act 1 and gathered their coats. Still, another woman told me, "I've seen this musical eight or nine times. It's very clever. I saw it on Broadway and Bernadette Peters played the Witch." A few may have flinched during some of the emotionally rougher sections of *Next to Normal* or found the hip-hop numbers in *In the Heights* a little too loud, but all seemed to thoroughly enjoy *Big Fish*, and of course the Broadway blockbusters *Les Misérables* and *Miss Saigon*. These Kelsey regulars often congratulate the actors who come out into the theatre after the show: "You did a good job! This was a lot of work! A lot of lines to remember!"

In addition, many Kelsey artists come out to support each other. Kitty explained, "It draws on itself because the people in show A come back and see show B, and the people in show B come to see show C, and so on. So you get crossover like that." She went on, "And then also you get the people who auditioned and didn't get cast, who come to see who *did* get cast to see if they"—the actors in the show—"did it any better than they"—those who weren't cast—"would have done it."

The rest of the audience is made up of friends and family of the cast and crew, and other local people who have heard of the show or are just curious to see a musical. Depending on the show, then, the audience varies by age, race, and musical theatre knowledge and experience. Typically, many people in the audience know one another, so there is always a feeling of neighborliness.

When I saw *Memphis*, for example, the theatre was packed with people of all ages, including children, and races. Two straight white couples in their seventies who sat in front of me were subscribers, and the two twenty-something African American women sitting next to me were first-timers who came to see their friend and sorority sister who played Felicia (the star). Behind me were a group of Chinese women (speaking Chinese) before the show started. On my other side, a freshman in college out of town—a young white woman—came home for the weekend to see her best friend perform. He was an exuberant young man in the ensemble, and she cheered loudly for him every time he came on stage. When many friends and family are in the audience, which is often the case for the nighttime performances, the response can be enthusiastic and loud, as it was for *Memphis*.

A few months later, *Fiddler on the Roof* enjoyed an entirely sold-out run, which a sign taped to the door of the theatre's lobby announced proudly. The auditorium buzzed—filled with the usual suspects of senior citizens, family and friends of the cast, crew, musicians, and creative team (no one Jewish, I'm fairly sure, but many Catholic Italian Americans). There were also many families and other spectators who knew and loved *Fiddler* and bought their tickets months in advance, as soon as the title was announced. I sat next to such a family—an Asian American mother and father and thirteen-year-old daughter, who wore a University of Maryland sweatshirt (her brother's college) and sat rapt through the entire three-hour show—and a friend of the girl's. They go to New York often to see Broadway shows, the mother told me, "but we love coming here. It's close and easy and the shows are terrific." Someone else sitting behind me told her friend that she saw *Fiddler* on Broadway in its last revival and "this production is just as good!" Then, as I was leaving, I passed a family of three generations, and overheard the grandmother saying, "This was our family. This is where we came from and how we got here." "That was Uncle Samuel?" one of the teenage kids asked. "Yes!" the grandmother answered. Needless to say, the whole audience went crazy for the bottle dance.

Why? Because it's in our community and it's live—a rare, ephemeral experience. As Dave, *Pippin's* lead guitarist, who watched the show from the orchestra "pit" above the stage, told me, "It's amazing to look down and see people in the audience absorbed and enjoying themselves. They come to forget about everything and see a show and that's what we give to them. And it's fun for us, too."

Kitty is an outspoken advocate for "the relevance of Community Theatre." She said, "Because of the choices and creativity one has to use to make a community theatre production work"—costs for one production range from $9,000 to $20,000, including $3,000 to $6,000 for royalties[35]—"sometimes the end result is actually a different, more basic and unencumbered version of the play, which turns out to reach and speak to the audiences even better than it did on Broadway."

Scene 8: After the Curtain Call

Time: *The next day*
Place: *Starbucks; at home at the computer; at home at the kitchen table*
Dramatis personae: *Kat (director), Kyrus (director), Frank (director)*

A few days after *Next to Normal* closed, Kat sat at a table in Starbucks, a script for *Fun Home* next to her latte, the cast album playing through earphones, and a pencil in her hand. She imagined the frame of a house on the Kelsey stage and remembered an antique couch they'd used for another show. She knew she would have no trouble finding a girl who could handle the leading role of Small Alison vocally and emotionally, and she had a few ideas for boys who could play the brothers. She felt the show's message was important and she loved the music, so yes. She decided she would call Pete, Pierrot's producer, tomorrow and agree to direct it next season. She was already getting excited about it.

A few days after *Into the Woods* closed, after he caught up on Kelsey Facebook page postings, sent a Kelsey Report e-newsletter with an audition notice, took care of some tasks for the next Kelsey Awards, and went to see various friends in other community theatre shows, Kyrus spent a few hours on the internet looking at photos and clips from different productions of *The Color Purple*, which he would direct for the Pennington Players next season. He started a file of the images he liked and the movement he thought was cool to pass on to Rachel, the choreographer. He also started a new spiral notebook—he liked to keep his ideas for one show in one place—and made a list of churches and other organizations to reach out to about auditions. He knew the African American theatre community would be ecstatic about this show, but he would have to work to find them and get them to come out to audition.

A few days after *Little Shop of Horrors* closed, after he and Shannon returned the Audrey II puppet to the theatre in Pennsylvania where they rented it and enjoyed some R&R watching football games at home, Frank opened his already-marked-up script for *The Hunchback of Notre Dame*. Rehearsals started in a week and he had a lot of big group scenes to block before then. He found some Post-it notes in a drawer and on each one, he wrote one character's name and stuck it on the table. He looked at the script and read the opening description: "The CONGREGATION walk on stage fully robed. CLOPIN, robed as well, walks through the center with a thurible." Then, "the stage is filled with the light of Notre Dame and the CONGREGATION face the audience and carry out the opening chords."[36] Not too many stage directions, which he preferred. He'd cast a sizable group of actors to play "statues" to set the scene in the cathedral and other characters he wanted to come and go in the opening for a sense of movement. So he arranged the Post-its as a bird's-eye view of the stage and the show's opening tableau, and snapped a photo with his phone. Then he skimmed the script for the next key stage picture, rearranged the Post-its, and took another photo. He went through the whole opening sequence this way, coding the photos to moments in the script. Then he went back to the beginning and staged out every step and every movement—like choreography for a marching band. Frank knew that he could be reactive in the rehearsal room and make changes if something didn't work live, but he always had a detailed plan from which to work.

The overlap and intensity of theatrical activity at Kelsey—on any given night, you can find a performance, a rehearsal where they're running the show, an early stage rehearsal, and auditions—is unusual because it's actually twelve different community theatres. But the liveliness and passion of engagement that you see at Kelsey is not unusual at all. The New Jersey Association of Community Theatres (NJACT), to which Kelsey's companies belong, has about 150 member theatres. These community theatres produce well over two hundred shows a year and the organization also sponsors an annual awards program like Broadway's Tony Awards (and like the Kelsey Awards), which are chosen by volunteer adjudicators who travel around the state to see productions.[37] Former NJACT president Patrick Starega said that close to a thousand plays and musicals are produced by New Jersey community theatres (both affiliated and unaffiliated with NJACT) every year.[38]

During a dress rehearsal for *Next to Normal*, I chatted with the young actor playing Gabe, the dead/undead son, who asked me what I was writing and what I was looking for. "I'm curious why people do this," I said. "Why do they drive long distances and spend their hours after work and after school here, making musical theatre?" He didn't miss a beat. "Yeah, why are we here?" he said. "We don't get paid anything and with gas, it actually costs us money to be here. So, yeah, why do we do it? How could we not do it? Because we love it."[39]

Figure 5.1. View of the set of *The Sound of Music* and the bay in the distance, from the top of the audience on a late spring day at the Mountain Play, Marin County, California.

5

The Sound of Music at Outdoor Summer Musical Theatres

It's not easy to get to the Mountain Play. Not only is Mill Valley (pop. 14,403), the affluent and quaint northern California town that sits at the base of Mt. Tamalpais, a ten-mile drive north of the Golden Gate Bridge from San Francisco.[1] But parking your car in the lot at Mt. Tam High School by 9 a.m. and schlepping your stuff—a cooler filled with wine and cheese and bread and fruit, plus sunscreen, plastic cushions for the rock-hard seats, and a sweater in case the weather changes—onto the yellow school bus with sixty of your new best friends is just the start of the day. You won't see your car again until 7 p.m. at the earliest. And yet, on late spring afternoons since 1913, thousands of people have ridden said school bus, or hiked or biked, or taken a steam locomotive (until 1929) the six miles uphill to a huge natural amphitheatre on Mt. Tam to see a play.[2] Without a doubt, it's worth it (Figure 5.1).

Halfway across the country in Austin, Texas (pop. 931,830), getting to Zilker Park, where they perform the annual Zilker Summer Theatre musical, is much easier, though it's still a long night.[3] You can drive or ride your bike or even take a bus to the park, which spreads over 351 acres in central Austin on the south side of Lady Bird Lake.[4] The always busy place includes hiking trails, playgrounds, grills and picnic tables, a funky snack bar, a little train for kids (and adults) that makes a circle around the park and through the trees and across Barton Creek, and, most famously, Barton Springs, the largest manmade, spring-fed pool in the world. Every day of the year, rain or shine, people swim in the sparkling-clear, nippy 70-degree water adjacent to the barebones theatre. In the summertime, when they do the show, the pool is packed with Austinites seeking respite from the broiling Texas heat. In the late afternoon, people start to spread out their blankets on the grassy hillside to get good spot (there will be an audience of a thousand people) and then go for another swim before enjoying their beers and picnic supper and the show. For free.

Beyond Broadway. Stacy Wolf, Oxford University Press (2020). © Oxford University Press.
DOI: 10.1093/oso/9780190639525.001.0001

Seventeen hundred twenty-five miles northeast of Austin, the Open Air Theatre in Washington Crossing State Park in western New Jersey—where General George Washington and his troops landed after they crossed the Delaware River on Christmas Day 1776—is still simpler to access, though a much smaller population lives within a reasonable ten-mile drive than in Austin or Mill Valley. The densely wooded park contains thirteen miles of hiking trails, group picnic and camping facilities, and places to fish, ride horses, and cycle. There are also historical sites: a museum of military collectibles and the Johnson Ferry House, an eighteenth-century farmhouse where Washington and his troops rested after their historic crossing. As well, the park hosts a 650-seat cement amphitheatre built into a natural dell.[5] Before the show, you can grill some burgers in the park or drive ten minutes to get a bite to eat in nearby, charming Lambertville. It might be hot and humid, or breezy and clear, or cold and rainy, and mosquitoes are common. An easy-to-miss, makeshift but weather-sturdy sign at the park's entrance off curvy, hilly County Road 546 announces the Open Air Theatre with a cartoon logo of a grinning crescent moon. Below, the title of that weekend's musical: *The Sound of Music*.

Broadway Meets Nature in *The Sound of Music*

One of the most popular and beloved musicals of all time, known better as the classic 1965 film with Julie Andrews than as a 1959 Broadway musical with Mary Martin, *The Sound of Music* was performed at these spectacularly beautiful, unusual outdoor theatres in 2011, 2012, and 2013. When audiences made the trek up the mountain, onto the hillside, or into the park, they were not only richly rewarded with the pleasure of watching actors sing "Do Re Mi" in nature. They also participated in a large-scale community event that most people recount with immense civic pride.

Just a few years after the 2008 economic crisis, all three theatres still struggled for financial solvency, so *The Sound of Music* was a clear choice for them. The tuneful score, the story's familiarity, and adorable singing children guaranteed full houses. Certain elements of all three productions resembled each other, as they would for almost any production of *The Sound of Music*, including seven children whose heights created a perfectly descending line, a big chorus of nuns, and a melodious, tear-jerking "Climb Ev'ry Mountain" finale. Each theatre's outdoor setting enhanced this particular musical like a dream, and each production met the audience's nostalgic, emotionally laden expectations of the show and also took advantage of the natural setting.

In 2013, the Mountain Play's hundredth anniversary, *The Sound of Music* sold out every performance. Because the weather cooperated and no performances were canceled, the show played to more than twenty thousand people and ensured a profitable season for the company. In 2012, Zilker Summer Theatre's production marked its exceptionally lucrative fifty-fourth season, playing to forty thousand people over thirty-two shows. In 2011, Downtown Performing Arts Center's production, which played six times over two September weekends, capped off an excellently attended second season in the park for the company.

The venues that we visit in this chapter are located in three different regions of the country with different theatre spaces, organizations, and performance dates and times. But they have more in common than their outdoor locations and summertime-only performances. Each theatre has a long history and an abiding commitment to provide accessible, affordable, family-friendly musicals. Each also offers opportunities for local artists to work in a unique setting with huge audiences. *The Sound of Music* allowed each theatre to capitalize on this musical's universal popularity as well as reflect the local setting and the local community.

Big outdoor summer musicals function equally as local theatrical ventures, as activities for families and groups, and as actions that connect people to their community and allow them to express civic pride. In some ways, outdoor summer musical theatre is a subset of community theatre, which we visited in the previous chapter. (In fact, many of the New Jersey community theatre groups that now rehearse and perform at Kelsey once did shows at the Open Air Theatre under a previous arrangement with the New Jersey State Park Service.)

But outdoor summer theatre is "community theatre" on a different scale: The audiences are huge and many spectators don't attend (indoor) theatre during the rest of the year. Audiences come to see the musical not only for its entertainment value but to perform their citizenship and engagement with their community. These organizations use the annual summer musical in the park to position themselves both as a theatrical venue and as a civic practice. Sometimes, the show becomes a means to an end, a way for people to get together for this occasion. Because of the casual, kid-friendly environment, outdoor summer musicals offer a way for children to be introduced to musical theatre. They can run around or talk, and everyone can sing along, and it's fine because no one can be heard over the loudspeakers.

A Brief History of Outdoor Summer Theatre

The Mountain Play, the Zilker Summer Musical, and the Open Air Theatre are only three among several hundred outdoor summer theatre venues across the United States.[6] Although theatre originated outdoors in Greek and Roman amphitheatres, and later at Shakespeare's Globe Theatre, open-air venues in the United States have always been more novelty than norm. In the 1910s, a handful of outdoor theatre spaces were built when the Industrial Revolution birthed an equally passionate defense of nature and call for people to spend leisure time active and outside. The Mountain Play's first actors in 1913, in fact, were members of the Mt. Tam hiking club.[7] In 1934, a few years before Zilker Park performances began, one Austin councilman closed off the area to cars "so that its [the park's] enjoyment by nature lovers will be complete and undisturbed."[8] In the mid-1960s, an early pamphlet of the Washington Crossing Association read, "Our members believe that . . . this 'theatre dell' in the park has a unique setting to stimulate the idea of outdoor recreation which can be geared towards cultural fulfillment as well as good summer entertainment."[9]

Though one might think of theatre—artificial, constructed, built—and especially Broadway musical theatre—contrived, glitzy, commercial—as nature's opposite, advocates for outdoor drama like *Theatre Arts Magazine* editor Sheldon Cheney found them perfectly complementary. In his 1918 treatise, *The Open-Air Theater*, Cheney argued that outdoor theatre is "the most genuine and most spontaneous expression of the life of the people."[10] "Nature is the great revivifier," he wrote, "and the mere calling of masses of people away from the roofed-in places has its salutary effect . . . the outdoor dramatic production . . . sends men and women back to their cities refreshed in mind and body."[11] Another early advocate for outdoor theatres, landscape architect Frank Albert Waugh, agreed, but nonetheless urged that theatres should be built to eliminate nature's distractions as much as possible: "There should be no competition of interests with what is going on on stage."[12] Waugh wrote in 1917, "The plague of mosquitoes is in fact one of the worst practical drawbacks to many an outdoor theatre. Civilization, it is true, is making visible progress in abolishing this pest, and perhaps the day will come when we may count it out altogether."[13] Wishful thinking.

Through the first half of the twentieth century, the number of outdoor theatres remained steady, but in the early 1960s, the movement saw a prose-lytizing resurgence, around when the Washington Crossing Open Air Theatre was built. The First National Outdoor Drama Conference convened in 1963, and a number of reports and architectural guides were published, all of which relished nature's grand scale and praised the ennobling diminution of the human form. In 1961, for example, the American Institute of Park Executives released a survey about outdoor theatres, which then numbered 1,362, with 777 more in the planning stage.[14] The report fretted over the growing popu-larity of television and its threat to theatre. Report author Foss Narum wrote, "The average American theatre-goer perhaps goes to the theatre more to be entertained than for any other purpose, so that serious drama is [. . .] a haz-ardous undertaking, financially speaking [. . .] The safest program in an out-door theatre, is the musical extravaganza, or the large aquatic show (a modern pageant), etc."[15] He continued, "Since an outdoor theatre usually plays to a larger audience than usual, and since the spatial properties of an outdoor the-atre are huge in dimension (including the whole sky as the ceiling), a type of production is needed which can use the immensity of space to the greatest advantage, namely a production which combines music, pageantry, action involving large groups, and the like."[16] Enter Broadway musical theatre.

In the twenty-first century, these theatres carry on this tradition. All three were founded by dedicated citizens who were both nature and theatre enthusiasts, and local audiences continue to boast about the beautiful setting and the high-quality productions. All are managed by a tiny paid staff and rely on many volunteers. All must contend with the very characteristic that defines this subgenre of community musical theatre and offers the biggest test and the biggest reward: thousands of people attending a musical out-doors. Here, big shows meet big audiences in big nature.

The Mountain Play, Marin County, California

I heard about the Mountain Play from a childhood friend of my brother's who has lived in the area for twenty years, and I could not believe that such a thing existed. A musical on top of a mountain? A natural amphitheatre with a view across the bay? An audience of more than three thousand people? I had to get there.

I bought our tickets online (as is the norm) and was confronted with a range of choices slightly baffling to someone who is only accustomed to choosing between the orchestra and the mezzanine. I found differently priced seating options, from open seating to unassigned seats in the shade to a specific seat labeled with my name in the reserved shady area, each of which cost progressively more. Sun? Shade? From New Jersey I was hard pressed to imagine this would be important. Still, I chose reserved seats in the shade, the first step of a series of rituals that were a part of the Mountain Play experience. Part theatre-going, part community celebration, part endurance test, my companion and I followed the flock and asked a lot of questions along the way.

We arrived at the parking lot of Mt. Tam High School, where we were supposed to leave our car for the day, on the early side, but the lot was already full. We somehow didn't see the person directing cars to the adjacent lot but instead followed a line of other cars down the road. With the Pickleweed Inlet of Richardson Bay on our right and the mountains on the left, we parked on a side street a quarter of a mile down the road. Everyone seemed to be making a beeline from their cars to the Safeway across the street, so we followed and bought some snacks, too, in an aimless, we-don't-know-what-to-expect kind of way.

When we got back to the high school, we saw a long line of people waiting in the morning sunshine to get on the school bus, and everyone was chatting and happy. We took our place in line and looked around to see what supplies other people had that we didn't. Our two plastic Safeway bags were sad next to everyone else's Coleman coolers and designer picnic baskets, but what could we do? Also, everyone wore baseball caps or sun hats (we did not), and despite the ever-mounting temperature, just in case the weather turned, most people carried fleece hoodies (we did not), and a number of people, ready to walk down after the show, held hiking poles (we did not). We did, though, have raincoats tucked inside our backpacks, too, just in case. The air was fresh, and we were in California about to see one of our favorite musicals. We were excited and a little nervous.

The bus ride took forty-five long and nausea-inducing minutes, up and around the corkscrew turns, treacherously lined with bikers going in both directions in an endless single-file line on the nonexistent shoulder, huffing and puffing their way up or flying down the mountain. The bus driver was understandably frustrated—although no doubt she had done this drive a hundred times, passing bikers—but no passengers on the bus seemed in a rush. The mood was festive, with packed-in spectators of all ages. We were on our way and the performance needed us, the spectators. The soon-to-be audience was all white (as far as we could see): families and groups of teenagers, old people, couples, a lot of little kids, and even babies.

The bus let us off in front of a small hut that served as the ticket booth, and people lined up to collect their tickets (Figure 5.2). We had paid a hefty $95 for reserved seats, but I couldn't remember if they were in the shade, which by then seemed an important perk. To the right of the ticket booth was a paved path leading slightly uphill and past a smattering of booths selling T-shirts and water, information about the park and a hand-drawn map for hiking down, as well as a place to rent stadium seats. The booths were simple and few and decidedly noncommercial—they urged you to donate to the park or join the local birdwatching club, which we liked. We passed a snack bar selling organic hotdogs, soda, wine, beer, and ice cream, which we would happily purchase during intermission.

Figure 5.2. The ticket booth for the Mountain Play, which is built for the run of the production, and then removed until the next year.

After a five-minute walk up the path, we arrived at the top of the amphitheatre with an expansive view of the bay. The size, scale, and beauty of the Mountain Play's setting, two thousand feet above sea level, are almost unimaginable. The space was huge and semicircular, a true Greek-style amphitheatre. A section of the seating was shaded by large, remarkable shade structures, which, according to Mountain Play executive director Sara Pearson, were built specifically to "provide relief from the sun while not touching the historic rocks or the soil around them." She explained that "it was an engineering feat" and "difficult to get the design approved by the State Park." While providing shade for nine hundred seats, the "tarps" obscured no one's view.

A thousand people already seemed well camped out, on their cushions and surrounded by coolers and plates of food and bottles of wine. Some hardy spectators hiked up the mountain, and many more planned to hike (including us, even without hiking poles) or ride mountain bikes down after the show. All were eating and drinking or walking around and chatting. It was fifteen minutes to show time.

A friendly volunteer showed us to our seats, which did indeed have our names on them. Though they were in the sun now, they would soon be in the shade. To house right and off to the side was a roped-off area with a "staff only" sign that led backstage and fifty portable toilets for the audience. To house left, just above the top row, sat a raised wooden tented platform, just large enough for a table with a massive, high-end sound board.

The set was a series of very tall flats painted—quite realistically—to look like the gray abbey walls. The flats extended along the impossibly wide eighty-foot stage and would later rotate to reveal the interior of the lovely Von Trapp family villa. Above and to the side of the set, we could see the city in the distance across the sparkling bay. The stage manager scurried around on the stage, looking like a tiny speck of a person. Two huge scaffold stands held enormous, rock concert–sized speakers on either side of the stage.

The set was designed by Ken Rowland, his twenty-sixth Mountain Play. Because nothing of the show can remain on the mountain, each year, the crew constructs the entire stage, including the turntables for scene changes, from scratch. They also build a structure for the sixteen-piece orchestra and storage areas. A local writer explained, "For several weeks of rehearsals and the six weeks of the run, a swarm of people descends on the amphitheatre to maintain the stage and sets, and then everything comes down, and the space reverts back to the calm of the wild." "It's like creating a little city up there," Rowland said.[17]

At 2 p.m. promptly, a fiftyish woman in jeans, a T-shirt, and a baseball cap, who turned out to be executive director Sara Pearson, used a handheld mic to give a "curtain speech." Standing in front of the booth, she thanked donors and supporters, thanked people for coming to see the show in the heat (the heat was a very big topic of the day), and thanked the crew and volunteers and everyone who helped to make the Mountain Play such a wonderful tradition. At that point—a moment before the show was to begin—people were still milling about and busily involved in their food. Northern Californians take their food and drink very seriously and few would let a mere curtain speech distract from cheese and crackers and wine. This was as much a social occasion as a theatrical one.

Then, the voices of a chorus of nuns rang out, as they slowly entered the stage in a line, singing the opening number, "Preludium," a Latin prayer-like chant. The sound grew through the song, which expanded from solo voice to chorus, both orchestra and actors loud and clear through the speakers. Visually, the actors seemed far away. But the scale was so huge that I couldn't translate the distance from where I sat to the acting space to anything I'd ever experienced in the past.

After this hymn-like song, which opens the stage version but not the more familiar movie, came the title song. Mountain Play veteran Heather Buck, who played Maria, entered from the top of the amphitheatre, as the audience had. It took most spectators a few lines to locate her because her disembodied voice came through the loudspeakers, but in the bright daylight, no follow spot guided our eyes. Plus, there were still (and through the whole performance) many people walking around at the top of the theatre.

Heather/Maria sang the first verse there, looking down at all 3,750 of us in the audience and the stage and across the bay. Then at, "My heart wants to sing/Every song that it hears," she slowly wended her way down the huge stone steps and onto the stage. This simple, even predictable entrance was nothing less than thrilling, an actor's physical co-joining of nature and art. As one reviewer observed, "Every time Maria talks about how much she loves to roam around the mountains of her youth, the Mountain Play's majestic home makes you really appreciate what she means."[18]

The Mountain Play's Story

The Mountain Play began in 1913 when a group of hikers who frequented the area, including Garnet Holme, then chair of the drama department at the University of California at Berkeley, noted that the natural amphitheatre had excellent acoustics and an extraordinary view across the bay that could provided a perfect backdrop for drama.[19] They did *Abraham and Isaac: "An Ancient Miracle Play"* and the Malvolio scenes from *Twelfth Night*.[20] The play's instant popularity led the men to form an association to oversee yearly productions. In 1916, Congressman William Kent, who owned the land, deeded the theatre to the Mountain Play Association (MPA). In 1936, the MPA gave the theatre to the state park that surrounded it, and from 1936 to 1946, the Civilian Conservation Corps (CCC) built "the massive serpentine stones that now form the 4000-seat Sidney B. Cushing Memorial Amphitheatre."[21]

For its first sixty years, the Mountain Play followed early outdoor theatre advocates' recommendation that noncommercial fare, especially classic and historical dramas, were most appropriate for the outdoors, and they presented Shakespeare, Ibsen, or adaptations of children's stories. A play was performed each and every summer, except for 1924, when the mountain was quarantined due to an outbreak of hoof-and-mouth disease, which threatened grazing cattle, and from 1942 to 1945, when the US Army Air Forces set up antiaircraft detection and radar warning sites on the West Peak, closing hiking trails and roads to the public. But all of the years that the park was open, a play was performed on the mountain. Even when a serial rapist and murderer nicknamed the Trailside Killer was terrorizing women in the area in the mid-1970s, the Mountain Play prevailed with a bicentennial musical revue, *Celebration '76*.[22]

Local residents always bragged about the Mountain Play, but by 1977, audiences had shrunk so much that the organization was on the verge of collapse. Marilyn Smith, a native of the adjacent town of Mill Valley, stepped up and agreed to serve as executive director of the Mountain Play on one condition: They would switch the repertoire to Broadway musicals.[23] The board, mostly made up of wealthy Marin businesspeople, demurred because of the high cost of producing musicals, but they had little choice. As all attest, Smith brought the Mountain Play back to life.

Smith knew that big, popular, commercial, and well-known Broadway musicals are well suited for a large outdoor venue. Audiences, especially those who aren't regular theatregoers, eagerly attend musicals with familiar music and stories that they know. When I saw *The Sound of Music*, everyone around me was singing along, loudly. During intermission, when Sara Pearson's voice came over the loudspeaker to announce that the next year's

Mountain Play would be another Rodgers and Hammerstein classic, *South Pacific*, a loud cheer went up among the older generation.

Once the Mountain Play's repertoire switched to musicals, Smith hired director James Dunn, who stayed with the organization for thirty years, and whose artistic style became a local legend and defined the Mountain Play brand. Years before musicals on Broadway flew in helicopters on stage or dropped chandeliers precariously close to audience's heads, Dunn grew famous in Marin for using real vehicles and featuring real live animals in all thirty shows he directed. The *Fiddler on the Roof* cast included live chickens, sheep, goats, and a cow. For *South Pacific*, he wanted a formation of real fighter jets to fly overhead, which Marilyn Smith made happen.

The Mountain Play's Producer

Executive director Sara Pearson joined the team in 2007, a few years before Dunn retired, and she acts as the lynchpin between the money, the people, the state, and the theatre for this one-show-a-year community theatre, with an enormous operating budget of $900,000 (in 2013 for *The Sound of Music*). Though she possesses considerable theatre experience, Sara spends much of her time fundraising and typically raises just enough money for next year's show. She searches out corporations and local arts grantors, who can be skittish about funding what they see as popular middlebrow fare. "People—theatre people—look at musical theatre as the most accessible—and I mean that in the worst possible way," she said. "Organizations that fund the arts . . . mostly fund new works or underrepresented theatre . . . [M]usical theatre is not seen as something, quote unquote, worth supporting. And it also happens to be the most expensive to produce." Also, the Mountain Play pays every person who works on the show. For most, it's a small, symbolic stipend, no matter the role, but the company also handles two Equity contracts each year. For the kids in the show, Sara told me, "to get a paycheck at all is really exciting. The biggest problem with them is that they don't cash them."

Sara also oversees a mass of volunteers from teenagers to retirees who are essential to the production, assigned to front-of-house duties that range from taking tickets to filling up spray bottles with water and ushering. As with many community theatres, roles within the operation are fluid, so someone who helps to build the set for this show might stage manage the next, or perform, or gather props. Participation builds a large base of performers, staff, and volunteers for the future.

And like other community theatres, entire families participate. Most Mountain Play productions include parents and children, siblings and cousins onstage or backstage. Both James Dunn and Ken Rowland's families were involved in a variety of roles "on the mountain," for many years, onstage and offstage. Ken also performed in some shows, as did his grandmother when she was twenty-one.[24] Sara keeps track of anyone who gets involved in any capacity, dividing her attention between producing this season's play and preparing for the short- and long-term future. By the time *The Sound of Music* opened, in addition to the forty-two actors and sixteen musicians, more than a hundred more people were involved backstage as designers, builders, stage managers, and techies of all stripes, what actor Ryan Drummond, who played Captain Von Trapp, called "an army of people backstage." The only unnecessary role: lighting designer.

Because ticket sales are crucial for the Mountain Play's continuance from one year to the next, the stakes are high in choosing each year's show—another of Sara's responsibilities. In her first year as executive director, they did a nudity-free production of *Hair* (surely California is the only place that *Hair*, in any version, could be considered family-friendly!), which was a big success. In 2009 when the recession hit, they also did a lesser-known—though still a classic (and more serious)—musical, *Man of La Mancha*. While ticket sales had been "generally in the neighborhood of $550,000 to $580,000," Sara said, "in 2009, sales dipped to $379,000." Whether because of personal finances or because spectators weren't enthusiastic about the title, only ten thousand people showed up—as opposed to the eighteen thousand tickets sold for the previous year's *Wizard of Oz*.[25]

A few years later, they did *Hairspray*, which audiences were excited about, but it rained and they had to cancel one performance. "When the show is performed on only six Sunday afternoons, losing one hurts," she said. "There are lean times and fat times, and you've got to ride them all out . . . If we hadn't survived as long as we had, we might have been more terrified and may have dropped the whole thing in fear. But one or two other times in Mountain Play history things waned dangerously then returned again triumphantly."[26] The story that the Mountain Play tells of itself is about survival against all odds, like a nature story.

In addition to overseeing the money, the people, and the choice and production of the show, Sara also works with the state park administration, whose priority is preserving the environment and keeping up to 3,750 people safe in notoriously unpredictable weather. The Mountain Play's contract with the park stipulates that they "leave no trace." Each summer, every item must be trucked up the mountain and built from scratch—from the deck for the stage and set to a small house for the musicians, the concession buildings, the costume and prop shop, and the dressing rooms—and then removed, returning the mountain to its natural state. In addition, the company hires a 24-7 guard to keep watch on the set, the orchestra "house," the massive speakers, and the sound booth, which is a deck with a scaffolding frame, tented with canvas. To minimize the toll on the environment, performances are limited to six a season, and the fire marshal will cancel a performance in hot dry weather if the fire risk is too high. In 2010, Sara said, they decided to stop refunding tickets if the performance is cancelled because of weather.

Which is the one thing Sara cannot control.

Weather that changes daily (or hourly) is the biggest challenge of producing outdoor musical theatre on the mountain. Mt. Tam can be 50 degrees and drizzling on Saturday and over 90 degrees with blinding sun by the start of Sunday's show. Actors, producers, spectators, musicians, and concession volunteers all tell proud and loving war stories about the weather and the general insanity of doing musical theatre outdoors. Mountain Play artists express a doggedness, an unshakable passion, even as they laugh and shake their heads recalling all that they've endured to make a show outside in the summer. "Mounting good musical theater on a mountaintop is an exercise in perennial optimism," said Ken Rowland.[27] The orchestra plays in a small built structure to protect them from the weather, but it's still challenging to keep instruments in tune. After the show, during the curtain call, the musical director Debra Chambliss steps outside of the building so the audience knows where the music has been coming from.

But the rewards are big, too: Thousands of people see the show rather than hundreds. As David Yen, who played Max in *The Sound of Music*, said, "What's a little physical discomfort? Backstage you put more clothes on or take them off. Then you go onstage and look out and see three thousand people in the audience." Ryan Drummond, Captain Von Trapp, called it "the crack cocaine of theatre." Maybe this is why actors return to do the show year after year.

The Mountain Play's Director of *The Sound of Music*

Among the Mountain Play's newcomers for *The Sound of Music*—in addition to some of the children and Mother Abbess Hope Briggs—was director Jay Manley. An experienced, award-winning director, well known in the area, Jay hadn't ever seen a Mountain Play production, so he spent a lot of time up there before rehearsals began to get a feel for the place. He held creative ambitions but readily admitted that the show comes with certain expectations about its look: a foreboding abbey and an elegant Salzburg mansion. Audiences know they'll see nuns in habits, Maria in an ugly dress, and the children in sailor clothes, play clothes made of curtains, and party garb. He needed to come up with a clever way to fake the finale's mountain climb.

Jay was fully cognizant of the emotional baggage of this show and equally aware of the theatre's need for the production to make money, so he elected to reproduce the show that audiences would expect but also made certain artistic choices that reflected the community, presenting one of Broadway's best-known and best-loved musicals as a locally grown performance. For example, when he was casting the show, Jay realized that there were many male performers in the community but few parts for men in the nun-heavy musical, so he decided to create a chorus of ten monks, the Benedictine Brothers, to join the women, their voices also providing a deeper sound in those songs. He also thought about how a show whose moods are evoked by darkness and light could work entirely in daylight. (From my perspective, it was kind of wonderful to see *The Sound of Music* in the bright light of day, and Jay's production captured the musical's every mood.)

Jay followed his predecessor's practice and incorporated real vehicles into the production: the Nazis' car and a motorcycle for Rolf. The audience roared with delight when the actors drove the vintage car on the stage. The new director's use of the old director's technique (and a perfect one for the setting) endeared him to the local crowd. Jay also made admirable use of the alarmingly wide stage, creating lovely pictures and blocking the actors to the edges of the stage. "When working outdoors, there is a lot more audience interaction and the audience becomes a dynamic part of the production," he said.[28]

Like all directors, Jay put his own interpretive spin on some of the characters. For example, he and Susan Zelinsky, who played Elsa, wanted to make her more likeable and sympathetic. They decided that when she leaves

Georg, it's because she knows he really is in love with Maria and it will be better for him.

The Mountain Play's Actors

This area north of the Golden Gate Bridge is not a suburb of the city but rather its own region between San Francisco and the Napa Valley, home to many talented and enthusiastic semi- or nonprofessional musical theatre artists. Ryan described the Mountain Play as "a Marin thing," "an amazing hidden gem." Many people in the cast had been in past musicals, including Susan Zelinsky, whose Elsa was her ninth role in a Mountain Play production. Others were first-timers, including an actor in the ensemble who rode his bike to and from rehearsals and the performance. He told me, "I've hiked up here since I was a kid and saw this show [the Mountain Play] twenty times and then someone said I should try out. And here I am!" The Mt. Tam cast was almost entirely white—as is the local community—though Hope Briggs, an African American singer who performed with the San Francisco Opera, played the Mother Abbess.

Many of the Mountain Play's artists work with other musical theatres as part of the local ecosystem. Almost all of the kids in *The Sound of Music*, for example, take classes at Marilyn Izdebski's studio (the backstage diva who is the subject of Chapter 2) and perform in her musicals during the school year and in the summer. The very next day after seeing *The Sound of Music*, I met some of the kids in the show auditioning for *Evita* at Marilyn's.

On the mountain, every acting choice must be large and clear. Longtime director James Dunn urged the actors to make everything "bigger, louder, funnier! Most important of all: Keep your heads up."[29] "This is not Stanislavsky," Dunn said. "Forget everything you ever learned about acting."[30] Actors David Yen and Susan Zelinsky explained how they kept their chins lifted so that the audience at the top of the theatre could see their faces. All of the actors talked about expanding their gestures and exaggerating their facial expressions.

A local archivist with friends in the production told me that it's the "ultimate experience for actors" to be in this "huge, rare performance space." "For actors," she said, "they're up on stage and there is actual dirt and an actual tree and an actual rock. And they're pretending, they're acting, but there is this actual stuff next to them."

The Mountain Play's Audience

The audience of the Mountain Play is divided between frequent theatregoers who enjoy this local event in a gorgeous setting and those who seldom go to theatre but are attached to the special occasion. For everyone, it's an annual ritual with family and friends to celebrate the unique natural jewel of Mt. Tam. As one local journalist wrote, "Among the organization's most significant contributions must be that for many theatregoers, their first trip up Mount Tam to see the Mountain Play has been their first live performance or live theatre. There's no way to accurately gauge the impact the Mountain Play has had on the community, other than to say, by reaching its 100th anniversary it has no rivals."[31]

Audiences are typically made up of families, often with several generations attending the play together, many of whom have been going for years and years. One couple in their sixties saw many Mountain Play shows when their kids were younger. Though they hadn't come for some years, *The Sound of Music* attracted them. This year, they joined their now-adult kids and a group of friends and brought a picnic: an elaborate spread of food and wine and real-glass glasses and nice cushions. Another family of four, parents and two teenagers, had lived in the area for years but moved to San Diego. The parents had wanted their kids to see the Mountain Play from the time they were little, so they drove up for the weekend.

One man in his sixties said he had grown up in New York City and went to the theatre all the time. He moved to San Francisco as an adult and "always" saw the Mountain Play. "Look," he said, as he pulled me over to the poster sitting on an easel with the list of all ninety-nine years of Mountain Play's productions. "This has been going on for ninety-nine years! See, they did *A Funny Thing Happened on the Way to the Forum* in 1978! And *The King and I* in 1987!"

Me: "Did you see all of these shows?"

Him: "Yes! Ever since 1975!"

Me: "And what do you think?"

Him: "They're great! They really improved a few years ago when they got a new sound system. Now you can really hear clearly and everyone is miked. And you know," he went on, treating me like a Mill Valley native, "today is the hottest day of the year. It's never like this. Usually you can sit up here and enjoy the show in the sun and the breeze." He was so excited for the show that he almost couldn't contain himself.

A woman sitting next to us had played in the orchestra of her high school production of *The Sound of Music* forty-some years before. Well oiled by a fews glasses of chilled white wine, she sang along—loudly!—through the whole show. It was fine, though, as the sound system projected the songs and dialog throughout the space. The Mountain Play's large and casual setting is the opposite of a quiet, attention-demanding, sit-still kind of theatre, which makes it an ideal introduction to the theatre for children (as well as enthusiastic adults). Kids can talk, wander around, sleep, or eat, and no one in the audience is bothered. Children's activities like face-painting and a puppet show take place before the show starts; all in all, the theatre-going is fun. Here the show supports the tradition of passing on knowledge of musical theatre. The setting is cross-generational, (relatively) accessible, and a civic ritual.

Once you're there, you experience a unique kind of spectatorship. Seeing a musical outdoors on the top of Mt. Tam feels more active than passive. It requires more concentration than seeing a musical indoors, more labor to stay engaged and pay attention to the action on stage. The gap of twenty-five feet between the stage and the first row of the seats and the rise of the amphitheatre means that for most spectators, the actors are a long distance away. And it's impossible to be on the mountain and not feel wonderfully distracted by the air and the view, the breeze and the smell of pine trees.

What struck me most about the entire occasion—and I found this to be true when I saw *The Sound of Music* at Zilker and at Washington Crossing, too—was that the audience's focus on the play itself ranged from very attentive to not at all. In general, people kept talking or moving around—there was a lot of coming and going from start to finish. The ritual of the experience, of being there with many other people, and the fact that people participate—they organize their stuff and gather their family or friends and troop up this mountain for the play—all of that matters as much as the show.

For those who live there (and for the 50 percent of the audience who come from outside of Marin), the ritual of seeing the Mountain Play holds great importance. Asking if you've "been up the mountain to the see the play" is as common as chatting about the weather during those precious few performance weeks in June. Audiences don't see themselves as spectators and consumers; they understand their role as supporting, investing in, and participating in the community's theatre. Even people who would otherwise scoff at seeing a classic musical tromp up Mt. Tam. "People go to the mountain to say that they've done it. It's like hiking to Machu Picchu to say you've done it," explained one local archivist. In the summer, this community the-atre becomes a civic practice.

The people involved with the Mountain Play seem unfazed by negative stereotypical associations of community theatre. Ryan Drummond called it "community theatre on steroids." It's "community theatre with professional standards," said Sara Pearson. One reviewer praised the "effort that is prima-rily community theatre reinforced by a sprinkling of professionals... [W]hen at its best (as it is this year) Marin's Mountain Play combines artistic rewards with a full day of healthy outdoor activity with family, neighbors, friends and thousands of boisterous people you've never seen before and never will again."[32]

As Sara Pearson described it: "We call ourselves a hybrid between pro-fessional theatre and community theatre . . . The range of expertise and—I hope not ability, I mean it's always high quality—but the range of expertise and experience is quite broad, and so a director needs to be able to work not only with professionals in the field but also people who may be doctors or lawyers or judges or housewives or others who really are not familiar with the professional world of theatre." She went on, "And wonderful things happen... there's kind of a hybrid with the kind of diversity on the stage... It's pretty cool."

A few times that day, I thought that going to see the Mountain Play was kind of like participating in a triathlon for the first time: There is a lot of equipment and a lot of rituals and you need to do it once to understand how it's going to go. We were hot and tired and overdressed and under-fueled but kept saying that we would know how to do it next time.[33] And we knew that, like the first time, it would be totally worth it and truly magical.

Zilker Summer Theatre, Austin, Texas

I returned to Austin four years after I moved away to join old friends and their two-year-old daughter, whom they were determined to make into a musical theatre fanatic before she turned three, to see *The Sound of Music* at the Zilker Summer Theatre. We drove fifteen minutes from their house in South Austin to Zilker, paid what felt like an exorbitant $8 to park, and walked ten minutes more across the park, past kids on swings and going down slides and big groups of families having picnics, their containers of food spread over several picnic tables and music playing. We carried a backpack of peanut-butter-and-jelly sandwiches and chips and Oreo cookies—that was what we could manage by way of a picnic—plus a blanket to sit on and sweatshirts for later, and found ourselves a little piece of ground about halfway up the already heavily populated wide hill. It was 90 degrees at 8 p.m. We were sweating.

We looked down onto the stage, which was a large, simple, permanent concrete platform (Figure 5.3). Though the Zilker Summer Theatre is a highlight of the season in the park, other groups use the venue to present Shakespeare, concerts, and kids' shows. The set for the abbey consisted of very tall flats on wheels, painted to look like stone. In the cramped wing space sat more movable flats painted to look like the von Trapp house and also the iconic staircase, intricately folded and interlocking like a 3D puzzle. A large permanent storage shed sat behind the stage, with dressing rooms off stage right. Downstage right and just off the stage level was an area for the six-piece orchestra—chairs and music stands and a portable keyboard. Like the Mountain Play, huge speakers sat on either side of the stage. A concrete patio ran along the base of the stage, with lawn chairs for older patrons and a seating area for people in wheelchairs.

I walked up to get a view from the top of the hill and found a little cabin with a wide porch that held the light and sound board. The stage manager—a young woman in her twenties—wore a headset and adjusted sound levels.

Figure 5.3. View of *The Sound of Music* on a summer night in Austin, Texas. Photo credit: Pauline Forgeard-Grignon.

Beyond the theatre and through the oak trees, I could see people swimming in the blue-green water of Barton Springs pool. The sky darkened, the stars came out, and I returned to meet my friends. The orchestra—a group of hip, shaggy men in their twenties who looked more like one of Austin's countless cool bands than the players for a classic Broadway musical—settled into their places and started to play.

Maria, played by then Austin newcomer Michelle Haché, entered from a hiking path far off stage left. (The director elected to open the show with this song, like the movie, rather than the nuns' sung chant.) The audience heard her singing "the hills are alive" through the speakers but couldn't see her, as she was too far for the follow spot to reach. Every one of the thousand people in the audience, young to old, craned our necks and looked around to see where she was. A few of us then detected the direction of the follow spot's straining glow. When Michelle/Maria finally came into view, we could see how far she had walked and how much farther she had to go as she continued the song and arrived on stage. Thought she wasn't on a mountain in Austria, this choice linked the character to a solitary existence in nature.

The Zilker Summer Musical's Story

In 1937, a city-sponsored summer music series featuring the Austin Municipal Band, whose concerts originally took place in different parks around town, premiered on a newly built stage in Zilker Park. There were risers for the band, a platform for guest entertainers, and a makeshift backdrop built of cedar posts and wire mesh covered in moonflower vines.[34] The series thrived for over twenty years, and by the 1950s, included film screenings, classical music concerts, and ballet performances. In 1957, the stage was elevated, and a proper soundboard made of plywood shell replaced the moonflower backdrop.[35]

In September 1959, the Recreation Department presented its first Broadway musical, *Seventeen*, at the Zilker Hillside Theater. Director of recreation Beverly Sheffield, for whom the hillside theatre would later be named, and his staff oversaw the production, which featured a cast of high school students and community members. The city saw the program as an opportunity "to give talent in the city a chance to prove itself through the production of good drama." The Zilker Summer Musical (ZSM) was born, the impetus "as simple as some high-school kids who wanted something to do over the summer."[36]

For the first two seasons, audiences paid admission to cover costs. But in 1961, the city agreed to fully fund the musical, which was *Anything Goes* that year, "for all to see and enjoy."[37] From that point on, the summer musical on the hillside was free. Soon, though, park attendance declined, a trend Sheffield attributed to television and air conditioning. Many park programs were discontinued, but not this one, and despite the financial struggles of the 1960s, the ZSM grew in scale and budget. During the 1970s, according to one ZSM director-producer, "The shows kept getting bigger and bigger and rehearsals were going longer and longer into the night, sometimes until 2 in the morning."[38] The 1980 presentation of *Jesus Christ Superstar* was not only the most expensive show to date but, during one performance, Jesus' cross fell, and the actor playing Jesus had to jump for safety.[39] Things had gotten out of hand.

Enter Bil Pfuderer, who directed a ZSM production of *Pippin* in 1978 and became the performing arts supervisor for the city of Austin in 1983. During his twelve-year tenure, Pfuderer brought professionalism and structure to the summer musical. He established a tight rehearsal schedule, hired a professional artistic staff, and shifted the orchestra from a group of high school students to an ensemble of union musicians. The quality of the productions significantly improved in the 1980s, but the budget skyrocketed to six figures.[40]

In the late 1980s, the national savings and loan crisis hit Austin's economy hard, including the parks and recreation department. In 1986, they announced a $60,000 cut in the ZSM's $61,000 allowance; that is, the city virtually eliminated their funding. At the time, about 75 percent of the show's budget came from the city, so the cut was a devastating blow.[41]

But it was not fatal. In 1986, business professionals and theatre supporters formed the nonprofit Friends of the Summer Musical (FOSM) to save this Austin treasure. Their lobbying efforts, which included a letter-writing campaign, an appeal, and a petition, convinced city council to reinstate a $12,000 contribution.[42] FOSM also expanded corporate donations and individual fundraising, including an annual twenty-four-hour rehearse-a-thon. In 1992, the city replaced the general revenue funds with money from its Cultural Arts Fund sourced by Austin's hotel and motel bed and occupancy taxes, which generated around $16,000 a year, depending on annual tourism.[43] At the same time, though, the city started charging FOSM $5,000 to $10,000 to rent the theatre, offsetting much of the city's contribution.[44]

In the 1990s, due to the lack of guaranteed funding, some productions were almost canceled. A month before the opening of *Annie* in 1990, for example, FOSM had only raised $50,000 of the production's $85,000 budget. Pfuderer cut scenes to reduce scenery and costume costs and asked some paid staff to volunteer their time.[45] As another fundraising tactic, in 1998, FOSM became Zilker Theatre Productions (ZTP) with the goal of becoming a year-round production company that could charge admission to indoor shows to generate the revenue needed for free outdoor shows. Their one indoor production—a concert version of *Floyd Collins*—failed, and the organization has since focused solely on the summer musical.[46]

In spite of insecure funding for productions, the theatre was rebuilt in 1995. The repairs and renovations improved conditions, but they also increased future production costs by 20 to 30 percent because every set thereafter needed wings to hide the new actor entrances and dressing rooms.[47] Between 2009 and 2018, $800,000 was spent on improvements, included new audience seating, alterations to comply with the Americans with Disabilities Act, a sewer line, a new stage floor, and a better electrical system.[48] Despite the financial challenges, the summer musical continues.

In 2018, *All Shook Up* marked ZTP's sixtieth anniversary. As has been the custom since the summer musical's earliest days, cast members collect audience donations nightly, which sometime covers 50 percent of the budget.

The Zilker Theatre Production's 2012 Producer

Over the years, the administrative organization to produce the summer plays changed hands several times. Peter Beilharz, who works as the bursar at nearby St. Edward's University, served as lead producer in 2012.

Like the Mountain Play, Zilker's engagement with the Park Service is part and parcel of the producer's normal work. Though the permanent concrete structure means there is less to negotiate year by year and show by show, performances nonetheless take place in close proximity to Barton Springs' fragile ecosystem. Peter reminded me that "there's the endangered salamander that lives underneath the spring." While the production team is extremely cautious, there is "ample opportunity for catastrophe," said Peter.

"At an outdoor play, you share the space with creatures that live there," he explained. "There's a family of raccoons that live under the stage and a bunch of feral cats that call it home [and] just run across the stage, you know. We've had bugs fly into people's mouths. Singing, a beetle flies in. I mean, little things like that."

As producer, Peter also works out the budget. Because of its central location, its accessibility, and its multi-month functionality as a performance venue, the ZSM costs much less than the Mountain Play—ZTP's *Sound of Music* cost $250,000 to produce, just over 25 percent of the Mountain Play's cost. Like the Mountain Play, ZTP pays everyone on the staff, including the stage manager and the artistic team, several professional designers who work at Austin's repertory theatre, Zach Theatre (costume designer Susan Branch Towne and lighting designer Jason Amato), and the musicians, professional rock players who enjoy this unusual side gig. Even the actors are paid, and everyone, no matter their age and experience, is paid the same amount, a minimal, mostly symbolic stipend. (The Mountain Play has a sliding scale for actors and typically writes two Equity contracts each season.) Like the Mountain Play, the ZSM survives only because of the many volunteers who help out before, during, and after the show.

The ZSM lives from hand to mouth on each year's earnings, and the revenue is entirely unpredictable because the show is free and spectators toss money in buckets passed during intermission and after the show. Years of experience enables Peter to estimate earnings, but he can't be sure until the dollar bills are counted. The performance earns nothing if there is a thunderstorm—though that's the only reason a show is canceled; Austinites are undaunted by 100-plus-degree heat.

Funding challenges have been a topic of debate and dissension among the producers, as some feel confident that a good show will garner plenty of income and others want steadier funding from local arts' grantors and corporations. To some degree, this conflict captures the essence of Austin's twenty-first-century schizophrenic identity: "Keep Austin Weird" versus tech center. Both are decidedly hip and cool identities, but one is based in Austin's long anti-establishment history and the other is newer, wealthier, and more commercial—either practical or a sellout. If the division in Mill Valley is between the high art classicists and the musical theatre types, in Austin, it's between the old-time hippies and the newer tech startup types. Still, despite some objections, the 2012 season ramped up corporate fundraising and private donation efforts.

Volunteers, on the other hand, are always welcome. Every year, the organization creates more opportunities and does more energetic outreach across the city for volunteers to get involved, offering free audition workshops, day-long events to build costumes and paint the set, and other community events, presenting the ZSM as a local project beyond the evening's performance.

Despite the challenges, Peter feels committed to outdoor free musical theatre in Austin. "So why bother doing shows outside? Why not take advantage of air conditioning, shelter, technical refinements, and all-around comfort of an indoor theatre?" he asked rhetorically. "Because an outdoor show is special." Peter values families' long history of attending the musical in the park. He relishes the experience getting there "three hours early" and seeing "families coming in laying their blankets for their show." They approach him "and tell me their stories about, 'Yeah, I've been taking my kids here . . . This is where my grandfather took me when I was a little kid.'" They tell him, "'I've been coming here for the past thirty years or so [. . .] I never miss it.'"

As much Peter values the theatre's longevity, he's mostly proud that it's free: "The reason why I do it's because . . . it's free because there are so many people who cannot afford theatre, you know . . . there are so many families who I talk to, you know, who say, like, this is the only theatre they go to . . . it's for those people who cannot have theatre." ZTP is "ingrained in the community because it's free," he concluded. In its fifty-fourth season, *The Sound of Music* played to Zilker's largest audiences ever, around forty thousand people over thirty-two weekend nights in June, July, and August. Each night's performance took in $8,000 to $9,000, when $3,000 to $4,000 is more typical. Some shows earned $10,000.

The Zilker Theatre Production's Director
of *The Sound of Music*

In Mill Valley, Sara's team researches musicals and selects a show that they present to the board for approval, and then she hires the director. In contrast, Zilker hires the package of director and show. They invite a number of directors to pitch projects, and that year, they selected M. Scott Tatum and his concept for *The Sound of Music*.

Directing the big outdoor show was Scott's first Zilker directing gig, though he was the lighting designer on two previous ZTP shows and worked in the park's theatre as a teenager. A longtime Austin resident and high school theatre teacher and director, Scott brought a self-reflexive, "progressive educator's view" to the process. "Everyone has those weird memories of the show, either they did it once before, or their aunt made them watch [the movie] during Thanksgiving," he said. This musical is "storytelling on a grand scale. It's theatre that can't fit into other spaces in Austin." He and his collaborators, many of whom he'd worked with before, "sat down and tried to get the big ideas, the big moments, and we made them the tent pole moments of the show." Then, they made "it very beautiful." At the same time, Scott intended to give their production more emotional depth. The script is "super-efficient," he told me, so they wanted to "find moments to make it more real."

Scott also wanted to bring newcomers into the ZSM family, so he organized an extensive outreach effort to local schools, churches, and community theatres, advertising auditions and other ways for people to get involved backstage. A month before auditions, Scott taught a free workshop on the basics of auditioning, which the organization continues to do. A record-breaking 380 people tried out for the show. As the production drew closer, they held set-painting workshops open to everyone. Again, these practices remain a part of Zilker's programs.

Scott cast the show with both Austin regulars and actors new to Zilker, and the multiracial, multiethnic cast reflected Austin's diverse community. Maria was played by a half-Persian woman; the Captain, an African American man; Elsa, a Korean American woman. The children, nuns, and smaller roles were played by mostly white and some Latino actors.[49] But the production didn't stress race. "It's a love story and about how music reawakens this man's ability to love," explained Scott. "It's a story about the arts."

Like everyone I spoke to in Austin, Scott remarked on the local roots and the significance of no-cost attendance. "It's made in Austin with Austin talent. It's an Austin institution. And it's free," he said.

The Zilker Theatre Production's Musical Director
of *The Sound of Music*

Co-music director for vocals, rehearsal pianist, and a pit player, Dustin Struhall prioritized the music-making above all. He dismissed what some see as *The Sound of Music*'s excessive sentimentality and stressed its value for singers. Golden Age musicals "are a good training ground," he told me. "Especially because Broadway is so pop now, what I like about doing things like *The Sound of Music* and *Carousel* and all these Golden Age of Broadway shows . . . is the legit style of singing." He continued, "I think it's imperative that people are exposed to that level of repertoire so that they really get a grounded sense of where their instrument is." He wanted each actor to work on their unique sound: "With younger ones, we're in the *Glee* generation, they all think it's that autotuned sound . . . and people think that's what they're supposed to sound like. And that's not the voice."

Dustin also wanted to use the songs to deepen the characters and their relationships. "I spent a lot of time working with [the nuns]," he said, "building them up as a group." He described one rehearsal in which he asked the actors to "share about who they are, as people in general." He was stunned to find out that "they all volunteer! They all help special needs people in one way or another, these real people, these ladies, are all involved in some charitable form in their life." Dustin "wanted them to bond," he said, "because I know how important those relationships are to making a good sound." Like Scott, and like director Jay Manley in California, Dustin anticipated a rough move from indoor rehearsal room to outdoor theatre: "As we got to the park, and it was easy to get sort of spacey, I really used those tools of 'what have we built together?' to bring them back together. Why are you out here? What is your purpose?"

The Zilker Summer Musical's Actors

In addition to telling the story clearly, delivering the expected stage pictures, and singing the hummable Richard Rodgers's melodies beautifully, the production, according to the creative team, should reflect Austin's progressive political leanings by giving the characters an edge. Max, played by Neal Gibson, was clearly gay, for example. Neal explained, "The main thing I tried to avoid was having Max come off as a caricature, so I tried to not play the role for the laughs . . . Just throw out the 'zingers' conversationally." He added that he and the actor playing Franz the butler created an erotic subtext between them.

Leslie Hollingsworth, a regular Austin actor and frequent ZTP performer, gave one of the sharpest performances of Elsa I've ever seen—nuanced and funny and smart. Her Elsa obviously detested the children and resented that she had to be nice to them. Because this production included the wonderful trio with Georg and Elsa and Max, "No Way to Stop It," which was cut from the movie and subsequently from many stage productions, Max and Elsa had bigger parts, so Leslie could develop Elsa as apolitical, self-centered, and nasty.

As for Maria, casting Michelle Haché put a welcome new spin on the role. Michelle is not a typical ingénue—she is dark-haired, a little older and physically strong, and trained as an opera singer. She played Maria as forceful and not in the least naive. "Maria's a teacher," Scott said. Michelle added, "She knows what's going on and she knows what is going to work for these kids. I think it's a very different Maria than a lot of people are used to." Michelle described her entrance, "I come across the hill and it's like, 'wait a minute, she's not blonde, and she's also not a tiny little stick figure of a girl.'" In the first few scenes, she said, audiences are "kind of quiet at first, and people are kind of trying to figure out, 'well, she's not blonde, he [Captain von Trapp] is African American,' but by the time we get to that point, they're like, down." In contrast the way the Captain is typically portrayed, Joshua Denning played him as gentler and more feminine. This offbeat spin on the show reflected the diversity and "Keep Austin Weird" philosophy of the city.

All of the actors talked about the rare and unique performance experience at Zilker. Performing outdoors "does require exaggerating one's movements and gestures somewhat so they will read at the top of the hillside," said Neal. "Quite frankly, it can feel awkward at times (for example, when you're twenty feet away from the person you're supposed to be having a normal conversation with)." Scott noted that the "conditions in which they perform are difficult," but the actors stressed the rewards more than the challenges. Leslie said, "It was such a great experience to, number one, be able to perform for so many audience members, which I think we as actors in community theatre don't really get an opportunity to do very often . . . [and] the family environment and the camaraderie that comes with Zilker is just amazing."

During intermission, the von Trapp kids and chorus members fanned out among the audience with colorful buckets to take donations of coins, dollar bills, twenties, or whatever spectators could offer. After the curtain call, the whole cast lined up along the front edge of the stage, money buckets in hand again, to greet the audience and take photos with them. ZTP theatre-makers are dedicated to the gift it gives to Austin. Leslie told me, "You start to become very passionate about what it stands for, being able to provide such a high-quality theatrical production." Costume designer Susan Branch Towne, who works at Zach Theatre, added, "It's a totally unique experience for good and for bad, but I keep coming back to it because it reminds me of why I loved it in the first place."

The Zilker Summer Musical's Audience

Audiences from all over Austin, of all races and ages, flock to see the ZSM. Some come once over the six-week run as a special occasion, but many return repeatedly during Austin's long, hot summer. I spoke to people who never go to the theatre otherwise and have been attending the ZSM for years and years. They see it as a big community event and an important way to expose their children to theatre. Scott described it as "embracing family time—whatever your family is."

I wandered around before the show started, tape recorder in hand, to gather some stories. I spoke to one Latina mother, who attended the show every night of the summer with her two daughters, aged four and six. "They love coming out here with a picnic and seeing all the kids on stage, and now they know all the songs, too," she said. A older white man said, "I come almost every year, and we come with another family, and now the family's grown and we have daughter-in-laws and son-in-laws and grandchildren—and we always get this front spot . . . 2 is usually when we come . . . we usually tag team, and we go jump in the springs and come back . . . [We've been coming for] at least fifteen years, maybe longer." A white woman in her twenties told me, "My favorite, favorite was *Guys and Dolls*, which I came five times for, I was just a *Guys and Dolls* groupie." Neal recounted that during the meet-and-greet after one show, "A mother and her little girl came up to Leslie and me. The kid seemed to be almost frozen, her eyes were wide open in amazement (or fear?) . . . The mother said, 'Please forgive her; she's never seen a live play before and she's having a hard time grasping that you're real people.'"

Dustin noted another contribution of the show that few people think about: hearing a natural human voice. He said, "I think it's important for Zilker to be around . . . so that people understand what the real thing sounds like—that it's not just what's on TV. That it's not what they hear on their CDs. That when you hear something live, here are the imperfections in it . . . it's an opportunity for people to see what real singing is, and what live performance is."

A middle-aged white woman put the experience in a larger context, explaining, "I love the idea of the community, the kids sitting right behind us all enamored . . . so the idea of living in a community that to me is that vital, that the family is here, and that they're swimming and coming here, it's unlike other cities—it's part of the ecosystem that exists right here, it's not just the show."

And a few people exclaimed, "It's 100 frickin' degrees, and look at all these people!"

Unlike the Mountain Play, the ZSM is performed at night, beginning after dusk and ending when the big Texas sky is filled with stars, as people make their way back to their cars by flashlight, hauling damp blankets, empty beer coolers, and sleeping children. Even though it's easy to get to Zilker, spectators have to commit to a long evening to attend the play. They often arrive as early as 4:30 p.m. (or earlier) to nab a good location on the hillside. They leave a blanket to mark their place, then walk around, have a picnic dinner, or go for a swim in Barton Springs. The show begins at 8:30, and *The Sound of Music* was over at 11:45 p.m.

The nighttime performance requires more personnel than a daytime show like the Mountain Play: a lighting designer, a master electrician to hang and focus lights, and several follow-spot operators, and of course, there are many more cues for the stage manager to call. The darkness also has a way of focusing the audience's perspective, shrinking one's sense of the space. As night falls, the southwestern heat subsides ever so slightly, and the actors and make-believe world seem to move closer to the audience.

Zilker toes its own blurry line between community theatre and "professional" theatre. Scott described it as "somewhere in between, with aspirations to be more." Joshua Denning called it "community theatre on a grand scale" and appreciated its accessibility: free theatre for homeless people and their children. Leslie said, "I call it 'community theatre' because it is literally artists in Austin, performing for Austin audiences." Producer Peter answered with an intentional contradiction: "Our goal is [for] it to be professional, but not be professional," by which he meant high quality and accessible for everyone. Neal said, "The majority of the audience for the Zilker Summer Musical could care less what category it fits into. What really matters is that every year there are thousands of people who have never seen a live musical, and/or who attended a previous summer musical but have never seen a musical theatre production anywhere else."

In the end, it's impossible to overestimate the importance of the show being free.

The Open Air Theatre, Titusville, New Jersey

A year earlier and 1,725 miles northeast of Austin, on a comfortably chilly late September night, I drove twenty minutes from my house along winding country roads to get to the Open Air Theatre in Washington Crossing State

Park. Except for the small sign, which I blew by once before retracing my route to find the park entrance, nothing suggested a fully functioning theatre in the woods. As soon as I passed the ranger's booth at the entrance, which warned about bear sightings, ticks, mosquitoes, and what to do in case of a thunderstorm, I joined a long line of cars in front me, slowly snaking their way down a sharply curving, gently sloped, tiny one-lane road. We were already deep in the woods. Crickets chirped and frogs croaked.

The road suddenly opened onto a wide clearing with an expansive grassy area that was the makeshift parking lot, with cars arranged more haphazardly than in straight lines. I pulled in alongside a minivan with one bumper sticker that read "My dog is my driver" and another, "LBI"—referring to Long Beach Island, a famous Jersey Shore destination. The parking was adjacent to the theatre. A small building on the right housed restrooms with proper flushing toilets (portable toilets, though plentiful and clean, were the only restroom facilities at both the Mountain Play and Zilker) and a ticket window to the left, which was the back side of the concessions hut.

Ten people stood in line in front of me. I handed my ticket, which I bought online, to the friendly volunteer mom, who was busy greeting people she knew (which seemed to be everyone) and telling her kids what they could and couldn't buy for snacks (popcorn yes, Coke no). I looked down and took in the venue from the top: an eight-hundred-seat concrete amphitheatre built within a natural dell. Wide cement steps led down to the stage, which was a wooden platform backed by a steep, densely wooded hill. Near the stage, house right, was a small building that looked like it might be a dressing room. At the back of the house, also to the right, was a small structure with the light and sound boards. Down on the stage, the set was simple: a few flats painted gray to suggest the abbey in the musical's opening scene. There were plenty of seats, which were wooden slatted benches with backs, and I walked down to sit near the front. Most of my neighbors brought stadium cushions or extra blankets to pad the hard surface. Yet again, I attended a performance with rituals I'd yet to learn. By the time the show started, all of the seats around me were taken by families with kids (including toddlers and babies), older couples, and groups of teenagers.

Just as dusk turned to night, the strings of bulbs that illuminated the audience area dimmed and bright lights came up on the set. A full orchestra's sound flowed from big speakers standing on platforms on either side of the stage. This was the second of six performances over two weekends. Lauren Brader, an Open Air Theatre regular, walked onto the platform and began to sing, "My day in the hills . . ." On every side of her, thick woods were visible, as if the force of Maria's bold spirit had opened a path in the dense forest.

The Open Air Theatre's Story

It all started when Hurricanes Connie and Diane destroyed Steel Run Dam in Washington Crossing State Park in 1955.[50] In order to rebuild the dam, park workers had to cut down swaths of trees on the nearby hillside. After reconstruction was completed in the fall of 1963, park superintendent Dirk van Dommelen and some locals interested in getting involved with the park toured the new dell and "saw how it presented itself as an amphitheatre."[51] These concerned citizens organized as the Washington Crossing Park Citizens Committee (WCPCC) and quickly approved a proposal for a the-atre. After all, they felt, a theatre would not only expand cultural program-ming and increase tourism, but also generate revenue that could be used to improve park facilities and fund other park activities.

The WCPCC members found creative ways to equip this new, somewhat improvised performance venue. They arranged benches, folding chairs, and logs with boards for seats; they made a wood-chip stage; they rigged generators in the trees to power the lights and sound; and they erected tents for dressing rooms.[52] They partnered with the Pennington Players for the first production, George Bernard Shaw's *The Devil's Disciple,* which opened to a packed house on July 24, 1964. The Washington Crossing Open Air Theatre (OAT) was born.

Through the 1960s and 1970s, the renamed Washington Crossing Association (WCA) presented concerts by high school choirs and bands, string quartets, and jazz groups, operas, Revolutionary War–based plays, and community theatre, including the Pennington Players' *Plain and Fancy,* the first Broadway musical presented at OAT. To accommodate the show's orchestra, a platform was erected over the waterless Steel Run Creek—what one local journalist called "a natural orchestra pit"—that separated the audi-ence from the stage.[53] Low attendance for concerts compelled the WCA to program exclusively theatre by community groups, who paid a performance fee and earned a split of any profit. The WCA covered the costs of news-paper ads, capital equipment, supplies, insurance and liability plans, wages, and refreshment stand supplies and used its portion of profits for other park projects or theatre renovations, such as building a proper stage in 1967.[54]

By 1977, Jack Rees, then in his tenth year as OAT's general manager, knew to schedule "four popular musicals a summer to break even" and that "musicals with outdoor settings do best."[55] From the 1980s through the early 2000s, most seasons featured one Shakespeare play, one to two operettas, and three to five Broadway musicals. Rees retired in 1986, and the WCA hired Kitty Peace, who programmed many of the community theatre companies that now perform at Kelsey.[56] (Kitty Peace is now Kitty Getlik, Kelsey's artistic director, in Chapter 4.)

In 1991, the relationship between the state of New Jersey and the WCA became strained when the state decided to formalize the license agreement for the WCA to operate the OAT.[57] The WCA felt this was unnecessary, since it had been running the theatre successfully for over twenty-five years. The agreement required the WCA to have a detailed management plan in place, which was not feasible because the organization was mainly operated by volunteers. After some negotiations, though, they signed the contract.

In 2000, the situation worsened. The state, under financial strain, mandated that the WCA pay $13,000 annually to rent the space. Previously, the WCA had paid the state $50 at most for a permit fee. The OAT might bring in $13,000 in a good season, but as a weather-dependent operation, it could not guarantee this figure. Kitty Peace held off the state for two years, but after she resigned as general manager in 2003, her successors signed the state's contract. They were unable to fulfill the agreement during the next two seasons, so in 2005, the state reopened bidding to operate the theatre. In March 2006, in a final desperate attempt to maintain control of the facility, the WCA placed a full-page ad in *The Trentonian* in which it asked the state to not raise its rent by 30,000 percent, noting its theatre had fifteen thousand patrons and was "the largest and longest established community theatre of its kind."[58] But the state ignored their plea, the nearby Bucks County Playhouse won the bid, and the WCA lost control of the space.[59] In 2008, the WCA officially disbanded.

After a few years in the space, the Bucks County Playhouse was caught failing to pay royalties and was kicked out of the park midseason. From 2010 to 2017, the Downtown Performing Arts Center (DPAC) produced shows at OAT.[60] DPAC presented Broadway musicals (as many as thirteen per summer) and children's shows. DPAC reignited the OAT tradition, and OAT, in return, helped DPAC achieve notoriety as a top-notch local performing arts organization. Eventually DPAC raised enough funds to move to its own indoor theatre and left OAT in the fall of 2017 to start Music Mountain Theater in nearby Lambertville.

In 2018, the OAT concession was open for bidding once again; the concession cost $4,500 plus insurance and other fees. As of July 2018, no shows were planned.

The Open Air Theatre's Producer

In 2010, DPAC took over the concession of the OAT in the park, which meant they paid a set amount to rent and run the theatre and kept the earnings from ticket sales and food. The park service maintained control of the space, though, helpfully quelling the theatre-makers' anxiety about environmental issues.

The year-round organization resembles other family-owned afterschool programs for children and teens, led by an ambitious and charismatic team: Ginny Brennan, her son Jordan, and his husband Louis Palena. Ginny works as producer and the two men direct, design, and choreograph. All three might be considered backstage divas (see Chapter 2). The school-year classes, which include jazz, tap, audition techniques, and musical theatre scene study, are geared toward kids, but the thirteen-show (twenty if you include the children's daytime shows) summer season in the park includes adult actors, too, many of whom are members of their resident company and others who also perform with various companies at Kelsey or other community theatres during the year.

DPAC presents a summer stock season at the OAT with a new production every two weeks. It's fast and furious and a phenomenal learning experience for those involved with more than one show. They hold auditions in the spring for the entire season, with the whole rehearsal schedule already laid out. Actors can specify which shows they're auditioning for; their choices are sometimes determined by which shows interest them, but more typically by practical constraints like vacation schedules or summer child care. Some actors perform in as many as four or five of the summer's shows. The season of *The Sound of Music* also included *Hairspray*, *Rent*, and *Once Upon a Mattress*.[61]

For the most part, they program light and family-friendly shows, and they need to turn a profit. "We haven't been able to sell plays, you know," said Ginny. "People want big musicals, they do. Musicals let people say, 'I'm gonna sit back and I'm gonna listen to the music and relax.'"

The unpredictable New Jersey weather and other outdoor challenges factor into their season selection and set and costume design. "We were limited to performances that we could get in and out of the rain quickly," Ginny said. "We had to deal with the humidity ruining our equipment, bugs, and mosquitoes, and all kinds of stuff." They regularly got rained out, and one night they had a snake in the concession stand. Ginny told me, "As wonderful as the space is [when] the weather is perfect, there's a little chill in the air . . . it's great. But when it's hot, or there's a thunderstorm any minute and you have to make a quick decision . . . Boom. Do we start the show?"

Weather also affects the bottom line when performances have to be canceled. As Wayne Irons of the Pennington Players explained, "Working at the Open Air Theatre was challenging financially. . . if the show didn't go on, we didn't make any revenue for that performance. The rights-holders would generally refund the royalties for a canceled performance, but all the other costs of the production then had to be amortized over the smaller revenue."

The Open Air Theatre's Directors of *The Sound of Music*

Like all of DPAC's shows at the OAT, Louis directed the book scenes, designed the set, and was tech director for *The Sound of Music*. Jordan choreographed the musical numbers, worked with the kids on their scenes, and designed the costumes. Their technical freedom was limited not only by the weather but by the schedule—a new show up every two weeks. "The set has to be interchangeable and multipurpose," Jordan said.[62] For this reason, the most they could do was "reference what [the place] looked like" and evoke the "time period," explained Louis.

In terms of casting, Louis was committed to "stay true to what it was intended to be." He calls himself a "traditionalist": families must look like they could be related, and he wanted the kids to "fit by height." "It's important to represent the family with historical accuracy," he told me.

Auditions are open, but since they have an ongoing community of actors, both kids and adults, they're not casting cold. Still, they said, *The Sound of Music* was only their second season (of seven seasons plus a few weeks) in the space, and they hadn't yet built a reputation among actors in the community. "If we could do it again now," Louis said, "We would be able to and would cast more people of color."

They "needed seven solid kids," but casting them was easy because we "have a lot of talent." Jordan hoped to give kids with whom they work during the school year an opportunity to perform, but they "cast the best kids to have the best show." He spent more time working with the youngsters during the speedy two-week rehearsal period, and they "expected the adults to know what they're doing." The actors received their scripts in advance and learned their lines before the first rehearsal.

Working in the outdoor space offered opportunities and challenges. It's "magical," Jordan said, and something "you can't get from indoor space," which they tried to take advantage of. For the party scene at the end of Act 1, for example, they allowed the woods that are visible at the back of the stage to serve as the backdrop behind the von Trapp villa's patio. You "have to divert people's attention away from nature or encompass it," Louis told me. Since most of the show takes place in the home or the abbey, they built and painted flats to represent the indoor settings. In addition, Louis said, because "the space is vast, you have to help the audience know where to focus." You "have to paint distinct pictures."

The Open Air Theatre's Actors

All of the actors who perform at the OAT are volunteers, "so they are all doing it for fun," said Jordan.[63] In this way, the work/leisure dynamic replicates that of community theatre (see Chapter 4). In addition, to be inclusive, they cast as large a chorus as they can manage, which a show like *The Sound of Music* allows. Their production included twenty adults and twenty-five children, who packed the small stage in the big production numbers like the "So Long, Farewell" party scene.

Actors who do more than one show in the summer must learn the material fast, work on their characters on their own, and hold two or three shows in their heads at once. Jessica Dowling, a recent college graduate, with a musical theatre major, played Liesl in the production when she was in high school, and her younger sister played Marta. "I loved every minute of it," she said. "The unpredictable weather was a challenge, though." *The Sound of Music* took place in late September, and one night it was unusually cold. "Gretl's teeth were chattering and we threw a sweater on her. We were freezing." On other nights, if it rained in the middle of the show, they would stop and wait for twenty minutes. For one performance of *Annie*, she said, it rained so hard that they took off the mics, put away the sound system, and finished the show singing as loud as they could, getting soaked. For another show, *Heathers*, the actors pulled out umbrellas and kept going.

As a young actor, Jessica credits her experience at the OAT with "learning to stay composed." "I'm deathly afraid of bugs" and during one performance of *The Sound of Music*, there was a "huge spider on my dress." She just tried to stay calm until the actor playing Rolf brushed it off.

Jessica was involved with DPAC for years, so she had many close friends there, including adult actors whom she looked up to. She knew people in all of the shows and every night in the audience. Many people introduce their children to theatre there because, she said, "Kids love it. They love being outdoors. They can yell out and it's fine. They feel they're a part of it. And they believed we were the characters!" Another actor, according to his usher and all-around-volunteer wife, "got dragged into doing shows because our kids do it." Now the whole family will "help build the set and they really feel part of it." His wife called him my "diva husband."

Only one thing is missing from this welcoming community event: musicians. DPAC rents licensed orchestral accompaniment recordings rather than rely on a live orchestra, which saves considerable rehearsal time, shrinks the number of people involved in the (already populous) production, and eliminates the expense of hiring musicians (since in this area, they're typically paid a stipend to perform in community theatre shows). Given the uncertainty of the weather, it also gets rid of one more area of stress and anxiety when it rains and thunderstorms.

The Open Air Theatre's Audience

The OAT attracts a large and regular community of spectators, as well as out-of-town visitors, people on vacation, park visitors who happen to see that a musical is being performed, relatives or friends of someone in the show, and fans who come to see a specific musical that they know and love.

A few African American spectators sat among the mostly white audience, and there were all ages, from cradled babies to people in their late seventies. Many older adults were there with kids and grandkids, and I saw couples, families, and groups of tweens and teens. Like the other two theatres, it was wonderful to see such a diverse age range. During intermission, huge lights illuminated the whole space, and everyone lined up to buy popcorn, Philly soft pretzels, nachos, candy, and ice cream novelties.

OAT offers a subscription series—a ten-show punch card—to encourage repeat customers through the summer. For many in the area, seeing shows at

OAT is a regular part of their summer routine, not unlike going to a community swimming pool or Little League baseball. The season-long audience—whatever motivates their attendance in the first place—forms their own community from late May through September, and many conversations revolve around how many and which shows they've seen and how this one compares to previous ones. They also remember actors and readily compare their performances across musicals. As one woman passed by the raffle table at the end of intermission, the volunteer selling tickets exclaimed, "Another good show!" and the spectator nodded in agreement. Many of the kids and teens wore OAT sweatshirts and gossiped knowingly about the show and the actors and the other plays that season.

Because the venue is smaller, more intimate, and more enclosed than the Mountain Play or Zilker, and because many in the audience are repeaters and know each other, the community feeling is strong. Though the rituals of seeing the show were less complicated than at the Mountain Play or Zilker, I felt my outsiderness more keenly there.

Single-ticket spectators have different stories. One couple in their seventies, for example, told me before the show started that the last time they came to the OAT was twenty years ago when they saw *Jesus Christ Superstar*. They recalled that the leading actor had laryngitis (that's all they remembered about the show, they said). They came to see *The Sound of Music* because a friend's "very talented" relative was in the show. A teenage girl told me that she came with her parents—their first time at the OAT—because they "wanted to do something fun before I go back to school next week" as a high school junior, and *The Sound of Music* is "one of my mom's favorite plays." Her family sees theatre in New York sometimes and "this play isn't as spectacular but it's good!" She doesn't participate in theatre at school, she said, but she always goes to see the plays. "It's fun to watch people pretending they are someone else," she said with a big grin.

Like the Mountain Play and Zilker, the OAT seemed the perfect way to introduce children to theatre. Small children were unconstrained, free to get up and walk around. The five-year-old girl sitting next to me knew all of the songs and sang along the whole time. Ginny said that "you'll see someone with a stroller up on top with a little baby who's crying while Daddy's sitting down in front of the stage with their four-year-old child. And they don't have to leave the theatre, they don't have to get up . . . the little child can run around a little bit and still get the experience. So, it works, it really works on a lot of levels."

The OAT seats 650 people, a little more than half as many as Zilker and one-fifth the number at the Mountain Play. In addition, the theatre is set in a deep dell, so it seems smaller than its capacity. It felt completely different watching this *Sound of Music* than seeing Zilker's production from close up for Act 1 and then, for Act 2, adjacent to the booth at the top of the hill with a thousand people spread all over the hillside between me and the stage. The Mountain Play, too, felt vast, especially with the bay visible beyond the flats of the set. At the OAT, there was something very odd and beautiful about the fifty actors crammed onto the small platform stage in colorful clothes waltzing to Richard Rodgers's music played by a full (taped) orchestra with huge beech, red maple, and cedar trees around them. When I looked up, I couldn't see many stars that night, but I did see rows of lights from planes—we sat below the flight path to Newark airport. City and country, nature and culture, Broadway music and crickets.

The DPAC, as the producing organization at the OAT, navigates the same labeling challenges that the Mountain Play and Zilker do. Are they professional? Are they a community theatre? As Ginny said, "We really want to be a professional theatre with ties to the community." She went on, "When I think of community theatre, I think of people who have either never been on stage or they were in high school and they loved it and it gives them an opportunity to perform . . . we look at ourselves as offering professional theatre yet being community-based, if that makes sense." Indeed it does.

"Climb Ev'ry Mountain"

Just as all three productions took advantage of the natural setting for Maria's entrance, they did as well for the iconic ending. At the Mountain Play, the actors playing Maria, Captain von Trapp, and the seven children exited upstage right, climbing up a rocky path toward a well-known hiking and mountain biking trail that eventually, six miles later, arrives in the town of Mill Valley. The actors in the Zilker production took the same route as Maria's entrance, stage left, and walked toward the hiking trail, soon out of the range of the spotlight as the orchestra played the last few notes. The OAT production had the actors exit behind the platform stage and up a steep hill with no trail, forging a path through the dark brush, with shadows cast by the spotlight shining onto and between the huge trees. It was impossible not to be moved by these stagings in nature. Each production offered a fresh understanding of the end of *The Sound of Music*.

Perhaps more than any musical in the classic Broadway canon, *The Sound of Music* retains its popularity, year after year, generation after generation. The producers at all three theatres told me that it's their most requested show, every single year. "Do Re Mi" and "Edelweiss" are part of America's cultural fabric.

But the experience is ultimately local, specific, and intimate, bound to the place, the people, and their local practices. Outdoors, on Mt. Tam overlooking the bay, or at Zilker on the hillside above Barton Springs, or in the deep forest at the Open Air Theatre, you can't forget where you are. The food (cheese and crackers vs. burritos vs. popcorn) and drink (wine vs. beer vs. soda) that people bring (or buy), the ways they interact with family and friends, their conversations and points of reference about local events, politics, and especially the weather saturate the event. All three cities value the outdoors and the arts, and audiences and theatre-makers express the community's values in a precise and visceral way. Mountain Play participants talks about their love for the mountain and share stories about hiking, camping, biking, or eating pancakes at the West Point Inn. Mill Valley places a premium on supporting the arts and asserting its cultural independence from San Francisco, and spectators are proud of this long-standing, unique nature-culture phenomenon. Zilker participants talk about their love for the park and for Barton Springs, and about the importance of the summer musical being free, open, and accessible, as it has been since 1958. Open Air Theatre spectators talk about the wonder of seeing a musical outdoors under the stars just thirty-five miles from Philadelphia.

The local also manifests itself in participants' lack of concern with Broadway (that is, the actual place). Audiences compare the show to community theatres and high school productions that they've seen. Artists in Mill Valley mention the community colleges that trained many of them; in Austin, they note Zach Theatre, which employs some of the designers and actors; at Washington Crossing, they talk about high schools and other community theatres that form a rich and vibrant musical theatre scene. Broadway is neither a destination nor a marker of professional achievement. These theatres converse with their long legacies of productions, with the memories of the locally known public figures, with the histories of the cities—Mill Valley, Austin, Washington Crossing—and how they've changed over the years. Outdoor summer musical theatre is a living organism in the local musical theatre ecosystem. And yet, even though these places in California and Texas and New Jersey don't look to Broadway, they sustain musical theatre by reproducing the repertoire. Most importantly, perhaps, they grow future audiences in the children who wander around or sing along. After all, the hills are alive with the sound of music.

Figure 6.1. A girl walks to rehearsal for the bunk show musical at summer camp.

6

Musical Theatre at Girls' Jewish Summer Camps

A hush falls over the audience as the house lights dim in the theatre barn at Attean Lake Camp in Maine.[1] A small follow spot takes a moment to find its mark: a twelve-year-old girl dressed in a top hat and tails, black leggings, and sneakers who stands at one corner of the arena-arranged space. A piano pings a minor key arpeggio twice and then repeats the final note twice again, offering the girl her starting pitch. She takes a breath, steps forward into the acting area, and begins to sing "Pure Imagination," the first song from the Anthony Newley and Leslie Bricusse musical *Willy Wonka and the Chocolate Factory*: "Come with me / And you'll be / In a world of pure imagination." As she moves along the edge of the space, she gains confidence. Her thin, airy voice gets louder, and she rotates her body with every line she sings, allowing the audience on all four sides to see her face as well as the long dark ponytail down her back. The light spilling from the follow spot reveals other actors, all twelve-year-old girls assembled in tableaux for the first few scenes of the musical: a grouping of "boys" at a candy store where they're buying chocolates in hopes of discovering a Golden Ticket; Charlie's powder-haired grandparents under mounds of quilts, and the "boy" Charlie and his parents flanking the bed. The actors sit, stand, or lie on makeshift set pieces of painted cardboard and furniture. As the Narrator character moves and sings, "If you want to view paradise / Simply look around and view it," the spotlight catches the audience: two hundred girls aged seven to fifteen, packed onto backless benches, wearing identical logo'd T-shirts and shorts, their sunburnt faces scrubbed and alert.

The building is a windowless wooden structure, with a high ceiling and four banks of risers. Open doorways on two sides look out to a purple night sky bursting with stars above a pristine landscape, dotted with small buildings and then, toward a large lake, a row of tented cabins in a neat line. Farther away and out of sight are rows of tennis courts, playing fields, horse stables, and a riding ring. Along the lake's edge, a dock floats, buoys mark out swimming lanes, and a line of canoes sit pulled onto the shore. In every

Beyond Broadway. Stacy Wolf, Oxford University Press (2020). © Oxford University Press.
DOI: 10.1093/oso/9780190639525.001.0001

direction in the distance is the pine tree forest. The setting is beautiful, both parklike and wild (Figure 6.1).

This performance of *Willy Wonka* took place at Attean Lake Camp, a private, non-orthodox, Jewish girls' seven-week sleepaway summer camp in Greenville, Maine. Attean Lake Camp was founded in 1917 and is one of a number of camps dating from the early twentieth century that dot the shorelines around the deep, cold, clear waters of Moosehead Lake and its tributaries in west central Maine. I spent a week visiting Attean Lake Camp and nearby Camp Holeb, Camp Kineo, and Camp Clearwater, all located within twenty minutes' drive of each other along the shore of Moosehead Lake, the largest lake in Maine, to see how musical theatre is produced and consumed at girls' Jewish summer camps.

As I discussed in the introduction, I went to Jewish summer camp as a child (and later worked at one as a counselor), but those were coed summer camps close to our home in Maryland. (My parents also met at summer camp, when my mom was directing a production of *Babes in Arms* and my father stopped by rehearsal to deliver some boys in his bunk to be in the show. But that's another story.) There was something exotic to me about Maine and about all-girls' camps, and, more than that, the fact, which I learned before visiting, that all of the girls were required to be in a show. Who forces girls to do musicals, and how does that work out?

The girls in *Willy Wonka*, like all of the girls who spend their summers at Attean Lake Camp, perform in one musical each year with their bunk—the group of girls of the same age who live together. The "bunk show" is a required activity at camp, along with soccer, tennis, sailing, arts and crafts, twice-daily swimming, and other sports and nature-oriented activities. The production of *Willy Wonka* was the fourth in a summer of six different musicals, one presented each week for all of the campers, counselors, and staff. The cast of *Willy Wonka* had been the audience for the previous weeks' shows, when the bunks of girls aged thirteen, ten, and nine performed their musicals, *Once Upon a Mattress*, *Sleeping Beauty*, and *The Jungle Book*. They would be the audience for the next two shows, as yet unannounced to sustain the excitement of the imminent surprise. Though the performance changes weekly, the rituals that surround the event have been the same since the camp opened more than a hundred years ago.

Musical theatre at girls' Jewish summer camps in Maine differs from some of the other venues we visit in this book in two ways. First, musical theatre at summer camp is embedded in a larger experience, a larger institution. In this way, it approximates school, where musical theatre is not a separate, independent entity but takes place within the larger school setting. Second, the participants here are bound not only by their engagement with the show but also by their similar identities. Third, summer camp is a closed and private setting. The show exists only for campers and staff, no outsiders allowed—except for me, a temporary guest.

When I was making my plans to visit, Stephanie Rosenthal, the director of Camp Holeb, told me that there would be no reason for me to arrive earlier than Wednesday to observe rehearsals for a Saturday evening show. "If you come on Monday or Tuesday, there won't be anything for you to see," she said. At the time, I was confused. At any other theatre that I knew, whether professional, university, community, or school, musicals typically rehearse for weeks if not months.[2] How could they prepare for a show in four days? That was my introduction to bunk show musicals—that they are produced at an alarming speed: five days from page to stage. I soon learned that the same schedule gets repeated each week of the summer, but that each week's process is artistically and emotionally unique because of the specific girls involved and the musical they're doing.

I drove along tiny winding roads shaded by huge pine trees, trying to find places not visible on my GPS. It was Maine and it was July and the days were very long.

Jewish Summer Camp and Broadway

Girls' Jewish summer camps in Maine seem to be far away from Broadway, from New York City, from culture and civilization. They're farther from a city than anywhere else we visit in this book. Unlike high schools or afterschool programs, summer camps might not register as hotbeds of musical theatre. Summer camp emphasizes sports and nature and the simple life without electricity and cellphones. The image of Broadway musicals performed in the woods of Maine seems contradictory. And yet, musicals are central to the experiential project of summer camp, and thousands of musicals are performed at summer camps of all kinds across the United States each year, forming a kind of cottage industry of youth amateur musical theatre production.

Jewish summer camp maintains a close association with Broadway because of Jews' contribution to the Broadway repertoire as composers, lyricists, and librettists, and as producers, directors, and choreographers. Jewish summer camps were the incubators for the early creative activity of numerous Broadway musical theatre artists, including Stephen Sondheim, who went to Androscoggin in Wayne, Maine, and Leonard Bernstein and Adolph Green, who met, became friends, and wrote musicals at Camp Onota in Pittsfield, Massachusetts.[3] The Broadway musical repertoire now serves as the source material for musicals at summer camps.

Other Jewish artists had memorable musical theatre experiences at summer camp. The novelist Chaim Potok, for example, author of the monumental novels *The Chosen*, *The Promise*, and *My Name is Asher Lev*, described how, in the 1930s, his parents were too poor to pay for summer camp. Like many Lower East Side parents, they were so frantic to get the boy out of the hot, steamy, and dirty city, where polio threatened children in the neighborhood's close quarters, that they sent him without hesitation to a free, non-Kosher summer camp sponsored by the local community center. He returned there for many years as a camper, then as a counselor, then as a division head at Ramah Poconos, and eventually as a camp director. At the end of a beautifully elegiac tribute to summer camp, Potok recounts the high point: "The time my senior campers in the Nyack Camp Ramah put on *Porgy and Bess* in Hebrew."[4]

Like afterschool program and high school musicals, this activity at summer camp holds value for both art-making and identity-making. These rough-edged performances allude to Broadway, haunted by professional productions or film musicals with which many campers are familiar. The girls' participation in theatre as both performers and audiences shapes them as engaged and knowledgeable spectators and fans (and possibly artists) who often go on to attend and support professional theatre. They learn how musicals are made by doing them, and they see many musicals and learn the Broadway repertoire over their years at camp. They acquire cultural capital and are disciplined and socialized into being attentive and enthusiastic spectators from a young age.

Musical theatre production at summer camp also supports the formation of positive (upper-middle-class) Jewish girlhood. Many of the skills that the girls acquire as they rehearse for their bunk show dovetail with those that summer camp espouses across all of its programs, namely individual bravery and risk-taking, and group cooperation and community-building. Theatre's face-to-face intensity aligns with summer camp's effort to foster direct, unmediated relationships among the girls and between campers and staff. Summer camps eschew technology (girls can listen to music on smartphones but have no Wi-Fi or phone access) and promotes the values of a simple life: getting back to basics, appreciating nature, and, most importantly, developing and valuing friendships. The bunk show also gives less athletic, more artistically inclined girls a chance to shine. As important, it strengthens the bunk group, as girls collaborate on something bigger than themselves. Each show performs the bunk's successful teamwork for the rest of camp. Girls develop the same skills doing musical theatre that they do playing sports and participating in other camp rituals.

Though girls' Jewish summer camps host an economically privileged and homogeneous population, they are, like every community, fragile and vulnerable. There are always resistances and cracks. Some girls hate camp, so they don't return. The very activities that enunciate community and inculcate most girls inevitably exclude others.[5] Still, each summer camp creates, recreates, and re-performs a self-referential community to reinforce its own importance. Musical theatre consolidates this community.

A Brief History of Summer Camps in the United States

Summer camps sprouted up in the late nineteenth century and flourished in the early twentieth when the Industrial Revolution compelled educational advocates to argue for the importance of outdoor activity for children and city dwellers feared polio outbreaks in the summer. Though the first summer camps were for boys and for Christians, by the 1910s, a number of Jewish girls' summer camps opened, including the ones I visited, which were among the first built in the United States. Kineo, Attean Lake Camp, Camp Holeb, and Camp Clearwater are categorized as "private, for-profit, non-Orthodox camps," or summer camps that have Jewish owners and directors and mostly Jewish campers, and that self-identify as Jewish.[6] Attean Lake Camp, for example, was founded and run for years by a pair of wealthy, enterprising Jewish sisters, daughters of a rabbi, who were schoolteachers in New York City.[7]

Their students took the train to Greenville, Maine, and then horse-drawn carriages to camp, shedding their city dresses and jewelry for comfortable uniforms intended to blur class distinctions. Sylvia Buden, who was Camp Kineo's director for fifty-seven years, from 1939 to 1996, described in her diary as a staff member in 1932 the process of collecting the girls' "city clothes and jewelry" at the beginning of the summer. Almost everyone to whom I spoke, staff and campers, both past and present, talked about the importance of the uniforms—now T-shirts and shorts bearing the camp's name—in diverting attention away from appearances and eliminating signs of wealth.

As the northernmost East Coast state, Maine carries associations of cold weather, a hardy and robust population, lobster (a delicacy everywhere else and a staple of the diet in Maine), and a site for wealthy New Yorkers to summer. For Mainers, anyone whose family has not lived there for generations is "from away," including the summer camp owners who bought property in the early twentieth century. The state is littered with summer camps, single-sex and coed, Jewish and Christian and nondenominational, all of which contribute substantially to the state's economy. A 2012 analysis of the economic impact of Maine summer camps found that they contribute almost as much as the fisheries industry, more than $332 million annually, plus another $171 million spent by campers' visiting parents each year.[8]

Summer camp planners aimed to create a pastoral utopia, or what Abigail A. Van Slyck calls "a manufactured wilderness."[9] To this day, girls live in tents on wooden platforms or rough-hewn cabins without electricity, though there is electricity in other parts of camp, including the theatre space. Other buildings—most original to each camp—include a dining hall, an infirmary, an arts and crafts lodge, as well as some covered wooden platforms so that some activities can proceed during Maine's frequent heavy summer thunderstorms. Each property also has multiple playing fields, tennis and basketball courts, horse stables, and a riding ring, but no swimming pool—girls swim in the lake. In addition, from their founding, these mini-civilizations in the rough always included a structure for theatre, some now with well-stocked costume shops, more-than-adequate lighting equipment, and fine set-making capabilities.[10]

By the 1920s, as the tradition of Jewish middle-class East Coast girls attending summer camp grew, camps got their business primarily through word of mouth.[11] Almost a century later, parents still send their daughters to a camp they've heard of and, for many girls, it's a family tradition. Paige, a longtime Kineo camper whose grandmother, two aunts, mother, and cousins went there, told me that her mother announced her sex to the family when she was born by saying, "It's Kineo class of 2012!" Weekly bunk show musicals help to embed this connectedness and validate this loyalty.

Jewishness and Feminism

Today, Jewishness and feminism are at once everywhere and nowhere at summer camp, informing minute details of the countless hourly, daily, and weekly rituals, but seldom spoken aloud or marked as Jewishness or feminism per se. The values espoused by Attean Lake, Kineo, Holeb, and Clearwater are humanitarian and liberal but also connected to the Jewish value of *tikun olam* (doing good in the world), of building community as a kind of family, of being kind and considerate. Just as Judaism marks daily life events—waking up, eating meals, going to sleep—with a prayer, every activity at camp is accompanied by one of hundreds of songs, many dating back one hundred years. At any moment of the day, somewhere at camp, you can hear girls singing.

Each camp holds a weekly service on Friday night, for which girls wear a more formal version of the uniform—a white shirt at Attean Lake, a collared gray shirt and uncuffed shorts at Holeb—and during which one girl presents a "sermon" on a topic, such as "beginnings," which she relates to camp values. Some (but not all) summer camps call the service "Shabbat" and include Hebrew prayers and songs. In the 1970s, Attean Lake's director replaced the concluding Hebrew song of the service, "Ein Keloheinu," with "Sabbath Prayer" from *Fiddler on the Roof*, which many Jewish summer camps did at the time, marking the strong affiliation among Jewishness, Broadway musicals, and summer camp.

Each girl's perception of her camp's Jewishness and/or feminism and their importance depends on her situation at home. Karen, for example, who attended Attean Lake for six years as a camper and two as a counselor, said, "I went to a private school that was WASP-y and so being around all Jewish girls at camp was important to me. I found a kind of community that wasn't what I had at home." Sara, who went to Holeb in the 1970s, told me something similar: "For me it was the first time I was around a majority-Jewish group, and I found girls who were just like me." Though some campers don't notice the Jewishness of their camp—a few eleven-year-olds who live in predominantly Jewish areas told me emphatically that Holeb isn't a Jewish camp—Jewishness is part of each camp's DNA.

The value of an all-girls' setting tends to be more overtly articulated by campers, counselors, and parents alike, whether or not it's named "feminism." As Sara, who now runs her own business, said, the fact that the camp is all girls "matters immensely. It helped build confidence in being yourself." Summer camp weaves together secular, cultural Jewishness and middle-class liberal feminism and encourages girls to form intense bonds with the place. This identity of being a girl, of being a Jewish girl, of being a Attean Lake or Kineo or Holeb girl, each camp hopes, will sustain campers through the other forty-four weeks of the year and keep them returning summer after summer. The bunk show is a crucial practice of this affective attachment.

The girls' Jewish summer camps I visited were founded thirty years before musical theatre emerged as an identifiable performance genre in the United States, but theatre was a regular part of summer camp programming from the start. As a 1923 manual for camp directors advised, "Dramatics, pageants, and aesthetic dancing have their appeal to youth. Careful attention should be given to details and all work should be undertaken seriously."[12] Performance, the manual continued, would "contribute toward the pleasure of their little community," and the participants would "profit richly by their experience."[13] Campers performed Shakespeare, pageant reenactments of "Indian" stories like Longfellow's version of Hiawatha, or plays based on folktales or myths.[14] For the first thirty-five years, Camp Kineo's repertoire, for example, included modern dance inspired by contemporary choreographers like Isadora Duncan (1877–1927) and vaudeville productions. In 1951, according to one camper's scrapbook, "Bunk 19" presented "a terrific marvelous performance" of Lerner and Loewe's *Brigadoon*, Kineo's first complete Broadway musical. From then on, musicals gradually replaced nonmusical shows.[15]

Bunk show musicals always maintained a timely association with Broadway, and each summer's repertoire followed New York's professional theatre's developments. *Brigadoon* premiered on Broadway in 1947, just four years before the group of thirteen-year-olds performed it at Kineo. In the summer of 1960, Kineo's season included *L'il Abner, The Boy Friend*, and *The King and I*, all well-known Broadway hits.[16] In 1967, when Jane (Paige's aunt) went to Kineo, she played Tevye in *Fiddler on the Roof*, which had opened on Broadway only three years earlier and was still playing to sold-out crowds. During the 1940s, 1950s, and early 1960s, Broadway musicals were a part of US popular culture. Songs played on the radio, scenes were performed on television on *The Ed Sullivan Show*, and cast albums regularly hit the top-forty Billboard charts. Given the upper-middle-class status and East Coast homes of most of the campers, they would have been familiar with the musicals they performed, whether they had seen them or listened to cast albums.

Though Broadway musicals are no longer mainstream popular culture, many of the girls have seen or know *Wicked, Spamalot*, and *You're a Good Man, Charlie Brown*, as well as Disney movies like *The Little Mermaid* and *Peter Pan*, all of which were performed at camp in recent years. As Holub camp director Stephanie told me, "If you do a show they know, it's already franchised and you've sold it to them." Summer camp musicals are in intimate conversation with professional musical theatre, highlighting only one of the many contradictions of this civilization-in-nature.

The prominence of musical theatre on summer camps' websites—typically listed right alongside athletics—confirms its centrality to the experience. Attean Lake Camp, for example, features a two-minute video in which the middle-aged female theatre counselor and several girls explain musical theatre's importance at camp. "Some of the girls have so much talent," the counselor exclaims, while we see an image of a girl playing the Little Mermaid, sitting on the edge of the stage in a bright green sequined mermaid's tail. Then the video cuts to the face of a teenaged camper who says, "Theatre at camp is amazing!"

In addition to the talking heads framed by camp's green slope down to the lake, the advertisement—which is its purpose, of course—includes moments of a rehearsal as well as performances. In one, the counselor leads fifty teenage girls, all wearing their matching camp T-shirts and shorts, rehearsing for "Sisterhood of Attean," a choreographed revision of the song "Brotherhood of Man" from *How to Succeed in Business Without Really Trying*. Then the scene of rehearsal cuts to the performance of the same song, with all of the girls dressed in black T-shirts, black pants, and Mardi Gras beads, their costume for this musical revue. The clip shows that the girls are taught theatre by an adult who is a professional, and that theatre is a process, from rehearsal to performance. Their choreography is simple and failproof, and they look like they're having fun.

The video also shows a section from a production of *Fiddler on the Roof*, performed on a raised stage with a simple set of a painted flat with several lighting instruments visible. The girls wear appropriate *Fiddler* faux shetl costumes, a pianist accompanies, and one of the campers portraying the eponymous character plays the violin on a catwalk above the space. All of these details attest to the camp's ample resources for producing musicals.

The selected images signal femaleness and Jewishness as primary identities to the target audience of prospective families. Parents obviously know that they are choosing to send their daughter to an all-girls' camp, but the images on the website of all girls performing in a musical, of girls playing the male roles of Tevye and the Fiddler, drive this fact home. By showing the clip of "Sisterhood of Attean," the camp reiterates the importance of the single-sex setting, of the value placed on girls. Attean Lake Camp chooses to highlight gender and Jewishness intertwined with musical theatre in its public image.

Like the video, the entire production process of bunk shows, from season selection to auditions to rehearsals to performance, balances the values of theatre-making, of individual girls' empowerment, of group bonding, and of the camp's affirmation of itself. At different points in the process, one objective might take priority over another, but the practices of this camp activity, repeated week after week and year after year, with only minor changes in the last century, aim to find equilibrium among those goals.

Making Musicals at Summer Camp

The work that takes place before the campers arrive is meant to ensure a readymade positive experience for the girls. The theatre staff consists of between three and six counselors, who are usually college theatre majors (aged eighteen to twenty-two) or high school teachers (in their twenties or early thirties) with enough training and expertise to direct a musical. Some of the counselors are Jewish and attended the camp themselves, and they bring years of experience, knowledge, and appreciation of the countless rituals, as well as a deep love for the place. A hefty percentage, though, and increasingly in the twenty-first century, are not Jewish, but are college students interested in a summer job working with children in a beautiful setting. Many counselors are from abroad, either university students or recent graduates from England, Israel, or Russia, who want to spend a summer in the United States. Sometimes these non-American young adults don't realize that they'll be stuck in far-flung places for eight weeks until they arrive. Other times it's a good fit and they and the girls benefit from one another.

Andy Davis, for example, led the theatre program at Kineo in 2012, his first year at the camp. He'd recently graduated from University of Maine and was getting ready to start a master's degree in English at the University of Vermont in the fall. That summer, he said, felt like his last hurrah for making theatre after years of performing in community theatre and high school and college plays. He'd worked at another summer camp for the previous two summers, but it wasn't an all-girls' camp or "so old and steeped in tradition." But the other camp was a JCC (Jewish Community Center) camp, so as a non-Jew, he learned to follow the rituals and expectations of that semireligious setting. At Kineo, he told me, "The signs of Jewishness are subtler but still clearly here," though he couldn't pinpoint how. They sing blessings before meals in English and never mention God, he explained. The girls wear white to services, which are held on Sunday, not on the Jewish Sabbath's Friday night or Saturday. The service is a nonreligious weekly meeting where a chosen senior camper talks about her experience and offer words of wisdom on a theme, such as loyalty, determination, or independence. And unlike the JCC camp, where many of the songs were in Hebrew, Kineo's songs are all in English. "And they never seem to stop!" he said. "The girls sing at every available opportunity. Sometimes I wonder how they manage to eat a single meal, given that they sing the entire time." Still, he repeated, Kineo is "definitely" a Jewish summer camp.

Within the group of theatre counselors, they need at least one person who can play the piano and one who possesses technical skills to hang and focus lights and one to create costumes. The head theatre counselor, who is the play's director, organizes the season of six shows during the preceding spring, choosing musicals that provide plenty of performance opportunities, significant ensemble numbers, and a reasonably positive and uplifting message. The repertoire is typically a mixture of classic Broadway fare, adaptations of movies, Disney shows, and newer musicals.

But season selection is more challenging than it may appear. Six bunk shows are performed each summer, and most girls attend camp for seven years. Because the shows shouldn't be repeated over one girl's years at camp, they produce forty-two different musicals before one is repeated. One girl, then, participates in seven different shows and sees thirty-five more over her years at camp, effectively becoming an experienced theatre spectator. (These numbers struck me as extraordinary for the campers and terrifying for the counselors who must choose the shows each year.)

In addition, since the audience is made up of girls aged seven to fifteen, the theatre counselor must find age-appropriate material or make it that way. Andy recounted when he learned about this requirement before he got to camp: "They did *Gypsy* here a while back, and I was like, '*Gypsy*? Like, how do you make that appropriate?' And they were like, 'Well, we just didn't do the second act.' I was just like, 'What?!' And then, I was just like, 'Okay.'" Everyone attends the weekly bunk show, so the repertoire must be accessible and acceptable, even if it's illogical. That the whole camp gathers and performs its unity is as important as which particular show is performed.

After the girls arrive at camp at the end of June, the bunk show season begins. Each week's show is announced on Sunday to squeals and cheers of excitement, and from then on, every aspect of the process encourages a sense of belonging. Auditions are intentionally low key: On Sunday afternoon, girls sing any song and can express their preferences for a big or small part, singing or not. With the smallest girls, Andy said, "They're really too young to be doing this at all, so I just have them sing together and I try to hear where the good notes are coming from." He explained, "We want to give everybody a chance and also make sure that the same girls don't have the biggest parts every year." Any girl might be cast in a male role, and those parts usually go to the strongest performers. Roles are often double-cast; in 1963, Jane played the Tin Man—a role "I really enjoyed," she said—in the second act of *The Wizard of Oz*, and another girl performed in the first act. Some shows are hard to cast, Andy said, when "there are a lot of girls who are capable of taking a big part and there aren't enough" big roles. To this end, the theatre counselor adds as many speaking, solo singing, or named characters as possible, sometimes dividing roles or giving chorus characters a name and a solo line to sing or speak. Every girl in the bunk is cast in the show. Andy said, "It's inclusive theatre and you never say, 'You didn't make the cut.'"

Parts are announced after dinner on Sunday, and the list is met with delight, with disappointment, and with some tears, too. One nine-year-old girl at Attean Lake Camp, for example, complained to me that she got a "bad part" last year and again this year and that she would "just be sitting around doing nothing." Every issue of Camp Kineo's yearbook *Dive* from 1916 on had at least one poem written by a girl who was unhappy with her part in the play. The counselors, staff, and older campers (who have visible leadership roles at camp and whose actions have great sway over the younger girls) try to quell sadness by stressing that "every single girl is important to the show" and "there are always opportunities to shine," and, as Andy said, they try to spread around bigger parts from year to year. Because the theatre staff turns over more frequently than the camp director, she'll give the final approval on the cast list with an eye toward fairness. Andy said, "Usually by the time you get into rehearsal, [the girls' discontent] is water under the bridge because you have to get it done." Some girls help backstage, too, and design and tech have become more popular in recent years. Bottom line: Everyone participates.

The process moves quickly from casting to rehearsing on an impossibly condensed schedule, which throws the girls and the counselors into a project that requires everyone's attention, engagement, and involvement. On Monday morning, they start rehearsing, and the girls' usual athletic activities are suspended for the next five days (Figure 6.2). Except for the required twice-daily swim, the show becomes the top priority.[17] A normal schedule is: Monday, learn music and start choreography; Tuesday, start blocking; by Wednesday afternoon, do a run and the actors can call for lines; Thursday

Figure 6.2. Girls rehearse for their bunk show at summer camp.

and Friday, finish and fix and run because there is no rehearsal on Saturday (it's Shabbat, though no one said that); and the show is Saturday night.

In the meantime, the tech staff, with the help of any girls interested in the backstage operations, hangs and focuses lights, builds the sets, and finds and alters, buys, or creates costumes. Here is how Tessa, the choreographer at Camp Kineo, described the week to me: "Monday is music day. Andy says, 'Oh, we can do anything.' And then by Wednesday it's like, 'Oh my god, we've got two more days to the show!' Thursday is like, 'This is awful.' Friday is like, 'We have to get the show on, get the show on,' and Saturday is tense. The [girls aren't] here all day, so we just get this place ready, finish off the set."

This breakneck speed is possible at a professional summer stock theatre but unheard of for amateurs, much less girls of all ages who might not do any theatre during the school year. Since there aren't enough hours to finish the show, the process is overlaid with the suspense of, Will the play actually happen? Will we succeed in getting it together? This social drama in camp's already-intense bubble invariably heightens emotions in every direction and deepens the bond that takes place in the group, since they are building something together from scratch in a very short amount of time. As Stephanie, director of Camp Holeb, described it, musicals create a "hyper-focus on one very important task that takes the self-container of camp and adds another container in it." Andy explained, "We talk to them about it before the summer starts, that this is their unity activity because it's part of the camp's philosophy. So it's their chance to get to know each other as bunkmates in a different way beyond living together but actually to cooperate on some kind of finished product." Tessa added that there is "pressure . . . well, not exactly pressure . . . but not many activities in camp have to produce a finished product. Like if the kid does riding and they get on the horse, that's success."

At Rehearsal

One afternoon-long rehearsal that I observed at Camp Kineo demonstrated the multiple values of theatre-making, individual empowerment, and collective bonding at play. That week, the bunk of fourteen-year-olds rehearsed for *Sister Act*, an adaptation created by Andy, which combined the 1992 Whoopi Goldberg movie and the 2011 Broadway production. The musical is about a lounge singer who is placed in a witness protection program in a convent, masquerading as a nun. She joins the choir and injects the dull music with pizzazz, transforming the dirge-like hymns to a full-out gospel celebration. Though this show might seem like a strange choice for a girls' Jewish summer camp, it actually worked well for a number of reasons: It's a fairly simple story with a lot of parts, it uses a broad and comedic style, and it has fun and catchy music. More subtly, it's also about an outsider who becomes an insider and transforms her environment for the better—a relevant story for adolescent girls. And it's about the transformative power of music when it's deeply felt and pleasurable, an apt metaphor for musical theatre at summer camp.

During the first section of the rehearsal, the campers work on an ensemble musical number with freshly learned choreography. Coached by three counselors, every exchange stresses group involvement. "Raise Your Voice," the musical's rousing turning-point number, happens when the new arrival, Deloris Van Carter, persuades the nuns to let loose and sing out. Eight girls—half the cast—are in this song, but all of the girls watch them and mimic their choreography alongside the two dance counselors who mirror the performers. Andy plays the piano, occasionally glancing over to see how it's going. The enthusiasm of the counselors and the energy of the girls on the sidelines are infectious. Though the performers possess unevenly strong voices, expressive faces, or choreographic grace, and some look positively mortified at the start, they're all eventually pulled into the pleasure of the song and the dance. By the end of the first run-through, every girl is smiling, singing loudly, and gesturing broadly. The final chord is admittedly off key, and Andy laughs, "Woo baby! Let's do that again! You're gonna be great!" And they do it again, better this time.

Having established the girls' strong investment in the process, Andy divides them into groups to work on different parts next: One group practices the music with counselor Barb, another group creates some schtick on their own, and a few others run lines with Tessa. What one director called "a six-ring circus" is the goal. As a camper told me, "A good rehearsal is if everyone has something to do the whole time."

A quartet remains with Andy to work on the book scene. Because cellphones and internet access are forbidden at camp, if the girls don't already know the musical they're doing, they can't access YouTube clips or productions and are dependent on the script, the director, and the other actors. "Okay," Andy begins enthusiastically, "let's just go through it once and see where we are." The girls say or read their lines, some slightly stilted and some already fully in character, hamming it up. "Okay, what's happening in this scene?" he asks. Blank faces. "What just happened right before this?" he rephrases. They jump to attention, each one chiming in where the action began and what each character is doing in this scene. Satisfied that they know what they're doing, he says, "Let's do it again." In that five-minute conversation I can see how much he is teaching them about theatre. Without using specific terminology, they learn about beats, objectives, and given circumstances.

As the rehearsal proceeds through the afternoon, he coaches each girl in character development. He works internally, asking, "What does your character want at this moment? Why is she saying this?" and externally, helping them find models for their characters. To the one who is playing Mother Superior, he says, "Do you know who Maggie Smith is?" (she played the role in the movie of *Sister Act*).

"No."

He thinks for a moment. "Meryl Streep?" he asks.

Enthusiastic nod!

"Okay," he concludes, "You're Meryl Streep."

At every turn but fully integrated into the scene work, he explains basics of blocking, of emotional connection, of physical grounding. "Good!" Andy says. "How do you feel?" The girls smile and look pleased with themselves, as each achieved something new this afternoon.

Then one girl raises her hand. "I have a question," she says, "What's Protestant?" I was already thinking that it was fascinating to see a bunch of Jewish girls playing nuns and one playing Deloris, who, according to the script, isn't an African American character, though Whoopi Goldberg and Patina Miller played her in the movie and on Broadway, respectively. But this moment foregrounds the insularity of this community. It is a question that could only be asked because none of the girls were Protestant. No one giggles or rolls her eyes. Instead, a quick lesson in religion ensues, mostly narrated by the twenty-four-year-old Tessa, who was the oldest grown-up there, with great gentleness and tact. And the rehearsal continues. Likely that camper, and perhaps others in the group, lives in a predominantly Jewish area or simply has not been exposed to other religions. This encounter highlights another contradiction of summer camp: that while girls are encouraged to "be brave," "go outside your comfort zone," and "try new things," these risks are circumscribed by layers of protection and support. Kineo camp director Wendy Hess later told me that a few of the girls told her how much fun they had playing nuns. Perhaps that afternoon's rehearsal and discussion promoted a small degree of cross-cultural understanding.

Watching the girls rehearse, I can see that they benefit from doing musical theatre in a variety of ways. First, they gain performance skills and musical theatre knowledge. Working on a show develops skills of multiple art forms, music and theatre and dance, and it demystifies the production process. Even if they don't do any theatre at home or school, over their years at camp, most girls perform in seven musicals, learning from the inside how musical theatre is made.[18] Whether girls sight-read music or learn by ear, the music is accessible and repetitive, harmonically straightforward, easy to learn, and fun to sing. They learn blocking and choreography, they memorize lines, and perhaps they achieve some characterization. As was clear with Andy's directing, girls learn the basics of acting. In addition, they develop their imagination, since working on a show encourages fantasy and allows the girls to pretend they're someone else, whether it's Meryl Streep or a nun.

Andy knows the girls are learning about theatre, but from his perspective as an educator and director, "It's a little frightening," he confessed. "It's a little piece of duct tape and prayers-to-God situation, you know?" At the same time, though, he feels he's grown as an artist. He's become a quicker decision-maker, which he knows has improved his directing. The process "doesn't really give you time to not make decisions. You just have to do it." He added, "In this building, I'm no BS and the girls might say that I'm harsh. But they produce the show and at the end of the week, they feel better about it." He paused to think for a moment and added, "I temper being harsh with being fair, but I'm also not going to let them sit back."

Musical theatre also encourages girls to try out different movement vocabularies, play across gender, take up physical space, and command center stage, especially because most musicals require a direct-address, face-front, and exuberant performance style with expansive physicality and broad expressiveness. These performance practices, embedded in a single-sex environment that values all kinds of physical activity and speaks to the importance of female power at every turn, promote a female-positive body image, in contrast to the female body-policing of everyday US culture. As Andy said, "For the shows we do, because it's always an all-female cast, I think that that brings up a lot of feminist issues unintentionally, or it really highlights the feminism that is going on. So, like, for this show: In a lot of ways, Deloris is portrayed as a kind of empty-headed, limelight-hungry woman, and by the end of the show she is completely changed and she's come into her own and she's realized things about herself." He believes that the girls learn from pretending: "I hope that by the end of seeing that and practicing that on stage, they take that away."

The single-sex environment matters. "Last week we did *Mulan* and it ended up being all about feminism," Andy said. The camp director and staff "find ways to empower women and try to inject the traditions of Kineo into that. Something about making this place important makes women important by virtue of what it is." As a director and a gay man, he feels freer as an artist. "Certain physical scenes are fine here," and "they're more apt to discuss things and try to figure out what they're doing." When the girls play male roles, "I don't want them to reproduce stereotypes of masculinity. I try to tell them, 'Watch the male staff.' Then they bypass the stereotype. And they're good at it. They like to mimic." Overall, he said, the girls value "their own merits and [are] not trying to impress a guy." They take "more personal responsibility" and there is "more substantial learning."

Preparing for a show teaches life skills valuable to the individual and the group. Girls are instructed to speak clearly, look their scene partner in the eye, breathe, listen, and project their energy outward. Rehearsing and learning lines, music, and choreography require concentration, discipline, patience, focus, and teamwork. The twelve-year-olds said that in their tents at night, they're practicing their lines alongside the Torah readings for their upcoming bat mitzvahs.

Finally, most musicals celebrate community and end with a rousing ensemble number. By learning, rehearsing, and performing group numbers, girls invest kinesthetically in the group, and the pleasure of performance reinforces its importance. As Tessa said, "They love the idea of bunk shows, and there is a massive amount of hype about bunk shows here."

Traditions

As much as rehearsals and the intense, occasionally frantic weeklong process of creating a musical enhance the bond among the bunk, the rituals leading up to and following the evening performance intensify their group solidarity by lodging the performance within the larger camp community. Wendy, Kineo's camp director, explained, "There are a lot of traditions that go along with the schedule. So rehearse, rehearse, rehearse. And then Thursday night they go out for dinner. It's the Bunk Show Dinner. They go into the real world. On Friday night is their dress rehearsal, which is when it comes together or not, right?" She continued, "And then Friday night their counselors do a special dessert for them in the dining room, called Bunk Show Treats. And then Saturday morning they're off, Saturday morning is team sports, so they always have team sports. And then they do it and it's amazing, right?"

Other summer camps have their own traditions. During Saturday lunch at Holeb, for example, the bunk that will perform that night sings to the melody of the Passover song "Dayenu": "Sets are built, scenes are learned, applause will be truly earned, it is certain that we know it's a great show. Props are made, costumes mended, cameras are recommended, thanks to drama, all is done, let's take one." At Kineo, Saturday's dinner meal is always pizza and brownies, and the girls in the audience wear special orange ties for bunk show night and sing altogether as they walk up to the theatre-in-a-barn. At Camp Clearwater, counselor Viv described how "on Saturday night they can't wait. There's singing in the dining hall, they have to wait at the bottom of the hill, and they ring a bell and race up. In thirty seconds they're up here." All of the bunk shows at every camp begin with songs and cheers to encourage and support the performers. These rituals stand in for Havdalah, the service that ends Shabbat. The bunk show is, as one twelve-year-old told me, "one of the few times when the whole camp is together." They join together as a secular congregation for the first activity of the new week: a musical.

The phenomenon of the bunk show is a rare theatre event where the audience and the performers not only know each other but are literally the same community. This week's audience was last week's performers and vice versa. They merely exchange places onstage or offstage week by week. The audience empathizes with the nervous actors, as the spectators either performed their bunk show in a previous week or know theirs is soon to come. As fourteen-year-old Hannah told me, "Theatre at [camp] plays a big role in our day because it is one of the only times the whole camp is together. I think that theatre here is much more personal [than at home] because it's imperfect and you know everyone on stage so well." Lily, thirteen years old, explained, "In your first year, you're like, 'Oh, the play is mandatory,' but then after that, it's a part of our camp. Every single girl is on the stage. Every single girl no matter what sport they play, they also do theatre. When someone is running down the field, you can think, she does theatre!" The place exchange of actors and audience week by week with no outsiders present (except for me and an occasional guest) makes this occasion more than just a play.

Bunk Show Time

The forty-five-minute performance of *Willy Wonka* that I attend at Attean Lake Camp captures the quartet of goals of artistry, individual empowerment, group bonding, and camp affirmation that the weekly musical is meant to achieve (Figure 6.3). The vast difference between the rehearsal I witnessed a few days earlier and the production is remarkable: the excitement, the occasion, the darkness outside, the packed house with girls younger than this age group who already idolize them and older girls whom this group idolizes. The entire camp performs its belief in the power of musical theatre, and it's electric.

The level of artistic achievement is impressive, as the theatre counselor and director, Megan, uses the whole building for a kind of environmental theatre experience, with scenes taking place on the floor in the round and all around the upper level, too. The staging is complex and ambitious. The tech staff, Zoe and Thomas, and a crew of interested girls decorated the whole space; they painted the floor and hung colorful quilts along the upper-level rail. They built other set pieces, too, including a complicated portable framed doorway through which the Golden Ticket–winning kids and their parents enter the chocolate factory. They also constructed colorful costumes with notable

Figure 6.3. The cast of *Willy Wonka* after their bunk show performance.

attention to detail, from the grandparents' powdered heads to Violet's fat blueberry costume to the Oompa Loompas' green hair and orange skin. I am struck by how much time, energy, and creativity went into this one-time-only, forty-five-minute performance.

Each and every one of the twenty-five girls in the show has something special to do. About three-fourths of them have speaking or solo singing roles, and the ten-girl ensemble who play Oompa Loompas reprise their number each time a kid behaves badly, so they're on stage a lot. The show clips along, no one seems to forget her lines, and they all keep up with the piano. Most of the girls project their voices fairly well, can carry a tune, and put over a song, and a few are strong actors and have created memorable and funny characters. All in all, each girl contributes to the production.

In spite of the considerable differences of presence and projection among the actors, the audience is attentive from start to finish, appreciative of every girl's performance, and applauds wildly after every song. The staff strives to ensure each girl's success, even if it means stopping the performance and starting a song again or whispering lines from offstage (which didn't happen during *Willy Wonka*). Viv at Camp Clearwater remembered, "A few weeks ago for *Peter Pan*, Peter forgot one of his lines, her lines, singing and she looked over at Michael (the director) and he just said, 'Woop!' and gave her the line and she started singing again." During my visits to camp, I heard over and over, "It's okay if you mess up," and "no one laughs at your mistakes," and "everyone cheers you on." Ideally, each girl comes away from the process with more confidence. As fourteen-year-old Grace wrote to me, "We are all surrounded by love and friendship, so our whole sense of reality goes out the window. In reality, people have stage fright, or don't like singing in public, but when we get on <u>our</u> stage, we don't feel that anymore. It all becomes fun, and almost easy." Michelle, thirteen years old, told me,

> For my birthday my grandparents always take me to plays and I never really liked them because, like, I always wanted to do theatre but I never had the courage. And then I came to camp, and last year was, like, the first time I had a relatively big part and it felt really good to have everyone cheer you on no matter how ridiculous you looked. Like, this year I was a boy in the play and I had to wear a moustache, and I didn't really care. And now I go to plays with my grandparents and I like it because I think, "Wow, I can do that."

Although some girls have bigger roles, the adults constantly stress the group's participation. After the bows, the audience immediately jumps off their benches to rush the stage and congratulate the actors, who look both thrilled and relieved. (At Camp Clearwater, they repeat a snippet of the show as an encore.) The other counselors gather their campers and escort them out and to their bunks. The actors remain, which they know to do because they've done it every year since their first bunk show at age seven, and they sit in the first row of seats, grinning from ear to ear, hair damp with perspiration, and makeup starting to drip. Laura, the camp director, praises them on their performance. "You exemplify the Attean Lake Camp spirit," she says. "We thank you for your dedication and effort." They let me add my congratulations, since I'd watched the girls rehearse and saw the show come alive in performance. Finally, Laura instructs them to get out of their costumes—"calmly!"—and then come back into the theatre for their treat of cookies (at Camp Holeb, they get cake).

I wasn't surprised that Laura didn't single out any one girl but only complimented them as a group because the bunk show is meant to unify the crew, to show the importance of team spirit, of working hard and having fun.

Musical theatre's choral effect of singing and dancing together intensifies the feeling of unity. As Andy said, "Bunk shows are a very charged affair."

Unlike musical theatre in many settings, which disappears as the applause fades, the bunk show is kept alive through a collection of hundred-year-old rituals that transform the potent experience into collective memory and nostalgia. At Camp Kineo, for example, during the next day's breakfast, someone will start a cheer and request a song from the previous night's performance, and the actors, back to their regular routine of camp activities but with the performance's afterglow, happily comply with what becomes their "bunk show song." Then, every Saturday night, as the girls walk up the hill from the dining hall to the theatre, each group sings their bunk show song. The last bunk show of the summer is the oldest girls', which is a revue of all of their bunk show songs over the years. The collection of songs, then, becomes each bunk's unique and multiyear repertoire, a part of this group's identity through their lives. Tessa explained, "By the time they get to Bunk 12 they're really serious about it and it's their last show. And they were crying because they didn't want it to be over."

Though the show itself happens only once, it leaves a musical trace that the girls (and later, as women) sing repeatedly year after year. This and other rituals affirm that, Jewishness aside, the true religion of camp is camp, and the bunk show musical contributes to the camp's fascination with, celebration of, dedication to, and even fetishization of itself.

Still, musical theatre at summer camp is not entirely utopic. The youngest girls are anxious when they audition, eager to do well, and invested in this process that is key to their becoming full-fledged campers. The older girls have solidified their identities, strengths, and weaknesses and know their role in the bunk show—big part, small part, tech crew—after doing it for a number of years. But the middle school years can be tough, as competition thrives and coolness is hard to leave at home. I happened to visit Camp Kineo during the week when the next-to-oldest girls were rehearsing. They were a very talented and invested group, and wanted to be around each other and work hard. In contrast, the week I went to Camp Holeb, the same age group was a crew with two girls who cared about theatre and ten who wanted to be playing basketball or hanging out, and the whole experience was miserable for the counselor/director. Tessa said that many of the little ones don't have the patience to rehearse and hate being cooped up. But for most of them, the performance makes it all worthwhile.

How musical theatre happens at this collection of girls' Jewish summer camps in Maine is one model, but other summer camps in Maine and across the United States follow different schedules and espouse different values, rituals, and practices. Ramah Wisconsin, for example, has a resident theatre company and specializes in devising and writing new musicals. Other Ramah campuses perform musicals in Hebrew. At some Christian camps, musicals and sports and "color war" complement Bible study and social justice activities. The pre-professional Stagedoor Manor, attended by professional performers like Lea Michele and Natalie Portman, among others, and French Woods focus solely on musical theatre training and performance.

Musical theatre, with all that it entails, is among the many rituals that take place over seven weeks at summer camp. These practices value direct, face-to-face relationships and foster homosocial intimacy and emotional ties. Ritual binds communities together as Jews, actors together as an ensemble, and girls together in gendered solidarity. "I'm still friends with the women I went to camp with," eighty-seven-year-old Mindy Cohen told me. "And the show was all."

Figure 7.1. Students rehearse for *The Lion King KIDS* as their teacher, front left, coaches.

7

Disney Goes to School

The Little Mermaid on Broadway was a bust.[1] Though the 1989 animated movie musical grossed $84 million domestically at its initial release, and by 2015 had earned $211 million worldwide and spawned an entire industry of kid-sized green rubber monoflippers, glittery corsets, and long red flowy Ariel wigs, the 2008 Broadway musical was panned—"an unfocused spectacle," Ben Brantley of the *New York Times* called it—and closed after only fifty previews and 685 performances.[2] After the jaw-dropping success of *Beauty and the Beast* (1994–1999) and *The Lion King* (1997, and still running strong as of 2019), which not only transformed the Broadway musical but also reshaped the entire Times Square neighborhood and the global economy of musicals, Disney thought the beloved *Mermaid* couldn't fail. And yet it did. And like everything that happens at Disney, it failed big: $20 million's worth.[3]

As soon as it was clear that *Mermaid* was going down the tubes, executives at Disney Theatrical Group (DTG) put their heads together to figure out how to salvage the product. They might have tossed the whole musical. They might have gone back to the drawing board and tried to make it into a bigger, brighter, and better Broadway show. Or they might have thought about a new audience for the product.

Fast forward to January 2013, the Junior Theatre Festival (JTF), which we visited in Chapter 1, at the Cobb Galleria Centre in Atlanta, Georgia. That year, twenty-one groups (more than 25 percent of the eight-two groups total) chose to perform a number from the newly released *Little Mermaid*—or rather, from *The Little Mermaid JR.*, a sixty-minute revision and adaptation of the Broadway script. More than four hundred tweens sang and danced to "Under the Sea" that weekend in nondescript conference hotel meeting rooms without lights or set, and wearing the requisite festival "costume" of jeans and matching JTF logo'd T-shirts. Backed by a fully orchestrated taped accompaniment to the calypso melody, the kids exhibited commitment and passion to rival that of Broadway's stars. These performances were just the tip of the iceberg of *The Little Mermaid*'s reincarnation as a Disney Junior show.

Beyond Broadway. Stacy Wolf, Oxford University Press (2020). © Oxford University Press.
DOI: 10.1093/oso/9780190639525.001.0001

Across the United States in 2013—the first year of *The Little Mermaid JR.*'s licensing—hundreds of schools, afterschool programs, and community theatres produced the almost new show. Between 2013 and 2018, Disney licensed more than 7,000 productions of *The Little Mermaid JR.*, which resulted in around eighteen thousand performances.[4] In addition, teachers and directors who purchased licenses received a Director's Guide with staging and choreography suggestions and production advice. Within a few short years of amateur licensing for a reworked, kid-friendly, hour-long *Little Mermaid JR.*, Disney had gone a distance to offset the Broadway production's loss.

The Little Mermaid's journey from Broadway to Atlanta—now performed by sixth- and seventh-graders—and then across America in a new, full-length professional production (about which more later), while the starkest example of DTG's creative savvy and economic acumen, is only one example of a Disney show that is raking in the bucks through kids' performances. Following the example of Music Theatre International (MTI)'s fast-growing Broadway Junior catalog—its pared-down versions of classic musicals, discussed in Chapter 1—Disney Theatricals recognized that children would be eager to play the characters they knew from the Disney movies they grew up with. As DTG president Thomas Schumacher asked with a grin, "Who wouldn't rather play Gaston [in *Beauty and the Beast*] than Sky Masterson [in *Guys and Dolls*]?"[5]

But that's not all. Fast forward again to May 2014 to Creswell Middle School of the Arts in Nashville, Tennessee, where I saw another *Little Mermaid JR.* This one was a lavish affair, with a gorgeously painted backdrop of "under the sea," brightly colored costumes, wigs, and a long, semitransparent, glittery piece of cloth stretched across a wide proscenium stage, representing the watery underworld. Ariel, played by an effervescent girl in a blazingly bright red wig and sparkling mermaid costume, listened half-heartedly to Sebastian, played by an expressive boy all in red (he's a crab), who belted the irresistibly tuneful tune. After the first verse, a troupe of kids playing sea creatures danced onto the stage, led by ten girl dancers who wore black or red halter tops and layered fabric dance pants and who executed a jazz routine upstage of Ariel and Sebastian. More kids leapt onto the stage, too, and a few carried clear umbrellas as "jellyfish." Everyone sang and moved on stage at once, bringing the song to life in an explosion of color and energy, though through the first verse, their singing was almost drowned out by children in the audience screaming about the bubbles released from the catwalk and floating into the light.

This delightful middle school performance was one of two complete casts of *The Little Mermaid JR.* who rehearsed for four months at the school, while many of their classmates built sets and costumes. Creswell was among the six Nashville elementary and middle schools selected that year to participate in Disney Musicals in Schools (DMIS), an ambitious program designed to seed musical theatre programs in underserved public schools across the United States. Creswell's student population is 86 percent Black, 10 percent White, 3 percent Hispanic/Latino, and 1 percent Asian, and 75 percent of the children are eligible to receive free and reduced-price lunches.[6] Administered locally by the Tennessee Performing Arts Center, DMIS was created for children who lack access to "in-school arts programs," according to Ken Cerniglia, DTG's dramaturg and literary manager, and Lisa Mitchell, senior manager of education and outreach.[7] The program aims to benefit kids who might not have been exposed to musical theatre previously and who likely wouldn't make it to the JTF extravaganza, which we visited in Chapter 1.

Disney's twenty-first-century trio of projects for children—licensable kid-friendly musical theatre adaptations of Disney movies and shows, supplementary production materials and teachers'/directors' guides, and public school outreach programs across the United States—has transformed child consumers into producers. By participating in—that is, by *doing* musical theatre—children become active agents and effective meaning-makers of musicals. They become Disney artists.

These activities bridge what might seem an impossible incongruity in Disney's philosophy and its artistic and educational practices: that this global conglomerate worth $152.1 billion, according to *Forbes*, and ranked number eight of the world's most valuable brands in terms of wealth and corporate power (in 2018), is also a leader in philanthropic support of the arts by way of musical theatre education across the United States.[8] Disney's stringent product quality control, which is only possible because of their vast resources for research and development and sustained oversight by the home office in New York City, virtually guarantees success for any production anywhere in the country. Their power—both economic and cultural—also explains how they, ironically, might diversify musical theatre socioeconomically and even, perhaps, challenge Broadway's hegemonic whiteness.

And Disney isn't alone. As Frank Bruni wrote in the *New York Times*, by 2015 corporations surpassed lawmakers and politicians in making real social change on issues such as same-sex marriage and immigration. Companies like AT&T, Marriott, and Microsoft, for example, "have produced compelling recent examples of showing greater sensitivity to diversity, social justice and the changing tide of public sentiment than lawmakers often manage to."[9] According to *Newsweek*, inclusiveness "may not be good politics in this day of polarization and micro-targeting, but it seems to be good business," and Bruni concluded, "Corporations aren't always the bad guys. Sometimes the bottom line matches the common good, and they're the agents of what's practical, wise and even right."[10] When public schools' arts funding is decimated, a corporation like Disney can step in. Disney's seemingly contradictory dual agendas—its capitalist commercial practices and its outreach aspirations—cohabitate surprisingly comfortably in DTG's rhetoric and practices.[11]

Critiques of Disney's insatiable desire to possess the souls of children and the pocketbooks of their parents abound, as do scathing attacks on their sexist, racist, and heteronormative representations and on their imperialist exoticization of African (*The Lion King; The Jungle Book; Tarzan*) and Middle Eastern (*Aladdin*) cultures. While I acknowledge these and other criticisms of the Disney corporation, here I want to look at their musical theatre ventures for and with children through a different, more positive lens.

My motivation is due in part to the fact that Disney's influence is here to stay, at least for now. A 2018 article in *Playbill* noted that over 100 million Americans—that's 38 percent of the US population—"have engaged with a licensed Disney show either as part of the cast, crew, or audience." "Disney musicals," writer Ruthie Fierberg concluded, "are so pervasive, so woven into the fabric of Americana."[12] As Schumacher said, "This is the new American songbook . . . We are this new era of Broadway," and he's not exaggerating.[13] Can they do something good? Embracing the contradictions in Disney's rhetoric and practices as well as my own ambivalence about their systematic, occasionally alarming reach and influence, I nonetheless want to explore Disney's unique musical theatre projects and their uniquely progressive—artistically, pedagogically, and socioeconomically—potential in this chapter.

Developing the Disney Junior and Disney Kids Catalog

In 2004, Disney began licensing their titles, which included *High School Musical* and *Beauty and the Beast*, for amateur productions through MTI, the largest global distributor of musical theatre titles. Between 2004 and 2018, Disney registered over ninety thousand productions, which led to more than

250,000 performances in the United States and Canada.[14] In fact, during that period, *Beauty and the Beast* saw more productions nationwide "than the four longest-running Broadway shows combined."[15] Concurrently, Disney started adapting musicals for children, both 60-minute Junior versions designed for middle school–aged youth and 30-minute Kids scripts for elementary school–aged children. By 2018 they'd licensed 68,418 productions that featured approximately 2.5 million student performers of Disney Junior titles *Aladdin JR., Aladdin JR. Dual Language Edition* (in English and Spanish), *Alice in Wonderland JR., Beauty and the Beast JR., High School Musical JR., High School Musical 2 JR., The Lion King JR., The Little Mermaid JR., Mulan JR., My Son Pinocchio JR.,* and *Peter Pan JR.,* and Disney Kids titles *101 Dalmatians KIDS, Aladdin KIDS, Cinderella KIDS, The Aristocats KIDS, The Jungle Book KIDS, The Lion King KIDS, Sleeping Beauty KIDS,* and *Winnie the Pooh KIDS.*[16]

DTG developed its own method for creating Junior and Kids versions as meticulously as they produced a multimillion-dollar show on Broadway. Though the end goal is the same as MTI's (and, later, iTheatrics')—to produce kid-friendly adaptations of full-length musicals and ancillary materials—they rely on an in-house team of dramaturgs and educators. Seeking a balance between what children need and what artists want, Cerniglia, Mitchell, and David Scott, the senior manager of theatrical licensing, calculate how to construct a script and musical score to ensure kids' successful performances, based on their reading levels and emotional maturity at different ages.[17] Like MTI's process, they work closely with each musical's composer, lyricist, and librettist to maintain the spirit and message of the original show or live-action or animated movie. Nothing is released to the public until it has been tested repeatedly through years of development: multiple table readings, workshops, and pilot productions at selected schools. Given that scripts and scores go out into the world with all of live performance's uncertainties, the members of the education team do everything they can to ensure success—and, of course, to regulate their product.

A sixty-minute Disney Junior or thirty-minute Disney Kids musical differs from an adult full-length show in a number of ways, many similar to MTI's Broadway Junior and Rodgers and Hammerstein's Getting to Know You series. First, unlike a typical musical's libretto, in which all of the sheet music appears at the end, these scripts place spoken text and vocal parts with lyrics in the show's order, so that children can easily follow the play and know when they're supposed to enter, speak, and sing. Second, the music is transposed to accommodate young voices and the harmonies are simpler to master. Third, the adaptations answer the practical, material demands of children's shows: They have bigger casts with flexible casting. Because teachers and directors try to involve as many children as possible and give them opportunities to "shine," as many teachers say, they look for shows with more characters (especially individualized characters with names), more speaking parts, more chances for individual children to sing a lyric or dance solo, and more expandable ensembles. *The Little Mermaid JR.*, for example, added two gender-neutral, flexibly sized groups of characters, the Tentacles and the Sea Chorus: "The Tentacles are extensions of Ursula, perhaps the poor unfortunate souls who are now trapped in her lair." The Director's Guide instructs, "Look for six or eight performers who work well together and can move as a unit." They can be played by boys or girls, with a singing range of just over an octave. For the Sea Chorus, "Look for performers who can move gracefully and are capable of being part of a scene without drawing focus." Disney reminds teachers/directors, "This can also be an opportunity to showcase some of your more skilled dancers. The Sea Chorus can double as Merfolk, Sea Creatures and Lagoon Animals."[18] The Junior script equalizes the roles, and actors in the chorus are "responsible for creating each world within the show." Finally, and crucially, Junior shows are shorter. In spite of two groups of choruses added to the cast of *The Little Mermaid JR.*, ten songs and two reprises are cut from the full-length version. Duration is a key concern so that a musical can fit into a school-day performance as well as hold young children's limited attention.

For experienced directors, the advice cuts both ways. On the one hand, they get foolproof instructions for a musical that kids know and love. On the other hand, as Neva Garrett, who directs Holly Performance Academy in Dahlonega, Georgia, said, "As a director, there are times for . . . bringing your own flavor and interpretation to a script. A Disney *Aladdin* is not that time. Disney's *Little Mermaid* is not that time. I'm not going to try to tell Hans Christian Andersen's tragic *Little Mermaid*, I'm going to do my very best to create Ariel and Sebastian."

DTG's time, effort, and money dedicated to creating the Junior and Kids versions have paid off in spades. Not only is youth adaptations' licensing a self-sustaining business, but more money returns in Broadway and touring company ticket sales. As Schumacher said, "If you play Gaston, then you want to see the show." In this way, Disney works its way into the everyday lives of schools and communities.

Production Support: The Disney ShowKits

The breathtaking, coast-to-coast success of Disney Junior and Disney Kids licensing makes it more than clear that kids all over America want to do musicals—that is, Disney musicals. In many communities, however, though the desire is there, the expertise and experience are not. To enable anyone to produce a musical and, again, to maintain control over the product, DTG crafted ShowKits, which resemble iTheatrics' kits for the Broadway Junior series: "step-by-step materials that will help you create your production," which are included with the license of any Junior or Kids title. As the website explains, "The Director's Guide offers advice on everything from how to create a rehearsal schedule to fun games to play with your cast to help them develop characters." It also includes a budget template and ideas for constructing simple, inexpensive costumes and sets. A choreography DVD "provides suggestions for how to block and choreograph major musical numbers." A karaoke-style "Accompaniment & Guide Vocal CD" has full professional orchestral accompaniment as well as tracks with "reference vocals": kids singing on the CD to help newbies learn their vocal parts. Like the scripts and scores, the ShowKits are carefully calibrated to deliver just enough but not too much information to instill confidence in teachers, directors, and kids and to ensure the production's success. Every aspect of the show must be clear and accessible to children, from the young performers to the backstage crew, and to the family, neighbors, and friends who attend the show.

The Lion King KIDS at E.K. Powe Elementary School, Durham, North Carolina

"I felt like I had a lot of responsibility when I was making the hyena's mask," said Lia, a fifth-grade girl whose class performed *The Lion King KIDS* at E.K. Powe Elementary School in Durham, North Carolina, like thousands of elementary schools across the country do each year. She added, "I knew it was a performance for the whole school and I had to run around and get all of the materials because I wanted it to be a really good mask."

Located in a leafy residential area near the Ninth Street commercial center in northwest Durham, the school is racially and socioeconomically diverse, its student population drawn from three adjoining neighborhoods, one high-poverty and predominantly African American and two middle-class, white, and African American. There are five hundred students, 25 percent Hispanic, 28 percent African American, 41 percent White, and 53 percent are eligible for free or reduced-price lunches. The school's resources are adequate but not more than that, and producing a Disney show for $800 plus a recording fee was a stretch. Still, the school is located in a city that values theatre: The Durham Performing Arts Center, two miles away, is the fifth most highly attended performing arts center in the country, after Radio City Music Hall in New York City, Atlanta's Fox Theatre, and Caesars Palace and Planet Hollywood in Las Vegas.[19]

A newly hired and enterprising drama teacher, Sara, decided to direct the musical—the first at the school—with all of the fifth-graders (Figure 7.1). Lia said, "It was a new thing for us, so there wasn't anybody we could ask. We went head on!" Students could choose between acting and contributing backstage, and during their "specialty" period, they would go to either drama or art to work on the musical. The show was created during the school day plus one Saturday-afternoon rehearsal a few days prior to the performance.

Those who wanted to perform auditioned and could request a particular role, and Sara knew she would double-cast to give more students speaking roles. One of the girls, Lucy, already had acting experience in several afterschool programs, and she hoped and assumed she would get the coveted role of Nala, the female lead. When Lucy received her envelope from Sara, who delivered casting assignments privately and individually instead of posting a cast list publicly, which some teachers prefer, Lucy was disappointed to see her assigned part: Ed the Hyena. Upset, she told her parents, "Ed barely has any lines and he is ugly!"

That night, though, Sara called their house and left a message: "I saw Lucy's face when she read her part, and I wanted to say that she could have played any of the parts she wanted. But for each of the other parts, there were a few students who could play each part—and that was why we double-cast them. But she was the only one who could play Ed, and that's why we need her in both casts." Sara's message went on, "It's a funny and important character and she can ham it up." Sara had noticed that Lucy was let down, and she made an effort to explain the casting and make the girl feel valued.

"Did she get over it?" I asked her father, who told me this story.

"Yes!" he said. "She loves it and she sees that it's an important part."

The backstage crew, which was Lia's group, painted the backdrop of the set and made the masks for the show, which looked quite beautiful, thanks in

Figure 7.2. Lia displays the mask she created for *The Lion King KIDS*.

part to Disney's template and instructions (Figure 7.2). Because her work was completed before the performance, Lia also worked on makeup, which was extensive for the many animal characters in the show. She took her responsibility seriously: "We had an hour before every show, and during that time, the chorus had to get makeup on. There were four makeup girls and maybe twenty or so chorus singers, so we had to keep running around. We had to switch colors a lot for their different skin tones. We had to make sure that we had the right materials for the face paint."

Other kids moved set pieces during the show, and Sara hoped that all of the students were engaged as much as possible throughout the process. When I asked Lia about acting versus backstage work, she said, "The actors have the most peer pressure on them because they have to say the words right and they have to come out on stage at the right time. It's not as much pressure backstage when it's like, I have to make a bush or I have to make a tree."

The dress rehearsal I attended on a sunny Saturday afternoon in May felt as chaotic and exciting as any a few days before opening. They practiced in a small auditorium with wooden seats that folded down and a proscenium stage. A large child-painted backdrop of trees and mountains hung upstage. Some kids stood on stage, and some sat in the audience, half-watching, half-whispering to each other behind cupped hands. Backstage, other children applied makeup, got dressed in their costumes, or prepared to move the set. Sara, a white woman in her early twenties, wearing jeans, sneakers, and a T-shirt, with her brown hair pulled back in a neat ponytail, knelt on the carpeted floor in the aisle that bisected the auditorium, her script and score in a loose-leaf notebook opened in front of her. The music teacher sat by a little table house left and operated the sound system with the taped, orchestrated music.

Four days and two rehearsals before the show, the kids knew their lines, their music, and their blocking, and most of them engaged intensely and energetically and seemed to be having fun. When they all lined up for the group numbers, though, I could see gaps in the line where a few students were missing from the rehearsal. The mics, as is typical anywhere other than a professional theatre, were inadequate, cheap headsets that went in and out and emitted ear-splitting feedback when the kids got too close to the speakers that were set on both sides of the stage. As with so many rehearsals and performances I've seen, I wished there were no mics to distract these children—and they could only be a distraction—from the pleasure of singing and dancing together on stage. The students with the clearest sense of purpose were the set-changers, two boys who arrived on stage promptly the moment after each scene ended and efficiently moved the "rocks"—desk chairs covered with brown cloth, one of Disney's inexpensive, clever set ideas—or the cardboard trees on wheels.

Sara seemed completely calm, and she never stopped the kids to correct them or coach them or give them direction as they stumbled through the thirty-minute show. During the chorus songs, she conducted the singing from the floor, every child's eye trained on her. The group was diverse across race and ethnicity and size and shape. One girl seemed to be on the autism spectrum. African American boys played Simba and Mufasa with charismatic intensity, and an African American girl played Rafiki with great comic flair. At that age, some of the kids looked like children and others like adolescents. Unsurprisingly, then, when it came time for "Can You Feel the Love Tonight?" all of them sprinted to the audience to watch the actors playing Simba and Nala slow dance, chortling with embarrassed fascination over this whiff of heterosexual romance.

Lia said of the experience, her first time doing theatre, "We had to put a lot of effort into it. It paid off at the end. I was relieved that it went so well." She said that she had fun and the next time, "I would be in the chorus if it was a show that had a chorus. Other than that I would be behind the scenes. I like doing the costumes and the setting."

The show had lasting effects for the kids and the school, too. First, this group felt special because they were the first to do a musical. It made Lia and her friends feel connected to the school, and it's one of her fondest memories a few years later. In addition, the class-wide project crossed friend groups and put kids in collaborative relationships that they might not seek out on their own. Because ticket sales covered the licensing and production costs, the school could produce another musical the next year. What began with *The Lion King KIDS* is now an E.K. Powe tradition.

After the performance, Lia told me, "During the first show when the K-2 grades saw it first, and it was at the end of the day, and my teacher was on bus duty, and a bunch of people were saying, 'Hey, we saw *The Lion King*!' My teacher was crying. I guess she's proud of us." Surely on that same day, there were thousands of other proud and crying fifth-grade teachers across the United States whose class performed the show.

Outreach: Disney Musicals in Schools

The scripts, scores, licensing agreements, and ShowKits for *Cinderella KIDS, Peter Pan JR.*, and all of the other titles are readily available to be purchased by anyone anywhere at any time, like they did at E.K. Powe. But what about communities where musical theatre is not a part of the academic or community landscape? In 2009, DTG began to reach this population in urban locales by launching a highly sophisticated, closely monitored, and blazingly ambitious outreach program to support the production of a Disney Kids show at approximately ten underserved public elementary schools in New York City each year.[20] At the time, a 2009 report by the New York City–based Center for Arts Education found that "the great majority of the city's public schools were failing to meet the minimum state requirements for arts education as set by the New York State Education Department."[21] DMIS was created in part to compensate for this deficiency.

The positive social, emotional, and intellectual effects of participation in the arts in general and musical theatre specifically have been well documented, with more studies to come. According to Lisa Mitchell's New York City–based study, participation in theatre develops "strong self-efficacy concepts," as children gain a sense of themselves in the world and their own agency.[22] In the 2009 report, public policy and arts advocacy expert Douglas Israel found that "children who perform in a school musical . . . are more likely to stay in school than their peers without access to the arts."[23] Arts education expert James Catterall observes, "Students with high levels of arts participation outperform 'arts-poor' students by virtually every measure. Since arts participation is highly correlated with socioeconomic status, which is the most significant predictor of academic performance, this comes as little surprise."[24] While all children benefit from engagement with the arts, Catterall argues, those from lower socioeconomic backgrounds profit exponentially.[25]

DMIS attempts to level the playing field. The program's gift to participating schools consists of three parts: first, free licensing rights to one of the thirty-minute Disney Kids titles, which includes scripts and scores for the whole cast; second, the ShowKit with Director's Guide and all of the other bells and whistles; and third, the semester-long presence of Disney-sponsored teaching artists to work with classroom teachers to produce the show. (Musicians and musical training are not a part of this program. To be sure, students should learn to play an instrument and, ideally, every performance would be accompanied by a live student orchestra. For DMIS to provide young children with opportunities to sing, dance, and act, though, professionally taped musical accompaniment is their best solution.) From the start, the DTG education team prioritized all three components: Licensing, informational materials, and people with expertise were all necessary for a school to produce its first musical.

But the program has higher aspirations. More than just produce one show, DMIS aims to seed self-sustaining musical theatre programs in schools; that is, "to develop a culture of theater production within high-need urban elementary schools."[26] Thus Disney decreases its support in subsequent years, which forces each school to harness local resources and find ingenious ways to sustain its production of a yearly musical. Remarkably, almost every school initially funded by DMIS has continued to produce shows.

New York City, with its intense concentration of theatrical energy, arts philanthropy, and a population of students who live right next door to Broadway but had never been there, was the perfect place to launch such a program. Still, it was a blip on the screen of DTG's ambitions, as they wanted to help start musical theatre programs all over the country. In 2010, they launched

Nashville's program, and by 2018, DMIS had expanded to nineteen additional cities: the Bay Area in California; Chicago; Cleveland; Dallas; East Lansing, Michigan; Kingman, Arizona: Las Vegas; Los Angeles; Louisville; Madison, Wisconsin; Newark, New Jersey; Oklahoma City, Oklahoma; Omaha, Nebraska; Orange County, California; Orlando; Philadelphia; Seattle; West Palm Beach, and one in London, England, with new sites being added each year.[27]

Disney's wide reach and visibility across every communication platform make it the ideal—and perhaps the only—artistic enterprise that could pull off such a bold and wide-ranging initiative. Although musical theatre production is an intimate, local practice that requires on-the-ground oversight, Disney's brand is global and ubiquitous. Most children are familiar with Disney characters and have seen the animated movies on which the Disney Kids shows are based. "Disney is the gateway art," said Kristin Horsley of the Tennessee Performing Arts Center. First-time DMIS schools often choose a musical that the kids already know, especially because many have never seen a play and don't know what live theatre is. DMIS, then, builds on preexisting knowledge, at once benefiting kids in underserved communities and generating a future base of consumers, potential theatregoers, and even possibly artists, all with loyalty to the Disney brand. More than that, this program imagines a radically diverse musical theatre future, ethnically, racially, and socioeconomically. With this project, Disney knits corporate profits into philanthropy.

Disney Musicals in Schools in Nashville

For its first out-of-New-York-City venture in 2010, Disney chose Nashville and the Tennessee Performing Arts Center (TPAC) as its local partner. Disney envisioned a "unique blend of a commercial theater producer, nonprofit arts center, school district, and corporate charity partnering to bolster arts education."[28] They model a team approach with each of the various stakeholders contributing; that is, Disney provides the materials as well as advice and support for the sponsoring local performing arts center, especially in the program's first year. "I was calling New York every five minutes," said Roberta Ciuffo West, TPAC's executive vice president for education and outreach, who oversees Nashville's program. She was only half-joking, well aware that Disney had worked out many of the kinks in New York and that the home office had clear goals and expectations for the program.

The local performing arts center staff are responsible for operations and oversight. They vet and select the schools, disperse the materials, hire the teaching artists, and answer questions and support the schools from auditions through rehearsals and performance. TPAC also produces the end-of-year Student Share, a celebratory performance in which each first-year school performs one musical number from their production in the 2,472-seat Andrew Jackson Hall in downtown Nashville for family, teachers, and students from other sponsored schools. This "professional debut" adds a layer of glossiness onto the hard work of doing a show, trains the students to be supportive spectators of their peers, and allows the students, teachers, and families to see the larger community of DMIS participants across the city. The teachers at each school, of course, do the bulk of the work.

Once Disney selected TPAC to pilot its nationwide venture, Ciuffo West sought applications from elementary schools in the Metropolitan Nashville Public Schools, visited a number of finalist schools, and, in consultation with Nola Jones, the school district's coordinator of visual and performing arts, chose five schools for the program's first year.[29] They looked for "need and readiness": evidence that producing a musical would be impossible without DMIS's resources and that the school's administrators, teachers, and staff were prepared to dedicate the enormous time and energy necessary to pull it off.

In addition, they intentionally sponsored schools in different neighborhoods across the city, though all had a significant percentage of students receiving free or reduced-price lunches and the majority were students of color. DMIS's purpose is "to primarily serve public-school students living at or below the federal poverty level."[30] Amy Kramer, a fourth-grade teacher at Buena Vista Enhanced Option Elementary School, said, "Most of our students have never had any experience like this before, any performing, [any] extracurricular activities. Many of them . . . aren't involved in anything after school." In 2014–15, eleven hundred students in twenty schools across Nashville participated in the program,[31] and 43 percent of the seventy-one elementary schools in the MNPS had applied. Ciuffo West hopes that all Nashville public schools will be funded in time.

A few months later, teachers from the selected schools gather at TPAC downtown for an orientation day, which includes a detailed overview of the program, budget and tech recommendations, and a display of all of the Disney Kids materials for them to examine and, by the end of the day, choose their show to take back to their school with much excitement and anticipation.

The group of adults who collaborate on each school's production possess complementary expertise: The teaching artists have considerable musical theatre experience, while the teachers know their school, its culture, and the children. DTG's Mitchell and her team designed a seventeen-week, ninety-minute biweekly rehearsal schedule in which teaching artists—two per school who visit once a week—take the lead for the first third of the rehearsal process; then they and the team of teachers partner evenly for the second third; then the teaching artists step back and the teachers oversee the production's final rehearsals, tech, dress rehearsals, and performances.

Ciuffo West hires teaching artists who are "artists first," many of whom are local professional musicians, dancers, or actors, and they all participate in an intensive three-day training to learn the Disney way. The school gathers a team of at least three to five teachers who volunteer to work on the show, which typically includes the school's arts specialist (every public school in Nashville has an arts specialist on staff, with expertise in music or art or theatre) and others who may or may not have any previous musical theatre experience.

The teachers quickly learn the ropes of theatrical production, while the teaching artists figure out the idiosyncrasies of the school and the children. Susan Scoby, a teacher at Gower Elementary, said, "Our [teaching artists] have been wonderful, and probably the most valuable they've been to us was through the audition process [when 150 children auditioned] because they had done that before." She added that the teaching artists were also able to see performance potential in students that teachers who know the kids might miss. "I would have never picked the boy playing Bagheera for a lead role and he's phenomenal," she said.

From the other side, the teaching artists benefit from and build on the learning and behavior practices already in place at the school. At Buena Vista, for example, the Disney musical rehearsal process began as all classes do at the start of the school year, with students articulating the "norms"; that is, the rules and expectations that they themselves propose and that all agree to follow, which included "Be brave" (meaning, don't be shy), "Respect," "Try our best," and "Keep practicing at home."

Still, such partnerings can be challenging on both sides. Occasionally teaching artists, who understandably become immersed in the process and attached to the kids, struggle to step back, especially when they have the skills to polish the show and bring the production to a higher aesthetic level. From the other side, elementary school teachers, who typically operate with considerable autonomy in their classrooms and control everyday practices and procedures, are unaccustomed to the degree of intense collaboration, co-operation, and compromise that musical theatre necessitates. Accustomed to teaching many subjects, they also might not expect the division of labor typical for theatrical production: assignments as director, musical director, choreographer, stage manager, and so on.

Finally, some classroom teachers might not anticipate the enormous amount of time required to stage and rehearse a musical, even a short thirty-minute show, including running lines and repeating choreography again and again. As noted in the introduction, some professional directors estimate one hour of rehearsal per one minute of production for nonmusical plays. DMIS appropriately allots almost twice that: a hundred minutes of rehearsal per minute of performance for a thirty-minute show. Whatever the adults' expectations or surprises, as they become more invested in the show and the stakes get higher, it can become harder to disentangle themselves or to compromise their vision or habitual ways of working.

The adults aim to create an atmosphere that is both serious and fun, creative and disciplined. Teaching artist Ginger Newman explained that she holds a "workshop" and plays theatre games with the kids rather than calling what they're doing "auditions." "You say the word 'audition' and they stiffen," she told me. During rehearsals, though, the kids learn and get accustomed to an expectation of "professionalism," including hearing theatre terms like "blocking" and "house right." When I visited Gower, teaching artist Marci Murphree gave the students a pep talk: "This is a dress rehearsal. Bring your best stuff: your best singing, dancing," and later, she told them, "I love the way it sounds in here. It's so professional." Later in the same day's rehearsal, drama teacher Miya Robertson coached a student, "Use your mother's voice when she can't find you. Use your acting skills."

Some lessons are learned the hard way. Master teacher Kathy Hull, who piloted *The Lion King KIDS* as well as Disney's linked elementary school curriculum, told me this story:

> One of my kids, he skipped a line or something and it caused someone to miss their cue. Evidently the child that missed her cue was his cousin. So she slaps him—backstage after the show was over. I put her out of the show.

[I said], "This is not right, not here, ever in any theater in the country, you would not be allowed to behave that way."

While the production is taken on with the utmost seriousness and highest expectations of the performance's quality, every adult to whom I spoke stressed the importance of "process over product." They want the process to be fun and for the children to grow artistically, socially, emotionally, and academically. To be sure, every child's answer to, "What did you think about doing the Disney show?" was, "It was fun!" "We got to learn new dances, we got to sing fun stuff," said a fourth-grade girl.

Here lies yet another contradiction in Disney's engagement with musical theatre and kids: On the one hand, every aspect of the DMIS program is designed to allow Disney to control its product. On the other, the DTG home office knows that theatre is messy and each production is entirely unique.

Moreover, for many children, it's a steep learning curve of both performance skills and theatrical culture. The teachers at Buena Vista explained that their students knew the story and songs from the movie of *The Jungle Book*, which was their first play in 2014, but that none had ever been to the theatre or knew what a live play was. (TPAC sponsors school visits to its theatres for kids to see a professional play, but some schools lack the resources to organize permission slips, bus rental, and so on to get the children downtown, said team leader and teacher Joe Ashby.) The children didn't know what it meant to learn lines or blocking, portray a character, or wear a costume especially made for them in front of an audience. Ashby found another school's production on YouTube, which the teachers watched with the children before starting rehearsals, and the students followed along in their scripts. By the second year's auditions for *Aladdin KIDS*, though, the whole school had experienced *The Jungle Book KIDS* and had seen their first play. This is how cultural capital is acquired.

Each school in Nashville navigates a balance among generating enthusiasm for the play, encouraging many students' participation, and dealing with inevitable attrition. Teachers at every school I visited shared stories about the number of kids who auditioned compared to how many performed in the end; in the first year, they lost half the cast along the way as kids learned that being in a play is hard work. It's not unusual for a role to be recast during the rehearsal process, even a day before the performance, as I witnessed at one school. A nine-year-old boy playing a leading role had missed a number of rehearsals and didn't know his choreography. He was unceremoniously replaced by a girl who knew the part well.

"You should be relieved," a teacher told the crying boy. "You looked like you didn't know what you were doing." Within ten minutes, the same boy was hamming it up in the chorus.

At another school 75 percent of the population is transient (many of them homeless), which means that three-quarters of the students who start the school year are gone by the spring, and around 270 children enter the school sometime midyear. To manage the play's rehearsals with the schools' shifting population, the adult team casts the leading roles with students who are likely to still be there in May and welcomes all students to rehearse for as long as they attend the school, or join the cast or crew whenever they arrive. In the Nashville schools, no casts have had fewer than thirty students, and some schools featured more than a hundred performers plus fifty more helping backstage. From the moment the show is announced to the final curtain call and enthusiastic applause, the adults underline teamwork and the importance of each and every character, of each and every student's contribution, which is supported by the numerous named characters in the Disney Kids scripts.

Some Nashville schools also adapt Disney's materials to the particularities of their population and resources. For example, many of the students at Harris-Hillman Special Education School are in wheelchairs or are non-communicative, so for their 2014 production of *The Aristocats KIDS*, their caregivers, tutors, or teachers stood behind and maneuvered wheelchairs, moved their limbs, or sang their parts. "They respond tremendously during rehearsal. I see a difference in the kids," observed teacher Stacy Subero, and teaching artist Ginger Newman enthused, "I've never encountered fearlessness like I have here . . . that's the one quality that we can't teach. And to walk into an environment and it's right there? It's been unbelievable."[32]

Though licensing forbids changing lines, DMIS allows roles to be cast in any way and for the chorus to be infinitely expanded. In the 2015 production of *Alice in Wonderland JR.*, at Wright Middle Prep, whose student population is predominantly Latinx and Kurdish, three different-sized girls (all Latinas) played Alice at the different stages of her adventure, and three other girls (also Latinas) were cast as the Cheshire Cat(s), with the lines divided among them, as they formed a kind of harmonious girl group.[33] At Buena Vista, they incorporated a step routine into the choreography of "Prince Ali," as Joe Ashby explained, so they could "bring some of the things they like to do into the world of Agrabah." In the end, all theatre—even when it's produced and overseen by a huge multinational corporation—is local.

Teaching artists, who, as visitors, work with the children once a week over the course of four months, observe remarkable changes, especially in the kids' confidence, expressiveness, and ability to articulate their ideas clearly. New York–based teaching artist Elizabeth Nestlerode said, "In just a few short months, kids who you could barely hear speaking their lines at the first read-through are standing up tall, speaking their lines loudly and clearly, taking pride in their part of the production." Tonya Pewitt, a Nashville teaching artist at Wright Middle Prep, talked about "how much the students were helping each other. If another person was having trouble with lines, lyrics, or dance moves another student was always willing to help." She observed that the program "helps with communication, reading, and public speaking. The students are having to commit to something and stick with it even when it gets hard, which is huge in character building." She continued, "The students are also getting to use their imagination. And instead of sitting at home they are at school being active. If they are struggling at home this is a great outlet for them." Teaching artists also note that some students who elect not to perform in the show often excel backstage as sound board operators, set builders, and assistant stage managers.

The teachers who see the children every day in class note academic and behavioral improvement. For the children, "doing Disney" is a privilege. Natalie Affinito, a math teacher who was Creswell's *The Little Mermaid JR.*'s musical director, explained, "You start to see some of these students open up more in the classroom, and you start to see the kids that maybe were a little bit too rowdy in the classroom, now they have an outlet to do that, they start to become more focused in the classroom."[34] Kathy Hull said of Hull-Jackson Montessori Magnet School's 2012 production of *Aladdin KIDS*, "They are so proud of themselves. And I think that they have come to realize their potential."[35] Sara Cottrill-Carlo, from Lakeview Elementary Design Center, said about their production of *Aladdin KIDS* in 2014, "I've seen them feel connected to the school in a way that I don't think they did before. And I think some that maybe whose grades aren't fantastic, who aren't getting a lot of praise in other ways, they're getting it here, and so they're having, you know, a higher sense of self-worth because they're part of something bigger."[36] Every teacher told stories of specific children who "blossomed" during the production. A teacher at Gower said of one very quiet and shy boy, "This has just been the first time he has been able to shine. He's in the fourth grade now and I've never seen him do what he's doing now."

The experience of doing a Disney musical is profoundly transformative for virtually every child. A fourth-grade boy who performed in *Aladdin KIDS* said, "I stopped being afraid. I'm thinking to myself, Yeah, this is going to be awesome!"[37] A third-grade girl from Buena Vista's *Aladdin KIDS* said that she enjoyed "the costumes and how we worked together to do it." Teaching artist Tonya Pewitt recounted a conversation with the mother of a boy who was a last-minute replacement for a leading role and was "extremely nervous": "I told her how much I think he has grown and how much more outgoing he has become. She told me, 'I can see a difference too, and I am so thankful that he is getting to do this. I know he has it in him, but I don't have the money to put him in anything like this. I am so grateful the school is offering something like this.'"

While the performance is a big occasion for every school, some teachers have been able to draw in parents or other members of the neighborhood community to help out. Kathy Hull, for example, schedules several Saturday afternoons for families to come to the school to help with the show. She sets up different stations for parents and children to make masks, sew costumes, and paint flats. Even though parents might belong to opposing local gangs, she said, they put their differences aside to work on the show. Still, Hull, as a master teacher, has taught several generations of families.

At other schools, they learn year by year how to work with and for the community. One group of teachers told me that in their first year of the program, they scheduled one performance on Friday during the school day, and one on Friday night and another on Saturday night for families and friends. But when Saturday came, half the cast didn't show up. "It wasn't a norm to bring their kids to school on a Saturday," said Joe Ashby, and some children who didn't live within walking distance lacked transportation. The next year, they planned the second performance for the end of the school day on Thursday as part of an already existing student "Showcase," where families are served dinner, look at student artwork displayed around the school, and then see the Disney show. The production adapts to the community's norms, and families and neighbors are more likely to get involved because they recognize the Disney brand.

The Student Share, which is the "professional debut" culmination of a school's first year in the program, reproduces the contradiction between process and product that weaves through the entire DMIS enterprise. Students look forward to singing and dancing on the big performing arts center's stage in their city, and the teachers and teaching artists polish one musical number that highlights the kids' talents (as much as no one wants to talk about talent) and perseverance as well as their skill as directors. Nashville's 2015 Student Share was hosted by rising-star country music duo, Maddie & Tae, and three hundred children from six schools performed.[38]

New York's Student Share, which is the model for other cities' events and which I attended in 2015, took place at the New Amsterdam Theatre, where *Aladdin* was playing at 97 percent capacity, having grossed $1.5 million that week (Figure 7.3).[39] This Student Share was an expertly managed affair, with hundreds of kids, their teachers, family members and friends, and invited guests from Disney, MTI, the New York City Department of Education, and other stakeholders. Emceed by a Broadway performer—Bonita Hamilton, who played Shenzi in *The Lion King*—the afternoon extravaganza featured each first-year DMIS school performing a musical number from their show, punctuated with patter from the host and a gorgeously produced, tear-jerking video about the DMIS program and its effects all over the country. Each group was introduced by two of their teachers and that school's teaching artists, who testified to the impact of the show on the students and the school.

From DTG president Thomas Schumacher, who opened and closed the event, through the host and the video, to the adults' introductions to their school's performance, "You're making your Broadway debut" was the mantra. This showcase transports the students and their performances out of their neighborhood and into the theatre district, connecting what they've been doing with the world of Broadway. When kids enter the theatre, they're overwhelmed. "Are you serious?!" exclaimed one girl in a bright yellow flower costume as she looked up and around the Smith Center, the location of the Las Vegas Student Share. "This stage is so big!" said a boy in a cap with raccoon ears.[40] If rehearsals at school emphasize good and responsible behavior, expressiveness, and cooperation, the Student Share opens up the fantasy of becoming a Broadway star.

Seeing fifteen different student groups at several Student Shares that I attended helped me to understand how teachers and teaching artists can wrangle eighty ten-year-olds and make a performance that is not only coherent but also charming and engaging for the audience. The general choreographic template was unified, simple movements for the very large chorus and basic blocking for the featured characters. A few schools had more complex choreography, such as two different groups doing different movements

Figure 7.3. Invitation to the DMIS Student Share Celebration in New York City.

at the same time, or a gesture that was passed down the line. The featured performers tended to be children with bold expressiveness and striking charisma on stage—kids of all sizes and shapes and races and personality types—who'd mastered the skill of seeming to speak to their scene partner while remaining physically open to the audience.

Gower Elementary's production of *The Jungle Book*, whose dress rehearsal I observed, had two sets of risers on the floors in front of the stage on which all of the children sat, in full view of the audience, when they were "offstage." The show, as most Disney Kids scripts, has many ensemble numbers, and the kids gestured or stood to perform simple, unified choreography from the risers. For other numbers, they came down off the risers and onto the cafeteria floor to dance in the big group songs. In this way, the whole cast was involved with the production and performed for the entire thirty minutes. When they weren't singing or dancing, the ensemble played observers of the action, standing in for audience members. The show—like the musical numbers performed in the Student Share—was conceived to make everyone look good, and it did.

DMIS has been astonishingly successful so far, balancing "quality control" of the brand with the idiosyncrasies of each locale. Each performing arts center operates under its city's structures and rules; each school system differs; each arts scene is unique. "We were surprised and delighted to see how much each city's DMIS program takes on its own local flavor," said DTG's Mitchell. "In Nashville, many of the teaching artists are musicians, so the music is fantastic; Seattle has a kind of cool grunge feel; and in Las Vegas, the kids are doing complex, undulating choreography since there are so many dancers and many of the teaching artists have been performers in Cirque du Soleil–style shows." Almost all of the participating schools have continued to do musicals, though some performing arts centers have had to kick in their own funding to supplement Disney's decreasing support of the schools. Cities are added each year with ever-expansive plans, but Disney's national ambitions for this aspirational project are the polar opposite of standardized testing.

Critiques of DMIS

From a pedagogical perspective, what might be the objections to and critiques of Disney's program? To start, most progressive educators scoff at the idea of Broadway musical theatre's repertoire providing the material for a reformist program. Broadway musicals have long been considered mindless, middlebrow, conservative, escapist entertainment, in part because they are typically produced at commercial venues with high (and expensive) production values, and in part because they seldom offer overtly political and left-leaning perspectives.[41] Even contemporary shows that challenged Broadway like *Rent* and *Hamilton* have come under sharp critique by academics for their neoliberal, individualist messages and ultimate pandering to the status quo. Broadway and social change seem to inhabit completely different political realms. If Broadway musicals aren't bad enough, the prospect of Disney musicals occupying the central place in a socially progressive program is incomprehensible.

Progressive educators take the opposite route and privilege Theatre in Education (TIE)'s devised practices, supported by the belief that children should tell their own stories, which become the basis of the performance (as I discussed in relation to high school musicals in Chapter 3). For kids who don't see their lives on stage, generating autobiographical scripts can be enormously validating. Young people can share their stories, shape them into performance, and publicly reveal their feelings and experiences.

But pointing only to original, devised, autobiographical work as a source of empowerment is reductive and fails to acknowledge that for some kids, pretending to be someone else and playing a role in a Disney musical is equally (if differently) empowering. As a fourth-grade girl from Nashville told me, "I loved being Jasmine [in *Aladdin KIDS*]. I got to wear a long scarf and pretend I was flying!" Playing Disney characters allows kids to launch themselves into an imaginary place. Further, they gain significant artistic and cognitive skills through imitation and emulation, not unlike the value of playing a musical instrument by reproducing the notes on the page or learning dance by following a teacher's movements. Some proponents of TIE assume that true creativity only emerges from the self—as if the "self" could be untainted, unmediated, and free from culture—who creates her own performance text. But each type of performance offers a different and valuable kind of creative expression.[42]

Further, the exceptionally high quality of Disney materials helps to bridge applied theatre's struggle between aesthetics and the social, and address the unfortunate but well-earned worry that much applied theatre is aesthetically weak, or what theatre and education expert Helen Nicholson describes as TIE's "unpredictable quality."[43] The scripts, scores, Director's Guides, and

CDs and DVDs that Disney supplies have been workshopped and tested before they are released and licensed. The shows are failproof, kid-friendly, and guaranteed for success. The stories are clear, the characters are winning and easy to play, the music is infectious, and the total effect is charming. With the ShowKits, it's virtually ensured that the show will be good. The kids will do well and be proud of themselves; family and friends will be entertained; administrators will be impressed. Success motivates.

But what roles are children succeeding in playing, especially in terms of gender? Even in elementary schools, more girls than boys participate in theatre, but the gender stereotypes that prevail in Disney products haunt these shows, too. The shows that DTG first developed as Disney Kids shows, including *The Jungle Book, 101 Dalmatians*, and *Aristocats*, feature many characters that aren't explicitly gendered. Teachers and teaching artists frequently cast cross-gender in shows like *The Aristocats KIDS*. Many teachers prefer those shows over the sexist, heterosexist classics *Cinderella KIDS* and *Sleeping Beauty KIDS*. Newer releases like *Aladdin KIDS* and *The Lion King KIDS* appeal to schools that are eager to get boys involved in musical theatre production, but these titles provide fewer leading roles for the always enthusiastic overabundance of girls. Also, those shows still rely on gender stereotypes and track a heterosexual romance.

When children inhabit these roles, they are forced to impersonate some characters who are poor role models for their developing personhood and to enact happily-ever-after fantasy tales that discourage political action. Nicholson argues that theatre in schools should "unfix commodified images of the world," which of course DMIS fails to do.[44] Several teachers at Gower Elementary School in Nashville told me that they were happy to be doing *The Jungle Book KIDS* because "at least it doesn't have princesses," one said. "Or a girl being saved by a man," said another. The very power of musical theatre performance shapes kids in particular physical and emotional ways.

Disney has added stronger female roles to its repertoire in recent years— Belle in *Beauty and the Beast*, the title character of *Mulan*, and the sisters in *Frozen*, for example—and from many conversations with the dramaturgs and educators at DTG, I know that they're eager to create more strong female roles for Disney Junior and Kids shows. At the schools I visited, in conversations and interviews with teachers as well as the rehearsals and performances I observed, girls played Baloo and Shere Khan but not Aladdin or Simba. The promise of Disney musicals' progressive political potential lies in part in the flexibility of gender in casting. Will elementary schools be brave enough to cast a boy as Cinderella or a girl as Mufasa in *The Lion King JR.*?

On the other hand, in terms of race, this program is impressively progressive. Disney musicals' troubling representations become differently inflected in actual elementary school productions in which virtually every character is played by a child of color, cast based on their energy and expressiveness and not their appearance or type. The racial population of the Nashville DMIS schools—and this is the case for all of the DMIS cities—leans heavily towards students of color and so ensures multiracial and "color-blind" casting, dominated by kids of color. Though critics may fret over the urban stereotype of the Hyenas in *The Lion King*, for example, such a view holds less sway in this context where every character in every musical is played by a child of color: a refreshing and moving vision of the twenty-first-century musical theatre stage. The charming production of *Alice in Wonderland JR.*, which I saw at Wright Middle Prep, boasted a cast of forty kids, almost all of them Latinx, Kurdish, or African American. For a spectator accustomed to a depressingly white Broadway, seeing so many children of color in a musical is nothing short of revolutionary.[45]

Another problem with DMIS might be that the personnel—the Disney representatives and the teaching artists—are outsiders to the school and inhabit what Kathleen Gallagher calls the colonizing stance of the white teacher as "noble savior." (Whether or not they're actually white, they hold power, privilege, and cultural capital.) She describes the "victory story" to which arts educators are attached: "A White teacher 'caring' and 'saving' Black youth; a school as safe haven; art making as the social leveller; and aesthetic engagement as social cohesion."[46] Artist-educators bring "altruistic" impulses, a term that Nicholson historicizes to underline its built-in power dynamics—a top-down model of control.[47] Progressives take issue with "outreach work" when visitors don't form a true partnership with the community, but merely duck in to make work and leave. Theatre of the Oppressed expert Kelly Howe critiques this "center-to-periphery power flow imagined in the word 'outreach' and in many of the projects for youth—often urban youth—designed by big money."[48] DMIS tries to offset this dynamic by employing local teaching artists—including many artists of color—and focusing the program on teaching teachers to make theatre; that is, DMIS tries to shift the power closer to the ground. Ideally, parents get involved as well.

Disney monitors a school's success to see if it can sustain its musical theatre program without teaching artists and Disney's free materials. In this way, the project attempts to foster long-term change rather than what's derisively termed "drive-by activism." To a degree, then, DMIS counters the "flash and dash" approach because its goal is not a single production of a musical but a long-term program at each school it sponsors.[49]

Activists also condemn outsiders who bring in the issues that they think matter to the community rather than the community deciding for itself what it wants its theatre to confront and represent. Worse still, DMIS's curriculum, built on the (re)production of Disney musicals, not only smooths over political discontents but also reinforces Disney shows' value as cultural capital and makes Disney's culture more central (if that's even possible) to kids' lives and to US culture.[50] When rich corporations fund philanthropic arts projects, they—not the people they purportedly serve—ultimately chart the theatrical repertoire for underserved communities. Children in DMIS gain valuable cultural capital as they learn what musical theatre is and how to do a show, but their knowledge and skill-building is formed in the service of Disney's products. Kids are groomed as loyal consumers as well as young musical theatre artists. The program is opposite of a typical applied theatre project that would foment social unrest and lead to change.

Ironically, though, Disney already infiltrates every class, race, and geographic sector of the country and so, weirdly (like all mass culture into which we're all entirely interpellated), feels like a relevant text for the schoolchildren. Disney's global presence in print, live, filmed, televised, and internet media enable the company to research, test, refine, and produce scripts and scores that will engage kids. Even children who have never been to the theatre recognize Disney characters, having seen the animated movies from which the Disney Kids shows are adapted. Still, the message of all Disney shows is liberal and individualist.

Does the program work to empower kids? In each sponsored city, Disney partly judges the program's success based on firsthand accounts by teachers and teaching artists, students, and performing arts center staff, many of which are articulated immediately following the production. But, as Kathleen Gallagher notes, a student's short-term experience does not always compel permanent change. Because of "the precariousness of engagement," she argues, teachers must involve students ten thousand times a day, each and every day. Students move on. Will these plays change the children later in their lives? Will these children change theatre? Only time will tell.

And what about the larger social, economic, and theatrical implications of this program? At once generously philanthropic and also colonizing—they only do Disney musicals after all—DMIS advertises the company, glossy with generosity and good will.

From the perspective of musical theatre education, DMIS promises the future racial, ethnic, and socioeconomic diversity of amateur and professional musical theatre. Perhaps the participating kids will become theatregoers; perhaps they will become artists; but providing them with cultural capital, the knowledge and experience of making theatre, and an intimate look at Disney's repertoire is undeniably empowering.[51] DMIS invites kids into the space of Broadway musical theatre through their own performances and develops their own creativity as well.[52] Neoliberal, yes. Corporate, yes. But empowering nonetheless.

DMIS challenges the assumption that corporations and activism are opposed. If we imagine a continuum of benefits/purpose/values, at one end, the measure of success for a corporation is profits. At the other end, success for activism is empowerment, equality, and justice.[53] But fifty African American, Latino, Kurdish, Asian American, and white children performing in a Nashville elementary school production of *The Jungle Book KIDS* dislodge this dichotomy. In this "community of solidarity," in Gallagher's words, "the social exchange is in the art."[54] Playwright Howard Barker rejects the notion of theatre's utility, arguing that neither profits nor politics should motivate art-making. Though DMIS is motivated by both profit and politics, a roomful of children singing "Bare Necessities" at the top of their lungs seems to make those goals temporarily disappear, and all that remains is laughter and pleasure and the power of making musical theatre together.

From licensing to developing supplementary materials to creating a national philanthropic musical theatre program, DTG has gradually expanded from corporation to church, from content to method, from providing product that is already desired to creating desire by introducing musical theatre to an ever more diverse population. From my progressive, feminist musical theatre scholar's perspective, it's hard not to drink (or at least sip) the Kool-Aid. Whatever my skepticism about global corporate capitalism or my frustration with Disney's parade of princesses, I suspect that any chance of a racially, ethnically, and socioeconomically diverse musical theatre is here, enabled by the organizational machinery, the adaptable repertoire, and the money of one of the richest corporations that owns Broadway.

As for *The Little Mermaid* that flopped, it didn't return to Broadway, but was successfully altered and revised by director Glenn Casale for a Dutch production in 2012, which he reworked again at Paper Mill Playhouse in New Jersey, followed by a three city "mini-tour" and a 2014 acclaimed production at the North Shore Music Theater in Beverly, Massachusetts.[55] The now frequently produced (by both professionals and amateurs) full-length licensable script is new and improved, thanks to the alterations instigated by the Junior adaptation. But I doubt if any production will be as engaging or impressive as the one I saw at Creswell Middle School of the Arts in Nashville.

Figure 8.1. Patrons eating dinner before *Kiss Me, Kate* at the Candlelight Dinner Playhouse.

8

Dinner Theatres: A Road Trip

Welcome to Colorado, the Centennial State

The sixty-mile stretch of I-25 in Colorado between Denver and Fort Collins is among the most breathtaking sections of interstate in the United States, with snow-capped mountains on the left and flat farm and ranch land as far as you can see on the right. This route, sometimes backed up with rush-hour traffic and sometimes empty for miles, traverses geographically the more liberal, wealthier, and highest-educated corridor of the state.[1] Two universities, Colorado State University in Fort Collins and the University of Colorado at Boulder, mark its north–south edges, and both cities regularly appear on lists of the 10 best places to live or retire. And within a radius of thirty-two miles from Loveland, you will find four thriving dinner theatres: Boulder Dinner Theatre (BDT Stage), Jesters, Candlelight Dinner Playhouse, and the Midtown Arts Center.[2] With a population of 4.5 million in the 415 square miles that make up this region—the Front Range—thousands of people attend dinner theatre each year.[3]

Dinner theatre complements, contradicts, conforms to, and complicates everything about the other theatres we've visited in this book. Like outdoor summer musicals, the theatrical production portion of dinner theatre is the main attraction, but not the only reason people attend. Like the Junior Theatre Festival, dinner theatres are commercial ventures that aim to make money through musical theatre production. Like community theatres, dinner theatres foster a close relationship with their audience. Like the backstage divas of afterschool programs, dinner theatre managers must be passionate, dedicated, and single-minded for the business to succeed.

And like every example in this book, dinner theatre re-performs the national repertoire of Broadway musicals, distributed by Music Theatre International (MTI), Rodgers and Hammerstein, Theatrical Rights Worldwide, and the other licensors. Productions are haunted by original Broadway productions, movie musicals, and YouTube clips. And still, like

Beyond Broadway. Stacy Wolf, Oxford University Press (2020). © Oxford University Press.
DOI: 10.1093/oso/9780190639525.001.0001

every venue in this book, dinner theatres produce shows that reflect the local context at every turn—in season selection, casting, advertising and branding, production values, the menu, and the total experience of the evening.

Here's how dinner theatres are different, though. First, as we'll see, dinner theatres are businesses. Corporations like Disney and licensors like MTI profit from people's participation in musical theatre, but a dinner theatre will close if there aren't enough patrons to pay the bills. Second, dinner theatre performers are professionals. Except for a few Equity contracts at the Mountain Play, all of the performers in this book are volunteers. Third, dinner theatre comes under more criticism and ridicule than other sites in this book, even more than community theatre. As we'll see, this contempt is connected to the fact that it's a business, that it hires professionals, and that it was invented in the 1970s.

My sister, Allie, joined me on a research trip to Colorado, which was the last journey for this book, but in some ways the first journey, too. When I was in elementary school, as I described in the introduction, I performed in two shows—*The Sound of Music* and *The King and I* (yes, I wore "Siamese" stage makeup and a black wig)—at the Burn Brae Dinner Theatre, located halfway between Baltimore and Washington, DC in a landscape that was, in the early 1970s, shifting day by day from farmland to suburbia.[4] Allie and I both took Saturday drama and dance classes that were held at the dinner theatre, taught by a formidable backstage diva, Toby Orenstein, who a few years later got kicked out of the theatre when her classes got too big and interfered with weekend rehearsals. With the help of our real estate broker and mildly stage-struck father—his never-fulfilled dream was to play Officer Krupke in *West Side Story*—Toby opened a new school in Columbia, Maryland, the planned utopian city where we lived because our father worked for the Rouse Company, which created and developed Columbia.

Toby also bought the Garland Dinner Theatre in Columbia and transformed it from an adult, light comedy venue to one of the most well-known homes for producing Broadway musicals in the DC metropolitan area. Toby's is a successful dinner theatre to this day.[5] Many of my drama class cohort went on to perform at Toby's, and a few went on to Broadway (Betsy True, Margo Seibert), to Off Broadway (Mark Waldrop), to film (Edward Norton, Traci Thoms), or to National Public Radio (Michele Kelemen). Many of us teach in high schools or universities. In other words, though neither Allie nor I had spent much time in Colorado, dinner theatre is in our blood.

For my sister and me and for many other musical theatre fans in the United States, dinner theatre was our introduction to live, professional musical theatre. When I was a kid, I didn't know the difference between Equity and non-Equity, or think about the salary of the actor who played Eliza in *My Fair Lady* and served us drinks in souvenir glasses before the show and brought us dessert during intermission and whether she had another job when she wasn't in a show. For me at age ten, it was theatre, it was musical theatre, it was dinner and a show, both in one place.

Now, many years later, I have more knowledge (for example, that many "professional" actors, Equity or not, don't earn a living wage) and experience and curiosity, too. It's why we're here—along the Front Range in northern Colorado—to have dinner, be entertained, and learn about what's happening at the dinner theatres.

Though a handful of dinner theatres still operate across the country, no other region hosts such a concentration of the musical theatre venue that some commentators believe died in the 1970s (which obviously is not true). This region of Colorado, then, seemed like the perfect place to compare a few of these operations. As with every venue in this book, I wanted to find out what musical theatre does at dinner theatres in Colorado, and what dinner theatres do to musicals.

A Short History of Dinner Theatres and their Critical Reception

Although precise details of its origins vary depending on the source, dinner theatre (or "dinner playhouse" as it was originally called) was invented in 1959 in Chicago or in 1960 in Washington, DC.[6] The first dinner theatres opened in downtown neighborhoods in cities, but they soon moved out—like a large segment of America's population at the time—to the quickly growing suburbs. Dinner theatres were marketed as a good value—an entire evening of food and entertainment, plus parking, all for one reasonable price.

Through the 1960s and early 1970s, dinner theatres popped up fast from coast to coast, joining shopping centers, parking lots, supermarkets, Little Leagues, and McDonald's as emblems of suburbia. These all-inclusive establishments opened outside of Hartford, Connecticut; in Pennsylvania Dutch Country; in Greensboro, North Carolina; and in Indianapolis, for example. Several successful dinner theatre chains were formed, too, including the Carousel, which had outlets in Ohio, and Prathers, located in Pennsylvania, Arizona, and Florida, plus a touring company.[7]

By 1973, at least 150 dinner theatres were in operation, and they were growing faster and employing more actors than any other type of theatre in the country, including Broadway, touring companies, and regional theatres. By 1977, there were more than 250 dinner theatres nationwide.[8]

1978 marked the pinnacle of dinner theatres' popularity, and that same year, the National Dinner Theatre Association was formed.[9] The building craze slowed by the 1980s—perhaps having reached a saturation point—and then, year by year, most dinner theatres went out of business. No one has fully accounted for dinner theatre's decline, though some speculate that a combination of changing tastes, an aging theatre-going population, the audience's aversion to committing four or more hours to an evening's activity, or the growth of regional theatres led to dinner theatre's waning popularity.[10]

Still, a handful of dinner theatres do survive and even thrive, including Toby's in Columbia, Maryland; the Chanhassen in Chanhassen, Minnesota (which I visited years ago—a successful Equity house and the largest restaurant in the state); and eight in Colorado, including the four my sister and I visited, each a popular destination and embedded in its community, economically and theatrically.

Dinner Theatre's "Taste" Problem

Back in 1970, I was thrilled when my parents took my sister and me to our first dinner theatre production—*The Music Man*—and my performance as Marta in the Burn Brae Dinner Theatre's production of *The Sound of Music* a year later was, as far as I was concerned, my professional debut. At the time, dinner theatres were a mainstay of the local entertainment scene. Little did we know, suburbanites that we were, that urban arts critics detested dinner theatres and were busy constructing images that would forever be linked with the quirky food-meets-theatre activity. The food is bland, inoffensive, or just plain awful (think tough roast beef and fluorescent Jell-O with a dab of Cool Whip), and what's on stage isn't much better: gaudy costumes, shaky sets, and performers whose voices crack on the highest notes, who act with enthusiasm if we're lucky and look worn and tired if we're not.

As dinner theatres gained popularity and profit in the 1970s, their growth and development were met with the anxious fury and utter disparagement of arts writers and theatre critics in East Coast city newspapers like the *New York Times*, the *Washington Post*, and the *Boston Globe*, who mapped out what we now understand as the negative "middlebrow" stereotype attached to dinner theatre.

For arts writers in urban centers, every aspect of dinner theatre threatened what they saw as "legitimate theatre." As one mid-1970s Boston journalist warned not atypically, "Professional theatre as we know it in Boston is doomed . . . What will kill Boston's professional theatre . . . is called Dinner Theatre."[11] Interestingly, the writer, Larry Stark, doesn't point to the many other likely reasons for "professional" theatre's decline in Boston at the time, including television, movies, the ailing economy, the energy crisis, or violence in the city. Rather he blames dinner theatre, which is "shooting for the lowest common denominator of taste."[12] In 1973, the *New York Times'* John Gruen observed that "dinner theaters are rampant"[13]—like a disease.

Why did arts writers hate dinner theatre and see it as the enemy?

The first problem with dinner theatre was that the owners were not theatre artists but rather businessmen of various stripes. As Gruen explained, "Dinner theatre owners are not culture mavens. They are mostly people who made money in other businesses, and decided it would be fun to get into the theater. . . . [T]hey've learned that a well-run dinner theater, with good service, good food, a Neil Simon comedy with one or two stars, can play to 90 percent capacity, and can clear as much as $400,000 a year."[14] Though Broadway theatre—dinner theatres' repertoire—has always been a commercial enterprise, owners' brazen profit motive offended many arts writers.[15] As the *New York Times* summarized, "It's a middle-aged, middle-class, middle-America invention, run mostly by people who wouldn't know the difference between Anouilh and ennui."[16]

Dinner theatre's second problem was its self-branding as a bargain, unapologetically exploiting the American obsession with value. One general manager in 1973 bragged that they offered "a sumptuous escape from reality at a bargain price."[17] Another article noted that "the key is five-star appeal at a modest price. The show, with a good meal, tax, tip, and parking, costs about $7."[18] East Coast urban critics were disdainful that dinner theatres supplied dinner, a show, and dancing for much less than the activities would cost separately, making theatre into a commonplace bargain rather than a rarified event. They objected to dinner theatre's value, its self-nomination as a "product," and the fact that operators advertised it that way, thereby appealing to practicality and economics, not to aesthetics and art.

In the 1970s, the idea of a theatregoer as consumer offended arts critics, even though it was always true for Broadway audiences. The image of the dinner theatre spectator is one who consumes—literally by eating huge servings of food and drinking expensive drinks in decorated souvenir glasses and by watching easily digestible theatre. The representation of the spectator as consumer contradicts a high-art ideal of one who seeks enlightenment, whether aesthetic, political, intellectual, or emotional. As Joli Jensen writes in *Is Art Good for Us?*, American culture since de Tocqueville is based on the assumption that taking part in the arts makes one better, smarter, and more civic-minded (the same argument made by educators and community theatre advocates).[19] But dinner theatre patrons didn't care about self-improvement. As one writer complained, "From entrance to exit, their [dinner theatre's] multitudinous consumers—many of whom have never seen a live play—will be responsibly, if mechanistically handled as part of an assembled 'no substitutions' mass. They need make no decision beyond beef stroganoff or turbot or chicken."[20] Moreover, since the dinner theatre experience is not above the body, but rather undeniably of the body, it bumps up against American culture's foundational defense of the arts.

City-based critics derided dinner theatre's suburban location. As a 1973 headline in the *New York Times* read, "Is Theater Dead? No, Out to Dinner." This journalist painted the picture: "In the middle of nowhere—approximately 15 miles outside Hartford, Conn.—there stands a large, sturdy, somewhat grim barn-like structure, flanked by an enormous parking lot."[21] This writer, like many others, assumed that culture and suburbia were incompatible, and the requisite huge parking lot—the source of abject horror for urban writers—became a synecdoche for the suburbs, dinner theatre, and that other frequently linked trend: shopping centers. As one writer noted, "Like the cross-country, all-purpose suburban shopping centers, dinner theaters have come along to offer neon-lit safety, convenience, economy—plus the attraction of a night on the town."[22]

Dinner theatres were enormously popular in spite of critics' disdain. In 1973, for example, owner Tony De Santis said that his theatre was filled "continually near capacity" and "no longer needs the critics, who usually snoot the show."[23] That Chicago operation, which was one of the longest-running and most successful, closed in 2003 when it was sold to Walmart. The 1973 critics might have been even more horrified by the theatre's eventual fate.

Colorado's Dinner Theatre Story

The history and reception of dinner theatres in Colorado are part of this national story, with a slight time lag. The Country Dinner Playhouse opened first in Denver in 1970, around ten years later than the East Coast early operations, and more soon followed. When the Chuckwagon Dinner Playhouse opened in Greeley in 1973, it drew a whopping thirty thousand patrons in its first year of operation.[24] The Boulder Dinner Theatre, which my sister and I visited, opened in 1977. Each business employed dozens of theatre workers (onstage and offstage and in the kitchen) and had a patron capacity of at least a thousand people a week.[25]

New dinner theatres continued to open into the twenty-first century, and many did well. According to the *Denver Post*, in 2004, Denver-area dinner theatres drew 22.1 percent of total theatre attendance in the state, brought in just under $10 million in revenue, and fed and entertained 351,794 people.[26] Some were misguided, though, such as the Pinnacle Dinner Theatre, which opened in 2004, with the plan to up the ante for food. The menu included "housemade mozzarella sliced with ginger-sweetened, fire-roasted tomatoes" and "beef tournedos finished with a wild mushroom cabernet reduction."[27] Ticket prices were steeper, too, by 30 percent. Audiences voted with their pocketbooks and insisted on the bargain that dinner theatre always promised, and the theatre folded in ten months "under a mountain of debt."[28]

Other terminations, however, were met with grief. The ignominious end of the Country Dinner Playhouse continues to hold apocryphal power among local artists. The longtime Denver institution's ticket prices remained at $12 for a buffet dinner and the show until 2005. But by 2007, changes in ownership and lease disputes ran the theatre into the red, and the then-owners declared bankruptcy, unbeknownst to the staff. When they showed up for work one day in the middle of a run of *Evita*, they found the doors padlocked.[29] (The actors performed the show in the parking lot for the patrons who showed up.) As if the theatre's unforeseen closing wasn't bad enough, a few months later, files of the theatre's financial records, including employees' names, addresses, and Social Security numbers, were found in the trash, not shredded. The "dumping" left everyone who had worked there publicly vulnerable (a decade before identity theft and credit card hacks became common) and with a bitter taste in their mouths well beyond their sudden, unexpected unemployment.[30]

Over its thirty-seven-year existence, the Country Dinner Playhouse, whose 470-seat house made it the second largest dinner theatre in the state, "entertained more than 5 million theatergoers" and "staged more than 220 productions."[31] Performers over the years included Mickey Rooney, Morgan Fairchild, "and nearly every significant local musical-theater performer in Colorado including Annaleigh Ashford" and Beth Malone, who starred in the original Broadway production of *Fun Home*.[32]

Here was this institution, everyone said, a place that had been there from the beginning and seemed timeless. Decade after decade, the venue never changed its approach to the food or the performance but chugged along and everything seemed fine. Its closure shocked the employees and actors who saw the place as home and their fellow workers as family. Its downfall underlined how the bottom line is business—in fact, a business twice as risky financially as running a theatre or a restaurant—and if it doesn't make money, it will close. Nonetheless, the workers felt betrayed by the owners, and some fell into depression or stopped acting altogether. It was a symbolic as well as a real loss for the community, and almost everyone I met during my visit referred to the Country Dinner Playhouse or told me this story.

When the Country Dinner Playhouse closed in 2007, seven dinner theatres remained across the state.[33] The newest addition, the Candlelight Dinner Playhouse, which we visited, opened its doors in 2008 and that same year, the Boulder Dinner Theatre celebrated its thirty-first anniversary.

Critics and Dinner Theatres in Colorado

Local Colorado arts writers' reception to dinner theatre tells a different story than the *New York Times*, at least at first. When dinner theatres arrived in 1970, Denver was still a relatively small city with a population of just over 514,000, inured from urban blight and suburban flight.[34] The area wasn't flush with theatres nor were there the same closely guarded hierarchies of high and middlebrow culture in the west, so Colorado arts writers welcomed new dinner theatre arrivals with enthusiasm. When the Dublin Dinner Theater opened in 1975, for example, *Gazette Telegraph* writer Patricia Renner said it was "long overdue in Colorado Springs," "a downright blessing" that "promise[d] to fill the void."[35] She praised "a thoroughly professional crew and a well-seasoned cast . . . Added to a brimming buffet, it's an unbeatable evening of all-around entertainment."[36]

Still, as Colorado dinner theatres proliferated in the later 1970s, critics—notably Barbara Mackay, the *Denver Post* theatre critic from 1976 to 1981—echoed the negative stereotypes articulated a decade earlier in New York, DC, and Boston. In a 1978 review of a production at the Country Dinner Playhouse, for example, Mackay reiterated "the usual expectations one has for dinner theaters: That they will give mediocre revivals of tried and true—but often tired—old musicals."[37]

By the late 1970s, even some prospective operators disavowed the label. One director, according to Mackay, "hesitates to call his new venture a dinner theater, because of the stigma so often attached to the business of feeding people mediocre food and then giving them theatrical pap."[38] When the Boulder Dinner Theater was about to open its doors in 1977, producer Jody Sarbaugh said, "We wanted to make this theatre different than any other dinner theatre in Colorado. We wanted to have a classy look as well as high quality in dining."[39] Similarly, Rick Seeber, musical director and producer at Eugene's Dinner Theater, explained in 1978, "We've always done stuff that's not normally done in dinner theaters: *Godspell, Company, Cabaret.* We have a lot of audiences who believe in seeing things that are not the run-of-the-mill dinner-theater productions, not just laugh-'em-up deals."[40] As the stereotypes of dinner theatre hardened among Coloradans, new operators tried to market themselves as unique. By doing this, though, they merely reinforced the negative stereotypes associated with their own businesses.

In recent years, local critics support the area's dinner theatres with a mixture of amusement, mild condescension, respect for their longevity against all odds, and occasional out-and-out praise for a production. Denver-based theatre critic Juliet Wittman described going to the Country Dinner Playhouse in February 2007, a mere three months before it closed, as a kind of time warp.[41] She found the food "the usual steam-table fare," and wrote, "There's the same mac and cheese and white bread and butter on the buffet, and what looks like the same man standing by the meat-carving station with a long knife, offering you your choice of ham or beef."[42] She admitted, "I was a little surprised by the professionalism of the performance, which featured good musicians and energetic actors with nice voices," and she observes appreciatively, "Where would we hear Cole Porter, Lerner and Loewe, and Rodgers and Hammerstein these days if there were no dinner theater?"[43]

To be sure, dinner theatre owners and managers are acutely aware of dinner theatre's negative stereotypes, the picture that Wittman paints. Michael Duran, the general manager at BDT Stage said, "People come to see a good show . . . we try to keep the quality up, so it looks good, it tastes good, it comes out hot. But really, it's all about the show." For Pat Payne, the production manager at Candlelight, "We know that five-star food isn't sustainable because you can't serve that many people fast enough. We're trying to find a balance, a happy medium: good food and spectacular show." As we'll see, the owners, managers, and artistic directors all feel pressured to make a profit while providing a good meal and great musical theatre for their audiences.

It seems to be working for audiences on the Front Range who appreciate the very qualities that irked arts critics: Dinner theatres are convenient, a good value, and offer a full night out, dinner and entertainment and parking. Moreover, many patrons are repeat customers who recognize the actors, and the actors can make a living and a life here. In this way, dinner theatres are an integral part of the local community. This is what I was curious to know: How and why do dinner theatres succeed and thrive in this area?

So Allie and I set off to experience four different versions of this unique, even peculiar cultural invention of the 1970s centered around musical theatre.

Thursday Night: *Kiss Me, Kate* at the Candlelight Dinner Playhouse in Johnstown

If you didn't know where the Candlelight Dinner Playhouse was, you would drive right by it.[44] Set behind a locally well-known and popular truck stop along Interstate 25—the highway that goes all the way from Las Cruces, New Mexico, to Buffalo, Wyoming—just outside of Loveland, the "Candlelight Dinner Playhouse, Professional, Broadway-Style Theater" is a big brick building fronted by an ample parking lot and adjacent to the Lazydays RV dealer. Built in 2008 and the newest theatre in the state by almost twenty years, the grand, high-ceilinged lobby speaks elegance and comfort, with thick blue flowered carpet on the floor, candelabras on the walls, a small staircase leading up to the dining room/theatre, and restrooms with numerous stalls to ensure that there's no delay during intermission. A kind and friendly host—a high school girl whose nametag reads Megan—welcomes us, asks our name, scans her reservation list for our assigned table, and leads us into the room. "Is this your first time at the Candlelight?" Megan asks brightly. "Yes," we say, exchanging looks. "Well, you're in for a big treat," she smiles. Hospitality from beginning to end is crucial to a dinner theatre's success because people spend an entire evening—sometimes more than four hours—there.

"We know," Allie and I reply, taking in the cavernous dining room. Like the lobby, the walls are deep blue, decorated with candelabras (the place earns its name!). It looks like a Las Vegas nightclub but more brightly lit. At the front of the room is a proscenium stage, as wide as a typical high school auditorium, and the unlit set for *Kiss Me, Kate*, Cole Porter's 1948 hit backstage musical adaptation of *The Taming of the Shrew* (Figure 8.1). We can see the brightly painted backdrop of the back of a theatre and two real sets of iron stairs going up to a second-level catwalk. In the room, 350 seats are divided among four tiers of tables set for two to six people, each raised a few feet above the one below for good sightlines. Megan leads us to our seats, two facing each other at a six-top on the second tier, which I had chosen online. It gives us a great view of the stage, but nonetheless puts us a good twenty feet away from its downstage edge, separated by the first, wide tier of tables and a sizable orchestra pit, which will later hold seven musicians. On our level, the adjacent tables are at least another table's distance from us and alongside our table runs a wide path for servers to bring and later clear the plates. In other words, compared to a normal restaurant or any theatre, there's a lot of space around us.

The Candlelight's layout is intentional in its design.[45] Built on an empty lot from the ground up and planned to be a dinner theatre from the start, which is rare in the business, the owners and architects made every decision to "capitalize on what worked in previous dinner theatres and improve on what didn't," Shauna Johnson, the Candlelight's technical manager (that's her official title but she is truly a jack of all trades), tells us. The wide alley on each level makes it easy for two servers carrying big food- and drink-laden trays to pass one another, for patrons to get up to use the restroom, and for everyone to feel that they can have a private conversation at their table. The actors also occupy these aisles several times during the show, most charmingly when Lois sings her flirtatious "Always True to You (In My Fashion)" to men in the audience. The unintended effect of the large space, though, is a dispersal of audience energy. We know the audience loves the show, especially when the group of fifty high school students hoots its approval after Lilly's "I Hate Men!" but "even with all of these people here, you can barely hear them clapping," Allie notices.

Because Allie and I grew up going to a dinner theatre with a buffet, we needed to learn the rules of table service and the local dinner theatre rituals. We loved the buffet as kids, but in Colorado, only the Country Dinner

Playhouse (RIP 2007) and the old-timey Chuckwagon in Greeley (1973–1977, destroyed by fire) fed its patrons buffet-style. No one we spoke to could explain why served meals are standard, but we suspected that table service implies the food is made to order, which the scale of the operation and time crunch—they have to feed three hundred people in an hour—would make impossible. We peruse the menu: a choice of soup or salad; a number of appetizers like spinach dip and shrimp cocktail for an extra charge; a few entrees, including meat loaf, fried chicken (for which the Candlelight is famous, our server tells us), and fish; fancier cuts of meat, including the prime rib, which Pat Payne assured me is their signature dish, for a surcharge; a selection of desserts for a charge; and an extensive wine, beer, and spirits list. Though we'd paid for our tickets, which included dinner, in advance, we see there are many ways to supplement the basic meal and rack up a substantial bill tonight.

After we've consulted the menu but before we've had a chance to introduce ourselves to our tablemates, Stephen, as his name tag reads, comes over, pad in hand and pencil poised to take our drink and dinner order. "Hi," he says, warmly and energetically, "I'm Stephen and I'm in the ensemble in tonight's performance. Can I take your food and drink order?"

While we wait for our food to arrive and eat crispy, sweet, and delicious chunks of cornbread, we chat with our tablemates. A couple in their late sixties who live forty-five minutes away brought their just-graduated-from-college son and his soon-to-graduate girlfriend who live in Pennsylvania "because we thought it would be fun. We thought it would be something different," the woman said.

"Do you normally come to dinner theatre?" I ask.

"No," they answer, "but we go to a lot of concerts and other theatre in our town."

Stephen delivers our food and we tuck into it quickly, as it's just twenty minutes to curtain. Allie ordered fried chicken and I got fish, and we agree that it's fine. As we would find in each dinner theatre, and as all of the owners and directors said, no one comes for the food. Still, like our table friends, we find the meal tasty enough, plentiful, reasonably priced, and utterly convenient.

Before we know it, the house lights go down to half, and Pat Payne, Candlelight's production manager, walks on stage, the bright lights looking harsh on a non-actor announcer. Pat delivers what we later identify as a standard ten-minute pre-show spiel, which is an important part of the evening's rituals at all dinner theatres. He encourages us to tell our friends to see the show if we like it, informs us how much longer it will be playing, announces the next season's shows, shares ways to save money with coupons and group sales, and leads us in applause for people who came to celebrate birthdays and anniversaries. This aspect of the ritual leans toward what might happen in a restaurant, where the waitstaff sings you happy birthday, and it also aims to reinforce the sense of belonging and comfort, which is crucial to the dinner theatre experience. Pat also asks the season subscribers to raise their hands, allowing everyone to see the regulars, which fosters our desire to be subscribers, too. At the end, he explains the tipping policy, since the tip is not included in the original ticket price and needs to be based on that cost plus tonight's additional food and drinks. Allie and I look at each other confused. Until our very last night in Colorado, we do not fully understand the correct way to calculate our tip.

Dinner theatre in the twenty-first century is marked by what allowed it to thrive in the 1970s: its lack of embarrassment about money and its pride in providing a bargain. Even as Candlelight gives off a sense of grandeur and luxury in its architecture and design, every moment of the experience reminds you that you're getting a good deal and a lot for your money. At all of the theatres we visited, there was not simply an ease in talking about money but pride in highlighting what a good value it is and advice on how to have the experience more cheaply. Candlelight's brand? Affordable, family-friendly elegance.

The orchestra tunes, the house lights dim to black, then the lights bump up and the overture to *Kiss Me, Kate* begins. The production is terrific, sharp, funny, and excellently sung. Everything on stage looks great—the set, the costumes, the lights. The dancing is wonderful and the performers are strong across the cast, from leads to ensemble players. I'm happy, too, because Allie is having a very good time.

At intermission, our Stephen is back in a flash, just as sweet and attentive and only a little sweaty from all of the dance numbers. He brings my sister's slice of chocolate cake and my box of caramel corn (a local specialty), and we and our tablemates agree that the show was "very good!" Stephen seems genuinely happy to see us.

"Are you acting now? Are you acting like a happy server?" I ask.

"No!" he answers. "One of the best things about this job is making contact with the audience."

Other actors we meet all week echo that sentiment. He brings our bill before intermission ends, and at the end of the night we have such a hard time figuring out the tip thing that we just give up and leave an amount in cash that we hope will be more than generous.

Act 2 follows with equal verve, bright costumes flashing, choreography conventional and well executed, comic shtick delivered with precision, Porter's luscious tunes sung beautifully. Certain sexual innuendoes and some of the musical's violence are downplayed—as Shauna told us earlier—because "the director didn't want to offend the audience." *Kiss Me, Kate* might not be among the best-known classics of the Broadway musical repertoire, but it seems a perfect choice for Candlelight's "family-friendly" mission. Though some might consider the musical dated, this production gives it freshness and energy. By the end of the night, our table family agrees that the whole evening was "really fun," which was, I think, a fair assessment. It was really fun. A patron's judgment is based more on the total experience and sense of pleasurable engagement than on distanced aesthetic critique. Dinner theatre demands its own metrics for judgment.

After the show, even though it's getting quite late, the fifty high school students and their teacher stay for a talkback with the actors. They assemble in one of the several meeting rooms that Candlelight included in their design to make the space rentable for corporate events and conferences and other group occasions. Shauna gets the conversation going, opening with, "Imagine if your hobby was your job," and goes on to tell the teenagers a bit about herself, her background, and how she got here. Eight of the actors show up a few minutes later, their faces scrubbed and in stylishly torn jeans, boots, and baggy sweaters. For thirty minutes, they give the youngsters their full attention and answer every question—"How do you learn your lines?" "How do you not get upset when you don't get cast?" "What's the most fun thing about this show?"—with kindness and generosity. One of the actors remarks, "I can see myself in you," but she doesn't need to say it aloud; it is clear in every word.

All but one of the cast and crew grew up in the area, went to college nearby, and plan to remain here. That they can live in a place they call home and make a living (or part of a living) as theatre-makers feels like a luxury. Though they are required to audition anew for every show at Candlelight—that is, shows are not precast—a small group of actors are frequently and regularly hired, either here or at BDT Stage. It's a small theatre community, they say, and everyone knows each other, more or less. Each season loses some actors to Chicago or New York or to different jobs altogether, and gains some newcomers—often local college graduates—too. Actors typically know their competition for a given role. When the show is too small or there's not a role for them, they can often still wait tables at the theatre to make money. One *Kiss Me, Kate* actor holds a regular job in BDT Stage's box office. Since all of the dinner theatres' shows run for six to ten weeks, they have steady work for a while.

The timing of Candlelight's 2008 opening, in the middle of the financial downturn, was more than unfortunate, but hands-on management, strict budgets, crowd-pleasing seasons, and high production values kept them afloat during the difficult early days. The operation is owned by Dave Clark, who is first and foremost, like many dinner theatre owners in the 1970s, a businessman. "I'm a theatre person now!" he says, and has the final word on all decisions. Dave is "a deliberate decision-maker," says Pat. The day-to-day operations are run by Pat and Shauna, who both came to the Candlelight after years of working at theatres and dinner theatres in the region. They operate a tight ship and understand both the artistic and business side of this complex venture.

After the talkback, Allie and I walk outside to the starry Colorado night, lights of the truck stop glowing in the near distance. We wonder: What made a group of twenty-first-century businessmen think that audiences on Colorado's Front Range would support another operation of an entertainment form that people in many parts of the United States think died altogether by 1980 or would consider obsolete? Earlier, Pat told us that in the winter of 2018, Candlelight sold out its run of *Beauty and the Beast*, which greatly strengthened the theatre's finances. For now, it seems that Candlelight, whose elegance, comfort, and affordability hearken back to dinner theatre's origins in the 1970s, is a welcome addition to the scene.

Friday Night: *Fun Home* at the Midtown Arts Center in Fort Collins

The small city of Fort Collins, founded as a military fort in 1864, is the home of the 31,856-student Colorado State University and eighteen microbreweries.[46] Its reputation is more conservative than Boulder, its funky neighbor fifty-five miles to the south, but more liberal than Cheyenne, Wyoming, forty-six miles to the north. The drive from Johnstown to Fort Collins is under twenty minutes (seventeen miles), but few spectators from Candlelight are likely to make the leap from there to here. True, like Candlelight, Midtown Arts Center is a dinner theatre, and true, there is some overlap in the season selection. And everyone (everywhere) wants to produce the surefire money-making Disney shows. But unlike Candlelight, Midtown Arts regularly produces contemporary, edgy shows seldom seen at dinner theatres any-where. In 2011, for example, it presented the Colorado premiere of *Next to Normal*, the Tony Award– and Pulitzer Prize–winning 2009 musical about a woman with bipolar disease who imagines she sees a teenage version of her son who died as a baby.[47]

Equally edgy is the musical we're there to see: *Fun Home*, Jeanine Tesori and Lisa Kron's 2015 Pulitzer Prize– and Tony Award–winning adaptation of Alison Bechdel's graphic novel about a lesbian cartoonist whose father is gay and who eventually kills himself.[48] Following *Fun Home*, Lynn Ahrens, Stephen Flaherty, and Terrence McNally's *Ragtime* is on the season, based on E. L. Doctorow's novel that intermixes fictitious characters with actual his-torical figures like Emma Goldman and Evelyn Nesbitt. The musical centers on the profound changes in the United States during the early twentieth cen-tury and features a newly independent white woman, an African American man, and a Jewish man. None of these musicals would be on the season at the other dinner theatres we visited in Colorado (and probably not at any other dinner theatre in the United States).

Midtown Arts is located, well, midtown, a few miles from CSU's campus and a historical downtown after which Disneyland's Main Street was mod-eled. The mountains are visible in the distance, and the town is flat on every side, with more than thirty-five miles of bike paths connecting the town end to end.[49] The venue is on a wide, busy street surrounded by strip centers, gro-cery stores, and chain restaurants. As of this writing (April 2018), plans are afoot to move the operation to a new building a few miles away because the parcel of land on which the current building sits was repossessed by the city to build low-income housing.[50]

In 2001, the ten-year-old Carousel Dinner Theatre (not one of the famous Ohio-based chain of dinner theatres, just coincidentally with the same name) in Fort Collins changed hands.[51] Local actor, director, and teacher Kurt Terrio bought the business, upgraded the building, and planned to main-tain a local acting company.[52] A few years later, he renamed the operation the Midtown Arts Center and moved it down the street to a four-plex movie theatre, which he renovated to be a dinner theatre. The building houses two dinner theatres, enabling two different shows to play at once, a good economic arrangement. When we visit, the two-woman show *Always . . . Patsy Cline* (which we saw in Boulder a few nights later) is in the smaller space. Midtown Arts also has several rehearsal rooms and houses a lucrative performing arts academy, owned and run by longtime actor and director Jalyn Webb, who plays Louise in *Patsy Cline*.

When we arrive that evening, we are (again) greeted warmly and led to our table with the same high school student enthusiasm that we recognize from the night before at Candlelight. The 236-seat house feels smaller (which it is, by 30 percent), more intimate, and more casual than Candlelight. The tables are closer together and wooden with built-in booths; there are no tablecloths. The proscenium stage is smaller, preset with a two-level set for *Fun Home*, Alison's drawing desk visible center on the top level (Figure 8.2). Our friendly server presents himself, tells us his role in the show: He plays the various male characters, including the father's boyfriend and a student. He asks for our drink orders as we peruse the menu and weigh our hunger against the cost of the extras. By the second night, Allie and I are learning the drill, and we order a few appetizers and, of course, dessert, which we know will arrive

Figure 8.2. After the show at Midtown Arts: the set of *Fun Home* and stacks of glasses, water pitchers, and used napkins on the tables.

during intermission. Unlike Candlelight, Midtown Arts starts everyone with a small green salad, which is on our table before we sit down. Eliminating the choice of one course saves time on the front end, which the bussers set, and reduces the servers' (many of whom are actors) labor.

The dinner, like the previous night's meal, is fine and tasty enough, but again, not a meal you would seek out intentionally. No matter: We are here for the show and excited to see a musical that no one would imagine as dinner theatre fare.

But first, Kurt gets up for the requisite pre-show spiel, and we start to understand how Midtown Arts is unique and how Kurt's public performance as the owner and director is fundamental to the place's identity. His ten minutes on stage are a laugh-out-loud comedy act and a masterful display of his ability to create a presumptive "we" in the audience. He knows that some spectators might not know that *Fun Home* is about a lesbian comic book artist coming to terms with her identity and her gay father's suicide. The advertising for the Broadway production, in fact, downplayed the gay themes and characters, hoping to woo possibly reluctant spectators with a mild synopsis: "After her father dies unexpectedly, Alison dives deep into her past to tell the story of the volatile, brilliant, one-of-a-kind man whose temperament and secrets defined her family and her life. Based on Alison Bechdel's autobiographical graphic novel." Midtown Arts used the same burb.[53]

But that night, rather than apologize for content that might offend some (and, of course, engage and touch others), Kurt casts all of us in the audience as his buddies, as insiders who of course want to see something provocative, complex, serious, and daring. He goes on a riff about how all great musicals end with death and then tosses the question to the audience.

"You know what I've always said, right? Sign of a good musical, what has to happen? Somebody has to die. It's true. Name a musical that's good where somebody doesn't die."

Playfully, audience members shout out show titles, challenging Kurt's claim. So that everyone can be in on the joke, he repeats their suggestions over the microphone, then refutes each one: "*Oklahoma*? Somebody dies. *Mary Poppins*? If you think that when she goes up in the umbrella at the end of the show, that's not symbolism, I've got bad news for ya [. . .] And one of the greatest musicals of all, *Les Misérables, everybody* dies." When someone suggests *The Full Monty* (a comedy about unemployed steelworkers who create a strip act), Kurt peers out into the house with fake incredulity, jokingly chiding, "Who said that? [. . .] This is a family theatre!"

Finally, he segues the joke into a plug for their upcoming production of *Ragtime*, with a promise that "more people are surviving at the end of the show than *Les Mis*." He goes on to "celebrate some life," applauding the birthdays of audience members, before asking if anyone is celebrating an anniversary. When he is met with silence, Kurt laughs, "No anniversaries? Nothing goes on beginning of March. Makes sense: It's Lent, it's cold. Are you sure, going once, twice, no anniversaries? Come on, folks. You're killing me."

It's hilarious. Allie cries with laughter. Kurt's monologue must work because as far as we can see, no one leaves during intermission.

From the time he bought the Carousel and rebranded it as Midtown Arts, Kurt insisted on programming shows that he wanted to direct. He balances contemporary musicals with more traditional, surefire hits but has built a reputation for doing Colorado premieres of new musicals, including, for example, *The Producers, In the Heights, Once*, and *Avenue Q*.[54] To attract audiences to a season of shows that might be unfamiliar to them, Kurt launched a "Leap of Faith" subscription, which enables patrons to buy super-cheap tickets before the season is announced. During the preshow spiel, he teases the audience, "I wish I could give you a hint of one of the shows next year, but it's just too early . . . unless you can really convince me." After much cheering, he concedes, "I will tell you this: We are doing no stories next year—from the *East Side*." The audience laughs knowingly, some whooping at the suggestion of *West Side Story*, others groaning at the pointedness of the hint. Kurt laughs, "Yeah. [The clues] get worse every year, don't they?"

With the promise of popular shows, half-price seats, and other season-ticketholder perks, Midtown Arts makes money from subscribers to keep the theatre running, and people feel like they're getting a great deal (which they are). Though Kurt programs a few edgy or challenging shows per season, many of their shows overlap with the ones at BDT and Candlelight, and there is fierce competition among the theatres to nab licensing rights first for a desirable show. The owners and managers of all three dinner theatres have cultivated long relationships with people at MTI and Rodgers and Hammerstein to get first dibs on popular shows, especially, these days, Disney musicals. Still, Kurt realizes that Midtown Arts' varied season means uneven attendance and occasional hate mail.

The production of *Fun Home* is excellent. A few of the actors are local, including Small Alison, who is truly terrific, but most are jobbed in from New York. Midtown Arts' casting practices differ entirely from the other dinner theatres in the area. Kurt (and sometimes Jalyn) travels to New York a few times a year to hold auditions, and he typically offers one or two Equity contracts. The actor who plays Bruce, the father, is Equity, for example. Kurt can entice young non-Equity actors with free local housing because Midtown Arts owns several homes for visiting artists. The actors can also double their meager salary by serving. Because shows run for eight to twelve weeks, New York–based actors can sublet their apartments and live in beautiful Colorado for a few months. Sometimes actors audition for several shows in a row and extend their stay.

Maybe Kurt could have found equally castable actors in the area—I suspect he could have. But, as he says, "Local actors have lives here and they want flexibility." He prefers to cast actors from out of town and have control over their lives for the months they're there. The local actor cast as Helen, the mother, in fact, does not perform the night we see the show because she has another commitment that night. Her understudy, a New Yorker who also is cast in *Ragtime*, takes on the role that night beautifully.

Kurt's colleague, Jalyn Webb, an effervescent, effusive, and acting-like-your-BFF blond, is a longtime performer and director at Midtown Arts, and she owns and runs its successful performing arts academy. She supplements her steady work at the theatre by teaching at the University of Northern Colorado in Greeley, from which many local dinner theatre actors have graduated. Many of her students, she says, "are so intense . . . that it's like, Broadway or nothing," she says. "They're so beaten down, you know." She explains, "I didn't go that route, I had such a strong sense of community, and my goal has always been to bring the best in theatre to the people that I care about, the people that live in my town and the people I have known for so long."

As for dinner theatre, she says, for a lot of people, "It is [a] tradition . . . it's a great evening out that's all rolled into one . . . a planned date night, you know, or their evening out. They buy this season ticket and they know every couple months, they have a night out with their spouse or partner . . . When you are in a town like Fort Collins, it's a unique experience."

We love the production of *Fun Home*, but the insertion of intermission, required by the dinner theatre's requisite dessert break, creates a weird pause in this seamless, short, emotionally intense one-act musical. After an hour, I start to wonder where the intermission will fall and identify a few places where I might have put it had I directed the show. When it eventually happens (after Bruce leaves his three children sleeping [he thinks] in a New York hotel room to go out and pick up a man), it feels jarring. But the lights come up, and we troop to the ladies' room and then return to chat with our server/actor, tell him how much we are enjoying the show, and eat our molten chocolate brownie with ice cream, glad that we decided to spring for dessert.

The break leaves Act 2 very short (and sad: Bruce dies), and then we meet some of the actors lined up in the hallway. Like Candlelight, the actors "meet and greet" after the show, and we overhear compliments and confessions, including more than once, "Some of my best friends are gay." Every encounter with the actor-servers deepens the audience's relationship with them and makes patrons want to return to see them in another show (though it's unlikely with Midtown Arts' show-by-show, mostly out of town cast). This series of face-to-face rituals before the show, during intermission, and after the curtain call breeds familiarity. To the audience, the performers glow with stardom's aura even as they seem natural and like us.

Saturday Night: *Always . . . Patsy Cline* at BDT Stage in Boulder

The song-packed two-hander, *Always . . . Patsy Cline*, is a surefire hit in a country and western music–friendly city like Boulder.[55] BDT Stage's producing artistic director Michael Duran hopes that ticket sales will be strong enough to support the many BDT actors who aren't performing but are waiting tables at the theatre during the fourteen-week run. Michael scheduled *Always . . . Patsy Cline* between two large-cast, guaranteed-to-sell shows in the season, *Annie* and *The Little Mermaid*, each of which would give many BDT actors the chance to perform and wait tables, too.

Since he began managing the operation in 2003, Michael has tried to balance the financial and the personal. He must keep the theatre profitable and also feels committed to employing his company of local actors. He wants them to work consistently and make enough money to have a house and a family—though everyone needs to audition for each show, and none are precast.[56] He chose *Always . . . Patsy Cline* in part because it could be produced relatively inexpensively. It's essentially a solo concert, with the musicians on stage, embedded in a story of a friendship between two women. And he knew it would be a crowd-pleaser with great numbers like "Crazy" and "I Fall to Pieces." "The problem," he says, "is that it's not an especially well-known musical and will take time for word of mouth to spark ticket sales."

As Michael (and everyone else I spoke to for this book) explains, "Ticket-buying habits have changed over the years, especially with younger people. No one wants to plan ahead or commit themselves, especially not to four shows a year." Disney musicals and certain classic shows do sell well in advance, but many smaller or newer shows—*Patsy Cline* included—take a few precious weeks to catch on as reviews are published and people recommend the show to their friends. We see the show the second night and love it. "I hope everyone here tells their friends to see it," Allie says brightly.

The dinner theatre sits a few miles from downtown Boulder and the University of Colorado's hilly campus. It was built in 1977 during the height of the dinner theatre craze when a group of parents whose children performed in a high school production of *Jesus Christ Superstar* wanted them to have more performance opportunities, so they purchased the land and created the Boulder's Dinner Theatre.

Prior to BDT's existence, Boulder residents had to drive at least an hour to the nearest dinner theater, Country Dinner Playhouse, so BDT brought this type of entertainment closer to home. During its first year in business, BDT experienced every disaster imaginable. An actor fell into the orchestra pit on opening night of *Fiddler on the Roof*; an actor got a concussion in the middle of a show; drunk patrons got feisty; a woman walked in off the street and started selling flowers to patrons during a show. But the operators learned how to manage the business as they went along and to curate a special experience for their audiences. As Jody Sarbaugh, co-founder and producer of BDT, explained, "We want people to . . . feel pampered from the time they first walk in until they leave."[57] What began as a fun idea at a local picnic became a real built-from-scratch dinner theater staffed by 25 people in 1977. By 1995, a hundred people worked on the staff.[58]

BDT Stage holds a steady, respected place in the Boulder theatre ecosystem, where they compete for audiences against numerous small theatres plus the Arvada Center, the Denver Theatre Center, and the Buell, Denver's large touring house. Actor Amy Adams performed in two shows at BDT Stage in her early career.

Like every dinner theatre, BDT Stage is fronted with a parking lot. Shrubs and decorative rocks surround the building and a large marquee on the building's side announces this show and the next one, *The Little Mermaid*. The lobby area is smaller than Candlelight or Midtown Arts, but with high ceilings, a big chandelier, photos on the walls of past productions, and décor that aims for sophistication. The dining/theatre space, too, is smaller and more intimate than the other theatres and seats 274 people. (BDT Stage seats thirty-eight more people than Midtown Arts but its footprint is smaller.) BDT Stage is also the only dinner theatre we visit with a thrust stage, which puts the audience on three sides of the action. Veteran BDT actor and director, Alicia K. Meyers, who is our server that night and plays Louise in the show, says that it sometimes feels cramped and is hard to serve, especially in such a short amount of time. But both she and Michael Duran love the theatre's intimacy and value the actors' close proximity to the audience, and they are right. We are seated in the first row and can practically feel the actors' every breath, but no seat in the place is too far away. We can see that our servers (Alicia plus another BDT regular who was directing *Little Mermaid*—they work in teams to serve around thirty-five people) have to squeeze by other tables to bring our food, but the space brings the play wonderfully close.

The menu at BDT Stage is more extensive than we had seen before, including a vegetable curry, which surprises me and which I happily order. Allie chooses fish, and not to break stride, we order dessert for later. Our table companions are a straight couple in their late seventies who just married—second marriage for each after their spouses died of lung cancer, and they met at a bereavement group. He is balding and wears a well-tailored jacket and tie. She is in a silk dress, several strands of pearls, a chunky diamond ring, and very blond hair. A friend gave them a gift certificate to the theatre as a wedding present, and the man is a fan of Patsy Cline's music. The man recalls with fondness the first time he saw a show at BDT Stage, thirty years ago when he was brought by his boss just after relocating to Boulder for a job.

"Do you normally come here?" I ask.

"No," the woman answers decisively.

"Why not?"

"The food," she says. "We would rather go out to dinner somewhere we choose in Denver and then see a show at the Buell."

But then the meal comes, and they are impressed. "Not what I expected!" she says, pleased.

BDT Stage's preshow spiel, delivered by the understudy for both women's roles, who had to be at the theatre every night anyway, hits the marks of the previous nights' announcements: encouraging people to tell their friends about this show, announcement of the next show (gasps of excitement in the audience for *The Little Mermaid*!), a push for group sales, announcements of birthdays and anniversaries, and explanation of the tipping policy, which Allie and I are finally starting to understand. The preshow talk is clear and to the point, and the actor delivers it in a professional no-nonsense way, telling us what we need to know.

The show is excellent. The story is sweet, touching, and feminist-lite. The actors' voices and acting are superb, and they have great chemistry between them. It is also wonderful to see musicians on stage after two nights of their being situated (more typically) in the pit.

The intermission conversation in the ladies' room is enthusiastic among women who said they are longtime subscribers. Our tablemates enjoy the evening, too.

"Now that you've had a good meal and liked the show here, would you come back?" I ask.

"Maybe," the woman answered, casting a sidelong glance toward her new husband.

This is a tough business, I think.

Alicia, who plays the musical's narrator Louise with warm affection toward the audience, a salty sense of humor, and an unabashed girl crush on Patsy, has been working at BDT Stage for more than twenty years as an actor, director, and choreographer. Her colleagues at BDT Stage are her co-workers, co-performers, and her family. "You love them and you want to strangle them," she says, thoughtfully. "We've all gone through everything together—death, children, traumas, relationships . . . I met my first husband there, and our daughter is ten now. We've given our lives to this place." And in return, she said, "The management takes care of the actors."

Alicia relishes the genuine if brief connection she forms with the audience each night, whether she is on stage and making eye contact in the small space or serving drinks and dinner. "At the beginning of the night, some people don't realize I'm a performer," she laughs. "Once they see me on stage, their attitude changes. During intermission is when you bond most with the patron." In some ways, she says, the serving aspect of the job is harder because of its unpredictability. "On stage, you've rehearsed and you know what will happen. With real people, it's always different." And the connections are real: "Some of my regular patrons request my section and some send me Christmas cards!"

After three days and nights, Allie and I summarize what we've learned: BDT Stage is the well-established and well-respected venue. It's been around for forty years and is a fixture in the community. People in the business admire Michael and credit him for rebranding the theatre when it was bought by new owners in 2003, and for raising the production values and improving the food. He's also respected for treating the actors well and not demanding too much time from the servers. To be clear: At dinner theatres, the actors are workers. The loss of the Country Dinner Playhouse left BDT to carry on as the oldest establishment.

Candlelight, which only opened in 2018, is the new kid in town, but with adult aspirations. Like BDT Stage, Dave, Pat, and Shauna are committed to hiring local actors and, if possible, giving people enough stable work so that they can stay in the area, buy a house and have a family, and perform. They're fostering a consistently family-friendly image, and eschew newer shows that Michael might add to the BDT Stage season for variety. Candlelight is still tweaking its ways of working. The week we are there, they decide to change the policy that requires the actor-servers to clear the tables at the end of the evening and instead releases them to go into the lobby and greet the audience on their way out. This adjustment improves the actor-servers' job (though it gives the high school kids who bus the tables more responsibility and a later departure from the theatre). As important, it provides the audience with one more direct encounter with the actors and the feeling they're being personally wished good night by the very people they saw perform.

Midtown operates a bit off to the side of the other two. It's further north geographically, but more significantly, it has a different philosophy, mission, and operating practices. The season includes new shows that might be risky for BDT Stage and out of consideration for Candlelight. Though Kurt hires some local actors, the majority of the cast is from out of town. Like any theatre operator, Kurt wants actors (any and all actors) to be able to work, but he's primarily concerned with producing shows that he likes and that challenge the audience and casts the shows from a national pool.

The three dinner theatres are run by men—and some formidable women behind the scenes—with remarkable determination, drive, and vision, as they somehow manage to keep these against-all-odds businesses solvent. We could see how these venues were similar enough to define a genre of performance in the region but different enough to attract different audiences. Is there overlap among the actors? Somewhat. Overlap among the audiences? Probably not. Competition? A bit. Mutual respect? Yes, from what they told me. A hope that they all succeed to raise the bar and keep dinner theatres alive and well in this area? For sure.

Sunday Afternoon: *Joseph and the Amazing Technicolor Dreamcoat* at Jesters in Longmont

For the Jesters' Sunday matinee of one of Andrew Lloyd Webber's best-known and most beloved shows, some people come straight from church and others barely have time to stop home and take a shower after last night at the bar.[59] In all of my conversations before and during our visit with theatre people about dinner theatres on the Front Range, no one mentions Jesters, and when I do, they raise their eyebrows or tell me gently via email, "Jesters isn't a professional dinner theatre. It's a community theatre that serves food." Co-owner and director Scott Moore—gray-haired, bearded, trim, and jovial—tells us the same thing when he shows us around the place after the afternoon's performance. But that doesn't detract from the pleasure of the midday meal and show. Like the other three professional venues, Jesters aims to create a feeling of conviviality and community.

Longmont is sixteen miles from Boulder and is a growing bedroom community of the college town and Denver, too. It boasts a charming main street, lined with coffee shops, clothing stores, real estate brokers, and two bookstores. There's also a local community theatre (the Longmont Players) and the Cheese Importers (an unusual, fantastic cheese and specialty food and housewares store plus a café), which is "Colorado family-owned and operated for over 30 years," a few blocks from Jesters.[60]

Scott and Mary Lou Moore bought and renovated the Jesters' building, which is a former lumberyard, into a theatre in 1999, though they started producing shows in Longmont in 1987. Mary Lou's family had owned the Wayside Inn, in Berthoud, one of the area's first dinner theatres, so she had some experience with this kind of operation. (Jalyn Webb from Midtown Arts made her stage debut at the Wayside Inn. Apparently, it was a restaurant "famous far and wide" for its fried chicken, and owner Fred Peterson added a theatre, renamed it Ye Olde Wayside Inn Dinner Theatre, and opened with a production of *South Pacific* in 1983. A fire destroyed this "Berthoud landmark" on Christmas Eve 1993. The restaurant was rebuilt in 1995 but without the theatre.[61])

Jesters' entrance is a storefront on the main street, marked by a large hand-painted sign with their logo—a jester, of course—and backed by a large parking lot and many rooms of various shapes and sizes, which they use for props and costumes, dressing, rehearsing, and living—that is, eating and sleeping. Scott and Mary Lou live at the theatre. "We sold our house after our kids left home and we were about to buy a new one and then we thought, why not save money and live here and use the money for the theatre?" Maybe that's why it has such a homey feeling. Everything about this place speaks family.

The lobby is very small, just a little ten- by twenty-foot entryway, where we are greeted warmly by the host, Scotty, one of Mary Lou's twin sons. Across from the entry stand is the bar, with drinks prepared by a man named George. The Pittsburgh native and Washington, DC transplant with a theatre background used to work for the Justice Department. He's in his seventies, a burly guy, bald, and wearing a plaid flannel shirt, and lives a block away from the theatre. "I'm a volunteer," he tells us. "I hang around and pour drinks and do shows when there's a part for me," including playing Roosevelt in Jesters' next show, *Annie*. "I just like it," he grins.

Scotty leads us to our table, which is so close to the low platform stage that we're practically sitting on it. He turns out to be one of our servers, too, and plays the role of Asher in this performance (his brother, Danny, plays one of the two Josephs). The other server is his wife, Lize, who designed and made the costumes for the show. Between the two of them, they handle all of the tables in the small, low-ceilinged room. Allie and I are happy to see entrée salads on the menu, so we opt to start with Italian minestrone, which is unexpectedly good, and then order entrée salads with chicken or salmon. Somehow, this time, we pass on the intermission dessert, though we go through two bags of Skittles, purchased at the bar, during the show. During our midday "dinner," Allie and I keep looking around nervously at the twenty people eating at the eighty-five available seats, concerned that the room will remain nearly empty for the show.

We needn't have worried. By ten minutes before curtain, the room is completely packed with couples, groups, and families, including several young children (Figure 8.3). Most people don't come for a full meal but order chips and salsa or drinks and then get dessert at intermission. (Jesters' menu offers more snacks and appetizers than the other dinner theatres, plus a children's menu, and their prices average around 30 percent less than Candlelight's.) Though all of the dinner theatres offer a "show-only" option, Jesters is the only one where people—especially folks who live in the neighborhood—seemed to really take advantage of it. We could see how Jesters is a dinner theatre but not like the others.

Scott Sr., who plays Judah, one of the few roles that is not double- or triple-cast in the show, comes on stage in his toga costume to do the preshow

Figure 8.3. Scott (with Mary Lou leaning against the set of *Joseph*) leads introductions of the cast of *Annie* at Jesters Dinner Theatre.

announcements—the only about-to-perform actor who does the spiel at any of the theatres we visited. All of the information is the same as at the others: upcoming shows, discounts and deals, birthdays and anniversaries, and a reminder to tell your friends to come if you like the show. Like Kurt at Midtown Arts, Scott seems entirely relaxed and at home, delivering a message that he composed in his own style. The audience's warm reception confirms that much of the audience knows him well.

The production is community theatre at its best. The cast is big—forty-eight people—all white except for one Asian American girl—including Joseph's twelve brothers and their wives, plus a group of children, and others filling out the ensemble. They all jam onto a truly tiny stage, not much bigger than a small patio and a mere twelve inches off the floor, with two twenty-foot walkways of sorts on each side of the main platform. End to end, the stage almost allows the whole cast to stand in a tight horizontal line. There is almost no set, but sheet-size backdrops, on which they painted a palm tree or the head of a sphinx, are hung and rehung to suggest each location. The nonstop costume changes—really too many to count—and crazy color combinations, including wigs, headpieces, hats, and boas in different styles for each number, while specific to *Joseph*, take me back to Marilyn's extravaganzas.

One of the most charming aspects of the production is that they don't use mics. The space is so small, there is no need. But it is such a pleasure to identify where the sound is coming from and to hear separate actors' voices in the group numbers. Mary Lou music directs all of the shows and plays the accompaniment on an electric piano from a room behind the stage, unable to see or cue the actors. The onstage sound is mic'd in and she just keeps playing, she says with a shrug. Occasionally Jesters rents "tracks" (taped accompaniment), but in the small space, a piano usually works fine. For several numbers, the actors come into the audience and sing or gesture directly to us. Allie blushes and we both find it endearing and sweet.

The performances are, unsurprisingly, uneven. There are a number of strong actors with excellent voices, good dancing skills, and sharp comic timing. Still, a fair number of the actors (more typical among the kids) have wandering gazes or wandering feet, both markers of an untrained performer. Or, as likely, they are under-rehearsed. Every show at Jesters is double- or triple-cast because they run for around ten weeks, and Scott and Mary Lou don't expect people to give up their entire weekend for more than two months to do the show. The actors know how many performances they've been assigned as soon as they're cast—sixteen or eighteen or twenty over the course of the run. During rehearsals, Scott explains, not every actor gets enough time to work on every scene. But every person in that theatre, onstage and offstage, is having a great time, including us. *Joseph* is a wonderful show—easy to sing, campy and over-the-top humor, with one big production number after another. The performers display genuine pleasure throughout the afternoon.

We strike up a conversation with the people seated at the table next to ours: a woman in her fifties named Carol, her two late-teenaged children, and her niece celebrating her twenty-fifth birthday. They come to Jesters frequently, though they live an hour away. "I like it here because it's intimate and not polished," Carol says. "It's a fun afternoon on a Sunday and isn't expensive." She attends professional theatre regularly in Denver and goes to BDT Stage, too. Her family started coming to Jesters because some children of a friend were in a show. And they just kept coming. We nod in agreement. Allie adds, "It's genuine and comfortable." The aesthetics here are barebones, nothing like what we've seen at the other venues, but it all feels so earnest and sincere that it's impossible to condemn its lack of polish; on the contrary, it feels like a virtue, an emblem of something real.

After the theatre clears out, Scott changes into his jeans and T-shirt, and Mary Lou gathers scripts for the thirty-five little girls (each role was triple-cast) who soon arrive for the first rehearsal of *Annie*, Jesters' next show.

In some ways, Jesters encapsulates much of what this book has been about: pleasure and performance, community and creative expression, labor and the local. This theatre defies easy categorization. It's part community theatre and part dinner theatre. It's a sustaining family business with volunteer actors. Jesters was derided by people at the other Front Range dinner theatres who don't consider it a peer—and that's true, it's not professional.

And yet, they do serve food and perform the rituals of other dinner theatres, in addition to the show. Their audience is as knowing as the audiences at community theatres and high schools, appreciative of the familiarity and the casual intimacy. To be sure, what happens at Jesters is the opposite of what the other dinner theatres strive for (and succeed in attaining): polished professionalism. But there's no doubt that Jesters is a valued institution in the community with a loyal following. The theatre also provides many (many many!) locals with the chance to perform.

After four days, Allie and I were impressed by the remarkable repertoire that we saw in one long weekend, each selection somehow perfectly calibrated to its theatre's identity: classic 1940s musical at Candlelight; newest and latest edgy show at Midtown Arts; country jukebox musical at BDT Stage; Andrew Lloyd Webber family-friendly hit at Jesters. These dinner theatres, we agreed, are part of a vibrant musical theatre landscape . . . beyond Broadway.

Postscript

In December 2018, nine months after our road trip to dinner theatres in Colorado, the *Loveland Journal* announced that the Midtown Arts Center would be closing its doors after this season.[62] I knew before I visited that the local housing authority repossessed the land on which the dinner theatre sat (which previously was a four-plex movie theatre), and when I was there, owner and artistic director Kurt Terrio drove me around two miles toward the university to show me a vacant lot next to a Chick-fil-A that he hoped would be the new and improved Midtown Arts Center. "This is a great opportunity because we can build the operation from the ground up," he said, with excitement and a gleam in his eye. "We've talked to architects and builders and it's going to be a very special place."

I absolutely believed Kurt, who is a fireball of fierce energy and intense, infectious enthusiasm, and I easily imagined the new venue rising up on the empty space, marquee glowing next to a parking lot filled with cars. At the same time, I detected a whiff of fatigue about him. When he told me the story of his life—his early sports-obsessed childhood, the one musical in middle school that caught him unawares and dragged him into musical theatre forever (a fairly typical story for boys)—he closed by saying that running a dinner theatre is enormously hard work, that you're always on the verge of going under, and that you have to "pander to your audience." He wisely and successfully balanced "family-friendly" shows and the Disney musicals that he fairly detested with the *Ragtime*s and *Fun Home*s that he really wanted to produce. Though he owned a dinner theatre—the most commercial of musical theatre ventures (and the most commercial venue that I discuss in this book)—Kurt never let go of an artistic and political idealism and insistence that a dinner theatre in northern Colorado could have a season that included "risky" shows and still put bread on his family's table (and the tables of the rest of the theatre's staff and artists).

When I spoke to workers at the other dinner theatres in the region, some raised their eyebrows at Kurt's audacity to think that *Next to Normal* could attract dinner theatre audiences who mostly want a fun night out (with parking). They also criticized his practice of hiring actors from New York, who are mostly young and underpaid, except they're provided with housing. Some others in the business found this policy exploitative of those actors who relocated to Colorado for a few months and dismissive of the many local musical theatre performers with long careers and families and homes in the area. Kurt was nonplussed about their criticism, as he saw his way as simply another business model to make ends meet. And all of the actors I spoke to who worked at Midtown Arts were thrilled to be cast in *Fun Home, Ragtime*, or anything else at Midtown, whether they were locals or out-of-towners delighted to live on the beautiful Front Range for part of a season. In some ways, then, Midtown Arts' (that is, Kurt's) business and artistic practices upset the ecosystem and local rules of dinner theatre production in the area. Still, every person to whom I spoke was glad for Midtown Arts' presence. Everyone, it seemed, agreed that more dinner theatre promotes more dinner theatre.

I was, then, both surprised and not surprised to hear of its closing.

The press cast the story as one of mutual profit, emphasizing that Kurt is ready to move on and that Candlelight will benefit because Midtown Arts is funneling its subscribers to the Loveland theatre. This part of the deal is significant because Midtown currently has a larger subscriber base.[63] I'm happy for Candlelight, as it's a beautiful and excellently run operation. They're understandably thrilled to have one less competitor, especially for the surefire hit titles like *The Little Mermaid* and *Beauty and the Beast* that they both competed for every season.

But artistically, it's a significant loss for the area's musical theatre scene. Candlelight's size, mission, and brand prevent it from presenting the kinds of shows that Kurt preferred and that motivated his business model. I have no doubt that Candlelight will continue to produce gorgeous, top-notch productions of *Tarzan* and *Oliver!* (both on the 2018–19 season). But I'm sad to think that if Allie and I visited northern Colorado two years later, we would not have experienced an evening at Midtown Arts Center or seen what will surely be the first and last time I'll see *Fun Home* in a dinner theatre.

Figure 9.1. The cast and crew of Worthington High School's production of *Into the Woods*.

Epilogue

On any given Wednesday morning seven years ago, my routine regularly took me down Main Street in Pennington, New Jersey, driving to the grocery store. I would pass the St. James Roman Catholic Church, Vito's Pizza, and Kathy's Korner Salon. A hand-painted sign planted by the sidewalk on the corner of Main and Route 31 announcing an event would momentarily catch my eye, but I wouldn't pay any attention. I would get to the grocery store, park, do my shopping, and on my way out, see a bunch of fliers on the community bulletin board for various activities, services offered, rooms for rent, and dogs to adopt. I would pick up a copy of *Town Topics*, the free local paper, and scour the real estate listing because I'm obsessed with real estate. And I would be on my way.

Today, my Wednesday routine still takes me down Main Street on my way to the grocery store. I pass the church, the pizza place, and the salon. Now, a hand-painted sign by the road catches my eye: a production of *Guys and Dolls* at Hopewell Valley High School with dates and times listed. I try to imagine my calendar: Can I go next weekend? I get to the grocery store, park, do my shopping, and on my way out, I see a flier on the community bulletin board, familiar Disney logo and all: *The Little Mermaid JR.* at Montgomery Children's Theatre. I think about plans for the next month: Am I free to see *The Little Mermaid*, again? (Can I bear to see *The Little Mermaid* again?) I pick up a copy of *Town Topics* and read among the weekly entertainment listings that *Jekyll and Hyde* is playing at the Bridge Players Community Theatre. I don't know that show and hope I can make it to South Jersey to see it.

What's changed? Has Pennington, New Jersey, suddenly become a hotbed of musical theatre performance? No. All of those signs, fliers, and ads were there seven years ago—for *Anything Goes* at the high school, *The Jungle Book JR.* at the children's theatre, *Les Misérables* at the community theatre. I just hadn't noticed them. Even though I am a musical theatre scholar who spends her life seeing musicals, writing about them, and teaching them, I failed to see what was right here in front of me all along.

More than that, seven years ago, even if I had paid attention to a poster for a high school musical, I probably would have chuckled and pitied the poor

Beyond Broadway. Stacy Wolf, Oxford University Press (2020). © Oxford University Press.
DOI: 10.1093/oso/9780190639525.001.0001

family and friends who would have to sit through what I presumed would be a second-rate production of *Grease*.

Because seven years ago, I was also under the sway of negative stereotypes about local musical theatre. Local, especially amateur, musical theatre was something serious theatre people derided, belittled, or ridiculed. Although I spent much of my own childhood and youth performing in local musicals, I'd forgotten why they mattered.

Even though my research for this book is officially over, the community where I live looks different through the lens of local musical theatre, as does everywhere I travel, whether I'm visiting family or friends or as a tourist.

For example, I recently traveled to the Big Island of Hawaii and found myself at a dress rehearsal for a local, youth theatre production of *West Side Story*, talking to people and taking notes about the place and the process. A week earlier and on a different part of the island, I'd noticed a prominently displayed poster for the production hung by the entrance of the Punalu'u Bake Shop, which is famous for their malasadas (a Portuguese donut-like fried pastry—delicious). The familiar scrawled black letters that spelled *West Side Story* against a red brick background grabbed me, but since my partner and I (there on vacation) were leaving before opening night and would miss the performance, I hoped we might be able to watch some of a rehearsal or talk to someone associated with the theatre.

When we arrived in Waimea, the hilly ranchland in the north central region of the island a few days later, we went straight to the Kahilu Theatre in Kamuela.[1] (Waimea is the actual name of the town, but because other islands also have towns named Waimea, some people [and the post office] call the town Kamuela. The name means Samuel in Hawaiian and honors Samuel "Kamuela" Parker, heir to the Parker Ranch estate. But the proper name, which all of the locals use, is Waimea.)

Looking out from the glass-walled, contemporary, high-ceilinged theatre lobby, we saw an endless expanse of green and gold rolling hills and a lot of sky, which changes from cerulean blue to gray clouds and light rain by the early evening on most Waimea days. Lucky timing, Chuck Gessert, the theatre's relatively new artistic director (this is only his third year), arrived just then, carrying a stack of mail and two cold drinks in sweating cans. He offered to sit and talk to us, and we were delighted. He had been working in Chicago, he said, directing an Equity company that was by all accounts successful, but he had struggled to make a living. He heard about this job in Waimea and decided to apply. The theatre's board advertised for an artistic director, Chuck said, but really, they needed someone to make the theatre viable for the long term.

The Kahilu Theatre was built by Richard Smart (1913-1992), the sixth generation and final heir to the Parker Ranch fortune. The Parker family, who descended from John Palmer Parker and Chieftess Kipikane, grand-daughter of King Kamehameha I ("who ruled the eight Hawaiian Islands as one kingdom for the first time"[2]), acquired thousands of acres of land in the 19th century. At one point, Parker Ranch was the largest privately-held ranch in the US, with 225,000 acres and 50,000 cattle.[3] They enabled local ranchers to purchase land for grazing cattle and developed a thriving town out of what was once grassland, building electric generators, a dam to ensure water supply, schools, a hospital, and eventually, a shopping center.[4] Parker Ranch relied on the skills of the *paniolos* (Hawaiian cowboys), who established local traditions, including a rodeo. To this day, Parker is a household name in Waimea.

As a young man, Richard Smart left the island to perform on Broadway and in cabarets and clubs in New York, Las Vegas, and Los Angeles for 30 years. He returned to Waimea to run the Parker Ranch operations, and then decided to build a theatre in his hometown, which he named after his mother, Thelma Kahiluonapua'api'ilani Parker (and whose portrait hangs in the theatre's lobby).[5] For 12 years, Smart directed or performed in numerous plays at the theatre, including *The Last of the Red Hot Lovers* and *On Golden Pond*.[6] (Two portraits of Smart that hang in the lobby, one above the bar and one on the opposite wall, suggest that he was something of a dandy.)

Before he died, Smart created the Parker Ranch Foundation to support education and healthcare in the town but neglected to leave an endowment to cover the theatre's operating costs.[7] Various theories circulate, as we learned when we visited. Perhaps Smart wanted the community itself to support the theatre? Perhaps the trustees of his estate refused to release funds to the theatre? Perhaps some funds were provided but mismanaged? Whatever the reason, the Kahilu Theatre had to fend for itself. After the real estate bubble burst, the theatre saw a $250,000 deficit and in 2012, shut down for a year.[8]

After massive fundraising efforts, including a $1.5 million (which equaled the original building's cost) grant-in-aid from the state, the theatre re-opened.[9] In the years since, the theatre has seen substantial upgrade and renovations and become increasingly vital to the community. The Kahilu Theatre fulfills many purposes: it's a touring venue for theatre, dance, and music performances; it's a performing arts community center; it's the home of classes for kids and adults, including theatre, circus arts, and the Prince Dance Institute. When we visited, it was the performing space for the Kahilu Theatre Youth Troupe, founded in 2010 and directed by Beth Bornstein Dunnington.[10] As *West Side Story* choreographer Angel Prince told me, "I don't know any space that functions like this, in Hawaii or on the mainland. The theatre must wear a lot of hats and fill many roles."[11]

Chuck gave us a lively, candid, editorialized talk as he toured us through the place, through the wide and welcoming lobby, past a box office counter stacked with brochures and staffed by a helpful young woman who answered questions. He pointed out the bar, with snacks and beer donated by the local Kona Brewing Company so the theatre can keep the five dollars they charge per bottle, and art galleries on either side of the lobby displaying work by local artists. In the theatre itself, we visited the huge lighting room (it would be impossible to call it a "booth," its size just one indication of the amount of space the theatre boasts); a fully functioning kitchen; a number of dressing rooms; over-large wings, one of which serves as storage for miscellaneous stuff and the other as a part-time dance studio with a sprung floor and space for classes; and of course, the 500-seat auditorium that was built in 1980.

This theatre would be a boon for many communities in the US—a lovely, ample, functional space. The problem, as Chuck explained, is that the Kahilu Theatre serves a community of only 9,200 people—around the same as Sedona, Arizona, or Brattleboro, Vermont—not even populous enough to count as a "micropolitan" area. Chuck shared his ambitious vision for the theatre: building renovations and education and programming plans, including presenting musicals. He had himself directed a sold-out production of *South Pacific* last year, but he and Beth, *West Side Story*'s director, were concerned (four days before opening night) that few people in the town seemed to be familiar with the musical and ticket sales were lagging. (It's perhaps unsurprising that their audience would be familiar with *South Pacific*, given that it takes place in a similar locale, on a remote tropical island in the ocean.)

After the tour with Chuck, we settled into the auditorium to wait for the rehearsal to start and met Angel Prince, *West Side Story*'s choreographer. Angel came to the Big Island fifteen years ago from New York City, where she "could not be an artist because I had to live." In New York, she told me, she held five different jobs at once: she taught acting, partner dancing, and basic computer programming, and worked for a PR company. No waiting tables, though. "When I graduated from college, I vowed never to wait tables or bartend again," she said. Still, she said, "I moved to New York to live a creative life." She realized she was sick of that routine, sick of not being an artist, and sick of the cold weather. Then, 9-11 happened. "I thought, why not move to paradise?" she told me. She researched all of the islands of Hawaii. She thought that Honolulu would be too big a city, Kauai was too small, and Maui was too expensive and touristy. Angel figured that the Big Island was, well, big (it's actually just smaller than the state of Connecticut). She sold her belongings and moved 4,898 miles to an island in the middle of the ocean. "I thought there would be an underground arts scene here. I was wrong!"

Still, Angel landed a job at the theatre soon after she arrived and started teaching dance classes, which grew exponentially and led to the creation of Prince Dance Institute, now with ten teachers and 200 students. She told me that "it's a juggling act" to teach dance in a working theatre, "but the energy is exciting." (Angel reminded me of the charming, energetic backstage divas whom I write about in Chapter 2.)

At rehearsal, Beth, the director, yelled, "Places!" and the run-through began. The cast of the show was made up of young people aged 12 to 24. All live in the area except two actors who were paid and jobbed in from the mainland. None of the other actors were paid, nor did they pay; that is, this organization is not a pay-to-play company. The creative staff was paid, and the eighteen musicians also received a small stipend. Many of them are players for the Kamuela Philharmonic Orchestra, which, according to Chuck, functions as a "community orchestra." "They're doctors who did music in school and love to play," he said. Financially, this production employed a structure similar to those used by community theatres I've studied (see Chapter 4).

The performance (well, rehearsal) was at once like every other *West Side Story* I'd seen and entirely unique. They used Robbins' choreography, which they'd licensed, and the performers, trained by Angel, executed it well. Most of the Sharks, including Bernardo, were played by native Hawaiians, embodying Waimea's racial divide. On an island with a powerful anti-colonialist history and a vibrant, living native Hawaiian performance culture, *West Side Story* might still resonate.

In the end, the show sold out, and the audience was a combination of people who knew the musical and those who were introduced to *West Side Story* for the first time that weekend. As Angel told me, "It blew my mind. These were people from the mainland, from California, educated and from a cosmopolitan area, who didn't know the show. But you have to be in a family that watches and values musicals." Most importantly, she said, "You need theatres with educational programs—to bring kids in to see plays and to take theatre to the schools . . . thank God for musicals like *Hamilton*, and for my generation, *Rent*—a revolutionary musical that finally made theatre relevant again."

My serendipitous visit to the Kahilu Theatre reinforced my sense that musical theatre production reflects local demographics and local dynamics and that the Broadway musical repertoire is at once expansive and flexible enough to resonate anywhere in the US. Even on this island in the middle of the Pacific Ocean thousands of miles from the US mainland, they're doing *West Side Story*. Chuck said, "People don't go to church anymore. The theatre is where people gather now. This is church now." As we were leaving, he said, "Trump is doing his thing in Washington," waving his arm in a "far away" gesture. "And here we are, as far from Washington as you can get, making theatre. That has to mean something." Jill and I nodded in agreement, "That has to mean something."

Our visit to the theatre reshaped how I understand *West Side Story* and how I, as a tourist, understood Waimea. I got a tiny glimpse into the local culture and got to interact with a few people in a setting that makes sense to me: a theatre. Musical theatre production became my entrée to this slice of life, and for a brief few hours I got to observe local practices in situ.

Because I live relatively close to New York, I can work a normal day and make it to the city in time for a quick dinner and to see a show. For a long time, Broadway was the epicenter of my musical theatre experience, as it is for many people who love this theatrical form (and who have the good fortune to live in the region and/or visit the city and see a show). I'm part of the thousands who support a "booming Broadway," whose attendance and box office numbers in 2019, according to Michael Paulson in the *New York Times*, were higher than ever. Paulson attributes Broadway's success to rising tourism in New York, diverse offerings (plays as well as musicals), and shows enjoying longer runs. I'm happy to be a regular audience member on Broadway.[12]

But researching this book has encouraged me to see that while much of musical theatre scholarship (and audiences and creators) gravitate towards Broadway, the heart of musical theatre in America is actually playing out in a dinner theatre in Colorado, at a high school in Wilmington, Ohio, or in a dance studio in San Anselmo, California. Musical theatre thrives in an elementary school in Nashville, on the top of a mountain in Mill Valley, California, in a barn in Attean Lake, Maine, in schools and community theatres in Pennington, New Jersey, and in every town in the US. (Musical theatre is also taking place in nursing homes and senior living communities, as visionary, eighty-year-old Freddie Gershon [MTI's co-chairman—see Chapter 1], is piloting *Into the Woods Sr.* Stay tuned for this sure-to-be-worthwhile expansion of adaptations of the musical theatre repertoire.[13]) By writing this book, my perspective has shifted outwards. I hope yours has, too.

When I began this book, I was curious about musical theatre practices and how they play out across the country. I found musicals far and wide, for and by kids and adults, and was, in the end, overwhelmed by the endless array of interesting places to visit and to study. Like any research project, a combination of intention and serendipity, opportunity and diligent sleuthing led me from one theatre to another. Each theatre formed its own subculture, with specific rituals, conventions, and practices that differed at each place. And yet, with the Broadway musical theatre repertoire at the center, each venue was surprisingly similar.

Beyond Broadway tells a story about entertainment, civic engagement, community connections, identity formation, and creative expression. It also tells stories about the value and importance of doing something for fun (and to be sure, fun doesn't mean it's not serious or that it's not done with absolute care and attention and diligence). These stories are about kids who do musical theatre with no professional aspirations, about adults who spend their leisure time working at a theatre, and about the professionals who sustain a vast national network of local, often amateur practices.

Each visit helped me to appreciate how local culture feeds and sustains, amplifies and brings to life the materials that come from Broadway. I also witnessed, over and over, how the Broadway musical repertoire—this common cultural vernacular that so many of us share—enables grassroots engagement, commitment, and pleasure.

I hope it's clear that this book is also meant to testify about and advocate for the power of local arts practices. In a 2011 *New York Times* article, Robin Pogrebin observes that "much of America's artistic activity does not happen in major recital halls and theaters," but rather in places like Lucas, Wichita, and Junction City, Kansas.[14] My travel across the United States proved this to be true. And the journey continues . . . beyond Broadway.

Acknowledgments

Writing this book was like producing a musical: There were so many people at every stage of the project who advised, supported, collaborated on, and contributed to the work. Thank you!

Norm Hirschy is the most extraordinary editor imaginable—smart, thoughtful, funny, articulate, and supportive. I can't imagine having written this book without his enthusiasm and encouragement.

My thanks to everyone at OUP who brought this book to life: an astute copyeditor, Newgen project manager Cheryl Merritt, and the production team. Thank you to Daniel Gundlach for doing an excellent job on the index.

During the years of researching and writing this book. I was fortunate to receive a Guggenheim Fellowship, two Bogliasco Foundation Fellowships, and a Starr Fellowship in Jewish Studies at Harvard University. Princeton University supported this work in the form of research leave time, research travel funding, and Anonymous Grants to support undergraduate research assistants who were crucial to this project: Maddie Meyers, whose sharp observations I appreciated; Katie Welsh, who aided me throughout the process with her extraordinary research skills and interviewing savvy; Emma Watkins, who, in the final year, was indispensable as an energetic researcher, a perceptive and thoughtful reader, and a superbly skillful editor; and Marissa Michaels, excellent proof-reader.

The Starr Fellowship allowed me to spend a terrifically productive semester at Harvard to participate in a seminar on Jewish music. I met a group of brilliant ethnomusicologists whose ideas and methods fundamentally shaped the project in its early days. I'm especially grateful to Kay Shelemay, Amy Wlodarski, and my intrepid writing group, Judah Cohen and Sara Warner, who helped me crank out those early chapter drafts week by week. Carol Oja, Megan Sandberg-Zakian, Barbara Grossman, Louise Burnham Packard, and Karen Engle made life that semester even better.

Through the research, I depended on the help of archivists, including Linda Oppenheim at Princeton's Firestone Library; Nancy Coombs at the Austin Historical Society; David Hays at the University of Colorado; and Linda Meyer, Lori Oling, and Naomi Lederer at Colorado State University. Roxxy Leiser at the University of Colorado helped with my research there.

I also relied on archives at the New Jersey Historical Society, the Marin Historical Society, and the Schlesinger Library at Radcliffe.

Outside of the archives, Carol Edelson at MTI, Steven Kennedy at iTheatrics, and Lisa Mitchell at Disney generously taught me about their worlds and went out of their way on many occasions to answer my questions. Ken Cerniglia at DTG helped me more times than I can count (and always on short notice).

Earlier versions of a few chapters were previously published as articles. I thank the peer readers and editors, including George Rodosthenous, Helen Nicholson, Jane Milling, Nadine Holdsworth, Donelle Ruwe, James Leve, and Liz Wollman.

Much of this work was presented as talks at UCLA, Washington University in St. Louis, Harvard, MoMA PS1, and at academic conferences: the Association for Theatre in Higher Education, the American Society for Theatre Research, Song, Stage, and Screen, and for at the Humanities and Human Flourishing Project's Theatre and Performance Studies working group. I appreciated invitations from Joe Scanlan, Ray Knapp, Mitchell Morris, Harvey Young, Daniel Fister, Caleb Boyd, and Ashley Pribyl. Audiences and co-panelists at those talks improved this work with their thoughtful, generous, and generative questions and comments.

This project introduced me to a new community of scholars based in the United Kingdom who research amateur theatricals. Meeting them and participating in their conferences completely transformed my sense of my work in the larger history of amateur theatre. These scholars—Nadine Holdsworth, Jane Milling, Judith Hawley, and David Gilbert—welcomed me with remarkable warmth, and special thanks to Helen Nicholson for her generosity and openness.

My US cohort of musical theatre scholars ("my people") have offered inspiration and support throughout: Joanna Dee Das, Liza Gennaro, Ray Knapp, Jeff Magee, Carol Oja, Doug Reside, Jessica Sternfeld, David Savran, Dominic Symonds, Tamsen Wolff, and Liz Wollman. Over the years, they have read much of this book. The field of musical theatre studies continues to grow, and I've appreciated the intellectual engagement with Sam Baltimore, Ryan Bunch, Bud Coleman, Daniel Dinero, Ryan Donovan, Bill Everett, Donatella Galella, Barrie Gelles, Eric Glover, Alosha Grinenko, Barbara Grossman, Kary Haddad, Kelly Kessler, Paul Laird, Mary Jo Lodge, Laura MacDonald, Arianne Johnson Quinn, Holley Replogle-Wong, Joshua Robinson, Arreanna Rostosky, Joshua Streeter, Bryan Vandevender, and many more!

I want to especially thank Liz Wollman, who helped me through many ethnographic crises, and David Savran, whose gracious and brilliant reading of the whole manuscript told me what it was about.

Closer to home, I thank (every day) my amazing students whom I get to learn from every day. I am grateful for my wonderful colleagues in the Programs in Theater and Music Theater at the Lewis Center for the Arts at Princeton: Michael Cadden (who was LCA Chair during the writing of this book), Jane Cox, Bob Sandberg, Brian Herrera, Elena Araoz, Vince Di Mura, Darryl Waskow, Carmelita Becnel, Chloe Brown, and the rest of the great Theater and Music Theater team. Thanks to excellent colleagues in the Department of Music: Wendy Heller, Gabriel Crouch, Stephanie Tubiolo, Marty Elliott, Michael Pratt, and Steve Mackey. The unbelievably fantastic staff at the Lewis Center improved my life daily—thanks to Rick Pilaro, Steve Rife, Dan Benevento, Crystal Henderson-Napoli, Cathy Sterner, Kim Wassall, Steve Runk, Tracy Patterson, Zohar Lavi-Hasson, Hope VanCleaf, Jaclyn Sweet, Rob Del Colle, Angel Gardner, and Amy Nash. Marion Young, Mary O'Connor, and Joe Fonseca make everything go right all the time. I'm also thankful for the staff in my other Princeton homes, Judith Ferszt, Sarah Malone, Reagan Maraghy, and Jordan Dixon in American Studies, and Maria Papadakis and Jackie Wasneski in Gender & Sexuality Studies.

I'm fortunate to have a local writing group that read and commented on many chapters of the book and are all-around superb supporters. Thanks to Wendy Belcher, Jill Dolan, and Tamsen Wolff.

Over the seven years of researching and writing this book, I had countless conversations with friends and colleagues who offered advice or shared their own story or helped to connect me to a new community. I sincerely thank Lilly Armstrong, Wendy Arons, Nick Barberio, Leonard Barkan, Alfred Bendixen, Susan Bennett, Susan Bernstein, Debbie Bisno, Amy Borovoy, Amy Campbell, Anne Cheng, Laurie Beth Clark, Mindy Cooper, Ellen Gainor, David Goldman, Elayne Grossman, Dirk Hartog, Holly Haynes, Christie Henry, A. M. Homes, Tera Hunter, Adam Immerwahr, Stan Katz, Chad Klaus, Danny Kleinman, Jason Klugman, John Kucich, Sonja Kuftinec, Regina Kunzel, Melissa Lane, Rena Lederman, Andrew Lovett, Laura Mamo, Lindsey Mantoan, Susan Marshall, Erica Nagel, Betsy Levy Paluck, Michael Peterson, Leslie Rowley, Chris Renino, Jan Runkel, Donna Ryu, Dianne Sadoff, Gayle Salamon, Marni Sandweiss, Eve Schooler, Starry Schor, Howard Sherman, Dara Strolovich, Timea Szell, Donna Tatro, Greg Thompson, Adin Walker, Dov Weinryb Grohsgal, Judith Weisenfeld, and Ginger Zakian. I also thank every other person I spoke to over those years, since pretty much every conversation led to local musical theatre.

I'm especially grateful to my dear friends Judith Hamera (and a great colleague) and Marcie Pachino (my first friend in life) for their endless enthusiasm and frequent wise counsel.

My family sustains me. I thank Allie (best sister), Tom (new neighbor), Jay, Josh (thoughtful interlocutor), Vanina (extraordinary editor), Jacob and Daniel (who offered last minute vocabulary advice), and Alice. My nieces, Liliana and Noë, gave me valuable information and performance examples. I am lucky to have a great in-law family who always asked me how it was going: Jerry, Randee, David, Rachael, Morgann, Ann, Bert, Ally, and Ben, who did musicals in school, much to my delight. My mother, Saralee, provided a daily, sometimes hourly, stream of encouragement. I cannot thank her enough.

In the final year of writing and revisions, three people (in addition to my family, that is) provided weekly cheerleading, wisdom, and specific feedback: Betsy Armstrong, Deborah Paredez, and Claudia Voyles. Our weekly runs (Betsy), check-ins (Claudia), and work-sharing (Deb) made finishing this book a reality.

What would my life be if I couldn't come home to Jill Dolan, who, though dogless, is my greatest supporter, advocate, cheerleader, teacher, co-pilot, and editor. She has been excited about this project from day #1, has read every word, has boosted me up, has prodded me to tell her more stories, and always acts like every story is interesting and new. Her critical generosity sustains me, and I aspire to live my life in the academy with her integrity, intelligence, and good will. She's also seen a lot of musicals!

All through the writing of this book, when anyone would ask me who I was writing it for, I would say, the people who do this, who do musical theatre locally. I also thank the many people who told me stories or allowed me to hang out with them or observe their theatre-making whose stories didn't make it into the book. I sincerely appreciate their time and attention and commitment, and their spirit is in the book even if their exact words are not.

Finally, I thank the hundreds of people who welcomed me into their rehearsal rooms for days or weeks or months and talked to me about what doing musical theatre means to them. Obviously there would be no book without their generosity and openness, so this book is dedicated to them.

Earlier versions of chapters were published as:

"Broadway Junior." In *Childhood and the Child in Musical Theatre*. Edited by James Leve and Donelle Ruwe. New York: Ashgate, forthcoming.

"Making Musicals for Serious Pleasure." In *A Critical Companion to the American Stage Musical*, edited by Elizabeth L. Wollman, 198–213. New York: Bloomsbury Methuen Drama, 2017.

"Not Only on Broadway: Disney JR. and Disney KIDS Across the USA." In *The Disney Musical on Stage and Screen*, edited by George Rodosthenous, 133–54. London: Methuen Bloomsbury, 2017.

"'The Hills Are Alive with the Sound of Music': Musical Theatre at Girls' Jewish Summer Camps in Maine, USA." *Contemporary Theatre Review* 27, no. 1 (2017): 46–60.

Notes

Introduction

1. As Christopher Small writes in *Musicking: The Meanings of Performing and Listening*, "Music is not a thing at all but is an activity, something that people do" (Middletown, CT: Wesleyan UP, 1998), 2.
2. Tim McDonald, personal email, April 24, 2013.
3. https://www.cbs.com/shows/tony_awards/video/, accessed June 22, 2018.
4. TV News Desk, "The 72nd Annual Tony Awards Sees Increase in Viewership from Last Year's Broadcast," BroadwayWorld.com, accessed January 31, 2019, https://www.broadwayworld.com/article/The-72nd-Annual-Tony-Awards-Sees-Increase-in-Viewership-from-Last-Years-Broadcast-20180611.
5. https://twitter.com/hashtag/tonydreaming?lang=en, accessed August 29, 2018.
6. https://variety.com/2018/tv/news/tony-awards-2018-ratings-1202840489/, accessed July 23, 2018.
7. Marvin Carlson, *The Haunted Stage: Theatre as Memory Machine* (Ann Arbor: U of Michigan Press, 2003), 66.
8. Ibid., 2.
9. John Koblin, "'American Idol' Prepares for Its Swan Song," *New York Times*, May 12, 2015, B1.
10. Brooks Barnes, "Sing Out, Hollywood!" *New York Times*, January 16, 2017, C1.
11. Ibid., C4.
12. Qtd. in Ibid.
13. Ibid.
14. David Kamp, "The Glee Generation," *New York Times*, June 13, 2010, STYLES 2.
15. Robert D. Putnam, *Bowling Alone: The Collapse and Revival of American Community* (New York: Simon and Schuster, 2000), 402.
16. Ibid., 411. Also see http://infed.org/mobi/robert-putnam-social-capital-and-civic-community/ and http://robertdputnam.com/bowling-alone/social-capital-primer/, accessed August 24, 2018.
17. Putnam, *Bowling Alone*, 411. Also see http://infed.org/mobi/robert-putnam-social-capital-and-civic-community/ and http://robertdputnam.com/bowling-alone/social-capital-primer/, accessed August 24, 2018.
18. Putnam, *Bowling Alone*, 411.
19. Ibid., 412. Also see Robert Wuthnow, *Loose Connections: Joining Together in America's Fragmented Communities* (Cambridge: Harvard UP, 2002) and Susan Arai and Alison Pedlar, "Moving beyond Individualism in Leisure Theory: A Critical Analysis of

Concepts of Community and Social Engagement," *Leisure Studies* 22, no. 3 (2003), 185–202.

20. Sherry Turkle, *Alone Together: Why We Expect More from Technology and Less from Each Other* (New York: Basic Books, 2011), 280.

21. Ibid., 280.

22. Ibid., 171–74.

23. https://www.americantheatre.org/2017/09/21/the-top-20-most-produced-playwrights-of-the-2017-18-season/, accessed August 13, 2018.

24. Lauren M. Gunderson, "The Oldest Tech, Theater, Might Be an Antidote to the Newest," *San Francisco Chronicle*, November 29, 2017, accessed December 13, 2017, http://www.sfchronicle.com/opinion/article/The-oldest-tech-theater-might-be-an-antidote-to-12393595.php.

25. On the amateur, see, for example, Michael Dobson, *Shakespeare and Amateur Performance: A Cultural History* (New York: Cambridge UP, 2011); Stephen Knott, *Amateur Craft: History and Theory* (New York: Bloomsbury, 2015); Nicholas Ridout, *Passionate Amateurs: Theatre, Communism, and Love* (Ann Arbor: U of Michigan Press, 2013); Ruth H. Finnegan, *The Hidden Musicians: Music-Making in an English Town* (New York: Cambridge UP, 1989); Andy Merrifield, *Amateur: The Pleasures of Doing What You Love* (New York: Verso, 2017). I returned to Finnegan's wonderful book repeatedly during my research. She sees "degrees of professionalism" among the musicians she studied. The amateur and the professionals reside along a "complex continuum," in "interrelationship and overlap." The players in her study differentiated themselves by skill and performance ability more than by money or income (13–17).

26. See Robert A. Stebbins, *Amateurs, Professionals, and Serious Leisure* (Montreal: McGill-Queen's UP, 1992); Chris Rojeck, Susan M. Shaw, and A. J. Veal, eds., *A Handbook of Leisure Studies* (New York: Palgrave Macmillan, 2006); Stephen M. Gelber, *Hobbies: Leisure and the Culture of Work in America* (New York: Columbia UP, 1999).

27. Wayne Booth, *For the Love of It: Amateuring and Its Rivals* (Chicago: U of Chicago Press, 1999), 12, 11.

28. Charles Leadbeater and Paul Miller, *The Pro-Am Revolution: How Enthusiasts Are Changing Our Society and Economy* (London: Demos, 2004), 12.

29. Carol Edelson, personal interview, New York, October 19, 2012. The other half is professional productions.

30. Some of this material is differently contextualized in Stacy Wolf, "Making Musicals for Serious Pleasure," *The Methuen Guide to Musical Theatre*, ed. Elizabeth L. Wollman (New York: Bloomsbury Methuen, 2017), 198–217.

31. "This Day in Music," *Billboard*, accessed January 31, 2019, https://www.billboard.com/articles/news/59279/this-day-in-music; "Leonard Bernstein *West Side Story* Chart History," *Billboard*, accessed January 31, 2019, https://www.billboard.com/music/leonard-bernstein.

32. Sofa Entertainment, "Broadway on *The Ed Sullivan Show*," The Official Ed Sullivan Site, accessed January 31, 2019, http://www.edsullivan.com/broadway-on-the-ed-sullivan-show/.

33. https://www.npr.org/sections/ed/2016/09/29/427138970/the-most-popular-high-school-plays-and-musicals, accessed August 12, 2018.

34. http://www.samuelfrench.com/, http://www.tamswitmark.com/about/, http://www.dramatists.com/text/contact.asp, http://www.rnh.com/our_history.html; all accessed August 31, 2015.

35. Ted Chapin, "In Conversation with John Doyle about the Musical *Follies*, Hal Prince, and Michael Bennett," Princeton University, September 26, 2016. He added, "You know, I'm a believer that people will do what they're asked to do. If you set the bar very low, they'll go there. If you set the bar up there," gesturing above his head, "who won't try to go there?"

36. Thomas L. Riis II, *Frank Loesser* (New Haven: Yale UP, 2008), 245.

37. Cross, "Don Walker," The Official Masterworks Broadway Site, accessed January 31, 2019, https://masterworksbroadway.com/artist/don-walker/. http://www.mtishows.com/content.asp?id=1_2_0, accessed August 31, 2015. Also see Riis, *Frank Loesser*.

38. https://deadline.com/2018/02/mti-drew-cohen-global-ceo-music-theatre-international-1202298077/, accessed July 12, 2018. Gershon became co-chairman of the company.

39. https://www.playscripts.com/, accessed July 24, 2018.

40. https://www.broadwayworld.com/article/Playscripts-Launches-Broadway-Licensing-with-Sean-Cercone-20170320. Also see https://broadwaylicensing.com/musicals/, accessed July 24, 2018.

41. Jim Rendon, "Broadway Hits the Middle School Circuit," *New York Times*, February 23, 2018, BU3, accessed February 25, 2018, https://www.nytimes.com/2018/02/23/business/broadway-hits-the-middle-school-circuit.html.

42. Qtd. in Rendon, "Broadway Hits the Middle School Circuit."

43. Ruthie Fierberg, "How Disney Shows Are Changing the Landscape of the American Musical Theatre," *Playbill*, August 10, 2018, accessed August 13, 2018, http://www.playbill.com/article/how-disney-shows-are-changing-the-landscape-of-the-american-musical-theatre.

44. "AllShows," Music Theatre International, https://www.mtishows.com/shows/all; "About Us," Rodgers & Hammerstein, https://www.rnh.com/about_us.html; "Our Shows," Tams-Witmark, http://www.tamswitmark.com/shows/; "Shows Archive," Theatrical Rights Worldwide online, https://www.theatricalrights.com/shows/; "Musicals," Broadway Licensing, https://broadwaylicensing.com/musicals/; all accessed August 11, 2018.

45. Their offices have since moved since I visited them in 2013.

46. Carol Edelson, personal email, September 13, 2018.

47. In August 2018, the position of director of education and development was added to Prignano's position. http://www.playbill.com/article/john-prignano-named-director-of-education-and-development-at-music-theatre-international, accessed August 29, 2018.

48. https://www.mtishows.com/marketplace/resource/pre-performance/the-original-production-choreography-videos, accessed July 24, 2018.

49. https://www.schooltheatre.org/resources/playsurvey, accessed August 10, 2018.

50. https://www.npr.org/sections/ed/2016/09/29/427138970/the-most-popular-high-school-plays-and-musicals, accessed August 10, 2018.

51. Fierberg, "How Disney Shows Are Changing."

52. Ibid.

53. Ibid.

54. Qtd. in ibid.

55. My thanks to Helen Nicholson, Jane Milling, and Nadine Holdsworth, who came up with this phrase to describe my work.

56. My thanks to Judith Hamera for this apt label.

57. http://public.imaginingamerica.org/blog/article/critical-generosity-2/, accessed January 30, 2019. My thanks to Jill Dolan for reminding me of critical generosity's usefulness here as a framework.

Chapter 1

1. Vanessa, Daniel, and all of the kids and adults connected with theatre groups in this chapter are composites based on interviews with Casper Children's Theater (WY), Center Stage Productions (MI), Holly Performance Academy (GA), Roy Waldron School Drama Team (TN), Spotlight Theatre Productions (FL), and Treehouse Theater (WI) in May and June 2014 and with Moorestown Theater Company (NJ) in January 2013. The names of the adults who work for iTheatrics and MTI are real. I observed some of these situations when I attended the 2013 JTF. Other situations are based on descriptions from interviews.

2. See http://www.broadwayworld.com/atlanta/article/Nicholas-F-Manos-Resigns-as-President-of-Theater-of-the-Stars-20130529 (May 29, 2013); Adam Hetrick, "Atlanta's Theater of the Stars Cancels 2013–2014 Season," *Playbill* (August 1, 2013), http://www.playbill.com/news/article/atlantas-theater-of-the-stars-cancels-2013-2014-season-207200; Adam Hetrick, "After 60 Seasons, Atlanta's Theater of the Stars Closes Its Doors," *Playbill* (September 11, 2013), http://www.playbill.com/news/article/after-60-seasons-atlantas-theater-of-the-stars-closes-its-doors-209397, all accessed August 24, 2015.

3. "Junior Theatre Festival '19." Brochure, August 11, 2018, http://juniortheaterfestival.com/wp-content/uploads/2018/03/JTF_2019_brochure-1.pdf.

4. Ibid.

5. Robert Viagas, "Junior Theater Festival Kicks Off! Darren Criss, Andrew Keenan-Bolger Are Guests," *Playbill*, January 15, 2016, http://www.playbill.com/article/junior-theater-festival-kicks-off-darren-criss-andrew-keenan-bolger-are-guests-com-379103.

6. Peter Filchia, "Filchia Features: The Night Before the Junior Theater Festival '14," January 31, 2014, http://mtiblog.mtishows.com/filichia-features-the-night-before-the-junior-theater-festival-14/, accessed August 24, 2015.

7. "Who Is Freddie Gershon?" (June 2012), http://www.freddiegershon.com/FreddiePrintBioJune2012.pdf, accessed June 10, 2013.

8. Qtd. in Dominic P. Papatola, "Children Will Listen: Juniorized: Sondheim Provided the Impetus for Smaller-Scale Versions of Shows," *The Sondheim Review* 12, no. 2 (Winter 2005): 13–14. http://www.sondheimreview.com/magazine/vol-12-no-2-winter-2005/, accessed August 24, 2015.

9. Also see Barbara Perlov, *Why We Tell the Story: A Report on The Shubert Foundation/ MTI Broadway Junior Program in the New York City Public Schools* (November 2009): 6–7. http://schools.nyc.gov/offices/teachlearn/arts/Bway%20JR/Why_We_Tell_FINAL-LD.pdf, accessed August 24, 2015.

10. https://www.tonyawards.com/en_US/news/articles/2012-06-03/201206031338746539021.html, accessed July 27, 2018.

11. Qtd. in Papatola, "Children Will Listen," 14.

12. http://schools.nyc.gov/offices/teachlearn/arts/Bway%20JR/Why_We_Tell_FINAL-LD.pdf, accessed August 23, 2015; http://itheatricals.com/bio_pdfs/Cynthiabio.pdf, accessed August 23, 2015; http://www.itheatricals.com/history.html, accessed August 24, 2015.

13. Papatola, "Children Will Listen," 13.

14. Perry Nodelman, *The Hidden Adult: Defining Children's Literature* (Baltimore: Johns Hopkins UP, 2008), 85.

15. Papatola, "Children Will Listen," 13.

16. Nodelman, *Hidden Adult*, 132.

17. MTI has also developed School Editions—full-length, cleaned-up versions for high schools—of some titles, including *Rent* and *Les Misérables*, for example. On the pilot production of *Rent School Edition* at Stagedoor Manor summer camp, see Mickey Rapkin, *Theater Geek: The Real-Life Drama of a Summer at Stagedoor Manor, the Famous Performing Arts Camp Theater Geek* (New York: Simon and Schuster, 2010).

18. http://itheatrics.com/our-team/, accessed August 27, 2015.

19. http://www.educationupdate.com/archives/2006/May/html/mad-lettheshow.html, accessed November 29, 2015.

20. Though MTI licenses and sells the product, Disney creates its own JR. and KIDS scripts and ShowKit materials.

21. Papatola, "Children Will Listen," 13.

22. Jim Rendon, "Broadway Hits the Middle School Circuit," *New York Times*, February 23, 2018, BU3. https://www.nytimes.com/2018/02/23/business/broadway-hits-the-middle-school-circuit.html, accessed February 25, 2018.

23. https://www.theatricalrights.com/shows/, accessed July 27, 2018.

24. http://itheatrics.com/adapting-broadway-musicals/, accessed August 27, 2015.

25. Sean Patrick Flahaven, the CEO of the Musical Company, which works with theatre writers and producers to publish music, license shows, and make cast recordings, supplied these statistics. https://www.nytimes.com/2018/02/23/business/broadway-hits-the-middle-school-circuit.html, accessed February 25, 2018.

26. Rendon, "Broadway Hits the Middle School Circuit."

27. Ibid.

28. http://www.playbill.com/news/article/mti-will-license-disneys-aida-and-beauty-and-the-beast-for-regional-and-ama-115365, accessed November 29, 2015;

http://broadwayentertainmentgroup.com/disneys-beauty-beast-celebrates-20th-anniversary-stage-first-%C2%AD%E2%80%90%E2%80%91ever-international-tour/, accessed November 29, 2015.

29. http://www.nbc.com/grease-youre-the-one-that-i-want/about; http://www.nbc.com/the-sound-of-music-live; http://www.nbc.com/peter-pan-live, all accessed November 29, 2015.

30. See Sean J. Bliznik, "We're All in This Together: Framing the Self-Representation of Adolescence in Disney's *High School Musical*," in *Children Under Construction: Critical Essays on Play as Curriculum*, ed. Drew Chappell (New York: Peter Lang Publishing, 2010): 149–66.

31. Rapkin, *Theatre Geek*, 145.

32. Ibid. Also see David Kamp, "The Glee Generation," *New York Times*, June 11, 2010 http://www.nytimes.com/2010/06/13/fashion/13Cultural.html?_r=0, accessed August 19, 2015.

33. https://www.mtishows.com/hairspray-jr, accessed January 28, 2019.

34. https://www.mtishows.com/hairspray-jr, accessed July 27, 2018.

35. https://www.dallasobserver.com/arts/at-plano-childrens-theatre-theyve-shampooed-all-the-black-kids-out-of-hairspray-7085541, accessed July 27, 2018.

36. https://www.broadwayworld.com/board/readmessage.php?thread=1041536, accessed July 27, 2018.

37. https://www.huffingtonpost.com/2012/01/31/all-white-production-of-h_n_1244955.html, accessed July 27, 2018.

38. https://www.broadwayworld.com/board/readmessage.php?thread=340554, accessed July 27, 2018.

39. Thanks to Steven Kennedy for sharing details of the process with me.

40. For a description of the process, see http://itheatrics.com/adapting-broadway-musicals/, accessed August 28, 2015.

41. Thanks to Robert Lee for sharing this and other details of the adaptation process with me.

42. http://www.mtishows.com/show_detail.asp?showid=000223, accessed August 30, 2015.

43. See Bruce Kirle, *Unfinished Show Business: Broadway Musicals as Works-in-Process* (Carbondale: Southern Illinois UP, 2005).

44. http://www.broadwayjr.com/store/showkitproduct.asp?oid=000223, accessed August 30, 2015. See "WELCOME TO THE MTI BROADWAY JUNIOR COLLECTION®" https://www.youtube.com/watch?v=xW4hDun9ZQM, accessed August 23, 2015. Also see http://www.mtishowspace.com/videos/154865/show-support-choreography-76-trombones-music-man-jr for an example of choreography for "76 Trombones," created by iTheatrics, accessed August 30, 2015.

45. Rendon, "Broadway Hits the Middle School Circuit."

46. http://www.mtishowspace.com/mod/ad/allshows.php, accessed August 23, 2015.

47. http://www.mtishowspace.com/show_support.php, accessed August 23, 2015; http://itheatricals.com/bio_pdfs/Cynthiabio.pdf, accessed August 19, 2015.

48. http://broadwayjr.com/audition/auditionlist.asp?ID=000223, accessed August 30, 2015.

49. http://www.mtishows.com/show_detail.asp?showid=000223, accessed August 30, 2015.

50. The importance of musicians takes on the opposite valence at adult community theatres, as they're typically paid (a small stipend) to play while actors perform without monetary compensation.

51. http://www.mtishows.com/show_detail.asp?showid=000223, accessed August 30, 2015.

Chapter 2

1. Qtd. in Stacy Wolf, *Changed for Good: A Feminist History of the Broadway Musical* (New York: Oxford University Press, 2011), 223.

2. "Past Marilyn Izdebski Productions Shows," Marilyn Izdebski Productions, accessed August 27, 2018, http://www.marilynizdebskiproductions.com/past-marilyn-izdebski-productions-shows.

3. "MARILYN, a short film by Sam Stoich," Marilyn Izdebski Productions, accessed August 27, 2018, http://www.marilynizdebskiproductions.com/marilyn-short-film-sam-stoich.

4. Wayne Koestenbaum and Simon Prozak, "'Opera Is a Closed Book': A Conversation with Wayne Koestenbaum," *Qui Parle* 21, no. 1 (Fall/Winter 2012): 248.

5. Ann Louise Wagner, *Adversaries of Dance: From the Puritans to the Present* (Urbana and Chicago: University of Illinois, 1997), 74. Also see Julia Cherry Spruill, *Women's Life and Work in the Southern Colonies* (New York: W.W. Norton & Company, 1972), 95, 260.

6. See, for example, "Dancing. – Miss Eliza Goodwin's Dancing School," *Nashville Union & American* (Nashville, TN), September 13, 1874, 4; "Dancing – 14 Words or Less, 20 cents," *St. Louis Post-Dispatch* (St. Louis, MO), September 30, 1900, 30.

7. Linda J. Tomko, *Dancing Class: Gender, Ethnicity, and Social Divides in American Dance, 1890–1920* (Bloomington: Indiana UP, 1999), ix.

8. See Elsa Posey, "Dance Education in Dance Schools in the Private Sector Meeting the Demands of the Marketplace," *Journal of Dance Education* 2, no. 2 (2002): 43–49.

9. Susan Leigh Foster, "Dance and/as Competition in the Privately Owned U.S. Studio," in *The Oxford Handbook of Dance and Politics*, ed. Rebekah J. Kowal, Gerald Siegmund, and Randy Martin (New York: Oxford UP, 2017), 57.

10. Winifred Ward, *Creative Dramatics: For the Upper Grades and Junior High School* (New York: D. Appleton and Company, 1930), 3. Ward was influenced by the progressive educational theories of American philosopher John Dewey and believed this process-based approach aided the intellectual and emotional development of the "whole child."

11. "Children's Playhouse Theatre Collection," Ball State University, accessed August 27, 2018, http://libx.bsu.edu/cdm/landingpage/collection/ChldPlyTCol. This web page also states that her studio is located "across from the old City Hall building, on the

southwest corner of Jackson and Jefferson." Many early advertisements for dance and theater studios gave these kinds of directions; studios were often off the beaten path and/or in unexpected locations (since women made do with the spaces they could find and afford), so directions often indicated the studio's location relative to major town landmarks like government buildings, suburban business parks, grocery stores, churches, Masonic halls, and schools. "Irene Thompson Belcher," *Find A Grave*, accessed August 27, 2018, https://www.findagrave.com/ memorial/92376489/ irene-belcher.

12. "Juvenile Players to Present Varied and Interesting Program," *San Mateo Times and Daily News Leader*, November 7, 1927, 3.

13. "Stage Beckons to Children," *Tucson Daily Citizen*, August 12, 1959, 27.

14. Micheline Keating, "Mary, at 83, A Marvelous Task Master," *Tucson Daily Citizen*, May 17, 1969, 31; Henry Kendrick, "Letter to the Editor: A Remarkable Lady," *Tucson Daily Citizen*, March 13, 1972, 23. Additionally, not unlike the two-day retirement gala held in Marilyn Izdebski's honor in April 2017, a community-wide "testimonial dinner" was held to publicly recognize MacMurtrie's significant impact on the community shortly before she passed away. "Testimonial to Honor Mary MacMurtrie," *Tucson Daily News*, September 13, 1971, 12.

15. *Dramatics 20-21* (Cincinnati: International Thespian Society, 1948), 15–16.

16. Kathleen Thompson, "Teaching More Than Dance," *Dance Teacher Now* 19, no. 5 (May 1997): 72. In 1962, for example, Miss Kathryn De Haven was running a "Teenage Musical Theater Workshop" at the Peninsula Conservatory of Music in Burlingame, California, in which students had "actual experience in production." Teens gained skills not only in acting and singing but also in "sets, lighting, and makeup," all of which they "developed in actual practice in the workshop productions." "Teen Theatre Workshop Due," *The Times* (San Mateo, CA), August 30, 1962, 27.

17. See Tom Rowan, *A Chorus Line FAQ: All That's Left to Know About Broadway's Singular Sensation* (Milwaukee: Applause Theatre and Cinema Books, 2015), Chapter 16.

18. See, for example, "Teen Theatre Workshop Due," *The Times* (San Mateo, CA), August 30, 1962, 27; "Conservatory Adds Class," *The Times* (San Mateo, CA), July 9, 1968, 7; Julia Prodis Sulek, "S.J. Arts Director Fondly Remembered," *Mercury News*, August 29, 2007, https://www.mercurynews.com/ 2007/08/29/s-j-arts-director-fondly-remembered/; Ruth Croft, "Tells Plans for Valley Musical Unit: Theater Group to Guide Young College Players," *Valley News* (Van Nuys, CA), March 29, 1974, 1.

19. See Thompson, "Teaching More Than Dance," 69.

20. "U.S. Census Bureau Quick Facts: Alafaya CDP, Florida; United States," United States Census Bureau, accessed August 15, 2018, www.census.gov/quickfacts/fact/table/ alafayacdpflorida,US/INC110216.

21. http://magiccurtainproductions.com/theaters/, accessed July 8, 2018.

22. Mary Rodgers, Marshall Barer, and Jay Thompson, Dean Fuller, and Marshall Barer, *Once Upon a Mattress* (New York: R & H Theatricals, 1959), 13, https://www.scribd. com/doc/147088418/Once-Upon-a-Mattress-Script.

23. Ibid.

24. "MARILYN, a short film by Sam Stoich."

25. Alexander Doty, "Introduction: There's Something About Mary," *Camera Obscura* 22, no. 2 (65) (2007): 2.

26. "MARILYN, a short film by Sam Stoich."

27. Ibid.

28. Ibid.

29. Ibid.

30. Ibid.

31. Ibid.

32. Ibid.

Chapter 3

1. "Low Budget Milky Whites," Blog, *Tumblr*, accessed July 20, 2018, http://lowbudgetmilkywhites.tumblr.com/.

2. Stephen Sondheim, *Look, I Made A Hat: Collected Lyrics (1981–2011)* (New York: Knopf, 2011), 59.

3. Ibid., 87.

4. Ibid.

5. Frank Rich, "Stage: 'Into the Woods,' From Sondheim," *New York Times*, November 6, 1987, C5, accessed July 20, 2018, https://www.nytimes.com/1987/11/06/theater/stage-into-the-woods-from-sondheim.html. On the 2002 revival, which Sondheim revised and which starred Vanessa Williams, see Bernard Weinraub, "Spring Theater; Back to the Woods, With Darker Lyrics and a Dancing Cow," *New York Times*, February 24, 2002, sec. Theater, accessed July 20, 2018, https://www.nytimes.com/2002/02/24/theater/spring-theater-back-to-the-woods-with-darker-lyrics-and-a-dancing-cow.html.

6. Rich, "Stage: 'Into the Woods,' From Sondheim."

7. Ibid.

8. Sondheim, *Look, I Made A Hat*, 58.

9. Ibid.

10. Carolyn Sung and Catherine E. Shoichet, "Freddie Gray Case: Charges Dropped Against Remaining Officers," *CNN*, last modified July 27, 2016, accessed July 20, 2018, https://www.cnn.com/2016/07/27/us/freddie-gray-verdict-baltimore-officers/index.html.

11. "Most Valuable Players Movie," last modified 2013, accessed July 20, 2018, http://mostvaluableplayersmovie.com/. "Purple Dreams (2017)," *IMDb*, last modified 2018, accessed July 20, 2018, https://www.imdb.com/title/tt2717718/. "I Can't . . . I Have Rehearsal," *NJTV*, May 3, 2017, accessed July 20, 2018, https://www.njtvonline.org/programs/i-cant-i-have-rehearsal/.

12. "About the Award," *The Jimmy Awards: The National High School Musical Theatre Awards*, last modified 2018, accessed June 27, 2018, https://www.jimmyawards.com/about/about-award/.

13. "FAQ," *The Jimmy Awards: The National High School Musical Theatre Awards*. Last modified 2018. Accessed June 28, 2018. https://www.jimmyawards.com/about/faq/. Neeti Upadhye, "Broadway's Biggest Night—for Teenagers," *New York Times*, June 27, 2017, accessed July 1, 2017, https://www.nytimes.com/video/theater/100000005185169/jimmy-awards-teen-musical-theater.html. Also see Rachel Syme, "Ever Heard of the Jimmys? It's the Tonys, for Teenagers," *New York Times*, June 27, 2017, accessed July 1, 2017, https://www.nytimes.com/2017/06/27/theater/jimmy-awards.html?_r=0.

14. "FAQ," *The Jimmy Awards*.

15. "2018 Play Survey," Educational Theatre Association, last modified 2018, accessed August 10, 2018, https://www.schooltheatre.org/resources/playsurvey.

16. Howard Sherman, "Keynote: School Theatre Can Be More," presented at the Florida Association for Theatre Education Annual Conference, Orlando, Florida, October 18, 2017, http://www.hesherman.com/2017/10/18/keynote-school-theatre-can-be-more/.

17. Ibid.

18. Ibid.

19. James Catterall, Richard Chapleau, and John Iwanaga, *Involvement in the Arts and Human Development: General Involvement and Intensive Involvement In Music and Theater Arts*, Champions of Change: The Impact of the Arts on Learning (Los Angeles: UCLA Graduate School of Education & Information Studies, University of California at Los Angeles, 1999), 15.

20. Ibid., 2.

21. Kathleen Gallagher, *Why Theatre Matters: Urban Youth, Engagement, and a Pedagogy of the Real* (Toronto: University of Toronto Press, 2014), 170.

22. Ibid.

23. Ibid.

24. Ibid.

25. Ibid.

26. Ryan John, "Part of It All: The High School Musical as a Community of Practice," *Visions of Research in Music Education* (2014): 15.

27. Qtd. in ibid.

28. Reed Larson and Jane Brown, "Emotional Development in Adolescence: What Can Be Learned From a High School Theater Program?," *Child Development* 78, no. 4 (August 2007): 1088.

29. Jay Greene, Heidi H. Erickson, Angela R. Watson, and Molly I. Beck, "The Play's the Thing: Experimentally Examining the Social and Cognitive Effects of School Field Trips to Live Theater Performances," in *Working Paper Series* (Arkansas: University of Arkansas, Department of Education Reform, 2017), 18.

30. Frederick Heide, Natalie Porter, and Paul Saito, "Do You Hear the People Sing? Musical Theatre and Attitude Change," *Psychology of Aesthetics, Creativity, and the Arts*, 6, no. 3 (2017): 224–230.

31. Rendon, "Broadway Hits the Middle School Circuit."

32. Elissa Nadworthy, "The Most Popular High School Plays and Musicals," *NPR.org*, August 1, 2018, accessed August 10, 2018, https://www.npr.org/sections/ed/2016/09/29/427138970/the-most-popular-high-school-plays-and-musicals.

33. Ibid.

34. Steve Spiegel, personal email, July 11, 2018.

35. Patrick Healy, "Critics May Rant, but 'Addams Family' Rakes It In," *New York Times*, April 13, 2010, sec. Theater, accessed July 20, 2018, https://www.nytimes.com/2010/04/14/theater/14addams.html. Broadway.com Staff, "*The Addams Family* to End Broadway Run on New Year's Eve," *Broadway.com*, last modified August 24, 2011, accessed July 20, 2018, https://www.broadway.com/buzz/157440/the-addams-family-to-end-broadway-run-on-new-years-eve/.

36. Charles Isherwood, "Talk About Your Spring Awakening," *New York Times*, July 13, 2008, accessed December 10, 2017, http://www.nytimes.com/2008/07/13/theater/13ishe.html?smid=pl-share.

37. Ibid.

38. Lucy Huber, "High School Girls in Musicals . . .," Twitter, @clhubes, July 7, 2018, accessed July 11, 2018, https://twitter.com/clhubes/status/1015620426876276737. Thanks to Laura MacDonald for alerting me to this tweet and the powerful comments that follow.

39. Nadworthy, "The Most Popular High School Plays and Musicals."

40. See Jennifer Chapman, "Knowing Your Audience," in *The Oxford Handbook of the American Musical*, ed. Raymond Knapp, Mitchell Morris, and Stacy Wolf (New York: Oxford University Press, 2011), 401. Chapman writes, "Like the popular titles from the community MT canon, all three shows have courtship rituals that reinforce gender stereotypes and all three have a wedding or offstage marriage as part of the plot" (401).

41. Howard Sherman, "Who Cares About Censorship on School Stages?," *American Theatre: Theatre Communications Group*, January 5, 2015, https://www.americantheatre.org/2015/01/06/why-i-care-about-censorship-on-school-stages/.

42. Josh Chapin, "Parents Want to Silence High School Musical," *NBC Connecticut* (Woodbridge, CT, March 11, 2013), https://www.nbcconnecticut.com/news/local/School-Musical--197251831.html.

43. Peter Crimmins, "Wielding Weapons on Stage, 'Les Misérables' Makes Students Confront Gun Violence," *WHYY*, February 23, 2018, accessed June 24, 2018, https://whyy.org/segments/wielding-weapons-stage-les-miserables-makes-students-confront-gun-violence/.

44. Howard Sherman, "How Not to Cancel Your High School Musical," *Hesherman.com*, December 4, 2013, accessed June 14, 2018, http://www.hesherman.com/2013/12/04/how-not-to-cancel-your-high-school-musical/.

45. Howard Sherman, "How To Defend Your High School Musical," *Hesherman.com*, November 29, 2013, accessed June 14, 2018, http://www.hesherman.com/2013/11/29/how-to-defend-your-high-school-musical/.

46. Ray Bendici, "'Rent' Production Is Back on at Trumbull High School," *Connecticut Magazine*, December 10, 2013, http://connecticutmag.gtxcel.net/Blog/Connecticut-Today/November-2013/RENT-Back-on-at-Trumbull-High/.

47. Patrick Healy, "Tamer 'Rent' Is Too Wild for Some Schools," *New York Times*, February 19, 2009, sec. Theater, https://www.nytimes.com/2009/02/20/theater/20rent.html.

48. Ibid. "In 2008, the superintendent of Bridgeport High School cancelled a production of *Rent: School Edition* because she was "concerned that families in her West Virginia school district would not find [the homosexual] content and other themes appealing. ('We're a bit back in the woods here,' she said.)"

49. Ibid.

50. Jeff Overley, "Instructor: Play Canceled Because of Gay Characters," *Orange County Register* (Newport Beach, CA), February 13, 2009, https://www.ocregister.com/2009/02/13/instructor-play-canceled-because-of-gay-characters/.

51. Howard Sherman, "You Can't Rewrite Your High School Musical," *Hesherman.com*, December 18, 2013, http://www.hesherman.com/2013/12/18/you-cant-rewrite-your-high-school-musical/.

52. Howard Sherman, "Obscuring The Better Angel of High School Theatre," *Hesherman. Com*, March 11, 2014, accessed June 18, 2018, www.hesherman.com/2014/03/11/obscuring-the-better-angel-of-high-school-theatre/.

53. Adam Hetrick, "Documents Reveal PA High School Canceled *Spamalot* Due to Gay Content," *Playbill*, last modified August 21, 2014, accessed July 25, 2018, http://www.playbill.com/article/documents-reveal-pa-high-school-canceled-spamalot-due-to-gay-content-com-327028.

54. Melanie Burney, "Cherry Hill Schools Grapple with N-Word in 'Ragtime': Will the Show Go On?," *Philly.com*, January 24, 2017, sec. Education, http://www.philly.com/philly/education/Cherry-Hill-school-board-to-hear-Ragtime-controversy.html.

55. Ibid.

56. Melanie Burney, "How Cherry Hill East Will Prepare Students to Handle N-Word in 'Ragtime,'" *Philly.com*, February 27, 2017, http://www.philly.com/philly/news/new_jersey/Cherry-Hill-East-Prepares-Students-to-Handle-N-Word-in--Ragtime-Production.html.

57. Ibid.

58. Sopan Deb, "Casting Controversy Derailed a High School Play. Then Came the Threats," *New York Times*, February 8, 2018, https://www.nytimes.com/2018/02/08/theater/hunchback-of-notre-dame-ithaca-high-school.html.

59. Maggie Gilroy, "Ithaca High School Pulls 'Hunchback of Notre Dame' over Casting Diversity Outcry," *Ithaca Journal*, January 29, 2018, sec. Local, https://www.ithacajournal.com/story/news/local/2018/01/29/new-project-planned-place-ithaca-musical-hunchback-notre-dame-cancelled-amid-outcry-diversify-castin/1074212001/.

60. Alex Chester, "Speaking Up: How Five Ithaca High School Students Protesting School Musical Became Targets of Hate and How They're Rising Above It," Onstage Blog, *The Acting Life*, February 15, 2018; http://www.onstageblog.com/columns/2018/2/14/making-waves-the-students-of-ithaca-high-school-speak-up-on-hunchback-controversy.

61. Bess Markel, "PTG's Production of 'In the Heights' Attracts Controversy," *Pioneer Optimist*, February 18, 2018, accessed June 24, 2018, https://pioneeroptimist.com/558/news/ptgs-production-of-in-the-heights-attracts-controversy/.

62. Jerlyn Hurtado Armas, "Submission: UCLA Theater Groups Need Consideration When Representing Cultures," *Daily Bruin*, accessed June 24, 2018, http://dailybruin.com/2016/03/01/submission-ucla-theater-groups-need-consideration-when-representing-cultures/.

63. Howard Sherman, "Intricacies and Intent Surrounding Race and Ethnicity in Casting," *Arts Integrity Initiative*, July 27, 2016, accessed June 14, 2018, http://www.artsintegrity.org/intricacies-and-intent-surrounding-race-and-ethnicity-in-casting/.

64. Qtd. in Howard Sherman, "What Does 'Hamilton' Tell Us About Race In Casting?," *Hesherman.com*, December 3, 2015, accessed June 14, 2018, http://www.hesherman.com/2015/12/03/what-does-hamilton-tell-us-about-race-in-casting/.

65. Emma Watkins, personal email, September 1, 2017.

66. Peter C. Wood, "Back(Lash) Into the Woods: Putting Women Back in Their Place," in *Text & Presentation, 2012*, edited by Graley Herren (Comparative Drama Conference Series 9; Jefferson, NC: McFarland & Company, Inc. Publishers, 2013), 138.

67. Worthington Chamber of Commerce. "Large Employer List," June 11, 2018.

68. "Referendum 2018 FAQs," Independent School District 518: Worthington, MN, accessed June 28, 2018, http://www.isd518.net/referendum-2018-faqs.

69. All of the students' names in this chapter have been changed for privacy.

70. Sondheim, *Look, I Made A Hat*, 59.

71. Wood, "Back(Lash) Into the Woods."

72. Sondheim, *Look, I Made A Hat*, 59.

73. Ibid., 63.

74. Mila Koumpilova, "Worthington Schools' Growth Defies Rural Trends, but Its Struggle to Help Minority Students Succeed Does Not," *Twin Cities Pioneer Press*, September 18, 2011, accessed June 28, 2018, https://www.twincities.com/2011/09/18/worthington-schools-growth-defies-rural-trends-but-its-struggle-to-help-minority-students-succeed-does-not/.

75. Ibid.

76. Ibid.

77. Ibid.

78. Ibid.

79. Sondheim, *Look, I Made A Hat*, 65.

80. Adam Hudlow, "Harmony, Voice Leading, and Drama in Three Sondheim Musicals" (PhD Dissertation, Louisiana State University, 2013), 55–57. Accessed May 19, 2018, https://digitalcommons.lsu.edu/cgi/viewcontent.cgi?article=1751&context=gradschool_dissertations.

81. Sondheim, *Look, I Made A Hat*, 66.

82. Ibid., 71.

83. Ibid., 69.

84. *Economic Overview: Clinton County, Ohio* (Clinton County Port Authority: Chmura Economics & Analytics, 2018).

85. Bob Driehaus, "DHL Cuts 9,500 Jobs in U.S., and an Ohio Town Takes the Brunt," *New York Times*, November 10, 2008, sec. Business Day, accessed May 17, 2018, https://www.nytimes.com/2008/11/11/business/11dhl.html.

86. "About," The Murphy Theatre, last modified 2018, accessed August 17, 2018, https://themurphytheatre.org/about-2/.

87. "2018 Season," The Murphy Theatre, last modified 2018, accessed July 19, 2018, https://themurphytheatre.org/tickets/.

88. Sondheim, *Look, I Made A Hat*, 72.

89. John Franceschina, *Music Theory Through Musical Theatre: Putting It Together* (Oxford: Oxford University Press, 2015), 25.

90. Sondheim, *Look, I Made A Hat*, 73.

91. Rich, "Stage: 'Into the Woods,' From Sondheim."

92. In *Drama High: The Incredible True Story of a Brilliant Teacher, a Struggling Town, and the Magic of Theatre* (New York: Penguin, 2013), 247, Michael Sokolove notes many kids learn to sing in church. Children also learn to sit still in church, which trains them to be good theatre spectators.

93. Stephen Sondheim and James Lapine, *Into the Woods* (New York: Theatre Communications Group, 1989), 128.

94. Sondheim, *Look, I Made A Hat*, 63.

95. Franceschina, *Music Theory through Musical Theatre*, 38.

96. Sondheim, *Look, I Made A Hat*, 75.

97. C. J. Pascoe, *Dude, You're a Fag: Masculinity and Sexuality in High School* (Berkeley: University of California Press, 2011), 78.

98. Sondheim, *Look, I Made A Hat*, 85.

99. Rich, "Stage: 'Into the Woods,' From Sondheim."

100. Ibid.

101. Ibid.

102. https://vanburen-mi.org/environmental/belleville_lake_4.htm, accessed February 2, 2019.

103. Penelope Eckert, *Jocks and Burnouts, Social Categories and Identity in the High School* (New York: Teacher College Press, 1989), 118.

104. Sondheim and Lapine, *Into the Woods*, 101–102.

105. Sondheim, *Look, I Made A Hat*, 98.

106. See Franceschina, *Music Theory Through Musical Theatre*, 24.

107. Sondheim, *Look, I Made A Hat*, 98.

108. "2018 Play Survey," Educational Theatre Association.

Chapter 4

1. Karolina Zachor, "Spotlight on: Kelsey Theatre's Dedicated and Versatile Staff," *Community News*, September 28, 2017, accessed July 21, 2018, https://communitynews.org/2017/09/28/spotlight-kelsey-theatres-dedicated-versatile-staff/.

2. Kelsey also produces non-musicals and children's shows, but musicals dominate the season.

3. In this chapter, I've changed people's names, show titles, or dates as requested for privacy. My account of the Kelsey Awards combines events from 2012-2018, and

the auditions, rehearsals, and performances in the "year-in-the-life of Kelsey" I describe are drawn from several seasons of shows from 2012- 2018.

4. "MCCC's Kitty Getlik Recognized for Contributions to Community Theater," *Mercer County Community College*. Last modified May 31, 2005, accessed February 21, 2014, http://www.mccc.edu/~humphrew/whatsnew/getlikaward.htm.

5. Leah Hager Cohen, *The Stuff of Dreams: Behind the Scenes of an American Community Theatre* (New York: Viking Penguin, 2001), 24.

6. Louise Burleigh, *Community Theatre in Theory and Practice* (Boston: Little, Brown and Company, 1917), xxxii. See Elizabeth Copeland Norfleet, "Louise Burleigh Powell: An Artist in the World of the Theatre, on Stage, and Behind the Scene," *Richmond Quarterly* 6 (Fall 1983): 22–8.

7. Percy MacKaye, *Community Drama: Its Motive and Method of Neighborliness* (Boston: Houghton Mifflin, 1917), 7.

8. See Dorothy Chansky, *Composing Ourselves: The Little Theatre Movement and the American Audience* (Carbondale: Southern Illinois University Press, 2004).

9. Jennifer Chapman, "Knowing Your Audience," in *The Oxford Handbook of the American Musical*, ed. Raymond Knapp, Mitchell Morris, and Stacy Wolf (New York: Oxford University Press, 2011), 392–407.

10. Robert E. Gard and Gertrude Burley, *Community Theatre: Idea and Achievement* (New York: Duell, Sloan, and Pearce, 1959).

11. Ibid., 3.

12. "About AACT," *American Association of Community Theatre*, accessed February 21, 2014, https://aact.org/aact/%20index.html. This number (46,000) encompasses both plays and musicals, but musicals likely make up a majority of the productions.

13. https://www.stillpointetheatre.com/, accessed January 29, 2019.

14. "Hale Centre Theatre—Utah's Professional Family Theatre." *Hale Centre Theatre*, accessed August 16, 2018, www.hct.org.

15. Mercer County (New Jersey), County of Mercer Comprehensive Farmland Preservation Plan (Mercer County Agriculture Development Board and Mercer County Department of Planning, 2007).

16. Susan Van Dongen, "The Shows Go On and On for Kelsey Artistic Director," *U.S. 1*, February 7, 2018, 34.

17. See David Brooks, "Opinion: The Golden Age of Bailing," *New York Times*, January 20, 2018, sec. Opinion, accessed August 16, 2018, https://www.nytimes.com/2017/07/07/opinion/the-golden-age-of-bailing.html. Though it happens less frequently with actors, there is a sense in our culture that you can overcommit yourself and quit later. In community theatre, though, missing too many rehearsals or overcommitting yourself without the directors' knowledge will lead to a bad reputation.

18. Virgil Baker, "The Community Theatre as a Force in Adult Education," *Educational Theatre Journal* 4, no. 3 (October 1952): 230.

19. See Michael W. Kramer, "Communication in a Community Theater Group: Managing Multiple Group Roles," *Communication Studies* 53, no. 2 (2002): 163–64.

20. Ibid.

21. Steven M. Gelber, *Hobbies: Leisure and the Culture of Work in America* (New York: Columbia University Press, 1999), 7.

22. Ibid., 6.

23. Susana Juniu, Ted Tedrick, and Rosangela Boyd, "Leisure or Work?: Amateur and Professional Musicians' Perception of Rehearsal and Performance," *Journal of Leisure Research* 28, no. 1 (1996): 46.

24. See Robert A. Stebbins, *Careers in Serious Leisure: From Dabbler to Devotee in Search of Fulfillment* (London: Palgrave Macmillan, 2014). Also see Robert A. Stebbins, "Serious Leisure: A Conceptual Statement," *Pacific Sociological Review* 25 (1982): 251–72, and Robert A. Stebbins, *Amateurs, Professionals, and Serious Leisure* (Montreal: McGill-Queen's University Press, 1992).

25. See Susan Arai and Alison Pedlar, "Moving beyond Individualism in Leisure Theory: A Critical Analysis of Concepts of Community and Social Engagement," *Leisure Studies* 22, no. 3 (2003): 185–202.

26. "Kelsey Theatre Staff," *Kelsey Theatre at MCCC*, accessed June 23, 2018, http://www.kelseytheatre.net/kelsey_staff.shtml.

27. For a reconceptualization of professional and amateur, see Charles Leadbeater and Paul Miller, *The Pro-Am Revolution How Enthusiasts Are Changing Our Society and Economy* (London: Demos, 2004).

28. Howard Sherman, "Theatre the Theatre Community Disdains," February 21, 2012, accessed October 11, 2012, http://www.hesherman.com/2012/02/21/theatre-the-theatre-community-disdains/.

29. Ibid.

30. See Michael W. Kramer, "Toward a Communication Theory of Group Dialectics: An Ethnographic Study of a Community Theater Group," *Communication Monographs* 71, no. 3 (2004): 326. Kramer writes, "Although community theater is not professional by definition, for some group members there existed a tension between behaviors that were fitting of a volunteer, nonprofessional group and *a desire to behave as professionals* . . . Although recognizing the group's voluntary nature, members also spoke about a desire that the group be as close to professional as possible" (326).

31. Chris Rojek, *The Labour of Leisure: The Culture of Free Time* (Los Angeles: Sage Publications, 2010), 3. Rojek's project in the book is to define these terms in the field of Leisure Studies.

32. Ibid.

33. Kyrus: "They have to go over stuff at home or we spend too much time going back over stuff . . . . They hold each other to a high bar and when everyone sees how prepared everyone is, it makes them all want to be prepared."

34. Juniu, Tedrick, and Boyd, "Leisure or Work?," 46.

35. Van Dongen, "The Shows Go On and On," 34.

36. Alan Menken, Stephen Schwartz, and Peter Parnell, *The Hunchback of Notre Dame (Papermill Playhouse Version)* (Disney Theatrical Group and La Jolla Playhouse, n.d.), 5.

37. "Kelsey Artistic Director Kitty Getlik Honored."

38. "New Jersey Community Theatre: A Conversation," Radio, *EBC Drama Club (NY/NJ Bengali)*, June 15, 2013.

39. One guy on the crew had auditioned for *Into the Woods*, didn't get cast, but wanted to be involved. One of his jobs was to lower Cinderella's dress from the grid, and, he told me proudly, "the other night it got a laugh and applause."

Chapter 5

1. http://www.city-data.com/city/Mill-Valley-California.html, accessed July 28, 2018.

2. For a wonderful, indispensable history, see Elisabeth Ptak with the Mountain Play Association, *Marin's Mountain Play: 100 Years of Theatre on Mount Tamalpais*, ed. Sara Pearson with Phyllis Faber and Mary Jo Sorensen (Mill Valley, CA: Mountain Play Association, 2013).

3. http://worldpopulationreview.com/us-cities/austin-population/, accessed July 28, 2018.

4. http://austintexas.gov/department/zilker-metropolitan-park, accessed October 7, 2013.

5. https://www.state.nj.us/dep/parksandforests//parks/docs/washington_crossing_brochure.pdf, accessed July 28, 2018.

6. The Outdoor Drama Association estimates that there are two hundred currently operating theatres. Given that none of these theatres are members of that association, the actual number of performance venues is no doubt much higher. Most outdoor dramas are regionally specific, tourist-attracting, yearly-repeating history plays, such as *The Lost Colony* in Manteo, North Carolina. Other venues produce Broadway musicals, for example, Theatre Under the Stars in Dallas, Texas, which hires a combination of Equity and non-Equity actors.

7. Ptak, *Marin's Mountain Play*, 29.

8. Minutes of the Parks and Public Playground Commission of Austin TX, File A 711.558 AUP234M 1928–1941, Austin Historical Society.

9. WCA Purpose and Program, undated (likely c. 1965), Washington Crossing Association Archives.

10. Sheldon Cheney, *The Open-Air Theater* (New York: Mitchell Kennerley, 1918), 7.

11. Ibid., 9.

12. Frank Albert Waugh, *Outdoor Theaters: The Design, Construction, and Use of Open-Air Auditoriums* (Boston: Richard G. Badger, 1917), 53.

13. Ibid., 43.

14. M. Foss Narum, *Outdoor Theaters*, Bulletin No. 4 (Wheeling, WV: American Institute of Park Executives, May 25, 1961), n.p.

15. Ibid., 10.

16. Ibid., 9.

17. Chad Jones, "Marin Tradition Weathers Economic Storms to Reach Centennial," *San Francisco Chronicle*, May 18, 2013, A1, accessed August 12, 2018, https://www.sfgate.com/entertainment/article/Mountain-Play-reaches-100-in-Marin-4527280.php.

18. Sam Hurwitt, "Theater Review: Mount Tam Alive with 'The Sound of Music,'" *Marin Independent Journal*, accessed May 23, 2013, https://www.marinij.com/2013/05/23/theater-review-mount-tam-alive-with-the-sound-of-music/.

19. Jones, "Marin Tradition Weathers Economic Storms."

20. "Marin History: Origin of the Mountain Play," *Marin Indpendent Journal*, https://www.marinij.com/2017/06/12/marin-history-origin-of-the-mountain-play/, accessed August 24, 2018.

21. https://www.flickr.com/photos/skipmoore/20063444501, accessed August 12, 2018.

22. Elizabeth Ptak, letter to the editor, n.d., https://www.mountainplay.org/about-us/history/past-productions/, accessed January 29, 2019.

23. http://millvalley.patch.com/articles/mountain-play-visionary-smith-dies, accessed May 4, 2013.

24. Jones, "Marin Tradition Weathers Economic Storms."

25. Ibid.

26. Qtd. in ibid.

27. Debra D. Bass, "Musical Vistas: Taking in an Outdoor Musical in a Spectacular Setting—Mount Tamalpais—With the Mount Play's 'My Fair Lady,'" *The Press Democrat*, May 20, 2004, D1.

28. Soren Hemmila, "Mountain Play Announces Its 2013 Director, Jay Manley," *Marinscope Newspapers* (October 10, 2012), accessed May 4, 2013, http://www.marinscope.com/news_pointer/news/article_d82f8ded-ff1a-512a-aeae-6158fb9e27cb.html.

29. Steven Winn, "Peak Performances: A Day in the Life of the Mountain Play, a Marin Springtime Tradition for 90 years," *San Francisco Chronicle*, May 21, 2003, D1.

30. Qtd. in Ptak, *Marin's Mountain Play*, 77.

31. Jones, "Marin Tradition Weathers Economic Storms."

32. Charles Brousse, "Theater: Mountain Play, Alive with 'The Sound of Music,'" *Pacific Sun*, May 31, 2013, accessed June 3, 2013, http://www.pacificsun.com/marin_a_and_e/theater/article_9310340c-c7ed-11e2-9eea-001a4bcf6878.html.

33. In September 2018, the Mountain Play reorganized its administration. Eileen Grady, who was on the staff for eight years, moved into the role of executive director and artistic producer, and Sara Pearson is the new director of leadership and development.

34. John Walch, "Forty Years: Zilker Musical Summer with a New Director and a Fresh Production of 'South Pacific,' Austin' Come-One-Come-all Musical Marks a New Chapter in Its 40-Year Run," *Austin American Statesman*, July 9, 1998, 32.

35. Beverly S. Sheffield, "The Zilker Hillside Theater" (Sept. 11, 1997) (Assistant Director of Recreation 1937–1940, Acting Director 1941–42, Director 1946–1973), page 1.

36. Walch, "Forty Years," 32.

37. Ibid.

38. Ibid.

39. Ibid.

40. Ibid.

41. Paul Matula, "Budget Cuts Drop Curtain on Zilker Park Musicals," *Daily Texan*, September 19, 1986, 9.

42. Alison Smith, "Mounting a Production: Public Sees Theater in the Waking When Cast Rehearses Carnival Around the Clock," *Austin American Statesman*, June 8, 1989, G2.

43. Pete Szilagyi, "City Proposes Cutting Summer Theater Budget: Shakespeare Program, Musical May Suffer," *Austin American Statesman*, June 25, 1991, C5. Pete Szilagyi, "Musical Seeks Long-Term Financial Cure: Private Task Force Works to Boost Monetary Support for 35th Annual Summer Show at Zilker Hillside Theater," *Austin American Statesman*, June 12, 1993, B1. Michael Barnes, "That Zilker Zip; Tight Performances in 'Joseph' Salvage This Summer's Musical," *Austin American Statesman*, August 23, 1995, B10. Michael Barnes, "Entertainment in the Park Is Free and Easy," *Austin American Statesman*, May 4, 1990, 19.

44. Walch, "Forty Years," 32.

45. Pete Szilagyi, "Zilker Prays Sun Will Come Out Tomorrow Funding Shortage Threatens Quality of Summer Production of Musical 'Annie,'" *Austin American Statesman*, May 30, 1990, E6.

46. https://www.austinchronicle.com/arts/2003-11-21/187237/.

47. Walch, "Forty Years," 32.

48. http://zilker.org/about-ztp/. Repairs were made possible by ZTP, John Faulk, the Parks and Recreation Department, and dozens of local businesses.

49. Like the Mountain Play (and other community theatres), Zilker sees many families who work on the show in various capacities. For example, the actors who played Liesl and Brigitta were sisters and their father played Herr Zeller.

50. "Open Air Theater Schedules Festival of Music, Drama," *Sunday Times Advertiser* (Trenton, NJ), May 28, 1967, 3. Also see Peter Osborne, *Where Washington Once Led: A History of New Jersey's Washington Crossing State Park* (Yardley, PA: Yardley Press, 2012), 252.

51. Osborne, *Where Washington Once Led*, 252.

52. "Natural Amphitheater: Players Will Put Crossing's Beauty Spot to Use," 1964, Unidentified Newspaper Clipping in WCA Archives Box; Lynne Martin, "Dramatic Progress on Natural Theater," *Evening Times* (Trenton, NJ), May 5, 1965. Also see Osborne, *Where Washington Once Led*, 252.

53. *The Evening Times* (Trenton, NJ), July 21, 1965.

54. Osborne, *Where Washington Once Led*, 254.

55. Jack Rees, a member of the Pennington Players, became the president of the WCA in early 1966 and served in this capacity for two seasons, during which time he also served on the Cultural Committee, chaired by Arno Saffron, and helped with the OAT productions. In the fall of 1967, he became chairman of the WCA's Cultural Committee and general manager of the OAT (1966 letter from Jack Rees, WCA Boxes). Ann Waldron, "*Oliver* to Close Open Air Season," *Philadelphia Inquirer*, August 21, 1977, 196.

56. These groups gained additional performance opportunities in the 1990s once Kitty became the artistic director of Kelsey Theatre at Mercer County Community College in 1995. (She had been a stage manager there since 1978.) When she took over the position, the college mandated that she find a way to break even during her first season; otherwise it would cut the program entirely. Kitty knew the box office split worked

well at the OAT, so she asked some of her OAT performance troupes if they also wanted to present shows at the Kelsey Theatre in the fall and winter and do the same box office split arrangement. Many groups agreed, Kitty broke even, and the Kelsey Theatre thrived.

57. Osborne, *Where Washington Once Led*, 324.

58. Osborne, 343. Their claims, though, were exaggerated for effect. The Mountain Play is considerably larger and older.

59. The Pennington Players' final production at OAT—after forty-one years—was *Into the Woods* in 2005. Bucks County Playhouse paid the state over $15,000 per year, which was charged in two installments.

60. DPAC paid a concession fee of about $4,100 to 4,500 per season, which it paid in four installments over the course of the summer.

61. http://www.montgomerynews.com/entertainment/hairspray-a-meaty-musical-for-the-whole-family/article_32a841aa-a3e9-527c-9275-27afc872735d.html, accessed July 14, 2018.

62. Ibid.

63. Ibid.

Chapter 6

1. The names and places in this chapter are pseudonyms.

2. Summer stock is the exception. See Martha S. LoMonaco, *Summer Stock! An American Theatrical Phenomenon* (New York: Palgrave Macmillan, 2004).

3. http://memory.loc.gov/ammem/collections/bernstein/lbpg01.html, accessed March 11, 2013. Bernstein and Green later teamed with Betty Comden (born Basya Cohen) to write *On the Town* (1944) and *Wonderful Town* (1954). See http://www.summercampculture.com/documentary-highlights-summer-camp-influence-on-broadway/, accessed February 27, 2013.

4. Chaim Potok, "Introduction," in *A Worthy Use of Summer: Jewish Summer Camping in America*, ed. Jenna Weissman Joselit with Karen S. Mittelman (Philadelphia: National Museum of American Jewish History, 1993), 7.

5. One might critique what Megan Boler calls "peer policing," a form of "pastoral power" over emotions, which "capitalizes on such structures of feeling as shame, humiliation, and desire for conformity." See Megan Boler, *Feeling Power: Emotions and Education* (New York: Routledge, 2004), 47.

6. Amy Sales and Leonard Saxe, "*How Goodly Are Thy Tents*": *Summer Camps as Jewish Socializing Experiences* (Hanover, NH: Brandeis University Press, 2004). See Joselit, *A Worthy Use of Summer*.

7. See Annie Pollard and Daniel Soyer, *Emerging Metropolis: New York Jews in the Age of Immigration, 1840–1920* (New York: NYU Press, 2012). Also see Melissa R. Klapper, *Jewish Girls Coming of Age in America, 1860–1920* (New York: NYU Press, 2005).

8. Ron Bancroft, "Maine's Crown Jewel," *Bangor Daily News*, July 1, 2012, accessed December 5, 2012, http://bangordailynews.com/2012/07/01/opinion/maines-crown-jewel/.

9. Abigail A. Van Slyck, *A Manufactured Wilderness: Summer Camps and the Shaping of American Youth, 1890–1960* (Minneapolis: University of Minnesota Press, 2006).

10. Ibid., 69.

11. Leslie Paris, *Children's Nature: The Rise of the American Summer Camp* (New York: NYU Press, 2008), 63.

12. H. W. Gibson, *Camp Management: A Manual for Camp Directors* (Cambridge, MA: Murray Printing Company, 1923), 174.

13. Ibid.

14. Ibid.

15. *Dive*, 1951. (Camp Kineo Archives, Schlesinger Library).

16. Ibid.

17. Having a rigid daily schedule at summer camps was a change introduced in the mid-twentieth century; early camps' programs were relatively unstructured. Van Slyck, *A Manufactured Wilderness*, 48–52.

18. See Jesse D. Ruskin and Timothy Rice, "The Individual in Musical Ethnography," *Ethnomusicology* 56, no. 2 (Spring/Summer 2012), 299–327.

Chapter 7

1. An earlier version of this chapter was published as Stacy Wolf, "Not Only on Broadway: Disney JR. and Disney KIDS Across the USA," in *The Disney Musical on Stage and Screen*, ed. George Rodosthenous (London: Methuen Bloomsbury, 2017), 133–54.

2. Jim Hill, "How Glenn Casale Helped *The Little Mermaid* Find Her Feet after this Disney Stage Show Stumbled on Broadway," *Huffington Post Blog*, July 23, 2014, accessed August 9, 2015, http://www.huffingtonpost.com/jim-hill/how-glenn-casale-helped-t_b_5612802.html Box Office Mojo; http://www.boxofficemojo.com/movies/?page=releases&id=littlemermaid.htm, accessed June 8, 2015.

3. Thomas Schumacher, public interview with Paul Bogaev, Princeton University, April 7, 2015. Schumacher said that on Broadway, 80 percent of shows fail, but for Disney, 80 percent succeed because they invest so much in research and development. They can channel profits from big moneymakers like *The Lion King* to fund new projects' extensive and long-term research and development. This extensive preparation explains why they're shocked when a show fails, like *The Little Mermaid* did.

4. Ken Cerniglia, personal email, August 30, 2018.

5. Schumacher, public interview with Paul Bogaev.

6. Nashville School Finder, accessed August 11, 2015, http://nashvilleschoolfinder.org/school/isaiah-t-creswell-middle-arts-magnet/.

7. Ken Cerniglia and Lisa Mitchell, "The Business of Children in Disney's Theater," in *Entertaining Children: The Participation of Youth in the Entertainment Industry*, eds. G. Arrighi and V. Emeljanow (London: Palgrave Macmillan, 2014), 140.

8. *Forbes*, accessed August 30, 2018, http://www.forbes.com/companies/walt-disney/.

9. Frank Bruni, "The Sunny Side of Greed," *New York Times*, July 1, 2015, A29.

10. Ibid.

11. DTG is well aware of this apparent contradiction. See Cerniglia and Mitchell, "The Business of Children," 142.

12. Ruthie Fierberg, "How Disney Shows Are Changing the Landscape of the American Musical Theatre," *Playbill*, accessed August 10, 2018, http://www.playbill.com/article/how-disney-shows-are-changing-the-landscape-of-the-american-musical-theatre.

13. Ibid.

14. Ibid.

15. Ibid.

16. Ken Cerniglia, personal email, August 30, 2018.

17. Cerniglia and Mitchell, "The Business of Children," 139.

18. Music Theatre International Shows, accessed June 5, 2015, http://www.mtishows.com/show_detail.asp?showid=000378.

19. https://www.dpacnc.com/news/detail/20162017-season-places-dpac-among-americas-top-five-theaters, accessed August 27, 2018.

20. Disney Musicals in Schools, Frequently Asked Questions, accessed July 19, 2015, http://disneymusicalsinschools.com/about/faqs. DMIS resembles another successful New York City–based musical theatre outreach program: Broadway Junior. Supported by the Shubert Foundation, Music Theatre International, and the New York City Department of Education, Broadway Junior was the brainchild of MTI co-founder and CEO Freddie Gershon and supports the production of Broadway Junior titles, including some Disney shows, at a handful of New York public middle schools each year.

21. Qtd. in Cerniglia and Mitchell, "The Business of Children," 140.

22. Ibid., 141. They cite Lisa Mitchell, *Self-Efficacy and Theatre Production in Urban Elementary Schools* (MS thesis, The City University of New York, 2011).

23. Qtd. in Cerniglia and Mitchell, "The Business of Children," 141. They refer to Douglas Israel, *Staying in School, Arts Education and New York City High School Graduation Rates* (New York: The Center for Arts Education, 2009), 3.

24. Qtd. in Cerniglia and Mitchell, "The Business of Children," 140–41. They refer to Edward B. Fiske, ed., *Champions of Change: The Impact of the Arts on Learning* (Washington, DC: Arts Education Partnership, 1999), 8.

25. Qtd. in Cerniglia and Mitchell, "The Business of Children," 141.

26. Ibid., 140.

27. http://disneymusicalsinschools.com/find-us, accessed August 30, 2018.

28. Cerniglia and Mitchell, "The Business of Children," 141.

29. Jones has a music background and has been instrumental (no pun intended) in growing music education in the Nashville public schools. During my visit in May 2015, she was awarded a sizable National Endowment for the Arts grant to maintain "Music Makes Us" in the schools. See http://mnpschildrenfirst.com/2015/05/06/metro-schools-and-music-makes-us-win-100000-grant-from-the-national-endowment-for-the-arts/ and http://musicmakesus.org/about-us, accessed August 17, 2015.

30. Cerniglia and Mitchell, "The Business of Children," 140.

31. See http://www.tpac.org/spotlight/country-duo-maddie-tae-to-host-disney-musicals-in-schools-student-share-on-may-14-at-tpac/, accessed July 19, 2015.

32. "Disney Musicals in Schools | Nashville: Harris-Hillman Special Education School," accessed June 8, 2015, https://www.youtube.com/watch?v=eRrnPKZNTxs&feature=youtu.be.

33. TPAC got permission from Disney to expand its program to include middle schools, which would perform Junior titles.

34. "Disney Musicals in Schools | Nashville: I.T. Creswell Arts Magnet Middle School," accessed August 11, 2015, https://www.youtube.com/watch?v=ijmmd4DluPo&feature=youtu.be.

35. "Disney Musicals in Schools | Nashville: Hull-Jackson Montessori Magnet School," accessed August 11, 2015, https://www.youtube.com/watch?v=Bz-1XBL4L4g.

36. "Disney Musicals in Schools | Nashville: Lakeview Elementary Design Center," accessed August 11, 2015, https://www.youtube.com/watch?v=0Hbv0zU_RSU.

37. Ibid.

38. "TPAC Spotlight," accessed August 14, 2015, http://www.tpac.org/spotlight/country-duo-maddie-tae-to-host-disney-musicals-in-schools-student-share-on-may-14-at-tpac/.

39. "Broadway World Grosses," accessed August 14, 2015, https://www.broadwayworld.com/grosses.cfm.

40. "The Smith Center's Disney Musicals In Schools," accessed August 14, 2015, https://www.youtube.com/watch?v=0fXSMyaLxwQ.

41. On the distrust of commercial theatre for progressive ends, see Helen Nicholson, *Theatre, Education and Performance: The Map and the Story* (New York: Palgrave Macmillan, 2011), 53, 81. On the nineteenth-century history of this distrust, see 20, 22, 28.

42. Gallagher also notes that one form of drama seldom reaches all students. See Kathleen Gallagher, *Why Theatre Matters: Urban Youth, Engagement, and a Pedagogy of the Real* (Toronto: University of Toronto Press, 2014), 167. She also underlines the value of playing with identities other than your own, 120. For a critique of the dominant form of participatory theatre, see Helen Nicholson, *Theatre & Education* (New York: Palgrave Macmillan, 2009), 62.

43. Nicholson, *Theatre & Education*, 51. Also see 79. For more on the tension between aesthetics and the social in applied theatre, see Gallagher, *Why Theatre Matters*, 168.

44. Nicholson, *Theatre & Education*, 49.

45. Some critics suggest that the racial demographic of Broadway changed in the 2015 season, thanks to, for example, *Hamilton, Allegiance, The Color Purple,* and *On Your Feet!* See Gordon Cox, "When Will Broadway's Onstage Diversity Carry over Behind the Curtain?" *Variety*, November 11, 2015, accessed November 12, 2015, http://variety.com/2015/legit/features/broadway-diversity-behind-the-scenes-1201636823/.

46. Gallagher concludes, "It is about a dominant Western ideology that fixes social differences through its colonization of cultural and artistic traditions." Gallagher, *Why Theatre Matters*, 130.

47. Helen Nicholson, *Applied Drama: The Gift of Theatre*, 2nd ed. (New York: Palgrave Macmillan, 2014), 36–38.

48. Kelly Howe, personal email, August 29, 2015.

49. For a critique of "flash and dash," see Nicholson, *Theatre & Education*, 41. Also see Doug Borwick, "Outreach ≠ Community Engagement," *Engaging Matters: An Arts Journal Blog*, March 20, 2013, accessed September 26, 2015, http://www.artsjournal. com/engage/2013/03/outreach-%E2%89%A0-community-engagement/.

50. For a compelling critique of theatre outreach projects that promote the acquisition of middle-class cultural capital, see Nicholson, *Theatre & Education*, 42.

51. Nicholson notes that kids appreciate learning about the backstage and how theatre is made. See *Theatre & Education*, 52.

52. For a more positive reading of the acquisition of cultural capital, see Nicholson, *Theatre & Education*, 59. On the need to develop creativity in a changing world, see 71–72.

53. See Nicholson, *Theatre & Education*, 7–11.

54. Gallagher, *Why Theatre Matters*, 122, 173.

55. Hill, "How Glenn Casale Helped."

Chapter 8

1. Ryan Heckman, "In Colorado, Living outside the Front Range Means Being Left behind," *Denver Post*, May 12, 2017, accessed May 20, 2018, https://www.denverpost. com/2017/05/12/at-the-continental-divide-an-opportunity-gap/. The Front Range, from Fort Collins to Colorado Springs, is the wealthiest and most highly educated region of Colorado (in addition to some of the wealthier ski resorts). Fifty percent of the population holds a bachelor's degree.

2. See https://www.axs.com/dinner-and-a-show-three-great-dinner-theaters-to-visit-outside-of-denv-18768, accessed September 7, 2017.

3. Daniel Tyler, "Front Range," Text, Colorado Encyclopedia, January 23, 2017, https://coloradoencyclopedia.org/article/front-range. The Official Site of Colorado Tourism, "Front Range Colorado," Colorado.com, 2018, https://www.colorado.com/front-range.

4. See http://www.washingtonpost.com/wp-dyn/content/article/2008/06/10/AR2008061003301.html, accessed June 27, 2019.

5. http://tobysdinnertheatre.com/, accessed August 20, 2018.

6. Almost nothing scholarly has been written about dinner theatre, except for a brief mention in an introduction to a theatre textbook. See Stephen Archer, Cynthia Gendrich, and Woodrow Hood, *Theatre: Its Art and Craft*, 5th ed. (San Diego: Collegiate Press, 2003), 50–51. Also see http://rickontheater.blogspot.com/2015/03/dinner-theater.html.

7. "The Barn Dinner Theatre," 2018, http://www.barndinner.com/shows. "Beef and Boards Dinner Theatre," 2017, http://www.beefandboards.com/. "Home: Info, Pictures, and More," Carousel Dinner Theatre, accessed August 8, 2018, http://www.

carouseldinnertheatre.com/. "The Carousel opened in Ravenna in 1973 and moved to Akron in March 1988, playing host to dozens of musicals and thousands of actors" (https://www.ohio.com/akron/lifestyle/carousel-dinner-theatre-closing-staff-says, accessed August 12, 2018). "Our Company," Broadway Palm Dinner Theatre, 2018, https://broadwaypalm.com/about/our-company/.

8. Cindy Wheeler, "Theaters Play It Up For Festival Week," *Colorado Springs Gazette Telegraph* (Colorado Springs, CO), August 20, 1977. Although I'm not dealing with Equity actors in this book, the statistics are telling and trickled down to non-Equity houses. According to Equity statistics, from 1969 to 1972, average employment on Broadway remained "almost static." But employment off Broadway for that period dropped 23 percent, touring companies dropped 22 percent, and regional theatres dropped 34 percent. Meanwhile, dinner theatres' employment increased by 34 percent. Frank Segers, "Dinner-Legit Boom Bolsters Stage; Employment Growing, Pay Rising; See It Attracting New Audiences," *Variety*, May 3, 1972, 250. The comparison became more pronounced when Equity created its first dinner theatre contract in June 1973, which formalized pay scales and working conditions, including a prohibition on actors' doing double duty as waitstaff. One month later, in July 1973 in Chicago, even though Equity actors no longer waited tables, more of them performed in dinner theatres than in non–food-related theatres. Jerome Landfield, "Dinner Theatres," *The Nation*, March 12, 1973, 350.

9. https://www.ndta.us/, accessed June 15, 2018.

10. See https://www.theproducersperspective.com/my_weblog/2013/05/why-did-the-dinner-theater-die.html, accessed June 15, 2018.

11. Larry Stark, "The Dinner Theatre Menace," no date, no publication, no page. Clipping files, "Theatres: Dinner-Style," New York Public Library.

12. Ibid.

13. John Gruen, "Is Theater Dead? No, Out to Dinner," *New York Times*, October 21, 1973, Section 2, 1.

14. Ibid., D4.

15. See Brooks McNamara, "Broadway: A Theatre Historian's Perspective," *TDR* 45.4 [T 172] (Winter 2001): 125–28.

16. Gruen, "Is Theater Dead?" See Pierre Bourdieu, *Distinction: A Social Critique of the Judgment of Taste*, trans. Richard Nice (New York: Routledge, 1984). David Savran writes, "The most salient characteristic of middlebrow [is] the unstable, unpredictable, and anxious relationship between art and commerce." David Savran, "Middlebrow Anxiety," In *A Queer Sort of Materialism: Recontextualizing American Theater* (Ann Arbor: U of Michigan P, 2003), 17.

17. Ann Fogle, "Dinner Theatres Cater to New Audiences in New Areas," *Show Business* 34, no. 38 (September 20, 1973): 1.

18. Landfield, "Dinner Theatres," 348.

19. Joli Jensen, *Is Art Good For Us? Beliefs about High Culture in American Life* (New York: Rowman & Littlefield Publishers, 2002), 27–30.

20. Linda Winer, "Catharsis à la Carte: Light on Plot, Heavy on Potatoes," *Chicago Tribune*, July 23, 1973, 26.

21. Gruen, "Is Theater Dead?" Section 2, 1.

22. Ibid. Another writer in 1973 put it like this: "The meal courses clip along, the plays are always divided into three acts barely longer than television segments, and the one-stop simplicity feels right in our supermarket world [. . .] Fear of the central city, rising suburban autonomy, and expressways make [dinner theatre] operations as natural as a shopping center" (Winer, "Catharsis à la Carte").

23. Landfield, "Dinner Theatres."

24. Jim Briggs, "1975 Was 'Tremendous Growth Year' for Chuckwagon Dinner Playhouse," *Greeley Daily Tribune*, March 9, 1976.

25. Jim Briggs, "Review of *South Pacific*, Colorado Music Hall Dinner Theater, Denver," *Greeley Daily Tribune*, June 29, 1973.

26. John Moore, "Country Dinner Playhouse Closes Doors," *Denver Post*, May 22, 2007, updated May 7, 2016, accessed January 24, 2018, https://www.denverpost.com/2007/05/22/country-dinner-playhouse-closes-doors/.

27. Kyle Wagner, "Dinner and a Show," *Denver Post*, June 6, 2005, accessed January 24, 2018, https://www.denverpost.com/2005/06/06/dinner-and-a-show/.

28. John Moore, "Country Dinner Playhouse Closes Doors," *Denver Post*, May 22, 2007, updated May 7, 2016, accessed January 24, 2018, https://www.denverpost.com/2007/05/22/country-dinner-playhouse-closes-doors/.

29. Ibid.

30. John Moore, "Moore: Country Dinner Playhouse Payroll, Customer Data Dumped," *Denver Post*, December 13, 2007, updated May 21, 2016, accessed January 24, 2018, https://www.denverpost.com/2007/12/13/moore-country-dinner-playhouse-payroll-customer-data-dumped/.

31. Moore, "Country Dinner Playhouse Closes Doors."

32. Ibid.

33. Ibid.

34. "Denver, Colorado Population 2018 (Demographics, Maps, Graphs)," *World Population Review*, June 3, 2018, http://worldpopulationreview.com/us-cities/denver-population/.

35. Patricia A. Renner, "Review of *Irma La Douce*, Dublin Dinner Playhouse, Colorado Springs, CO," *Colorado Springs Gazette Telegraph*, April 5, 1975.

36. Ibid. Also see Jim Briggs, "Show Goes on by Candlelight at *Hello, Dolly* Opening," *Greeley Daily Tribune*, July 23, 1973, 33; Briggs, "1975 Was 'Tremendous Growth Year'"; Barry Morrison, "Denver after Dark: Theater Is in Orbit," *Denver Post*, April 21, 1978, 76.

37. Barbara MacKay, "Country Dinner Playhouse Serves Good Comedy-Drama," *Denver Post*, May 2, 1978, 37.

38. Barbara Mackay, "Dinner-Theatre Owner Oakley Tries 'Little Different' Venture," *Sunday Denver Post*, May 28, 1978, 194.

39. "Rehearsing for New Dinner Theater," *Louisville Times*, July 21, 1977, 10.

40. Barbara MacKay, "Seeber on Theater: 'It's No Hobby,'" *Denver Post*, June 4, 1978, 313.

41. Juliet Wittman, "*Clue: the Musical*," *Westword*, February 1, 2007, accessed January 24, 2018, http://www.westword.com/arts/clue-the-musical-5091574.

42. Ibid.

43. Ibid.

44. http://www.coloradocandlelight.com/, accessed June 17, 2018.

45. See https://www.denverpost.com/2008/06/05/dinner-theater-gets-new-shine-in-johnstown/, accessed December 25, 2018.

46. https://midtownartscenter.com/, accessed June 17, 2018. https://www.fcgov.com/visitor/fcfacts.php, accessed March 27, 2018. "Colorado State University—Profile, Rankings and Data," *US News Best Colleges*, accessed August 8, 2018, https://www.usnews.com/best-colleges/colorado-state-university-1350. "Breweries in Fort Collins, Colorado," *Fort Collins Brewery Guide*, 2018, http://fortcollinsbreweryguide.com/breweries.aspx.

47. John Moore, "Carousel Dinner Theatre Will Be First to Stage 'Next to Normal,' 'Avenue Q' Here," *Denver Post*, April 21, 2011, accessed May 20, 2018, https://www.denverpost.com/2011/04/21/carousel-dinner-theatre-will-be-first-to-stage-next-to-normal-avenue-q-here/.

48. See https://www.denvercenter.org/blog-posts/news-center/2018/01/18/fun-home-is-finding-a-home-on-stages-all-over-colorado, accessed June 17, 2018.

49. "Park Trails," City of Fort Collins, accessed August 8, 2018, https://www.fcgov.com/parks/trails.php.

50. See https://www.coloradoan.com/story/money/2018/03/28/midtown-arts-center-building-closer-becoming-low-income-housing/465380002/, accessed June 19, 2018.

51. Steve Porter, "New Owners Ride the Carousel Theatre," *BizWest*, November 20, 2001, accessed May 20, 2018, https://bizwest.com/2001/11/30/new-owners-ride-the-carousel-theatre/.

52. Ibid.

53. http://www.playbill.com/production/fun-home-circle-in-the-square-theatre-vault-0000014079, accessed June 17, 2018.

54. Moore, "Carousel Dinner Theatre."

55. http://www.bdtstage.com/, accessed June 17, 2018.

56. http://www.dailycamera.com/entertainment/ci_26972974/boulders-dinner-theatre-rebrands-itself-bdt-stage accessed June 17, 2018. Also see Juliet Wittman, "Michael Duran Serves Up Some Meaty Fare at BDT Stage," *Westword*, January 9, 2018, accessed January 23, 2018, http://www.westword.com/arts/michael-duran-serves-up-some-meaty-fare-at-bdt-stage-9864168.

57. http://oralhistory.boulderlibrary.org/interview/oh0744/

58. Ibid.

59. http://jesterstheatre.com/, accessed June 17, 2018.

60. http://www.cheeseimporters.com/, accessed June 15, 2018.

61. http://www.reporterherald.com/business-top-stories/ci_29175500/veterinary-clinic-buys-berthouds-wayside-inn, accessed August 25, 2018.

62. See http://www.reporterherald.com/loveland-theater/ci_32155432/midtown-arts-center-close-candlelight-will-benefit, accessed December 25, 2018.

63. https://www.denvercenter.org/midtown-arts-center-will-close-next-year-after-merger-with-candlelight/, accessed December 25, 2018.

Epilogue

1. http://kahilutheatre.org/, accessed July 9, 2019.
2. https://parkerranch.com/legacy/history-of/, accessed July 9, 2019.
3. http://www.hawaiihistory.org/index.cfm?fuseaction=ig.page&PageID=445, accessed July 9, 2019.
4. https://parkerranch.com/legacy/history-of/modern-history/, accessed July 9, 2019.
5. http://kahilutheatre.org/About-Us, accessed July 9, 2019.
6. https://keolamagazine.com/people/kahilu-theatre/, accessed July 9, 2019.
7. https://parkerranch.com/legacy/history-of/going-forward/, accessed July 9, 2019.
8. https://keolamagazine.com/people/kahilu-theatre/, accessed July 9, 2019.
9. https://keolamagazine.com/people/kahilu-theatre/, accessed July 9, 2019.
10. http://wakingupinhawaii.com/kahilu-theatre-youth-troupe-shows/, accessed July 9, 2019.
11. Angel Prince, personal conversation, July 8, 2019.
12. Michael Paulson, "All Signs Point to a Booming Broadway," *New York Times*, May 30, 2019, C3.
13. Nancy Coleman, "Along in Life and 'Into the Woods,'" *New York Times*, July 6, 2019, C1, C4.
14. Robin Pogrebin, "Arts Outposts Stung by Cuts in State Aid," *New York Times*, August 1, 2011, accessed February 2, 2019. https://www.nytimes.com/2011/08/02/arts/kansas-and-other-states-cut-arts-funds.html.

Selected Bibliography

Ahmed, Sara. *The Cultural Politics of Emotion*. 2nd ed. Edinburgh: Edinburgh University Press, 2014.

Ames, Raina S. *A High School Theatre Teacher's Survival Guide*. New York: Routledge, 2005.

Anderson, Benedict. *Imagined Communities: Reflections on the Origin and Spread of Nationalism*. Rev. ed. London: Verso, 2016.

Anderson, Leon, and Mathew Austin. "Auto-Ethnography in Leisure Studies." *Leisure Studies* 31, no. 2 (2011): 131–46.

Anshel, Anat, and David A. Kipper. "The Influence of Group Singing on Trust and Cooperation." *Journal of Music Therapy* 25 (1988): 145–55.

Arai, Susan, and Alison Pedlar. "Moving beyond Individualism in Leisure Theory: A Critical Analysis of Concepts of Community and Social Engagement." *Leisure Studies* 22, no. 3 (2003): 185–202.

Armstrong, Elizabeth A., and Laura T. Hamilton. *Paying for the Party: How College Maintains Inequality*. 1st Harvard University Press paperback ed. Cambridge, MA: Harvard University Press, 2015.

Arrowsmith, Keith. *The Methuen Amateur Theatre Handbook*. London: Methuen Drama, 2001.

Averill, Gage. *Four Parts, No Waiting: A Social History of American Barbershop Harmony*. New York: Oxford University Press, 2010.

Baker, Virgil. "The Community Theatre as a Force in Adult Education." *Educational Theatre Journal* 4, no. 3 (October 1952): 227–30.

Ball, Mike, and Greg Smith. "Technologies of Realism? Ethnographic Uses of Photography and Film." In *Handbook of Ethnography*, edited by Paul Atkinson, Amanda Coffey, Sara Delamont, John Lofland, and Lyn Lofland, 302–19. London: SAGE Publications, 2001.

Baumol, William J., and William G. Bowen. *Performing Arts—The Economic Dilemma*. New York: MIT Press, 1968.

Becker, Howard S. *Art Worlds*. 25th anniv. ed., updated and expanded. Berkeley: University of California Press, 2011.

Bendix, Regina. *Backstage Domains: Playing "William Tell" in Two Swiss Communities*. New York: Peter Lang, 1989.

Bennett, Jeff. *Secondary Stages: Revitalizing High School Theatre*. Portsmouth, NH: Heinemann, 2001.

Berger, Harris M., and Giovanna P. Del Negro. "Reasonable Suspicion: Folklore, Practice, and in the Reproduction of Institutions." *Cultural Analysis* 15, no. 1 (2016): 145–67.

Bergero, Bennett M. "The Sociology of Leisure: Some Suggestions." *Industrial Relations: A Journal of Economy and Society* 1, no. 2 (1962): 31–45.

Bishop, G. W. *The Amateur Dramatic Year Book and Community Theatre Handbook*. London: A. & C. Black, Ltd., 1928.

Blau, Judith R. *The Shape of Culture: A Study of Contemporary Cultural Patterns in the United States*. New York: Cambridge University Press, 1989.

Bliznik, Sean J. "We're All in This Together: Framing the Self-Representation of Adolescence in Disney's *High School Musical.*" In *Children Under Construction: Critical Essays on Plays as Curriculum*, edited by Drew Chappell, 149–66. New York: Peter Lang Publishing, 2010.

Booth, Wayne. *For the Love of It: Amateuring and Its Rivals.* Chicago: University of Chicago Press, 1999.

Bourdieu, Pierre. *The Field of Cultural Production: Essays on Art and Literature.* Edited by Randal Johnson. New York: Columbia University Press, 1993.

Bramham, Peter, and Stephen Wagg, eds. *The New Politics of Leisure and Pleasure.* New York: Palgrave Macmillan, 2011.

Burleigh, Louise. *Community Theatre in Theory and Practice.* Boston: Little, Brown and Company, 1917.

Butz, David, and Katheryn Besio. "Autoethnography." *Geography Compass* 5, no. 3 (2009): 1660–74.

Buur, Jacob, and Rosa Torguet. "Ethnographic Findings in the Organizational Theatre." *Ethnographic Praxis in Industry Conference Proceedings* 2013, no. 1 (2014): 143–60.

Cabedo-Mas, Alberto, and Maravillas Díaz-Gómez. "Positive Musical Experiences in Education: Music as a Social Praxis." *Music Education Research* 15, no. 4 (2013): 455–70.

Campbell, Patricia Shehan. *Songs in Their Heads: Music and Its Meaning in Children's Lives.* 2nd ed. New York: Oxford University Press, 2010.

Campbell, Patricia Shehan, and Trevor Wiggins, eds. *The Oxford Handbook of Children's Musical Cultures.* New York: Oxford University Press, 2013.

Catterall, James, Richard Chapleau, and John Iwanaga. "Involvement in the Arts and Human Development: General Involvement and Intensive Involvement in Music and Theater Arts." Champions of Change: The Impact of the Arts on Learning. Los Angeles: UCLA Graduate School of Education & Information Studies, University of California at Los Angeles, 1999.

Cerniglia, Ken, and Lisa Mitchell. "The Business of Children in Disney's Theater." In *Entertaining Children: The Participation of Youth in the Entertainment Industry.* Edited by Gillian Arrighi and Victor Emeljanow. New York: Palgrave Macmillan, 2014.

Chansky, Dorothy. *Composing Ourselves: The Little Theatre Movement and the American Audience.* Carbondale: Southern Illinois University Press, 2004.

Chapman, Jennifer. "Heteronormativity and High School Theatre." *Youth Theatre Journal* 21 (2007): 31–40.

Chapman, Jennifer. "Knowing Your Audience." In *The Oxford Handbook of The American Musical*, edited by Raymond Knapp, Mitchell Morris, and Stacy Wolf, 392–407. New York: Oxford University Press, 2011.

Chase, Guilbert. "Gentlemen Amateurs." In *America's Music: From the Pilgrims to the Present*, 72–93. Urbana: University of Illinois Press, 1992.

Cheney, Sheldon. *The Open-Air Theatre.* New York: Mitchell Kennerley, 1918.

Clifford, James. *Routes: Travel and Translation in the Late Twentieth Century.* Cambridge, MA: Harvard University Press, 1997.

Clough, Patricia Ticineto, and Jean Halley, eds. *The Affective Turn: Theorizing the Social.* Durham, NC: Duke University Press, 2007.

Coakley, Jacob. "Composers and Curriculum." *Stage Directions* 23, no. 6 (2010): 44.

Cochrane, Claire. "The Contaminated Audience: Researching Amateur Theatre in Wales before 1939." *New Theatre Quarterly* 19, no. 2 (May 2003): 169–76.

Cochrane, Claire. "The Pervasiveness of the Commonplace: The Historian and Amateur Theatre." *Theatre Research International* 26, no. 3 (2001): 233–42.

Cohen, Anthony Paul. *The Symbolic Construction of Community*. London: Routledge, 1985.

Cohen, Gary P. *The Community Theater Handbook: A Complete Guide to Organizing and Running a Community Theater*. Portsmouth, NH: Heinemann, 2003.

Cohen, Judah M. "'And the Youth Shall See Visions': Songleading, Summer Camps, and Identity among Reform Jewish Teenagers." In *Musical Childhoods & the Cultures of Youth*, edited by Susan Boynton and Roe-Min Kok, 187–207. Middletown, CT: Wesleyan University Press, 2006.

Cohen, Judah M. "Singing out for Judaism: A History of Song Leaders and Song Leading at Olin-Sang-Ruby Union Institute." In *A Place of Our Own: The Rise of Reform Jewish Camping*, 173–209. Tuscaloosa: University of Alabama Press, 2006.

Cohen, L., and Sonja Kuftinec. "A Cornerstone for Rethinking Community Theatre." *Theatre Topics* 6, no. 1 (March 1996): 91–104.

Cohen, Leah Hager. *The Stuff of Dreams: Behind the Scenes of an American Community Theatre*. New York: Viking Penguin, 2001.

Conquergood, Lorne Dwight. *Cultural Struggles: Performance, Ethnography, Praxis*. Ann Arbor: University of Michigan Press, 2013.

Cook, Nicholas, and Richard Pettengill, eds. *Taking It to the Bridge: Music as Performance*. Ann Arbor: University of Michigan Press, 2013.

Cousins, Heather. "Upholding Mainstream Culture: The Tradition of the American High School Play." *Research in Drama Education* 5, no. 1 (2000): 85–94.

Curley, Eileen. "Parlour Conflagrations: Science and Special Effects in Amateur Theatricals Guidebooks." *Popular Entertainment Studies* 6, no. 1 (2015): 26–41.

Dalrymple, Jean. *The Complete Handbook for Community Theatre: From Picking Plays to Taking the Bows*. New York: Drake, 1977.

Davis, Tracy C. "The Context Problem." *Theatre Survey* 45, no. 2 (November 2004): 203–9.

DeNora, Tia. *Making Sense of Reality: Culture and Perception in Everyday Life*. London: SAGE Publications Ltd., 2013.

DeNora, Tia. *Music in Everyday Life*. Cambridge, UK: Cambridge University Press, 2000.

DiMaggio, Paul, and Francie Ostrower. "Participation in the Arts by Black and White Americans." *Social Forces* 68, no. 3 (March 1990): 753–78.

Dobson, Michael. *Shakespeare and Amateur Performance: A Cultural History*. New York: Cambridge University Press, 2011.

Dorbian, Iris. "Keeping Theatre Alive in Schools." *Stage Directions* 23, no. 10 (October 2010). http://stage-directions.com/2735-keeping-theatre-alive-in-schools.html.

Duneier, Mitchell. "How Not to Lie with Ethnography." *Sociological Method* 41 (2011): 1–11.

Eckert, Penelope. *Jocks and Burnouts, Social Categories and Identity in the High School*. New York: Teacher College Press, 1989.

Elkington, Sam. "Ways of Seeing Degrees of Leisure: From Practice to Pedagogy." *Leisure Studies* 32, no. 4 (2013): 447–61.

Emerson, Robert M., Rachel I. Fretz, and Linda Shaw. *Writing Ethnographic Field Notes*. 2nd ed. Chicago: University of Chicago Press, 2011.

Ettenberg, Sylvia C., and Geraldine Rosenfield, eds. *The Ramah Experience: Community and Commitment*. New York: Jewish Theological Seminary and the National Ramah Commission, 1989.

Feher, Michael. "Self-Appreciation; or the Aspirations of Human Capital." *Public Culture* 21, no. 1 (2009): 21–41.

Ferguson, Ann Arnett. *Bad Boys: Public Schools in the Making of Black Masculinity*. 1st pbk. ed. Ann Arbor: University of Michigan Press, 2001.

Fernández-Kelly, María Patricia. *The Hero's Fight: African Americans in West Baltimore and the Shadow of the State*. Princeton, NJ: Princeton University Press, 2015.

Filichia, Peter. *Let's Put on a Musical! How to Choose the Right Show for Your Theater*. 2nd ed. New York: Second Stage Books, 2007.

Fine, Michelle, Lois Weis, Craig Centrie, and Rosemarie Roberts. "Educating beyond the Borders of Schooling." *Anthropology & Education Quarterly* 31, no. 2 (2000): 131–51.

Finnegan, Ruth H. *The Hidden Musicians: Music-Making in an English Town*. Cambridge, UK: Cambridge University Press, 1989.

Fordham, Signithia. *Blacked out: Dilemmas of Race, Identity, and Success at Capital High*. Chicago: University of Chicago Press, 1996.

Forsyth, Ann. *Reforming Suburbia: The Planned Communities of Irvine, Columbia, and The Woodlands*. Berkeley: University of California Press, 2005.

Foster, Susan Leigh. "Dance and/as Competition in the Privately Owned U.S. Studio." In *The Oxford Handbook of Dance and Politics*, edited by Rebekah J. Kowal, 53–76. New York: Oxford University Press, 2017.

Francombe, Jessica. "Learning to Leisure: Femininity and Practices of the Body." *Leisure Studies* 33, no. 6 (2013): 580–97.

Freidenreich, Fradle Pomerantz. *Passionate Pioneers: The Story of Yiddish Secular Education in North America, 1910–1960*. Teaneck, NJ: Holmes & Meier Publishers, Inc., 2010.

Friedman, Marilyn. "Feminism and Modern Friendship: Dislocating the Community." In *Communitarianism and Individualism*, edited by Shlomo Avineri and Avner de-Shalit, 101–19. Toronto: Oxford University Press, 1992.

Gallagher, Kathleen. *Theatre of Urban: Youth and Schooling in Dangerous Times*. Toronto: University of Toronto Press, 2007.

Gallagher, Kathleen. *Why Theatre Matters: Urban Youth, Engagement, and a Pedagogy of the Real*. Toronto: University of Toronto Press, 2014.

Gard, Robert E., and Gertrude Burley. *Community Theatre: Idea and Achievement*. New York: Duell, Sloan, and Pearce, 1959.

Gelber, Steven M. *Hobbies: Leisure and the Culture of Work in America*. New York: Columbia University Press, 1999.

Gilbert, Charlene. *Children Will Listen: When Children and the Arts Come Together*. Documentary. PBS, 2005.

Gleason, Kendall Lione. *Wyonegonic: The First 100 Years*. Gwynn, VA: Gleason Pub., 2001.

Goertzen, Chris. "Powwows and Identity on the Piedmont and Coastal Plains of North Carolina." *Ethnomusicology* 45, no. 1 (2001): 58–88.

Goffman, Erving. *The Presentation of Self in Everyday Life*. New York: Doubleday, 1990.

Goldman, William. *The Season: A Candid Look at Broadway*. New York: Harcourt, Brace & World, 1969.

Gonzalez, Jo Beth. *Temporary Stages: Departing from Tradition in High School Theatre Education*. Portsmouth, NH: Heinemann, 2006.

Graff, Ellen. *Stepping Left: Dance and Politics in New York City, 1928–1942*. Durham, NC: Duke University Press, 1997.

Greene, Jay, Heidi Erickson, Angela Watson, and Molly Beck. "The Play's the Thing: Experimentally Examining the Social and Cognitive Effects of School Field Trips to Live Theater Performances." In *Working Paper Series*, 1–27. Arkansas: University of Arkansas, Department of Education Reform, 2017.

Gross, Edwin, and Natalie Gross. *Teen Theatre.* New York: McGraw Hill, 1953.

Grote, David. *Play Directing in the School: A Drama Director's Survival Guide.* Colorado Springs, CO: Meriwether, 1997.

Gunderson, Lauren. "The Oldest Tech, Theater, Might Be an Antidote to the Newest." *San Francisco Chronicle*, November 29, 2017. http://www.sfchronicle.com/opinion/article/The-oldest-tech-theater-might-be-an-antidote-to-12393595.php.

Haar, Charles M. *Final Report: President's Task Force on Suburban Problems.* Cambridge, MA: Ballinger Publishing Co., 1974.

Hailey, Charlie. *Camps: A Guide to 21st-Century Space.* Cambridge, MA: MIT Press, 2009.

Hamera, Judith. *Dancing Communities: Performance, Difference, and Connection in the Global City.* Basingstoke, UK: Palgrave Macmillan, 2007.

Hanna, Judith Lynne. "Issues in Supporting School Diversity: Academics, Social Relations, and the Arts." *Anthropology & Education Quarterly* 25, no. 1 (March 1994): 66–85.

Harrop, Peter, and Dunja Njaradi, eds. *Performance and Ethnography: Dance, Drama, Music.* Newcastle upon Tyne: Cambridge Scholars Publ., 2013.

Heathcotte, Toby. *Program Building: A Practical Guide for High School Speech and Drama Teachers.* Glendale, AZ: Mardale Books, 2003.

Heide, Frederick, Natalie Porter, and Paul Saito. "Do You Hear the People Sing? Musical Theatre and Attitude Change." *Psychology of Aesthetics, Creativity, and the Arts*, 6, no. 3 (2012): 224–30.

Hemmings, Annette. "Navigating Cultural Crosscurrents: (Post)Anthropological Passages through High School." *Anthropology and Education Quarterly* 37, no. 2 (2006): 128–43.

Hess, Amanda. "The Cult of the Amateur." *New York Times*, November 10, 2015. http://www.nytimes.com/2015/11/15/magazine/the-cult-of-the-amateur.html?_r=0.

Highmore, Ben. *Ordinary Lives: Studies in the Everyday.* London: Routledge, 2011.

Hochschild, Arlie Russell. *The Managed Heart: Commercialization of Human Feeling.* 2nd ed. Berkeley: University of California Press, 2012.

Horowitz, Alexandra. *On Looking: A Walker's Guide to the Art of Observation.* [Kindle.] New York: Scribner, 2013.

Horowitz, Rob. "Evaluation of the Broadway Junior Arts Connection Program in Three New York City Public Schools." New York: New York City Department of Education, 2009.

Howard, Vernon A. "Virtuosity as a Performance Concept: A Philosophical Analysis." *Philosophy of Music Education Review* 5, no. 1 (1997): 42–54.

Hurley, Erin. *Theatre & Feeling.* New York: Palgrave Macmillan, 2010.

Israel, Douglas. "Staying in School, Arts Education and New York City High School Graduation Rates." New York: Center for Arts Education, 2009.

Jackson, Anthony. *Theatre, Education and the Making of Meanings: Art or Instrument?* Manchester: University of Manchester Press, 2007.

Jackson, Shannon. "Just-in-Time: Performance and the Aesthetics of Precarity." *TDR: The Drama Review* 56, no. 4 (2012).

Jackson, Shannon. *Social Works: Performing Art, Supporting Publics.* New York: Routledge, 2011.

Jensen, Joli. *Is Art Good For Us? Beliefs about High Culture in American Life.* New York: Rowman & Littlefield Publishers, 2002.

John, Ryan. "Part of It All: The High School Musical as a Community of Practice." *Visions of Research in Music Education* 24 (2014): 1–29.

Johnson, Margaret F. *The Drama Teacher's Survival Guide: A Complete Tool Kit for Theatre Arts.* Colorado Springs, CO: Meriwether, 2007.

Joselit, Jenna Weissman, and Karen S. Mittelman, eds. *A Worthy Use of Summer: Jewish Summer Camping in America.* Philadelphia: National Museum of American Jewish History, 1993.

Juniu, Susana, Ted Tedrick, and Rosangela Boyd. "Leisure or Work?: Amateur and Professional Musicians' Perception of Rehearsal and Performance." *Journal of Leisure Research* 28, no. 1 (1996): 44–56.

Katz, Jack. "Ethnography's Warrants." In *Contemporary Field Research: Perspectives and Formulations.* Edited by Robert M. Emerson. Prospect Heights, IL: Waveland Press, 2001.

Kenrick, John. *Complete Idiot's Guide to Amateur Theatricals.* New York: Alpha, 2006.

Khan, Shamus Rahman. *Privilege: The Making of an Adolescent Elite at St. Paul's School.* Princeton, NJ: Princeton University Press, 2011.

Klapper, Melissa R. *Jewish Girls Coming of Age in America, 1860–1920.* New York: New York University Press, 2005.

Kleinman, Daniel Lee. *Impure Cultures: University Biology and the World of Commerce.* Science and Technology in Society. Madison: University of Wisconsin Press, 2003.

Knapp, Margaret M. "Narrative Strategies in Selected Studies of American Theatre Economics." In *The American Stage: Social and Economic Issues from the Colonial Period to the Present,* edited by Ron Engle and Tice L. Miller, 267–77. Cambridge, UK: Cambridge University Press, 1993.

Knott, Stephen. *Amateur Craft: History and Theory.* New York: Bloomsbury, 2015.

Kramer, Michael W. "Communication and Social Exchange Processes in Community Theater Groups." *Journal of Applied Communication Research* 33, no. 2 (2005): 159–82.

Kramer, Michael W. "Communication in a Community Theater Group: Managing Multiple Group Roles." *Communication Studies* 53, no. 2 (2002): 151–70.

Kramer, Michael W. "Shared Leadership in a Community Theater Group: Filling the Leadership Role." *Journal of Applied Communication Research* 34, no. 2 (2006): 141–62.

Kramer, Michael. "Toward a Communication Theory of Group Dialectics: An Ethnographic Study of a Community Theater Group." *Communication Monographs* 71, no. 3 (2004): 311–32.

Kreutz, Gunter, Stephan Bongard, Sonja Rohrmann, Volker Hodapp, and Dorothee Grebe. "Effects of Choir Singing or Listening on Secretory Immunoglobulin A, Cortisol, and Emotional State." *Journal of Behavioral Medicine* 27, no. 6 (December 2004): 623–35.

Krug, Edward. *The Shaping of the American High School: 1920–1941.* Madison: University of Wisconsin Press, 1972.

Larson, Reed, and Jane Brown. "Emotional Development in Adolescence: What Can Be Learned from a High School Theater Program?" *Child Development* 78, no. 4 (August 2007): 1083–99.

Law, Lois. "Training in Citizenship through Play-Production." *High School Thespian* 8, no. 2 (October 1936): 5, 16.

Lazarus, Joan. *Signs of Change: New Directions in Secondary Theatre Education.* Portsmouth, NH: Heinemann, 2004.

Leadbeater, Charles, and Paul Miller. *The Pro-Am Revolution: How Enthusiasts Are Changing Our Society and Economy*. London: Demos, 2004.

Lederman, Rena. "Pretexts for Ethnography: On Reading Fieldnotes." In *Fieldnotes: The Makings of Anthropology*. Edited by Roger Sanjek. Ithaca, NY: Cornell University Press, 1990.

Lee, Stacey J. *Up against Whiteness: Race, School, and Immigrant Youth*. New York: Teachers College Press, Columbia University, 2005.

Lees-Maffei, Grace. "Introduction: Studying Advice: Historiography, Methodology, Commentary, Bibliography." *Journal of Design History*, Domestic Design Advice, 16, no. 1 (2003): 1–14.

Levin, Theodore Craig. *The Hundred Thousand Fools of God: Musical Travels in Central Asia (and Queens, New York)*. Repr. Bloomington: Indiana University Press, 2007.

Livingston, Tamara E. "Music Revivals: Towards a General Theory." *Ethnomusicology* 43, no. 1 (1999): 66–85.

Lofland, John, David A. Snow, Leon Anderson, and Lyn H. Lofland. *Analyzing Social Settings: A Guide to Qualitative Observation and Analysis*. 4th ed. Belmont, CA: Wadsworth/Thomson Learning, 2006.

London, Todd, ed. *An Ideal Theater: Founding Visions for a New American Art*. 1st ed. New York: Theatre Communications Group, 2013.

Lorge, Michael M., and Gary P. Zola, eds. *A Place of Our Own: The Rise of Reform Jewish Camping*. Tuscaloosa: University of Alabama Press, 2006.

Lynk, William M. *Dinner Theatre: A Survey and Directory*. Westport, CT: Greenwood Press, 1993.

Macgowan, Kenneth. *The Theatre of Tomorrow*. New York: Boni and Liveright, 1921.

MacKaye, Percy. *Community Drama; Its Motive and Method of Neighborliness*. Boston: Houghton Mifflin, 1917.

Mackenzie, Frances. *The Amateur Actor*. New York: Theatre Arts Books, 1966.

MacNutt, Barry. *Noble Life: Memories of a Summer Camp in Maine*. Lincoln, NE: iUniverse, 2007.

Maine Summer Camps and Outdoor Adventure Programs. Portland, ME: Maine Youth Camping Association, 2006.

Massie, Eleanor. "Love Songs and Awkwardness: Non-Professional Performers and Affective Labour." *Performance Paradigm* 11 (2015): 59–75.

Merrifield, Andy. *Amateur: The Pleasures of Doing What You Love*. New York: Verso, 2017.

Messner, Michael A. *It's All for the Kids: Gender, Families, and Youth Sports*. Berkeley: University of California Press, 2009.

Milofsky, Carl. *Smallville: Institutionalizing Community in Twenty-First-Century America*. Medford, MA: Tufts University Press, University Press of New England, 2008.

Mitchell, Lisa. "Self-Efficacy & Theatre Production in Urban Elementary Schools." MA Thesis, City College of New York, 2011.

Modica, Marianne. *Race among Friends: Exploring Race at a Suburban School*. New Brunswick, NJ: Rutgers University Press, 2015.

Morrill, Calvin, David A. Snow, and Cindy H. White, eds. *Together Alone: Personal Relationships in Public Places*. Berkeley: University of California Press, 2005.

Motter, Charlotte. *Theatre in High School: Planning, Teaching, Directing*. Lanham, MD: University Press of America, 1984.

Naple, Nancy A. "The Outside Phenomenon." In *In the Field: Readings on the Field Research Experience*. Edited by Carolyn D. Smith and William Kornblum. Westport, CT: Praeger, 1996.

National Endowment for the Arts, and Mathtech, Inc, eds. *Conditions and Needs of the Professional American Theatre*. National Endowment for the Arts Research Division Report; 11. Washington, DC: National Endowment for the Arts, 1981.

Nettl, Bruno. *Heartland Excursions: Ethnomusicological Reflections on Schools of Music*. Urbana: University of Illinois Press, 1995.

Nicholson, Helen. *Theatre & Education*. New York: Palgrave Macmillan, 2009.

Nicholson, Helen. *Theatre, Education and Performance: The Map and the Story*. New York: Palgrave Macmillan, 2011.

Nodelman, Perry. *The Hidden Adult: Defining Children's Literature*. Baltimore, MD: Johns Hopkins University Press, 2008.

Nolan, Kathleen. *Police in the Hallways*. St. Paul: University of Minnesota Press, 2012.

Norfleet, Elizabeth. "Louise Burleigh Powell: An Artist in the World of the Theatre, on Stage, and behind the Scene." *Richmond Quarterly* 6 (1983): 22–28.

Norris, Joe, Laura A. McCammon, and Carole S. Miller. *Learning to Teach Drama: A Case Narrative Approach*. Portsmouth, NH: Heinemann, 2000.

Ogden, Holly. *Vivid Moments Long Remembered: The Lifetime Impact of Elementary School Musical Theatre*. Germany: VDM Verlag Dr. Müller Aktiengesellschaft & Co., 2009.

Olsen, Laurie. *Made in America: Immigrant Students In Our Public Schools*. New York: New Press, 1997.

Opelt, James. *Organizing and Managing the High School Theatre Program*. Boston: Allyn and Bacon, 1991.

Orenstein, Peggy. *Cinderella Ate My Daughter: Dispatches from the Front Lines of the New Girlie-Girl Culture*. 1st Harper pbk. New York: Harper, 2012.

"Organized Summer Camps: Their Value to Maine." Portland, ME: Center for Research and Advanced Study, University of Maine at Portland-Gorham, 1975.

Osborne, Peter. *Where Washington Once Led: A History of New Jersey's Washington Crossing State Park*. 1st ed. Yardley, PA: Yardley Press, 2012.

O'Toole, John. "Drama and Curriculum." *Landscapes: The Arts, Aesthetics, and Education* 6 (2009): 97–116.

Page, Stephen J., and Joanne Connell. *Leisure: An Introduction*. Harlow, UK: Financial Times Prentice Hall, 2010.

Paris, Leslie. *Children's Nature: The Rise of the American Summer Camp*. New York: New York University Press, 2010.

Pascoe, C. J. *Dude, You're a Fag: Masculinity and Sexuality in High School*. Berkeley: University of California Press, 2012.

Patterson, James, Donna McKenna-Crook, and Melissa Swick. *Theatre in the Secondary Classroom: Methods and Strategies for the Beginning Teacher*. Portsmouth, NH: Heinemann, 2006.

Perlov, Barbara. "Why We Tell the Story: A Report on the Shubert Foundation/MTI Broadway Junior Program in the New York City Public Schools." New York: New York City Department of Education, 2009.

Perry, Pamela. *Shades of White: White Kids and Racial Identities in High School*. Durham, NC: Duke University Press, 2002.

Perry, Rachel, and Elizabeth Carnegie. "Reading Pro-Am Theatre through a Serious Leisure Lens: Organisational and Policy-Making Implications." *Leisure Studies* 32 (2013): 383–98.

Poisson, Camille L. *Theater and the Adolescent Actor: Building a Successful School Program.* Hamden, CT: Archon Books, 1994.

Pollard, Annie, and Daniel Soyer. *Emerging Metropolis: New York Jews in the Age of Immigration, 1840–1920.* New York: New York University Press, 2012.

Posey, Elsa. "Dance Education in Dance Schools in the Private Sector: Meeting the Demands of the Marketplace." *Journal of Dance Education* 2, no. 2 (2002): 43–49.

Potter, Claire Bond, and Renee C. Romano, eds. *Doing Recent History: On Privacy, Copyright, Video Games, Institutional Review Boards, Activist Scholarship, and History That Talks Back.* Athens: University of Georgia Press, 2012.

Prell, Riv-Ellen. "'How Do You Know That I Am a Jew?': Authority, Cultural Identity, and the Shaping of Postwar American Judaism." In *Jewish Studies at the Crossroads of Anthropology and History,* edited by Ra'anan S. Boustan, Oren Kosansky, and Marina Rustow, 31–57. Philadelphia: University of Pennsylvania Press, 2011.

Prell, Riv-Ellen. "Jewish Summer Camping and Civil Rights: How Summer Camps Launched a Transformation in American Jewish Culture." Lecture, Jean and Samuel Frankel Center for Judaic Studies, University of Michigan, Ann Arbor, 2006.

Prentki, Tim, and Sheila Preston. *The Applied Theatre Reader.* New York: Routledge, 2009.

Ptak, Elisabeth, and The Mountain Play Association. *Marin's Mountain Play: 100 Years of Theatre on Mount Tamalpais.* Edited by Sara Pearson, Phyllis Faber, and Mary Jo Sorensen. Mill Valley, CA: Mountain Play Association, Global PSD, 2013.

Putnam, Robert D. *Bowling Alone: The Collapse and Revival of American Community.* 1st Touchstone ed. New York: Simon & Schuster, 2001.

Putnam, Robert D., Lewis M. Feldstein, and Don Cohen. *Better Together: Restoring the American Community.* 1st Simon & Schuster paperback ed. New York: Simon & Schuster, 2004.

Rapkin, Mickey. *Theater Geek: The Real Life Drama of a Summer at Stagedoor Manor, the Famous Performing Arts Camp.* New York: Simon and Schuster, 2010.

Rappel, William J., and John R. Winnie. *Community Theatre Handbook.* Iowa City, IA: Institute of Public Affairs, 1961.

Rauch, Eduardo. *The Education of Jews and the American Community: 1840 to the New Millennium.* Tel Aviv University, 2004.

Rice, Timothy. "Call and Response: Disciplining Ethnomusicology: A Call for a New Approach." *Ethnomusicology* 54, no. 2 (2010): 318–25.

Richardson, Michael. *Youth Theatre: Drama for Life.* New York: Routledge, 2015.

Ridout, Nicholas. *Passionate Amateurs: Theatre, Communism, and Love.* Ann Arbor: University of Michigan Press, 2013.

Ridout, Nicholas. *Stage Fright, Animals, and Other Theatrical Problems.* New York: Cambridge University Press, 2006.

Robinson, Ken. *Do Schools Kill Creativity?* TED Talk, 2006.

Rojek, Chris. "Is Marx Still Relevant to the Study of Leisure?" *Leisure Studies* 32, no. 1 (2013): 19–33.

Rojek, Chris. *The Labour of Leisure: The Culture of Free Time.* Los Angeles: Sage Publications, 2010.

Rojek, Chris, Susan M. Shaw, and Anthony James Veal. *A Handbook of Leisure Studies*. Basingstoke, UK: Palgrave Macmillan, 2006.

Romano, Renee C. "Not Dead Yet: My Identity Crisis as a Historian of the Recent Past." In *Doing Recent History: On Privacy, Copyright, Video Games, Institutional Review Boards, Activist Scholarship and History That Talks Back*, edited by Claire Bond Potter and Renee C. Romano, 23–44. Athens: University of Georgia Press, 2012.

Romero, Edwina Portelle. *Footlights in the Foothills: Amateur Theatre of Las Vegas and Fort Union, New Mexico, 1871–1899*. Santa Fe, NM: Sunstone Press, 2011.

Rose, Mike. *Possible Lives: The Promise of Public Education in America*. New York: Houghton Mifflin, 1995.

Ruskin, Jesse D., and Timothy Rice. "The Individual in Musical Ethnography." *Ethnomusicology* 56, no. 2 (2012): 299–327.

Sales, Amy L., and Leonard Saxe. *"How Goodly Are Thy Tents": Summer Camps as Jewish Socializing Experiences*. Hanover, NH: Brandeis University Press, 2004.

Salvato, Nick. "Out of Hand: YouTube Amateurs and Professionals." *TDR: The Drama Review* 53, no. 3 (2009): 67–83.

Sanjek, Roger, ed. *Fieldnotes: The Makings of Anthropology*. Ithaca, NY: Cornell University Press, 1990.

Sarna, Jonathan. "The Crucial Decade in Jewish Camping." In *A Place of Our Own: The Rise of Reform Jewish Camping*, 27–51. Tuscaloosa: University of Alabama Press, 2006.

Shay, Frank. *The Practical Theatre; a Manual for Little Theatres, Community Players, Amateur Dramatic Clubs and Other Independent Producing Groups*. New York: D. Appleton and Company, 1926.

Shelemay, Kay Kaufman. "Musicals Communities: Rethinking the Collective in Music." *Journal of the American Musicological Society* 64, no. 2 (2011): 349–90.

Shelemay, Kay Kaufman. *A Song of Longing: An Ethiopian Journey*. Urbana: University of Illinois Press, 1991.

Sherman, Howard. "Call to Action: Support 'Sweeney' at Timberlane High." *Hesherman.com* [blog], March 31, 2014. http://www.hesherman.com/2014/03/31/call-to-action-support-sweeney-at-timberlane-high/.

Sherman, Howard. "How Not to Cancel Your High School Musical." *Hesherman.com* [blog], December 4, 2013. http://www.hesherman.com/2013/12/04/how-not-to-cancel-your-high-school-musical/.

Sherman, Howard. "Intricacies and Intent Surrounding Race and Ethnicity in Casting." *Arts Integrity Initiative* [blog], July 27, 2016. http://www.artsintegrity.org/intricacies-and-intent-surrounding-race-and-ethnicity-in-casting/.

Sherman, Howard. "Theatre the Theatre Community Disdains." Accessed August 24, 2018. http://www.hesherman.com/2012/02/21/theatre-the-theatre-community-disdains/.

Shookhoff, Carol. "Three Broadway Junior Case Studies." New York: New York City Department of Education, 2009.

Sinn, B. A., and Kenneth B. Webb. *A Brief History of the American Camping Association. Light from a Thousand Campfires*. Martinsville, IN: American Camping Association, 1960.

Small, Christopher. *Musicking: The Meanings of Performing and Listening*. Middletown, CT: Wesleyan University Publishing, 1998.

Smith, Carolyn D., and William Kornblum. *In the Field: Readings on the Field Research Experience*. Westport, CT: Praeger, 1996.

Smith, Stephen Lloyd, and Kate Darlington. "Emotional Ecologies as Brands: Towards a Theory of Occasioned Local Feelings." *Place Branding and Public Diplomacy* 6, no. 2 (2010): 112–23.

Sokolove, Michael. *Drama High: The Incredible True Story of a Brilliant Teacher, a Struggling Town, and the Magic of Theatre*. New York: Penguin Books, 2013.

Spradley, James P. *Participant Observation*. New York: Holt, Rinehart and Winston, 1980.

Stebbins, Robert A. *Amateurs, Professionals, and Serious Leisure*. Montreal: McGill-Queen's University Press, 1992.

Stebbins, Robert A. *Careers in Serious Leisure: From Dabbler to Devotee in Search of Fulfillment*. London: Palgrave Macmillan, 2014.

Stebbins, Robert A. "Serious Leisure: A Conceptual Statement." *Pacific Sociological Review* 25 (1982): 251–72.

Stebbins, Robert A., and Sam Elkington. "History of the Serious Leisure Perspective (SLP)." The Serious Leisure Perspective (SLP). Accessed December 13, 2017. http://www.seriousleisure.net/historystebbins-bio.html.

Stebbins, Robert A., and Sam Elkington. *The Serious Leisure Perspective: An Introduction*. Abingdon, UK: Routledge, 2014.

Steichen, James. "HD Opera: A Love/Hate Story." *Opera Quarterly* 27, no. 4 (December 1, 2011): 443–59.

Stern, Lawrence. *School and Community Theater Management: A Handbook for Survival*. Boston: Allyn and Bacon, 1979.

Stoke, Martin. "Introduction." In *Ethnicity, Identity, and Music: The Musical Construction of Place*, edited by Martin Stoke, 1–28. Providence, RI: Berg Publishers, 1994.

Stone, Ruth M., and Verlon L. Stone. "Event, Feedback, and Analysis: Research Media in the Study of Events." *Ethnomusicology* 25 (1981): 215–25.

Sugarman, Jane C. "Building and Teaching Theory in Ethnomusicology: A Response to Rice." *Ethnomusicology* 54 (2010): 290–301.

Tawa, Nicholas E. *High-Minded and Low-Down: Music in the Lives of Americans, 1800–1861*. Boston: Northeastern University Press, 2000.

Taylor, Millie. "Experiencing Live Musical Theatre Performance: *La Cage Aux Folles* and *Priscilla, Queen of the Desert*." *Popular Entertainment Studies* 1, no. 1 (2010): 44–58.

Taylor, Millie, and Dominic Symonds. *Studying Musical Theatre: Theory and Practice*. New York: Palgrave Macmillan, 2014.

Thornton, Sarah. *Seven Days in the Art World*. New York: W.W. Norton, 2009.

Turino, Thomas. *Music as Social Life: The Politics of Participation*. Chicago: University of Chicago Press, 2008.

University of Maine at Portland-Gorham. "Children's Summer Camps; Their Economic Value to Maine. A Study of the Annual Maine Use, Revenue, Tourism and Expenditures Generated by Children's Summer Camps, and the Value of Their Investment." Portland, ME: Allagash Environmental Institute, 1976.

Van der Poel, Hugo. "Sociology and Cultural Studies." In *A Handbook of Leisure Studies*, edited by Chris Rojek, Susan M. Shaw, and A. J. Veal, 93–108. New York: Palgrave Macmillan, 2006.

Van Maanen, John. *Tales of the Field: On Writing Ethnography*. 2nd ed. Chicago: University of Chicago Press, 2011.

Van Slyck, Abigail A. *A Manufactured Wilderness: Summer Camps and the Shaping of American Youth, 1890–1960*. Minneapolis: University of Minnesota Press, 2006.

Verley, Joy. *An Essential Manual for High-School Theater Directors: How to Structure and Organize a Youth Theater Program*. Hanover, NH: Smith and Kraus, 2001.

Wachsmann, Klaus. "The Changeability of Musical Experience." *Ethnomusicology* 26, no. 2 (May 1982): 197–215.

Wade, Bonnie C. *Composing Japanese Musical Modernity*. Chicago: University of Chicago Press, 2014.

Warde, Alan, and Lydia Martens. *Eating Out: Social Differentiation, Consumption and Pleasure*. New York: Cambridge University Press, 2000.

Water, Manon van de, and Annie Giannini. "Gay and Lesbian Theatre for Young People, or the Representation of 'Troubled Youth.'" In *We Will Be Citizens: New Essays on Gay and Lesbian Theatre*, edited by James Fisher, 103–22. Jefferson, NC: McFarland, 2008.

Waterman, Christopher A. "'I'm a Leader, Not a Boss': Social Identity and Popular Music in Ibadan, Nigeria." *Ethnomusicology* 26, no. 1 (1982): 59–71.

Waterman, Christopher A. "'Our Tradition Is a Very Modern Tradition': Popular Music and the Construction of Pan-Yoruba Identity." *Ethnomusicology* 34, no. 3 (1990): 367–79.

Watkins, Daniel. "Greetings from Band Camp: For a Price, Fearless Amateurs Suffer for Their Art." *New York Times*. July 15, 2012.

Watson, Beccy, and Sheila Janet Scraton. "Leisure Studies and Intersectionality." *Leisure Studies* 32, no. 1 (2013): 35–47.

Waugh, Frank Albert. *Outdoor Theaters: The Design, Construction, and Use of Open-Air Auditoriums*. Boston: Richard G. Badger, 1917.

Webb, Duncan M. *Running Theaters: Best Practices for Leaders and Managers*. New York: Allworth Press, 2004.

Weber, William. *Music and the Middle Class: The Social Structure of Concert Life in London, Paris, and Vienna*. New York: Holmes and Meier Publishing, Inc., 1975.

Welton, Martin. "Shows of Feeling." In *Feeling Theatre*, 20–50. New York: Palgrave Macmillan, 2012.

Wilson, William. "Documenting Folklore." In *Folk Groups and Folklore Genres: An Introduction*, edited by Elliott Oring, 225–54. Logan: Utah State University Press, 1986.

Wolf, Stacy. *Changed for Good: A Feminist History of the Broadway Musical*. New York: Oxford University Press, 2011.

Wolf, Stacy. "Not Only on Broadway: Disney JR. and Disney KIDS Across the USA." In *The Disney Musical on Stage and Screen*, edited by George Rodosthenous, 133–54. London: Methuen Bloomsbury, 2017.

Wong, Deborah Anne. *Speak It Louder: Asian Americans Making Music*. New York: Routledge, 2004.

Wuthnow, Robert. *Loose Connections: Joining Together in America's Fragmented Communities*. Cambridge, MA: Harvard University Press, 2002.

Young, John Wray. *Community Theatre: A Manual for Success*. New York: Samuel French, 1971.

Zola, Gary P. "Jewish Camping and Its Relationship to the Organized Camping Movement in America." In *A Place of Our Own: The Rise of Reform Jewish Camping*, 1–26. Tuscaloosa: University of Alabama Press, 2006.

Zolberg, Vera L. *Constructing a Sociology of the Arts*. Cambridge, MA: Cambridge University Press, 1990.

Index

For the benefit of digital users, indexed terms that span two pages (e.g., 52–53) may, on occasion, appear on only one of those pages.

Printed in the USA/Agawam, MA
May 8, 2020

754659.001